MOON ®

HUDSON
RIVER VALLEY

FIRST EDITION

NIKKI GOTH ITOI

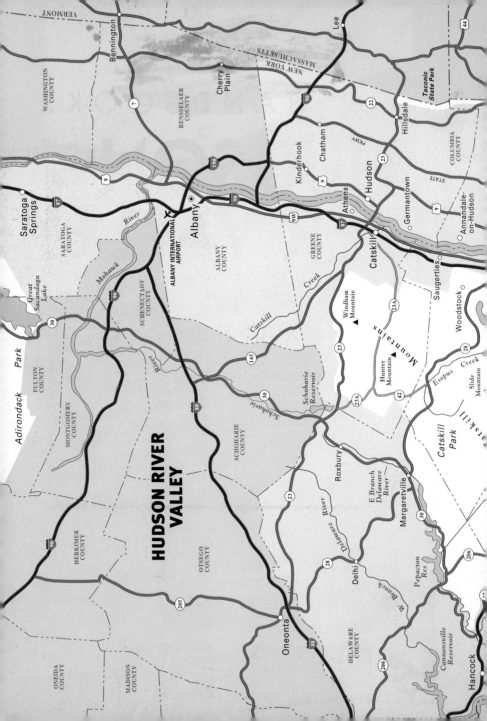

CONTENTS

Discover the Hudson River Valley

Explore the Hudson River Valley

MAPS

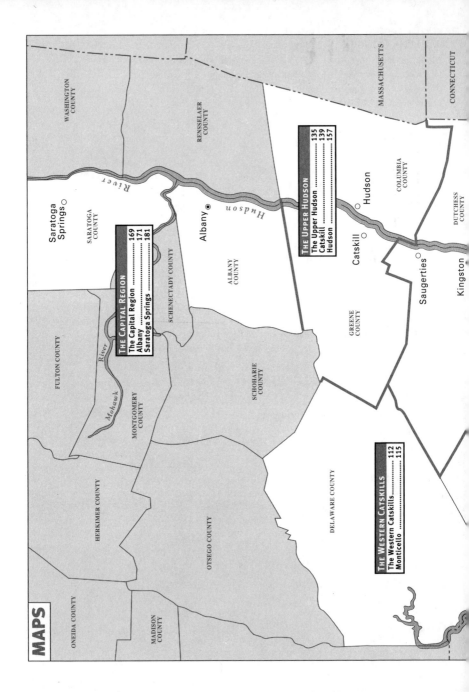

ONEIDA COUNTY

MADISON COUNTY

HERKIMER COUNTY

FULTON COUNTY

OTSEGO COUNTY

MONTGOMERY COUNTY

SCHENECTADY COUNTY

SCHOHARIE COUNTY

DELAWARE COUNTY

Mohawk River

Hudson River

Saratoga Springs

SARATOGA COUNTY

Albany

ALBANY COUNTY

WASHINGTON COUNTY

RENSSELAER COUNTY

GREENE COUNTY

Catskill

Saugerties

Kingston

Hudson

COLUMBIA COUNTY

DUTCHESS COUNTY

MASSACHUSETTS

CONNECTICUT

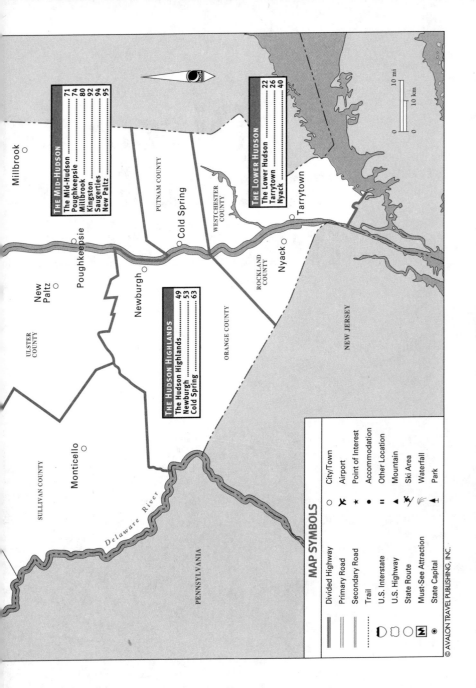

THE MID-HUDSON
The Mid-Hudson 71
Poughkeepsie 74
Millbrook 80
Kingston 92
Saugerties 94
New Paltz 95

THE LOWER HUDSON
The Lower Hudson 22
Tarrytown 26
Nyack 40

THE HUDSON HIGHLANDS
The Hudson Highlands .. 49
Newburgh 53
Cold Spring 63

Millbrook

New
Paltz

Poughkeepsie

Newburgh

Cold Spring

Nyack

Tarrytown

ULSTER
COUNTY

PUTNAM COUNTY

WESTCHESTER
COUNTY

ROCKLAND
COUNTY

ORANGE COUNTY

SULLIVAN COUNTY

Monticello

Delaware River

PENNSYLVANIA

NEW JERSEY

10 mi

10 km

0

MAP SYMBOLS

Divided Highway		○	City/Town
Primary Road		✈	Airport
Secondary Road		★	Point of Interest
Trail		●	Accommodation
U.S. Interstate		=	Other Location
U.S. Highway		▲	Mountain
State Route		🎿	Ski Area
Must-See Attraction		⚑	Waterfall
State Capital	●	⛽	Park

© AVALON TRAVEL PUBLISHING, INC.

Discover the Hudson River Valley

F

or nearly four centuries, travelers have ventured up the Hudson River in search of opportunity, inspiration, and a breath of fresh air. Measured by the numbers, the river is unexceptional—only 315 miles long, 3.5 miles across at its widest point, and 216 feet at its deepest. But the fertile valley that extends east and west of it holds a treasured place in history as one of America's first vacation destinations. It is here that Washington Irving wrote "The Legend of Sleepy Hollow" and Thomas Cole created the landscape paintings that signaled the dawn of the Romantic Era. In 1827, William Cullen Bryant dedicated a poem to the Hudson River at dawn: "A Scene on the Banks of the Hudson."

Old-world roots, dramatic scenery, and an ever-changing economy give the Hudson River Valley the depth and complexity of an aged red wine. Dutch names alternate with Algonquin Indian words to produce tongue twisters like Kinderhook and Rhinebeck, Taghkanic and Minnewaska. Timeless legends of haunted houses and enchanted woods entertain children and adults alike. At the conclusion of an 1859 journey from the river's source to its end, Poughkeepsie resident Benson John Lossing wrote of the Hudson:

> *It is by far the most interesting river in America, considering the beauty and magnificence of its scenery, its natural, political, and social history, the agricultural and mineral treasures of its vicinage, the commercial wealth hourly floating upon its bosom, and the relations of its geography and topography to some of the most important events in the history of the Western hemisphere.*
>
> The Hudson: From the Wilderness to the Sea,
> *originally published by H.B. Nims & Co., 1866.*

Today, the region continues to evoke a sense of wonder. You can't ride the train along the Hudson's eastern shore without contemplating the Revolutionary War, the viability of community-supported agriculture, or the fate of the American shad. All the while, you feel the unmistakable presence of those who came before: Alexander Hamilton, Ulysses S. Grant, Henry James, and Mark Twain, to name a few.

Carved by a glacier 75 million years ago, the river originates from Lake Tear of the Clouds in the rugged Adirondack Mountains and becomes navigable at Troy, above Albany. From the Federal Dam at Troy all the way to New York Harbor, the Hudson is a 150-mile-long estuary that ebbs and floods with ocean tides, mixing salt water with fresh as far up as Kingston in Ulster County. The Algonquins called it "Muhheahkantuck" meaning the river that flows both ways, or great waters constantly in motion. In winter, chunks of ice near the shore might flow south, while those in the middle flow north.

The constant mixing supports the largest single wildlife resource in New York State, according to environmentalist Robert

Boyle, author of *The Hudson River: A Natural and Unnatural History*, (W.W. Norton & Company, 1979). Deciduous trees, rocky bluffs, and gentle foothills line both shores. Mallard ducks paddle across narrow inlets while fishing boats troll for striped bass. Beyond the river's edge, narrow country lanes lead to historic parks, working fruit and dairy farms, and mountains that stretch 4,000 feet into the sky.

The Industrial Revolution wreaked havoc on the river, but water quality has improved substantially in recent decades, thanks to the persistent efforts of community and environmental groups. Local governments have preserved large tracts of pristine wilderness, and once-deserted villages have reinvented themselves with revitalized waterfronts and restaurants that give farm-fresh cuisine an international twist. From wine trails to snowboard terrain parks, the valley continues to adapt to changing traveler interests.

At its heart, the Hudson River Valley is a place of contrasts—where dairy farmers mingle with concrete factory workers, where hunters share the forest with conservationists, and where the cosmopolitan meets small-town America. Along this historic river, the familiar still has the power to surprise.

The region covered in this book includes 12 New York State counties, which are commonly divided into six regions: the Lower Hudson River Valley, Hudson Highlands, Mid-Hudson River Valley, Upper Hudson River Valley, Western Catskills, and Capital Region. You can drive or train the length of the valley, approximately 180 miles from New York City to Albany, in well under three hours; however, the region offers ample entertainment for a weekend- or week-long adventure in any season.

Whether you explore the area by car, bike, train, motorcycle, foot, or private plane, you will find boundless opportunities for outdoor recreation and entertainment on either side of the Hudson River. Out-of-state visitors often combine a Lower Hudson Valley excursion with a trip to New York City, or a tour of the Upper Hudson with a New England itinerary. Local residents may want to plan a series of weekend getaways to explore each county in the region. Wherever you choose to begin, be sure to venture away from the river's edge to the hills and mountains that lie beyond.

Generally speaking, the Hudson River Valley gets prettier the farther north you travel, so if you're looking for a real contrast to New York City, it's best to keep going at least until you reach the highlands near Cold Spring. That said, public transportation, international cuisine, and first-rate museums are more prevalent the closer you get to the Big Apple, and the Lower Hudson River Valley does have its share of beautiful outdoor spaces.

Most itineraries will cover more than one county in the region, especially if you stay near the river. You can visit one or two sights and enjoy a good meal in any of these counties in a one-day trip. For the weekend traveler, a couple of museums or historic sights would leave time for an outdoor adventure as well. If you want to take in most of the available sights and attractions, Dutchess, Ulster, and Greene Counties will require the longest stay for exploration—allow two to three days for each of these counties. Also, remember that destinations are more spread out in rural counties like Sullivan and Delaware, so you'll need extra time to get from place to place. For those who plan to explore the region from top to bottom—whether by car, train, or bike— a full week would allow plenty of time for a cross-section of activities.

Some of the most spectacular river views are only accessible by train, but for travelers who want to explore the area's hidden gems, a car affords more flexibility and spontaneity. Motorists have many options in this area, from winding country roads to open interstates. Route 9 and its many permutations (9D, 9G, 9H, 9J) hug the eastern shoreline, except for Route 9W, which runs parallel on the Hudson's west side. A faster choice is the scenic Taconic State Parkway, which runs north to south through Westchester, Putnam, Dutchess, and Columbia Counties. Farther east, Route 22 runs along the New York State border with Connecticut and Massachusetts. The speediest way to get from the wilderness to the sea is the New York State Thruway (I-87), a multilane toll road that connects New York City to Albany.

The most popular accommodations for today's leisure travelers are rustic country inns and upscale bed-and-breakfasts. The region also has the usual assortment of standard motels and moderately priced chains, including Travelodge, Best Western, and Days Inn. Camping is permitted in many state and county parks, as well as at private campgrounds, with more choices the farther north you travel.

WHEN TO GO

The best times to visit the Lower Hudson Valley are late spring to early summer, and early to mid-fall. July and August tend to be hot and muggy, especially close to New York City. For cooler temperatures in summer, or winter activities, head to the Upper Hudson, the Catskills, or the Capital Region.

The fall foliage season begins in mid-September and can last until late October, depending on the weather. A heavy rain or snow will end the season early. Most years, the colors are best around Columbus Day weekend in mid-October. The prime leaf-peeping window varies by as much as a week or two from the lower to upper parts of the valley (and from lower to higher elevations), so if you can't catch the peak in one county, you can often travel north or south to see an earlier or later show.

November can be cold, damp, and dreary. Winter storms can make a mess of the valley October–April. Snow typically begins to fall in December, with a cold snap of below-zero temperatures often occurring in January. Winter conditions last through February, when the maple-sugaring season begins.

Many small-town sights, restaurants, and accommodations have variable hours in the off-season, and it's a good idea to call ahead to confirm hours of operation. Reservations are essential during the fall foliage season and when major festivals, car shows, or county fairs are in town. For outdoor adventures, wear layers, as temperatures can change rapidly with elevation and proximity to the river. Field guides, sports equipment, rain gear, sunscreen, and insect repellent will also come in handy.

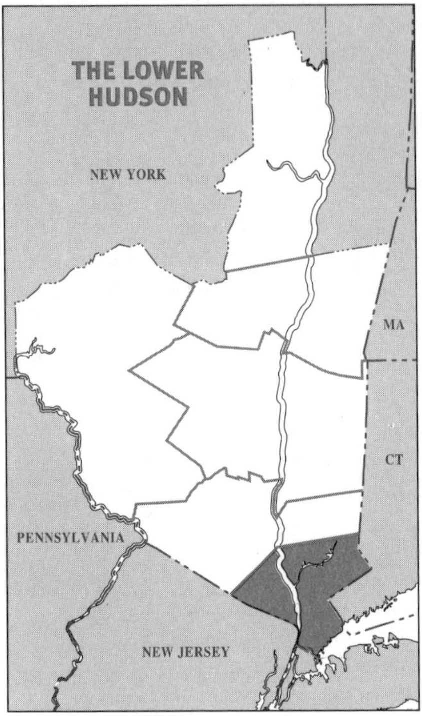

THE LOWER HUDSON

THE LOWER HUDSON

NEW YORK

PENNSYLVANIA

NEW JERSEY

MA

CT

The Hudson River Valley begins at the borders with New York City and New Jersey and includes densely populated Westchester and Rockland Counties. City dwellers often say there's little to see in this congested area except shopping malls and upscale bedroom communities; however, several attractive mansions and gardens line this stretch of the river, including Kykuit, the magnificent Rockefeller residence in the Pocantico Hills. And along with the historic estates come several wilderness areas that are all the more impressive for their proximity to Manhattan. Outstanding international cuisine and lively nightlife are additional highlights of the area. To see all of Westchester, from the Hudson to the Connecticut state line, would take several days and include a countless number of commuter towns. Fortunately, most of the county's top sights, including Washington Irving's Sunnyside estate and Katonah's Museum Mile, are clustered along Route 9W on the Hudson and Route 22 to the east. Any Rockland County itinerary should include a visit to Harriman State Park. The quaint villages of Tarrytown and Piermont, on opposite sides of the river, are an easy daytrip from Grand Central Station.

THE HUDSON HIGHLANDS

Above the lower Hudson, the Hudson Highlands encompass Orange and Putnam Counties along the most distinctive stretch of the river. A solid granite mountain range called the Appalachian Plateau crosses the Hudson here, and the river has carved a narrow and deep path through the range. The resulting fiords and vistas resemble the banks of the Rhine. To complete the picture, a dreamy mist often clings to the peaks of Storm King and Breakneck Mountains on opposite shores. One day is plenty of time to spend along both sides of the river, but Orange County extends more than 30 miles west to the Delaware River and Pennsylvania state line. A good way to see this part of the region is to plan an itinerary along Route 17 and continue on through Sullivan and Delaware counties in the Western Catskill region. Don't leave Orange County without seeing the historic West Point campus. For outdoor recreation in winter and summer, head to Greenwood Lake on the New York–New Jersey state line.

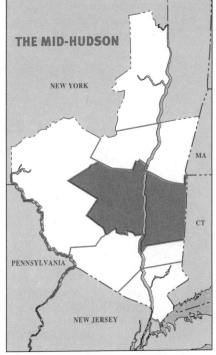

THE MID-HUDSON

NEW YORK

PENNSYLVANIA

NEW JERSEY

MA

CT

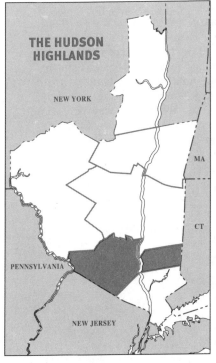

THE HUDSON HIGHLANDS

NEW YORK

PENNSYLVANIA

NEW JERSEY

MA

CT

THE MID-HUDSON

The "Gunks" of Ulster County and the riverside mansions of Dutchess County define the Mid-Hudson River Valley region. Here, the valley expands into rolling hills and farm fields interspersed with lakes, streams, and forests. Plan your trip around a visit to a gourmet restaurant or local arts festival. Wine trails on either side of the river guide visitors along rural back roads. Outdoor adventurers could spend a week in Ulster County without exhausting the possibilities: hiking, rock climbing, tubing, and downhill or cross-country skiing are just a few of the options. Make time to summit Slide Mountain, the Catskills' highest peak. Scenic drives through both counties cover miles of idyllic countryside. The towns of New Paltz, Saugerties, or Woodstock make a convenient home base for exploration. This part of the valley features several cultural highlights as well: Dia:Beacon is a nationally recognized museum for artwork from the 1960s to the present, and the Culinary Institute of America trains first-rate chefs, many of whom stick around to influence local menus.

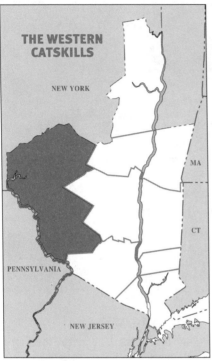

THE WESTERN CATSKILLS

Fly fishing and yoga retreats are the activities of choice in the sparsely populated western Catskill region. Although Sullivan and Delaware Counties do not directly border the Hudson River, they make an easy extension to many Hudson Valley itineraries. Communities here are a mix of long-time farming families and newer second-home owners. Several historic covered bridges span the Willowemoc and Beaverkill Rivers, while hundreds of lakes and streams entertain anglers and bird watchers alike. Do spend an hour inside the Catskill Fly Fishing Museum, even if you're not the fishing type. Its informative exhibits demonstrate how delicate flies are tied and document the life and works of the founders of the sport in a way that will appeal to any outdoor enthusiast. Most travelers will want at least a full weekend to explore the back roads of these two counties; serious fishing and hiking enthusiasts could easily find a week's worth of entertainment.

THE UPPER HUDSON

The Catskill and Berkshire Mountains frame the upper section of the Hudson River Valley. In between, small lakes and dense hardwood forests alternate with rolling hills and cultivated fields. Rural communities dot the landscape, welcoming visitors with historic sites, antique shops, and the promise of outdoor adventure. The sites and activities in each of these counties could fill a long weekend or more. The dramatic topography of the Catskills inspired the first generation of Hudson River School painters, who depicted natural wonders like Kaaterskill Falls in colorful Romantic landscapes. Nearby, skiers and snowboarders can carve turns at Windham and Hunter Mountains, both of which host a variety of cultural programs in the off-season. Across the river, Columbia

County is more closely affiliated with the Berkshire Mountains of New England. Several historic mansions are worth a half-day visit, including the Livingston family home at Clermont and the Persian-style Olana, which belonged to painter Frederick Church.

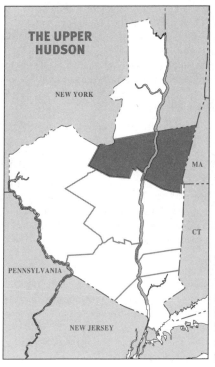

THE CAPITAL REGION

The capital region of Albany and Saratoga marks the end of the navigable Hudson River and the gateway to the Adirondack wilderness. There is much more to New York's state capital than meets the eye—art, history, government, fine dining, and easy access to outdoor areas are some of the highlights. Add to the list a lively entertainment scene that revolves around the college culture, and you have a surprisingly dynamic urban community. A day is adequate for seeing most of the sights; if you decide to stay longer, you can take your time in the museums and enjoy a wider variety of Albany's culinary experiences. By contrast, Saratoga Springs is a well-developed resort town steeped in the cultures of horse racing, apple picking, and natural spa treatments. Saratoga Springs is ideal for a weekend getaway or as a conclusion to an Adirondack backpacking trip.

The ideal Hudson River Valley itinerary includes a little bit of everything—outdoor adventure, good food, history, and culture. Here is a sampling of the very best.

THE HUDSON HIGHLANDS

WEST POINT

It's all business these days at the security gate to the U.S. Military Academy at West Point. Visitors are still welcome but must ride a tour bus to see the campus. If you have even a passing interest in early American history, it's worth the logistical hassle.

THE MID-HUDSON

DIA:BEACON

Aficionados from across the country are arriving at Beacon's new Dia museum to contemplate art from the 1960s to the present. River views and the innovative restoration of an old factory make for a memorable tour.

MINNEWASKA STATE PARK

It's tough to play favorites among the region's state parks, but dramatic rock formations and the presence of rare scrubby pines make Minnewaska State Park one of the very best. Access 12,000 acres from the main entrance at Lake Minnewaska, off Route 44/55.

THE LOWER HUDSON

KYKUIT

To experience the sheer splendor of a bygone era, visit the hilltop Rockefeller estate outside of Tarrytown in Westchester County.

RHINEBECK

From the historic 1766 Beekman Arms to the rows of Victorian, colonial, and Greek revival buildings, Rhinebeck lays on the charm. Boutique shops and gourmet restaurants can keep visitors entertained for days, and country inns make for quaint overnight stays.

the Rockefeller mansion at Kykuit

THE UPPER HUDSON

KAATERSKILL FALLS

At 180 feet, these waterfalls are inspiring—many painters of the Hudson River School thought so. Take a challenging, hour-long hike to see them for yourself.

THE CAPITAL REGION

SARATOGA PERFORMING ARTS CENTER (SPAC)

Enjoy an outdoor concert in an amphitheater surrounded by tall pines and the healing waters of natural hot springs.

Excellent outdoor recreation is one of the top reasons people come to the Hudson River Valley. You can escape the crowds in summer or winter on the expansive network of trails in the Catskills or in one of the region's state parks. Approximately 100,000 acres of wilderness are preserved in more than a dozen state parks, including Bear Mountain, Harriman, Minnewaska, and Saratoga Spa. Catskill State Park encompasses another 900 square miles of "forever wild" state land. And the expansive Taconic State Park encompasses 5,000 acres at the base of the Taconic Range, near the Massachusetts and Connecticut state lines. Hiking, boating, and fishing rank among the most popular activities.

WINTER SPORTS

New Yorkers flock to **Windham, Hunter,** and **Belleayre Mountains** for downhill skiing and snowboarding, and many state parks—especially **Harriman, Minnewaska,** and **Saratoga Spa**—maintain trails for Nordic skiing, snowshoes, tubing, and toboggans. Resorts with snow-making equipment open in late November or early December, as soon as temperatures dip below freezing. Spring conditions typically last through the end of March.

HIKING

Most state parks maintain their own trail systems and camping facilities, and some 200 miles of trails traverse the Catskill Forest Preserve. High above the Hudson River Valley are **Kaaterskill Falls** and the **Escarpment Trail,** a magical wilderness setting where the Hudson River School of painters found inspiration and the Catskill Mountain House entertained prominent guests. **Slide Mountain** in Ulster County is the highest peak in the Catskills and a challenging day-hike. Minnewaska State Park and Taconic State Park also have miles of trails that invite exploration.

Rock climbers head for the **Shawangunk Range,** including Minnewaska State Park and the Mohonk Preserve outside of New Paltz. To the south, geologists and climbers share the vertical cliffs of the **Palisades Park.**

Camping is unrestricted below 3,500 feet, although backpackers are encouraged to camp in designated areas to minimize the impact on the forest.

CYCLING

Cyclists enjoy endless miles of rolling hills on quiet country roads, and several counties have converted long stretches of abandoned train tracks into paths for walking, jogging, or biking. **Piermont** and **New Paltz** are popular cycling towns, and many local clubs plan group rides on summer weekends. You might tour one county at a time, or attempt the 180-mile multiday ride from New York

© GARY GOTH

at the base of the Catskill High Peaks

© PAUL ITOI

Minnewaska State Park

City to Albany. Include as many bridge crossings as possible, and allow time to take in some of the sights along the way. Several companies also offer guided bike tours of the area.

SWIMMING AND BOATING

The Hudson and its tributaries support all manner of water sports. Boats are available for rent at marinas on both shores—the Village of Catskill is a good place to launch. Tubing on the Esopus in Ulster County is especially popular in summer. Sailing school is an option out of Kingston. Greenwood Lake in Orange County and several lakes near Saratoga Springs have beaches for swimming and facilities for boats.

FISHING

Anglers can fish the tidal Hudson River, freshwater creeks and streams, or reservoirs. Guided tours are available in many locations, including the Willowemoc and Beaverkill Rivers near Roscoe (Trout Town U.S.A.) and the Pepacton Reservoir. Popular catches include American shad, striped bass, perch, herring, and sturgeon in the Hudson; and wild trout and bass in lakes, streams, creeks, and ponds throughout the region. The Catskill Fly Fishing Museum in Sullivan County pays tribute to the fathers of the sport in a series of informative exhibits. Bass tournaments draw large crowds to the river near the town of Catskill in summer.

A love of food is a prerequisite for enjoying all that the Hudson River Valley has to offer. The region's eateries range from classic diners to contemporary American restaurants, and from game-inspired, farm-fresh menus to upscale Italian, French, and international cuisine. Ethnic foods are easier to find the farther south you go. Many towns now offer gourmet coffee shops, bakeries, and bagels too. To make food the focus of you trip, consider enrolling in a cooking class, or design your route to follow a wine trail.

COOKING CLASSES

The main campus of the nation's premier culinary college sits on 80 acres overlooking the river at Hyde Park. The Culinary Institute of America runs five restaurants, a bookstore, and courses for cooking professionals and enthusiasts. Its facilities include 41 kitchens and the largest collection of culinary books and reference materials of any library in the country. For serious training, enthusiasts can enroll in one of the CIA's Boot Camp programs.

Vintage Hudson Valley organizes culinary events at restaurants across the valley, including Allyn's in Millbrook, Le Chambord in Rhinebeck, and Aubergine in Hillsdale. Four-hour-long "celebrity chef classes" cost $150, and midweek "inn-to-inn vacations" run $380, not including accommodations.

FRESH PRODUCE

Every county in the region has its share of apple orchards, berry patches, organic farms, and corn fields. Flavors differ from one hillside to the next, in what locals like to call micro-terroirs. Farmers markets and farm stands are a popular pastime for both locals and visitors.

The Hudson Valley specializes in a number of delicious fruits and vegetables. Fern-like fiddleheads appear on many menus in the early spring. For those who like to forage for their food, spring rains bring wild mushrooms, including morels and chanterelles. In summer, the local garlic harvest begins in Saugerties, and farm stands overflow with fresh-picked corn, tomatoes, and other vegetables. Strawberries and cherries ripen through June and July, and blueberries last July–September. You can pick apples July–November, whereas pumpkin patches do a steady business in September and October.

Greig Farm runs one of the most developed farm markets in the valley, including a garden shop, bakery, and winery. Columbia County's V.R. Saulpaugh and Sons has evolved from a green bean operation into a more diversified grower. Look for the stand along Route 9G in Germantown. Two more standout markets are the Nyack Farmers Market in Rockland County and Warwick Farmers Market in Orange County.

GOURMET RESTAURANTS

You'll find pockets of high-end cuisine across the region, with the highest concentrations of restaurants in Westchester, Dutchess, Ulster, and Columbia Counties. Several towns, including Tarrytown, Cold Spring, Rhinebeck, and Saratoga Springs, are known for their wide selection of gourmet restaurants.

A handful of venues are worth planning a trip around, by virtue of the outstanding cuisine they prepare and the unparalleled dining experiences they offer. Here is an abbreviated list of the best: Blue Hill at Stone Barns in Westchester, American Bounty on the CIA campus, the DePuy Canal House in Ulster County, The Basement Bistro in Greene County, and Aubergine in Columbia County.

© PAUL ITOI

tasting room at Clinton Vineyards

WINERIES

Hudson Valley grape growers introduced French American hybrid grapes in the 1970s to please an increasingly sophisticated consumer base. The switch put the region on the New York State wine map, producing award-winning Italian-style whites, as well as pinot noirs and cabernet francs. The Dutchess Wine Trail includes Alison Wines, Clinton Vineyards, and Millbrook Winery & Vineyards, and covers miles of pretty countryside. Meanwhile, the wineries themselves produce some of the highest-quality labels in New York State.

On the other side of the Hudson, the Shawangunk Wine Trail is a 30-mile loop connecting nine family-owned wineries. The trail runs along back roads between the New York State Thruway, I-84, and Route 17 between New Paltz in Ulster County and Warwick in Orange County. Some of the most popular stops include Rivendell Vineyards and Winery, Applewood Winery, and the Warwick Valley Winery & Distillery.

Fall Foliage

Time a visit with the changing of the seasons to catch one of the most spectacular displays of color anywhere on the planet. The leaves begin to turn in mid-September and peak around Columbus Day in October, depending on temperature, rainfall, and elevation. The clear, crisp days of autumn offer prime conditions for hiking.

ON FOOT

The hardwood forests of the Catskill and Shawangunk ranges explode in shades of red, orange, and yellow. One of the most popular fall hikes is a triple-summit over the Catskill High Peaks of Thomas Cole, Black Dome, and Blackhead Mountains. Dress in layers and be prepared for fast-changing weather conditions.

BY CAR

The most scenic driving routes are the Taconic State Parkway, Route 9W through the Hudson Highlands, and the Route 23/23A loop through Greene County. Route 44 in eastern Dutchess County and Route 28 through western Ulster County also put on an amazing show.

AERIAL VIEWS

Skydiving in the Hudson River Valley is the best around, and what better time to attempt a jump than during the leaf-peeping season? Operators include Saratoga Skydiving (Capital Region) and Skydive the Ranch (Mid-Hudson).

autumn at Ward Pond

COURTESY OF WESTCHESTER COUNTY OFFICE OF TOURISM

The Hudson River Valley has a number of outstanding and eclectic museums, as well as many unique venues for enjoying the arts—whether on canvas or on stage.

THE LOWER HUDSON AND HUDSON HIGHLANDS

Begin an arts tour of these regions in Westchester County along Katonah's Museum Mile. See what's showing at the Katonah Museum of Art and then stay for an evening performance at the Caramoor Center for Music and the Arts. Next, head north to Putnam County for the riverside summer Shakespeare Festival at Boscobel. Or cross the Hudson to explore the Storm King Art Center, a 500-hundred acre museum, sculpture park, and nature center set in the dramatic Hudson Highlands.

THE MID-HUDSON AND UPPER HUDSON

In Dutchess County, save time for the region's newest cultural attraction, Dia:Beacon, which occupies a restored early-20th-century factory in the town of Beacon. Then continue on to Columbia County and explore the Shaker Museum and Library, which contains one of the largest collections of Shaker artifacts.

THE CAPITAL REGION

Albany has a number of first-rate museums, including the science-focused New York State Museum. Also, a number of works from the impressive New York State Art Collection are on display throughout the Empire State Plaza. In Saratoga Springs, don't miss the Tang Teaching Museum and the Saratoga Performing Arts Center, an amphitheater inside Saratoga Springs State Park.

the grounds at Dia:Beacon museum

COURTESY OF WESTCHESTER COUNTY OFFICE OF TOURISM

American victory in 1779 boosted morale and severely damaged British forces. Heading north, the United States Military Academy at West Point has been a training ground for army officers since 1802. The academy sits on the bluffs overlooking the river. Located in Newburgh, Washington's Headquarters became the first national historic site in the United States. Conclude this tour in Kingston, a colonial city that was torched by the British.

HISTORIC MANSIONS

A handful of majestic estates line the Hudson River, representing several centuries of architectural and cultural trends. Most of them are open to the public. Kykuit, the sprawling estate of John D. Rockefeller is located in the Pocantico Hills near Tarrytown. In Dutchess County, Hyde Park claims the Vanderbilt Estate as well as FDR's home and library, while Columbia County contains the Livingston family's Clermont in Germantown and the Persian-style Olana near the city of Hudson.

HUGUENOT STREET

Within walking distance from downtown New Paltz, six original stone houses mark the settlement of a group of French Huguenot Protestants who arrived in the late 17th century. Some of the homes are preserved as they looked in the 18th century, while others were renovated a century later. The result is an informative progression of styles.

REVOLUTIONARY WAR SIGHTS

Route 9W leads to a treasure chest of military history sights, beginning with the Stony Point Battlefield Museum in Rockland County, where an

Explore the Hudson River Valley

The Lower Hudson

Not surprisingly, the Hudson Valley's most densely populated counties border New York City. Although no longer much of a getaway destination itself, the Lower Hudson Valley is packed with historic mansions and restored gardens at every bend in the road. John Jay, Frederick Philipse, the Vanderbilts, and the Harrimans all left their mark, but the grandest estate of all was the sprawling Rockefeller residence in the Pocantico Hills. As a legacy of these large estates, Westchester and Rockland Counties were able to preserve wilderness areas that rival many upstate parks and preserves, even as they struggled to cope with rapid industrial and housing development.

Today, both counties support diverse populations that represent the very highest and lowest income brackets, as well as many different nations and cultures. Local restaurants prepare menus you only expect to find in New York City or San Francisco, including specialties from Brazil, China, India, and Japan, as well as Italy, Spain,

Must-Sees

Look for **N** to find the sights and activities you can't miss and **N** for the best dining and lodging.

N Sunnyside: The romantic home of author Washington Irving is set amidst rolling hills, a babbling brook, and the purple and white flowers of wisteria that climbs all the way up to the gabled roof (page 25).

N Kykuit: John D. Rockefeller built a 6-story, 40-room mansion in the Pocantico Hills near Tarrytown, with breathtaking views of the Hudson River and Palisades across it (page 27).

N Katonah Museum Mile: Katonah is home to three first-rate museums, all located within a mile of each other: the Caramoor Center for Music and the Arts, the Katonah Museum of Art, and the John Jay Homestead (page 30).

N Piermont Village: Three miles south of the Tappan Zee Bridge, on a steep hillside between Route 9W and the riverbank, is the upscale village of Piermont, a haven for cyclists, foodies, and creative types (page 39).

Sunnyside mansion

COURTESY OF WESTCHESTER COUNTY OFFICE OF TOURISM

N Stony Point Battlefield State Historical Site: Located on Haverstraw Bay is the site of a small but important victory in the American Revolution, with a riverside park and museum that includes the oldest lighthouse on the Hudson (page 41).

N Harriman State Park: The first section of the Appalachian Trail was cleared here in 1923, and today, hikers can access several lakes, plus 200 miles of trails, inside the park (page 41).

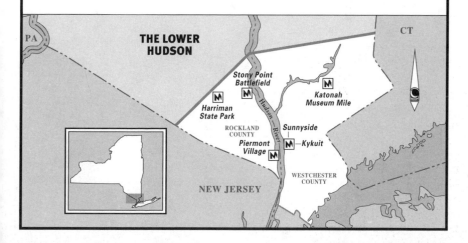

THE LOWER HUDSON

The Lower Hudson

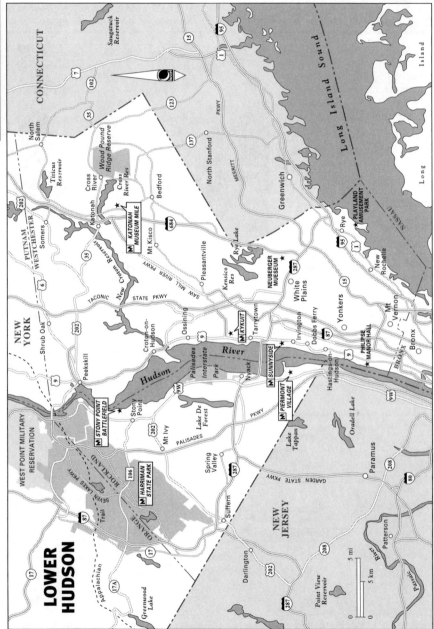

LOWER
HUDSON

© AVALON TRAVEL PUBLISHING, INC.

and France. And unlike in other parts of the Hudson River Valley, night owls who visit the Lower Hudson have many choices for evening entertainment, from the Westchester Broadway Theater in Elmsford to the Performing Arts Center in Purchase.

The Tappan Zee Bridge connects the two counties at the widest part of the Hudson River, while the Bear Mountain Bridge spans the river at Westchester's northern border.

PLANNING YOUR TIME

Whether you want to add an easy day trip to a longer New York City stay or find a new stopover on your way to a regular weekend getaway farther north, Westchester and Rockland Counties offer many choices for historic tours, outdoor entertainment, and fine-dining experiences. And the well-developed New York and New Jersey transit systems make it easy to leave the car behind.

If you have one day to explore the area, bring a picnic to the gardens of the former Rockefeller estate at Kykuit, in Sleepy Hollow, and choose a

restaurant for dinner in Tarrytown. Alternatively, plan to tackle a section of the 26-mile Old Croton Trailway by foot, bike, or horseback.

In Rockland County, head to the Piermont area for the perfect mix of entertainment, food, and outdoor recreation. Then drive north on Route 9W to visit a series of Revolutionary War sights and scenic river overlooks. Or forget the history lesson and get away from it all with a backcountry hike in Harriman State Park.

Longer itineraries allow you to visit multiple historic homes, such as Jay Gould's Lyndhurst and Washington Irving's Sunnyside, or to contemplate the works of art in one of several well-funded museums. Add half a day to sample the wild mushrooms at the Nyack Farmers Market or attend a White Plains Antique Show. Add another day to tour the gardens in Somers and Purchase. When planning an overnight visit, beware that choices in accommodations will be limited primarily to business hotels. If quaint and memorable lodging is a priority, consider visiting the Lower Hudson on a day trip from New York City or when passing through to parts north.

Westchester County

Bordering the Bronx, the southern edge of Westchester County is just 15 minutes from Manhattan by train. The county boasts the largest population and the highest population density in the Hudson Valley region—and a surprising blend of wealthy suburbs, ample green space, and historic sites. Yonkers, Mount Vernon, New Rochelle, Rye, and White Plains are the largest cities, and White Plains is the county seat.

The New York Assembly established Westchester County in 1683, and the first English settlements popped up in the eastern part of the county at Rye, Mamaroneck, Eastchester, and Bedford. The manor of Frederick Philipse, deeded through a royal grant, covered more than 52,000 acres between Yonkers and Tarrytown. Roads, taverns, and ferries were built in the 18th century, and by the end of the century, Westch-

ester had become the wealthiest and most populous county in New York.

The American Revolution took its toll, however, through the battles of Pelham and White Plains. Westchester found itself stuck between the American headquarters, near Peekskill, and the British, in New York City. It took decades for local communities to rebound from the expense and disruption of war.

Westchester County became a commuter base as early as the 19th century, when rail travel made it possible to reach New York City in just a few hours. As transportation evolved from steamboat to rail to car, Westchester grew at a frenzied pace. Its river towns began to produce medicines, cars, beer, sugar, and elevators, among other goods. Expansion of the New York City watershed created more jobs and further accelerated growth. Today's population is more than 900,000 and counting. But along with the crowds came upscale shopping, first-rate cultural attractions, and outstanding international cuisine.

ALONG THE RIVER—ROUTE 9

Yonkers

Start a tour of Westchester's river towns from the West Side Highway in Manhattan and follow Route 9A north to Yonkers. This diverse city of 188,000 people is a major transportation hub and is the fourth-largest city in New York State. Its name derives from *jonkheer,* the Dutch word for "young nobleman," in reference to Dutchman Adriaen Van Der Donck, who built a sawmill where the tiny Nepperhan River (later renamed the Saw Mill River) empties into the Hudson. Four miles of frontage on the eastern bank of the Hudson offer beautiful views of the Palisades in New Jersey and Rockland County.

Legendary jazz singer Ella Fitzgerald was raised in Yonkers, and a statue of her greets passengers arriving at the train station. Nearby, where Main Street meets the river, is the hundred-year-old **Yonkers Recreational Pier,** newly renovated to hold community events and festivals.

Two notable museums are within walking distance of the train station. Two blocks east on Warburton Avenue is **Philipse Manor Hall** (29 Warburton Ave. at Dock St., Yonkers, 914/965-4027, www.philipsemanorfriends.org; Apr. 1–Oct. 31 Wed.–Sat. noon–5 P.M., Sun. 1–4 P.M.; adults $4, seniors and students $3, under 12 $1, under 5 free; onsite parking free). This Georgian mansion housed three generations of the Philipse family until loyalist Frederick Philipse III was arrested in 1776 and forced to flee to England. The building dates to 1682, and exhibits inside trace the history of Yonkers.

Also on Warburton Avenue, the **Hudson River Museum** (511 Warburton Ave., Yonkers, 914/963-4550, www.hrm.org; May–Sept. Wed.–Sun. noon–5 P.M., Fri. noon–9 P.M.; adults $4) was founded in 1919 with a focus on Hudson River art, history, and science. Exhibits include landscape paintings from the Hudson River School of Painters, historic photographs, sculpture, and prints. After browsing the collection

of 19th- and 20th-century art, enjoy river views from the museum café. Then learn about the natural history of the Hudson and the summer night sky inside the Andrus Planetarium.

Inside the Glenview Mansion, which is also part of the museum, six rooms are furnished in turn-of-the-20th-century style. The sitting room holds one of the highlights of a house tour: a delicately carved and inlaid sunflower pattern in the woodwork, representative of the rare American Eastlake interior style. In addition to these varied exhibits, the museum hosts an annual jazz series each summer.

Hastings-on-Hudson, Dobbs Ferry, and Irvington

If you have one day to spend on the **Old Croton Trailway** (see sidebar, *Old Croton Trailway State Historic Park*), choose the section that connects the three river towns above Yonkers: Hastings-on-Hudson, Dobbs Ferry, and Irvington. Artists and commuters have made these towns their home, and the route leads to one delight after another—from historic homes and shady lanes to local parks and river views, with the Palisades always looming in the distance. Farmers markets, bookstores, antiques, and other shops provide good diversions from the trail.

The most famous resident of Hastings-on-Hudson began his career as an architect and later became a painter associated with the first generation of the Hudson River School. Like his fellow Romantic artists, Jasper Francis Cropsey (1823–1900) depicted the Hudson River, Catskill Mountain House, and Lake George, as well as other natural wonders in the northeast, in a series of colorful and fantastical landscapes. The **Newington Cropsey Gallery** (25 Cropsey Lane, Hastings-on-Hudson, 914/478-7990, www.newington-cropsey.com; by appointment Mon.–Fri. 1–5 P.M.), located near the train station, contains an exhaustive collection of Cropsey's works, including oil paintings, watercolors, drawings, and architectural renderings. A guided tour of the gallery takes about 45 minutes. Also in town, the yellow 1835 **Cropsey Homestead** (49 Washington Ave., Hastings-on-Hudson, 914/478-1372; Apr.–Nov. except Aug. Mon.–Fri. 10 A.M.–1 P.M.), called Ever Rest, has been furnished and decorated to reflect the 19th-century sensibility. The separate artist studio dates to 1885, and many of Cropsey's sketches and studies are on display inside the home and studio.

During the same time period, a 19th-century photographer and astronomer named John William Draper (1811–1882), who took some of the earliest pictures of the moon, built a federal-style farmhouse on 20 acres in Hastings. His two sons later built a famous observatory that hosted the likes of Thomas Edison and Samuel Morse. Today, the **Draper Observatory Cottage** (41 Washington Ave., Hastings-on-Hudson, 914/478-2249) holds the Hastings-on-Hudson Historical Society, with an archive of books, maps, paintings, and other town memorabilia. After browsing the museums, enjoy a picnic and the riverside views at MacEachron Waterfront Park, next to the train station.

Much of the 2002 movie *Unfaithful,* starring Diane Lane and Richard Gere, was filmed in neighboring Dobbs Ferry. Settled by Irish, Italian, and other European immigrants during the Industrial Revolution, this town of 10,000 residents was named for a ferry service that operated in the 1700s. Journalist and railroad financier Henry Villard (1835–1900) joined the well-to-do here in 1879. Many of the original homes feature long-lasting Vermont slate roofs. A handful of art galleries are located along Main Street and Broadway.

Irvington takes its name from Washington Irving, but the town is better known as the home of the first African American millionaire and philanthropist, Madam C. J. Walker (1867–1919), who made her fortune selling hair and beauty products. Walker commissioned Vertner Woodson Tandy, considered the first licensed black architect in New York State, to build her dream home on Broadway in 1917. The resulting Italianate structure, called Villa Lewaro, featured river views from the dining room and hosted many black leaders of the time, from Langston Hughes to W. E. B. DuBois. Villa Lewaro is privately owned today by Helena and Harold Doley.

Tarrytown

Soon after he moved to the neighboring hamlet of Sleepy Hollow, John D. Rockefeller reportedly tried to purchase and shut down Tarrytown's only tavern. It was a rare instance where the Puritan business mogul was unable to impose his will on those around him, and Tarrytown remained a lively center for commerce and the arts.

In September 1780, three Tarrytown militiamen captured Benedict Arnold's partner in treason, British Major John Andre, and found in his boot copies of George Washington's plans for fortifying West Point. Andre was tried, convicted, and hung across the river in Nyack. A sign in Patriot's Park commemorates the arrest.

Today, a stroll along Main Street, with its coffeehouses and antique shops, is the perfect interlude between tours of the surrounding homes and gardens, and it is a convenient stop for nourishment while exploring the Old Croton Aqueduct. Route 9 turns into Broadway as you approach the center of town. Follow Main Street toward the river to find a public parking lot.

Ⓜ Sunnyside

A few miles south, Sunnyside (West Sunnyside Lane, Tarrytown, 914/631-8200, www.hudsonvalley.org; Apr.–Oct. daily 10 A.M.–5 P.M., Nov.–Dec. daily 10 A.M.–4 P.M., Mar. weekends only 10 A.M.–4 P.M.; adults $9, seniors $8, children $5, under 5 free), the romantic home of celebrated author Washington Irving, comes right out of the pages of a children's storybook. Defined by rolling hills, a babbling brook, and the purple and white flowers of wisteria that climb all the way up to the gabled roof, Sunnyside captures the imagination in much the same way that Irving's tales "Rip Van Winkle" and "The Legend of Sleepy Hollow" did.

Guides in Victorian-era costumes welcome visitors into the enchanted home to experience a day in the life of the writer. Among the furnishings on display are Irving's desk and many of his books.

Nationally known and loved in his own lifetime, Irving wrote far more than the stories we remember today: among his last works was an exhaustive biography of his namesake, George Washington. After a life of international travel and diplomacy, he found this peaceful retreat in

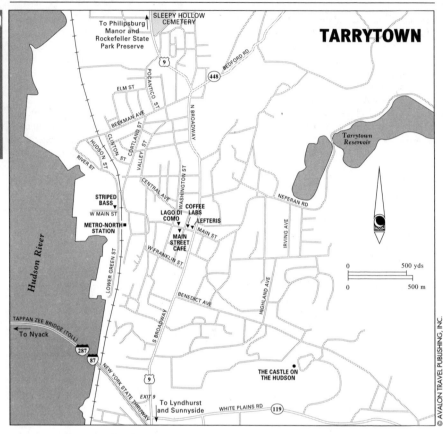

To Philipsburg
Manor and
Rockefeller State
Park Preserve

SLEEPY HOLLOW
CEMETERY

TARRYTOWN

9

BEDFORD RD

448

ELM ST

POLANTICO ST

BEEKMAN AVE

N BROADWAY

CLINTON ST

HUDSON ST

CORTLAND ST

VALLEY ST

RIVER ST

Tarrytown
Reservoir

CENTRAL AVE

WASHINGTON ST

NEPERAN RD

STRIPED
BASS

W MAIN ST

COFFEE
LABS

LAGO DI
COMO

LEFTERIS

MAIN ST

IRVING AVE

MOON

METRO-NORTH
STATION

MAIN
STREET
CAFE

Hudson River

W FRANKLIN ST

LOWER GREEN ST

HIGHLAND AVE

BENEDICT AVE

0   500 yds

0   500 m

TAPPAN ZEE BRIDGE (TOLL)

To Nyack

287

87

NEW YORK STATE THRUWAY

S BROADWAY

THE CASTLE ON
THE HUDSON

9

EXIT 9

To Lyndhurst
and Sunnyside

WHITE PLAINS RD

119

Tarrytown, a place he remembered well from his childhood. Sunnyside was built in 1835. Visitors can tour the inside, walk the grounds, and picnic under the trees. Visitor services include a café and museum shop.

Lyndhurst

The Old Croton Trailway connects Sunnyside to the adjacent Lyndhurst property, the former residence of financier Jay Gould (635 S. Broadway, Tarrytown, 914/631-4481, www.lyndhurst.org; mid-Apr.–Oct. Tues.–Sun. 10 A.M.–5 P.M., Nov.–mid-Apr. weekends and holiday Mon. only 10 A.M.–5 P.M.; adults $10, seniors $9, students $4, under 12 free). Designed in 1838 by renowned architect Alexander Jackson

Davis, the mansion, with its asymmetrical lines, reflects the Gothic Revival style. Gould was third to own the home, after New York City mayor William Paulding and businessman George Merritt.

The carefully planned gardens on 67 acres are as visually interesting as the ornate rooms inside. Also on the premises, Gould built the largest private conservatory in his day, while his daughter, Helen Gould Shephard, later designed the circular rose garden that still blooms today. A popular way to arrive in summer is by boat from Manhattan (NY Waterways, 800/53-FERRY or 800/533-3779), www.nywaterway.com; adults $49, seniors $47, children $25, including transfers and site admission).

COURTESY OF WESTCHESTER COUNTY
OFFICE OF TOURISM

Lyndhurst mansion

Philipsburg Manor

A tour of the three-story, white **Philipsburg Manor** (150 White Plains Rd., Tarrytown, 914/631-8200, www.hudsonvalley.org; Apr.–Oct. daily 10 A.M.–5 P.M., Nov.–Dec. daily 10 A.M.–4 P.M., Mar. weekends only 10 A.M.–4 P.M.; adults $9, seniors $8, children $5, under 5 free), at Upper Mills, is an interactive production, with theatrical guides dressed in colonial garb. It is also a sobering experience, designed to give visitors an appreciation for the manual labor required to run an international trading company in the 19th century. The Philipse family was one of the earliest and largest slaveholders in the northeast, and in 2004, the museum's directors decided to shift the focus of their exhibits to address the African American experience on the farm. Accordingly, today's tour begins in the basement kitchen and former slave quarters, and then progresses through the house with a narrative that brings the enslaved perspective to life.

Across Route 9 from Philipsburg Manor is the **Sleepy Hollow Cemetery,** with the gravesites of Washington Irving, William Cullen Bryant, Andrew Carnegie, Walter Chrysler, William Rockefeller, and others. The property runs for several miles along Route 9, surrounding the **Old Dutch Church** and its historic burying ground.

Kykuit

Land prices were at a historic low in 1893 when John D. Rockefeller bought his first 400 acres in the **Pocantico Hills** (po-CAN-tee-co) north of Tarrytown. Stunning views of the Hudson River

and surrounding hills and mountains drew the oil magnate to an area he described as "a place where fine views invest the soul and where we can live simply and quietly." The family's country estate expanded to 1,600 acres by the turn of the 20th century and 3,000 at its peak.

Rockefeller built 75 homes and 70 miles of roads, all strategically placed to show off the surrounding views. He designed much of the landscape himself, and except for a central private area, he insisted that the grounds be kept open to the public, as long as visitors abided by his rules: no cars, no drinking, and no smoking. As the estate grew, Rockefeller paid handsomely to relocate a small college, a neighborhood of homes, and even a stretch of the New York Central Railroad to the outskirts of his property. A small farm supplied food for the family, and golf became Rockefeller's preferred pastime at Pocantico. He designed a 12-hole course and played year-round, rain or shine.

For the first decade, Rockefeller lived in and remodeled the modest home that had come with the property. When that residence burned down in 1902, the family built a hilltop mansion at Kykuit (pronounced KYE-cut), which means "lookout." It was designed to maximize sunlight in winter. Conceived as an English country house, the structure evolved into a six-story, 40-room ordeal in the American Renaissance style. It was completed in 1913.

A walking tour of Kykuit (Pocantico Hills, Tarrytown, 914/631-8200, www.hudsonvalley.org; Wed.–Mon. 9 A.M.–4 P.M.; adults $22, seniors $20, children $18) takes about two hours. The only access is via shuttle bus from the visitors center at Philipsburg Manor. Tickets are sold same day only, on a first-come, first-served basis. The adjoining **Rockefeller State Park Preserve** (Rte. 117, 1 mile east of Rte. 9, Tarrytown, 914/333-0102, www.friendsrock.org; Apr.–Oct. daily 8 A.M.–sunset, Nov.–Mar. weekends only; $6 parking fee) is open year-round for hiking, fishing, horseback riding, and cross-country skiing.

Route 442 out of Sleepy Hollow leads to Bedford and the **Union Church of Pocantico Hills** (Rte. 448/Bedford Rd., Sleepy Hollow, 914/631-8200, www.hudsonvalley.org; Apr.–Dec.

COURTESY OF HISTORIC HUDSON VALLEY

The Rockefeller mansion at Kykuit

Wed.–Mon. 11 A.M.–5 P.M., Sat. 10 A.M.–5 P.M., Sun. 2–5 P.M.; admission $4). Take the Eastview exit from the Saw Mill River Parkway. This church features stained-glass windows designed by Henri Matisse and Marc Chagall, as Rockefeller family memorials. Matisse completed the design for a rose window just days before he died in 1954. The series of one large and eight small windows, completed in 1965, are the only church windows Chagall ever created.

Ossining and Croton

Continuing north along Route 9, Ossining is best known as the location of **Sing Sing Prison,** which you can see from a small riverfront park near the train station. Ossining's Main Street is busy and attractive in a no-nonsense sort of way, though a new Bikram yoga studio suggests the town may be shedding its working-class image. The Old Croton Aqueduct runs straight though the middle of town. And just beyond, **Teatown**

Lake Reservation (1600 Spring Valley Rd., Ossining, 914/762-2912, www.teatown.org; free admission and parking) is a nature preserve with 14 miles of secluded trails and environmental exhibits. The nature center there is open Tuesday–Saturday 9 A.M.–5 P.M. and Sunday 1–5 P.M.

The next river town, **Croton-on-Hudson,** is a major point of transfer for rail commuters coming to and from the northern counties. Croton also boasts the third-largest reservoir in the New York City Watershed. By the turn of the 20th century, New York City needed more water than the original aqueduct could provide, and work began anew. Irish, German, and Italian immigrants labored hard to build the dam that created the **New Croton Reservoir**. It measures nine miles long—touching the towns of Cortlandt, Yorktown, Somers, Bedford, and New Castle—and holds 19 billion gallons at full capacity. The dam is located on Route 19, off Route 9A north of the village of Croton.

OLD CROTON TRAILWAY STATE HISTORIC PARK

Yonkers is the southern terminus for the most unique outdoor space in all of Westchester County: the Old Croton Trailway State Historic Park. In the early 19th century, a thirsty New York City, plagued by fire and illness, turned to abundant upstate resources for a clean and ready supply of water. The Croton River delivered, and the city has feuded with rural upstate towns over rights to water ever since.

Engineers diverted the river through a 26.2-mile aqueduct to the Bronx. They built a stone tunnel 8.5 feet tall by 7.5 feet wide that sloped just enough to use the force of gravity. They then laid the length of it with brick, adding a stone shaft at every mile for ventilation. Completed in 1842 at a cost of $12 million, the Old Croton Aqueduct served the growing city well until the turn of the next century. When New York needed more, a replacement in 1905 tripled its capacity.

The oldest aqueduct in the New York City watershed is now a National Historic Landmark and a long corridor of a state park. It's also just the perfect length, surface, and terrain to prepare for a marathon. In fact, joggers hit the trail at dawn most days of the year. Historic mansions, riverside villages, and Hudson River views distract them from the work at hand, while the stone markers at every mile ensure they stay on pace.

You don't have to be an endurance athlete to appreciate the trail: Cyclists, walkers, cross-country skiers, and horseback-riders of all levels enjoy the path and its ever-changing scenery. Access is convenient to most of the train stations along the Metro-North Hudson Line, including Hastings-on-Hudson, Dobbs Ferry, Irvington, and Greystone in Yonkers. Parking is available at the train stations and also at the Ossining Heritage Area Visitor Center. The community organization **Friends of the Old Croton Aqueduct** (www.aqueduct.org) publishes a detailed color map of the trail for $5.75.

At the junction of the Croton and Hudson Rivers and within walking distance of the Croton-on-Hudson train station, the fieldstone **Van Cortlandt Manor** (S. Riverside Ave., Croton-on-Hudson, 914/631-8200, www.hudsonvalley.org; Apr.–Oct. Wed.–Mon. 10 A.M.–5 P.M., Nov.–Dec. weekends only 10 A.M.–4 P.M.; adults $9, seniors $8, children $5, under 5 free) hides behind a row of hardwood trees. As the Dutch-style home of a prominent colonial family, the museum contains many original Georgian and Federal period furnishings. On the grounds outside, caretakers plant seasonal heirloom vegetable and herb gardens.

Peekskill

At the northern edge of Westchester County and just below the Hudson Highlands lies the city of **Peekskill,** yet another strategic location during the American Revolution that later became a large manufacturing center and busy river port. After some tough years of decline, Peekskill is quietly attracting artists and small businesses again. Its **Riverfront Green** is a good place to launch a kayak for a paddle around Peekskill Bay.

CENTRAL WESTCHESTER COUNTY

Several old highways traverse the length of central Westchester County, following smaller rivers that empty into the Hudson: the Saw Mill River Parkway connects Manhattan's Upper West Side to the Taconic Parkway in Mount Pleasant; the Bronx River Parkway connects Mount Vernon to the Taconic at I-287; and the Hutchinson River Parkway runs from Pelham Manor to I-684. In the center of all the traffic is White Plains, a land of corporate headquarters, chain hotels, shopping galleries, and business conference centers.

Named for the fog that hung over its wetlands when the first settlers arrived, White Plains has secured its place in history: It was the site of a major Revolutionary War battle, and George Washington set up a command from the 1720 **Jacob Purdy House** (60 Park Ave., White Plains, 914/428-1776; by appointment only). Unless you seek upscale stores outside of New York City, however, you'll find few sights that require a special trip.

Neuberger Museum of Art

East of White Plains, near the Westchester County Airport, is an outstanding modern art museum (735 Anderson Hill Rd., Purchase, 914/251-6100, www.neuberger.org; Tues.–Fri. 10 A.M.–4 P.M., Sat.–Sun. 11 A.M.–5 P.M.; adults $5, free admission on the first Sat. of the month). In 1969, Purchase College, part of the State University of New York, received a generous donation of 20th-century American art. Roy R. Neuberger enabled the college to begin a collection that now features contemporary and African art, as well as its initial base of modern masterpieces. The permanent collection at the Neuberger Museum of Art includes works by Edward Hopper (see Nyack), Georgia O'Keefe, Jackson Pollack, and Mark Rothko. Take Exit 28 from the Hutchinson River Parkway.

Pleasantville

In a quiet town off the Saw Mill River Parkway, Frank Lloyd Wright introduced the carport and radiant heat as key elements of his Usonian vision for the American residential neighborhood. Isolated examples of the functional suburban style are scattered across New York; however, the only full-scale cooperative that Wright developed is found in Pleasantville, north of where the Taconic State and Saw Mill River Parkways meet.

Pleasantville's **Usonia** was designed with 47 homes on about 100 acres of thickly wooded property. Wright used light, glass, and open designs to blur the lines between inside and out. Two of the homes are relatively easy to find today, but visitors must look from a distance, because both are private residences. Look for the Reisley House, at 44 Usonia Road. Exit I-684 at Route 120, then turn left onto Bear Ridge Road, and left again onto Usonia Road. The circular Friedman House is located around the corner, at 11 Orchard Brook Drive.

Chappaqua

For much of his 30-year tenure as founding editor of the *New York Tribune*, journalist Horace Greeley (1811–1872) owned a country home in Chappaqua. Today, the town is better known for its high-profile residents, Bill and Hillary Clinton.

A contemporary of Abraham Lincoln, Greeley was an influential writer and political figure who campaigned against slavery, hired Karl Marx as a European columnist, and ran for president against Ulysses S. Grant. To learn more about Greeley's life and works, visit the **New Castle Historical Society** (100 King St., Chappaqua, 914/238-4666, www.newcastle-ny.org; Tues.–Thurs. 1–4 P.M., Sat. noon–4 P.M.), or pick up a copy of his autobiography, *Recollections of a Busy Life,* available in paperback from University Press of the Pacific.

Katonah Museum Mile

New York City's need for water left an indelible mark on the hamlet of Katonah. When city officials flooded the Cross River in the 1890s to add new capacity to the Croton Watershed System, they threatened to swallow the homes that had stood on its bank since the first Europeans arrived. A group of resolute townspeople pooled their resources and moved dozens of buildings to the opposite shore. They planned a simple grid, and the new town thrived as a place of commerce and leisure. As a result, present-day Katonah blends a Victorian look and feel with a modern sensibility.

This community of 5,000 people supports a remarkable group of cultural institutions, three of which comprise the town's Museum Mile, along Route 22. The **Caramoor Center for Music and the Arts** (149 Girdle Ridge Rd., Katonah, 914/232-1252, www.caramoor.org) began as the summer home of Walter and Lucie Rosen, both passionate musicians and patrons of the arts. The Rosens purchased the estate in 1928, and they had exquisite taste in furniture, tapestries, china, and jewels—many of which are on display in the 20 rooms that are open to the public today. They invited musicians to perform in the Old World setting of a Spanish courtyard, and over the years, their private concerts evolved into an annual summer festival. A tour of the house and gardens is intriguing, but to really experience the place, you must attend a performance.

North of Caramoor on Route 22, the **Katonah Museum of Art** (Rte. 22 at Jay St., Katonah, 914/232-9555, www.katonah-museum.org; Tues.–Sat. 10 A.M.–5 P.M., Sat. noon–5 P.M.; adults $3) is known for developing small, high-quality shows that often pair a well-known artist with an emerging local one. In this way, the museum draws a large following while giving exposure to newer works. Exhibits change frequently and have recently included prints by Richard Diebenkorn.

Katonah's third museum is a good place to dive into the early history of the nascent U.S. government. At the conclusion of a distinguished career, diplomat and negotiator John Jay retired to his family's farm in Katonah. A descendant of the Van Cortland family (see Croton), Jay had worked with the Founding Fathers to ensure the future of the new republic. After a succession of international posts, George Washington appointed him first chief justice of the U.S. Supreme Court. His former residence is now the **John Jay Homestead** (Rte. 22, Katonah, 914/232-5651; Wed.–Sat. 10 A.M.–5 P.M., Sun. noon–4 P.M.; adults $7), located on Route 22 between Katonah and Bedford Village. Katonah is at the junction of the Saw Mill River Parkway and I-684, or Exit 6 off I-684.

COURTESY OF WESTCHESTER COUNTY OFFICE OF TOURISM

hikers on a wooden walkway in Ward Pound Ridge Reservation

Cross River

Westchester County's largest park has been a wildlife sanctuary since 1924. Located east of Katonah at the junction of Routes 35 and 121, **Ward Pound Ridge Reservation** (Rtes. 35 & 121, Cross River, 914/864-7317; admission $8) encompasses 4,700 acres of wildflowers, hiking trails, campsites, and picnic grounds, plus an interpretive **Trailside Museum and Wildlife Center** with Native American exhibits.

Somers

IBM and Pepsico draw business travelers to the suburban town of Somers, but a couple of unusual sites are worth a peek if you happen to pass through. Apply the concept of heirloom vegetables to fauna, and you've got **Muscoot Farm Park** (Rte. 100, Somers, 914/864-7282; daily 10 A.M.–4 P.M.). Its rare farm-animal breeds and vintage-equipment exhibits on 777 acres portray the life of the American farmer in the early 20th century. In something of a cross between a petting zoo and a museum, the farm raises pigs, horses, sheep, and ducks. It is also a good place to look for wild butterflies. From Exit 6 on I-684, follow Route 35 west to Route 100. The entrance is a mile down the road, on the right.

Also in Somers is the eclectic **Museum of the Early American Circus** (Rtes. 100 & 202, Somers, 914/277-4977; Thurs. 2–4 P.M., the second and fourth Sun. of each month 1–4 P.M.; admission by donation), one of a couple dozen museums in the country dedicated to the history of this all-American pastime. Several of the town's residents—including one Hachaliah Bailey, of Barnum and Bailey fame—were instrumental in developing the circus as we know it today. They imported some of the first exotic animals and built the first circus tent. The Somers Historical Society has documented their activities in a three-room museum on the 3rd floor of the old Elephant Hotel.

North Salem

Michael Bloomberg and David Letterman are among the well-to-do who vacation in rural North Salem, across the interstate from Somers and close to the Connecticut border. The **Hammond**

COURTESY OF WESTCHESTER COUNTY OFFICE OF TOURISM

vine tending at the North Salem Vineyard

Museum and Japanese Stroll Garden (28 Deveau Rd., North Salem, 914/669-5033, www
.hammondmuseum.org; Wed.–Sat. noon–4 P.M.;
adults $5, seniors $4, under 12 free) blends Eastern and Western aesthetics to create an enchanting outdoor experience. Water lilies, a reflecting
pool, and the red maple terrace take visitors back
to 6th-century Japan. And a delightful combination of rock and sand, waterfalls and evergreens,
stimulate the senses. Inside the Hammond Museum is a collection of Mandarin fans, as well as
several hundred portraits taken by music and theater critic Carl Van Vechten. A miniature replica
of Mount Fuji is also in the works.

THE LONG ISLAND SOUND

You can't exactly hear the surf crashing from
Larchmont or Mamaroneck—and the water is
generally too polluted for swimming—but
Westchester is the only county in the Hudson
Valley that boasts oceanfront property on Long
Island Sound. Much of this area is congested
with suburban sprawl, but if you're headed out to
the Connecticut coast, a couple of sights may
be worth a stop.

New Rochelle

Revolutionary writer and human-rights champion Thomas Paine (1737–1809) lived his later
years and passed away in New Rochelle, and the
town has preserved his former home and some of
its original furnishings. A contemporary of Benjamin Franklin, who helped him get to America
from England, Paine mastered the art of controversy in his writing. His "Common Sense"
pamphlet challenged colonists to fight for independence. Upon returning to Europe midcareer,
he wrote two well-known political treatises,
The Age of Reason and *The Rights of Man*. The
Thomas Paine Cottage (983 North Ave., New
Rochelle, www.thomaspaine.org) is open year-round to visitors.

Rye

Roughly a million visitors a year come to Rye's
Playland Amusement Park (Playland Parkway,
Rye, 914/813-7010, www.ryeplayland.org; weekends and some midweek days May–Sept., longest
hours in July–Aug. Tues.–Sun. noon–11 P.M.;
$21 for 24 tickets), along a boardwalk on the
Long Island Sound. The park has been entertaining thrill-seekers since 1928, and its art deco

buildings are now recognized as a National Historic Landmark. New rides for the 2004 season included a rollercoaster called Super Flight that barrels along at 25 miles per hour, taking sudden twists and turns to create the illusion of flight.

SPORTS AND RECREATION

Winter Sports

Despite its population density, Westchester maintains 17,000 acres of public parks for recreation throughout the year. Many of them are ideal for cross-country skiing after heavy winter storms. Take a loop around the lake on three miles of trails at **Cranberry Lake Preserve** (Old Orchard St., White Plains, 914/428-1005). Some sections of the gently graded **Old Croton Aqueduct** are also skiable. Try Croton Dam Plaza in Croton or North Tarrytown, near Rockefeller State Park.

Hiking

Westchester wilderness lends itself more to a walk in the woods than a backcountry experience. But several large green spaces make it possible to get well away from the bustle of everyday suburban life. Many of Westchester's parks are open to residents only and require the purchase of a county parks pass (www.westchestergov.com/parks/parkpass.htm; $45 for three years). Both **Tibbetts Brook Park** (Midland Ave., Yonkers, 914/231-2865) and **Sprain Ridge Park** (Jackson Ave., Yonkers, 914/231-3450; adults $5.75 with a required Westchester County Park Pass) have trails for hiking and biking. More than 230 species of migrating birds have been sited at the **Marshlands Conservancy** (Rte. 1, Rye, 914/835-4466; nature center 9 A.M.–4 P.M.; Westchester County Parks Pass not required), on Long Island Sound.

Mountain Biking and Road Riding

In addition to the parks above, Westchester County maintains a network of trailways for cyclists—paths that are mostly paved and closed to motorists. The **South County Trailway** is a 14.1-mile path that runs north to south in the southern part of the county. Pick up the northern end by the Eastview park-and-ride at Route 100C. The **North County Trailway** starts at the

same park-and-ride and runs north for 21 miles. There is a relatively steep climb up from the Croton Reservoir. The **Bronx River Parkway** also closes to traffic for Bicycle Sundays, May–September. **TrailMasters Touring** (914/325-5916, www.trailmasterstouring.com) offers tours and clinics to riders of all levels.

Golf

New York City executives support some 50 public and private golf courses across the county. The newest course is the **Hudson Hills Golf Course** (400 Croton Dam Rd., Ossining, 914/864-3000; www.hudsonhillsgolf.com; weekends $100, weekdays $85). Architect Mark Mungeam, who led the overhaul of Chicago's Olympia Fields Country Club for the 2003 U.S. Open, designed the course. You'll have to fight the city crowd for tee times.

In 2004, the **Centennial Golf Club** (185 John Simpson Rd., Carmel, 845/225-5700, www.centennialgolf.com; weekends $125, weekdays $95) deployed a golf-cart GPS system as a convenience to players. The Larry Nelson 7,100-yard course strictly enforces a pace-of-play policy, so if you waggle like Sergio and fall behind, you may be gently reminded to keep the game moving. Greens are fast but roll true. First-rate service compensates for the steep fees.

Dunwoodie Golf Course (Wasylenko Lane, Yonkers, 914/231-3490, www.westchestergov.com/parks/golf/dunwoodie.htm; $37 weekends $44 weekdays, reduced rates with parks pass) is county-owned, and some patrons say it shows in the greens. The short 5,815-yard, par 70 course offers plenty of challenges, with elevation changes and a deep rough. Extensive course renovations began in August 2004.

All 18 tees were recently renovated and expanded at **Maple Moor Golf Course** (North St., White Plains, 914/995-9200; $37 weekends $44 weekdays, reduced rates with parks pass). Some greens are slow on this 6,226-yard, par 71 course, but there's enough action to keep it interesting. Don't let the highway noise on the front nine distract you.

Swimming and Boating

Kayak Hudson (Five Islands Park, New Rochelle,

888/321-4837, www.kayakhudson.com; Mon.–
Wed. 6 A.M.–6:30 P.M., Thurs. 6 A.M.–10 P.M.,
Fri. 6 A.M.–11 P.M.) takes paddlers on guided trips
on the Hudson River and Long Island Sound.

Fishing and Hunting

Freshwater fishing in Westchester revolves
around the reservoir system. With a New York
Watershed permit, you can catch large bass
and the occasional trout. Rent a canoe to open
up the possibilities. **Mohansic Lake** (201 Haw-
ley Rd., North Salem, 914/864-7310) is a zoo
on summer weekends, but it is known to have
aggressive bass and large crappie. **Kensico
Reservoir,** three miles north of White Plains,
has rainbows, browns, and lakers up to about
15 or 20 pounds.

ACCOMMODATIONS

Westchester has mastered the science of the business conference hotel. Although there are a few exceptions, for more charming accommodations,
you're better off heading north to Putnam County,
or south to New York City.

$150–200

Crabtree's Kittle House (11 Kittle Rd., Chappaqua, 914/666-8044, www.kittlehouse.com;
$147) is first and foremost an outstanding
restaurant, but its 12 moderately priced rooms
are an added convenience if you plan to sample
more than a taste from its enormous wine cellar. Rooms are decorated simply in pastels and
floral linens, and with white trim and dark
wood furniture.

Dolce Tarrytown (E. Sunnyside Lane, Tarrytown, 914/591-8200, tarrytownhouse.dolce.com;
$150–180) is a good option for staying close to
the action in Tarrytown but within an easy drive
of New York City. The hotel has 200 modern
rooms and is part of an international chain of
properties. High-speed wireless Internet service
caters to business travelers who appreciate the
proximity to nearby corporate headquarters. The
Presidential Suite offers a striking view of the
Hudson. In winter, rooms in the King House
also have river views.

With 300 rooms set on 30 acres, the **Renaissance Westchester Hotel** (80 West Red Oak
Lane, White Plains, 914/694-5400; $130) is a
comfortable Marriott property that primarily
hosts business travelers.

Over $200

One of the priciest places to stay in the Hudson
Valley region is the **Castle on the Hudson** (400
Benedict Ave., Tarrytown, www.castleonthe-
hudson.com; $350–725). Built by the son of a
Civil War general on a hilltop outside of Tarrytown, this ultra-luxurious inn features a 75-foot
tower that is the highest point in Westchester
County. Its rooms feature high ceilings and
plenty of natural light. Elegant drapery and furnishings create a decidedly Old World atmosphere. Dinner at Equus Restaurant onsite will
be an experience to remember, if only for the
views and the bill.

FOOD

Restaurants are plentiful and diverse in Westchester, serving cuisines from Indian to Southwest.
French and Italian themes are most common,
and the county offers a number of casual cafés
and local farm stands. That said, there are lot of
expense-account traps to avoid—unless, of
course, you're on an expense account.

Along the River–Route 9

In an unlikely location near a Citgo gas station and a Toyota dealership, **Nyauta** (27
Meyer Ave., Yonkers, 914/476-5900, www
.nyauta.com) has affordably priced Indian cuisine. Spices ground on the premises and homemade cheese and yogurt add a special touch.
Also in Yonkers, Hunan Village is a top choice
for gourmet Chinese.

Up the hill from the Hastings train station,
tiny **M Buffet de la Gare** (155 Southside Ave.,
Hastings-on-Hudson, 914/478-1671; Tues.–Sat.
6–9:30 P.M. and Thurs.–Fri. noon–2 P.M.; dinner
menu mains $22–33) serves a mouthwatering
cassoulet, along with other French specialties
such as venison, duck confit, and coq au vin.

For outdoor dining on a warm summer eve, try

Harvest on Hudson (1 River St., Hastings-on-Hudson, 914/478-2800, www.harvest2000.com; dinner daily and lunch Mon.–Fri.). Set in an inviting Tuscan farmhouse, the restaurant prepares Mediterranean foods, including heirloom tomatoes from a garden onsite.

Tarrytown's Main Street has a full menu of choices for casual and fine dining. The "Labs" **Ⓜ Coffee Labs** (7 Main St., Tarrytown, 914/332-1479; drinks $2–5) refer to Labrador retrievers, which the owners evidently adore. This is your stop for Fair Trade coffees and a great selection of teas. Try the Rooibos winter blend on a snowy afternoon.

Lefteris (1 Main St., Tarrytown, 914/524-9687, www.lefterisgyro.com; daily 11 A.M.–10 P.M.; mains $5–16) packs in the crowds at the corner of Main and Broadway. Neighboring shop owners use this busy Greek restaurant as a barometer for the business level on any given day. Sit outside and enjoy the traditional Greek salads and excellent people watching.

Continuing toward the river, **Main Street Café** (24 Main St., Tarrytown, 914/524-9770; lunch and dinner daily) attracts a mix of locals and out-of-towners with a diverse menu and outdoor seating along Main Street. You can walk to the Tarrytown Music Hall from family-run **Lago di Como** (27 Main St., Tarrytown, 914/631-7227, www.lagodicomorestaurant.com; Tues.–Sat. noon–2:30 P.M. and 5–10 P.M., Sun. 4–9 P.M.; mains $14–35) after a meal of northern Italian specialties.

At the docks in the Tarrytown marina, **Striped Bass** (236 W. Main St., Tarrytown, 914/366-4455, www.stripedbassny.com; lunch and dinner daily) offers a Caribbean menu and live jazz on weekends.

Also centrally located is **Horsefeathers** (94 N. Broadway, Tarrytown, 914/631-6606, www.horsefeatherstarrytown.com; lunch and dinner daily from 11:30 A.M.), known for its literary decor and a tome of a menu, which is arranged by chapters and includes 100 types of beer. Burgers and pub fare prevail. Across from the Tarrytown Hilton Inn, **El Dorado West** (460 S. Broadway, Tarrytown, 914/332-5838) is a classic diner that's open late.

On a hilltop outside of town, **Equus Restaurant** (400 Benedict Ave., Tarrytown, 914/631-3646, www.castleonthehudson.com) may be the place to celebrate a special occasion. Part of The Castle at Tarrytown, the restaurant offers an outstanding, if pricey, wine list and a seasonal prix fixe menu consisting of four courses. Sunday brunch and high tea are good alternatives to a full lunch or dinner.

One of Westchester's newest experiments in fine-dining, **Ⓜ Blue Hill at Stone Barns** (630 Bedford Rd., Pocantico Hills, 914/366-9600, www.bluehillstonebarns.com; Wed.–Sun. 5–10 P.M., Sat. till 11 P.M., Sun. brunch 11 A.M.–2:30 P.M.; two courses $46, three courses $56, four courses $66), takes the concept of seasonal cuisine up a notch. True to the Rockefeller vision of a self-sustained farm, the restaurant raises its own livestock, as well as herbs and produce, on the premises. Chef Dan Barber hails from the original Blue Hill in New York City and a genuine family farm in the Berkshires. Dinner and brunch are served in a converted dairy barn with window views designed to offer harried city people a chance to take in the quiet countryside.

At **Zeph's** (638 Central Ave., Peekskill, 914/736-2159), Victoria Zeph prepares a creative menu that reflects an ever-changing variety of international influences, from French and Chinese to Moroccan, Caribbean, and Thai. The setting is a converted gristmill outside downtown Peekskill.

Central Westchester County

Bengal Tiger (144 E. Post Rd., White Plains, 914/948-5191; lunch and dinner daily) and **Coromandel** (30 Division St., New Rochelle, 914/235-8390; daily noon–2:30 P.M., Thurs.–Sun. 5–10 P.M., Fri.–Sat. till 11 P.M.) rank among Westchester's best for Indian-inspired fare.

Take a break from the shopping to dine at **P.F. Chang's China Bistro** (The Westchester Mall, 125 Westchester Ave., White Plains, 914/997-6100, www.pfchangs.com; mains $7–18), part of a national chain of upscale Chinese restaurants.

Finch Tavern (592 Rte. 22, Croton Falls, 914/277-4580, www.finchtavern.com; Tues.–Fri.

11:30 A.M.–2:30 P.M. and 5:30–10 P.M., Fri.–Sat. till 11 P.M., Sun. 11 A.M.–2 P.M. and 5–9 P.M.; mains $17–30) opened in 2002 in a historic home along Route 22 with a menu of fish, meat, and pasta dishes that are designed to highlight local flavors.

Locals praise **Iron Horse Grill** (20 Wheeler Ave., Pleasantville, 914/741-0717, www.ironhorsegrill.com; Tues.–Sat. 5 P.M.; mains $25–29) for contemporary American dishes including breast of pheasant and tenderloin of venison. The 60-seat restaurant occupies a converted train station.

A stroll along Katonah's main thoroughfare reveals a handful of tempting places to eat. **Blue Dolphin Ristorante** (175 Katonah Ave., Katonah, 914/232-4791; lunch & dinner Mon.–Sat.; mains $12–18) prepares fresh daily seafood specials, making it a local favorite. Expect to wait for a table on weekends. Across from the train station, **Willy Nick's Café** (17 Katonah Ave., Katonah, 914/232-8030) has patrons raving about its oversized waffles, steel-banded retro tables, and blintzes.

N Crabtree's Kittle House (11 Kittle Rd., Chappaqua, 914/666-8044; lunch Mon.–Fri., dinner daily; mains $18–32) has an unparalleled selection of wines, with more than 50,000 bottles in its cellar. Order a special bottle in advance to have it brought up to temperature or let sediment settle out. A creative American menu leads to some fabulous wine and food pairings. Try a half-bottle of Condrieu with the scallop appetizer.

Power business lunches take place at **Mulino's** (99 Court St., White Plains, 914/761-1818; Mon.–Thurs. 11:30 A.M.–11:30 P.M., Fri. till midnight, Sat. 5 P.M.–midnight; $25–30), known more for its free starter plates than for standout northern Italian food. **Little Spot** (854 N. Broadway, White Plains, 914/761-1334; mains $5) is a roadside find, serving "freedom fries," split chili dogs, and milkshakes to rave reviews.

Fresh fish and reasonable prices bring in the crowds at **Eastchester Fish Gourmet** (837 White Plains Rd., Scarsdale, 914/725-3450; 11:30 A.M.–2:30 P.M., daily dinner at 5 P.M.; mains $8–12). Expect a wait unless you show up early.

The Long Island Sound

La Panetière Restaurant (530 Milton Rd., Rye, www.lapanetiere.com; lunch Mon.–Fri., dinner daily; mains $17–26) excels in the service department. The menu is Provençal, and the atmosphere defines "elegant."

The Bayou Restaurant (580 Gramatan Ave., Mount Vernon, 914/668-2634, www.thebayourestaurantny.com; daily 11:30 A.M.–11 P.M., Thurs.–Sat. till 1 A.M.; mains $13–20) prepares Cajun delights and live music performances.

ENTERTAINMENT AND EVENTS
Performing Arts
Built by music lovers for music lovers, **Caramoor Center for Music and the Arts** (149 Girdle Ridge Rd., Katonah, 914/232-1252, www.caramoor.org) features classical and jazz performances in two theaters. The **Performing Arts Center** (735 Anderson Hill Rd., Purchase, 914/251-6200, www.artscenter.org; Mon.–Fri. 10 A.M.–6 P.M.) holds 600 jazz, cabaret, and classical music events annually. You can catch Tony Bennett on a summer weekend or watch the *Wizard of Oz* with the kids.

Another popular evening venue is Elmsford's **Westchester Broadway Theatre** (1 Broadway Plaza, Elmsford, 914/592-2222, www.broadwaytheatre.com; $56–77), a dinner theater that produces musicals, comedy, and children's shows. Choose from matinee or evening performances. The standard dinner menu includes chicken marsala, prime rib, and roast pork loin.

Musicians from Dave Brubeck to Bruce Springsteen have performed on the stage of the 1885 **Tarrytown Music Hall** (13 Main St., Tarrytown, box office 866/302-5739, information 914/631-3390, www.tarrytownmusichall.org). A local nonprofit rescued the theater from near demolition in the 1970s, and although the building is showing its age outside, it continues to host concerts, plays, musicals, operas, dance performances, and recordings inside. In 2004, the theater began showing movies again, after a 27-year hiatus.

Bars and Nightlife
Get your blues fix at **Isabel's Café** (61 Main St., Tarrytown, 914/332-1992). The owner has pulled

bands off stage if he finds the music below par at this well-loved local establishment. The food is American with a Scandinavian slant. Call ahead for a table. **New Roc City** (33 LeCount Pl., Yonkers, 914/637-7575, www.newroccity.com) has it all under one roof: ice rink, minigolf, a multiplex theater with an IMAX screen, and even a grocery store.

Festivals

Caramoor International Summer Music Festival (149 Girdle Ridge Rd., Katonah, 914/232-1252, www.caramoor.org; July–Aug.) is a summer concert series with a wide range of productions from classical music to Latin jazz fusion. Many shows sell out, so check the website early for tickets.

Yonkers Hudson Riverfest (Yonkers Waterfront, Yonkers, www.yonkersriverfest.com) is a daylong environmental and multicultural festival held every September. Tens of thousands of visitors come each year. A new "ferry-go-round" provides ferry service to five communities for events, fireworks, and arts and crafts. Also on the river, the Clearwater Festival takes place in Croton each June (see the *Mid-Hudson* chapter).

SHOPPING

Westchester and shopping go all the way back to the Great Depression, when the first department store opened in White Plains. Today you can find it all, from antiques and flea markets to Neiman Marcus. If you're on a quest for unusual antiques, head to Bedford Hills, Cross River, Tarrytown, or Larchmont. With more than 100 stores, the **Cross County Shopping Center** (6-K Mall Walk, Yonkers, 914/968-9570), in Yonkers, is one of the oldest and largest malls in the county, while The Westchester, in White Plains, and Vernon Hills Shopping Center, in Eastchester, are among the most upscale.

The **Charles Department Store** (113 Katonah Ave., Katonah, 914/232-5200; Mon.–Fri. 9 A.M.–6 P.M., Sat. 9 A.M.–5 P.M.) is a throwback to the era of the family-owned department store. The store is managed by the grandsons of the founder and sells everything from shoes to coffeepots.

Antiques and Galleries

For a wide selection of fine jewelry, browse the shops in **Kohl's Shopping Center** (515 Boston Post Rd., Port Chester, 914/939-1800; Fri. 10 A.M.–8 P.M., Sat.–Sun. 10 A.M.–6 P.M., Thanksgiving–Christmas daily). Take Exit 21 from I-95 or Exit 11 from I-287.

Hundreds of vendors set up outdoor booths at the **Yonkers Raceway Market** (914/963-3898; Mar.–Dec. Sun. 9 A.M.–4 P.M.) each Sunday. Goods for sale include new merchandise, as well as antiques and collectibles. From the New York Thruway, take Exit 2 northbound or Exit 4 southbound.

Yellow Monkey Antiques (Rte. 35, Cross River, 845/763-5848, www.yellowmonkey.com; Tues.–Sun. 10 A.M.–5:30 P.M.) has more than 7,000 square feet of showrooms that focus on British Pine antiques that are shipped in large quantities from Europe.

For one weekend each November, antique collectors and interior designers descend on the Westchester County Center for the acclaimed **White Plains Antique Show** (198 Central Ave., White Plains, 914/698-3442; admission $5). In its 69th year in 2004, the show includes collections of American, English, Swedish, and Continental furniture; vintage posters; Steuben glass; estate jewelry; and fine china and ceramics.

Riverrun Rare Book Room (12 Washington St., Hastings-on-Hudson, 914/478-1339; daily 11 A.M.–5 P.M.) is a haven for aficionados, with 200,000 titles in two stores and two warehouses. The collection includes signed books, vintage paperbacks, and modern first editions.

Inside a municipal building on Maple Avenue, **The Gallery at Hastings-on-Hudson** (7 Maple Ave., Hastings-on-Hudson, 914/478-4141; Wed.–Sun. noon–5 P.M.) produces rotating exhibits of art from Westchester County.

Farm Stands

In Tarrytown, family-owned **Mint Premium Foods** (18 Main St., Tarrytown, 914/703-6511; Mon.–Sat. 11 A.M.–10 P.M.) carries gourmet cheese, olive oils, and meats, as well as organic teas and honey. **North Salem Vineyard** (441 Hardscrabble Rd., North Salem, 914/669-5518, www.northsalemwine.com; Sat.–Sun. 1–5 P.M.) grows Seyval Blanc, Foch, de Chaunac, and Chancellor grapes and has a tasting room on weekends year-round.

The **Tarrytown Farmers Market** (914/923-4837; Jun.–Oct. Sat. 8:30 A.M.–2 P.M.) takes place at Patriot's Park off Route 9. Look for the **Hastings-on-Hudson Farmers Market** (914/923-4837; mid-June–mid-November Saturday 8:30A.M.–2P.M.) in the town library parking lot off Maple Avenue.

INFORMATION AND SERVICES

The **Westchester County Office of Tourism** (222 Mamaroneck Ave., White Plains, 800/833-9282, tourism@westchestergov.com) also runs a tourism information center at Exit 9 off the Bronx River Parkway, near Leewood Drive.

GETTING THERE AND AROUND
By Bus
The Bee-Line System is a countywide bus service with more than 55 different routes and express service. Routes serve many of the county's recreational facilities and also provide connection to trains.

By Train
It's hard to avoid the Metro-North commuter line in Westchester. It was practically built to serve this county's suburbs, and today, there are 43 station stops on three lines providing continual service to Manhattan's Grand Central Station and points within the county.

By Car
You can rent a car at the Westchester Airport in White Plains. But be forewarned: Traffic is bad and getting worse in Westchester—both from cars passing through and from those that belong to local residents. The Tappan Zee Bridge regularly backs up during the rush hour commute. Drive off-peak when you can and allow extra time to reach your destination at any time of day. Tune in to frequent metropolitan area traffic reports on the radio at AM 880 "on the eights" (1:08, 1:18, 1:28, etc.) and AM 1010 "on the ones" (1:01, 1:11, 1:21, etc.).

Rockland County

With the Hudson River, New Jersey, and Orange County as its borders, Rockland County is the smallest county in the state, outside of the five boroughs of New York City. Located just 16 miles from New York City, Rockland has protected almost a third of its 176 square miles from development, thanks in part to generous donations from the wealthy families who built the first mansions along its riverbank. The terrain encompasses approximately 30 miles of Hudson River frontage, plus Bear Mountain and Harriman State Parks, which contain most of the Ramapo Mountain Range.

Rockland County's first European settlers arrived to join the Native American population in the 17th century. Initially a part of Orange County, Rockland separated in 1798 because the Ramapo Mountains made it difficult for residents to reach the county courthouse in Goshen.

Rockland communities endured two key battles during the Revolutionary War: British forces captured Fort Clinton at Bear Mountain in October 1777, but two years later, colonial forces overwhelmed the British at Stony Point. Benedict Arnold's partner in treason, British Major John Andre, was captured in Tarrytown across the river. In his possession were the plans for West Point that he had received from Arnold. Andre was taken to the village of Tappan for trial. A jury found him guilty, and he was hanged.

Like most of the neighboring Hudson River communities, Rockland grew around the industries of milling lumber, making bricks, harvesting ice, mining, and quarrying. In the 1920s, internationally accomplished artists and performers settled in the area, including painter and muralist Henry Varnum Poor, playwright Maxwell Anderson, and composer Kurt Weil.

Artist Edward Hopper hailed from Nyack, along with actress Helen Hayes.

The opening of the Tappan Zee Bridge, Palisades Interstate Parkway, and New York State Thruway, all in the 1950s, ended Rockland's days as a rural getaway. The county began to absorb much of the sprawl from New York City, and business conference centers became plentiful. Fortunately, Rockland has managed to develop without compromising its treasured green space. Dozens of historic markers remind visitors of the churches, farms, cemeteries, and homes that hold a significant place in the American past. At the same time, numerous immigrant communities have helped create a vibrant scene for restaurants, performing arts, and museums. Several world-class shopping malls line the Route 59 corridor near Nanuet.

Four townships hold most of the county's historic and outdoor attractions: Clarkstown, Haverstraw, Ramapo, and Stony Point. New City is the county seat.

ALONG THE RIVER—ROUTE 9W

Rockland County begins about 10 miles north of the George Washington Bridge (I-95), a main artery out of New York City. From the bridge, the Palisades Interstate Parkway cuts diagonally across the county, and Route 9W hugs the riverbank. Near the New Jersey state line, the dramatic Palisades cliffs plunge into the river, creating a playground for geologists and rock climbers alike.

Piermont Village

Rockland's major river crossing, the Tappan Zee Bridge (I-287), is the longest span across the Hudson, connecting Rockland residents to Westchester County and points east. With 85,000 cars a day passing through, the bridge is the busiest crossing in the region.

Three miles south of the Tappan Zee Bridge, on a steep hillside between Route 9W and the riverbank, is the upscale village of Piermont, where you can savor a $40 prix fixe brunch at **Xaviers** (506 Piermont Ave., Piermont, 845/359-7007), paddle a canoe through 1,000 acres of marsh, and then return to town for an

evening of live music. Piermont has long been a haven for creative types. Woody Allen's 1985 film *The Purple Rose of Cairo* was filmed here, as was *At First Sight* (1999), starring Mira Sorvino and Val Kilmer.

These days, many residents also commute daily into Manhattan and ride their Italian-made bicycles on the weekends. A row of lively bistros and boutiques takes up most of Piermont Avenue in the village center, where a mile-long pier juts out over the marsh and into the Hudson.

Initially built to handle steamboat traffic, and later, railroad commerce, the **Piermont Pier** became the site of a successful paper mill during the 20th century. During World War II, tens of thousands of U.S. troops boarded ships to Normandy from the pier, earning it the name "Last Stop USA." The soldiers received their last training and inspections at **Camp Shanks,** four miles west of the pier. The camp also housed German and Italian prisoners of war until the end of the conflict. It's hard to get a sense of the magnitude of the camp from the small museum that remains today. Exhibits inside a model barracks depict life during the war.

Today, the Piermont Pier is a public park that attracts anglers, walkers, and anyone in search of a cool breeze. Just south of the pier is **Tallman Mountain State Park** (Rte. 9, Bear Mountain, 845/359-0544; admission $7), a favorite spot for viewing birds and wildflowers on land that once belonged to John D. Rockefeller's Standard Oil Company. Additional facilities include a public pool and tennis courts. Take Exit 4 from the Palisades Parkway to reach the Piermont area.

Tappan

Students of the Revolutionary War must pay a visit to several sites in the village of **Tappan,** a few miles southwest from Piermont. George Washington turned the Dutch colonial **DeWint House** (20 Livingston Ave., Tappan, 845/359-1359; free admission)—now a registered national landmark and the oldest building in Rockland County—into temporary headquarters during the trial of Major John Andre, the British spy who was accused of conspiring with Benedict Arnold. The trial took place at the county courthouse, which stood on the Village Church Green, next door to the 1835 **Reformed Church of Tappan** that stands today.

Near a stoplight at the center of town is the **The Old '76 House,** built in 1755. Andre was held captive here until his execution. The building is now a restaurant and tavern (see *Food*).

Nyack

On the other side of the Tappan Zee Bridge lies the busier commercial center of Nyack ("Point of Land"), part of the Clarkstown township. Home to a vibrant mix of artists, immigrants, and commuters (many of whom know each other by name), Nyack draws day-trippers out of the city with the **Edward Hopper House Art Center** (82 N. Broadway, Nyack, 845/358-0774, www.edwardhopperhouseartcenter.org; Thurs.–Sun. 1–5 P.M.; donation requested), as well as dozens of galleries, shops, and restaurants. Most of the businesses are gathered around the intersection of Main Street, (which slopes downhill toward the river), and Broadway, which runs parallel to it. Look for a visitor information booth near the Clock Tower, where Main Street crosses Cedar.

Realist painter Edward Hopper spent his childhood in a modest clapboard house on Broadway, a few blocks north of the main retail strip. After attending high school in Nyack, he moved to New York City, but returned home frequently throughout his career. A small museum in the family home, now a restored New York State Historic Site, documents Hopper's life and displays works by local artists. In summer, jazz concerts are often held in the garden.

A short drive beyond the Edward Hopper House leads to a row of riverside mansions—many of them owned by celebrities, including Rosie O'Donnell—protected by imposing brick and stone fences. At the end of this exclusive neighborhood is **Nyack Beach State Park** (Broadway, 845/268-3020; open year-round; admission $8), where local residents come to walk, relax, and fish. A two-mile trail for jogging and biking follows the river north to Hook Mountain. Trains rumble in the distance, and to the south, you can see the Tappan Zee Bridge.

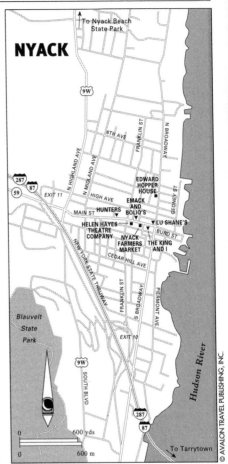

New City

Between Rockland Lake State Park and Haverstraw, Route 304 West leads to New City, where the **Historical Society of Rockland County** produces historical exhibits inside the **Jacob Blauvelt House** (20 Zukor Rd., New City, 845/634-9629, www.rocklandhistory.org; Tues.–Sun. 1–5 P.M.; admission $5). This two-story brick farmhouse was built in 1832 in the Dutch style. Six rooms and an 1865 carriage house are currently open to visitors. Exhibits cover a broad span of time and address a range of topics relevant to the local experience. Native American culture,

Dutch bibles, Civil War diaries, 19th-century furnishings, the agrarian lifestyle, and former industries (such as making bricks, harvesting ice, mining, and quarrying) are all represented. Take Exit 10 from the Palisades Parkway.

Haverstraw Bay

Natural resources and innovation in the process of brick making positioned Haverstraw at the forefront of the construction industry through most of the 19th century. In 1771, clay was discovered in the Hudson offshore from Haverstraw, and the ability to mold bricks into a standard size allowed Rockland County to play a pivotal role in the building of New York City. At its peak before the advent of steel and the Great Depression, the local industry supported 42 independent brickyards. The **Haverstraw Brick Museum** (12 Main St., Haverstraw, 845/947-3505, www .haverstrawbrickmuseum.org; Wed. 1–4 P.M., Sat.–Sun. 1–4 P.M.; admission $2), open three afternoons a week, documents the history of the industry. A ferry to the Ossining Metro-North station departs from Short Clove Road.

Stony Point Battlefield State Historical Site

Located on Haverstraw Bay is an all-important Revolutionary War site: the Stony Point Battlefield State Historical Site (Park Rd. off Rte. 9W, Stony Point, 845/786-2521, www2.lhric.org/spbattle/spbattle.htm; Wed.–Sat. 10 A.M.–5 P.M.; free admission) is a riverside park and museum that includes the oldest lighthouse on the Hudson (1826). On the night of July 15, 1779, Brigadier General Anthony Wayne led a small group of colonial soldiers in a midnight assault on the British troops who had taken control of the point. In a textbook operation, Wayne's men waded silently through marsh and mud to catch the British by surprise. A small but important win, the victory restored morale among American troops.

It takes about 10 minutes to walk from the parking lot to the lighthouse, where visitors are rewarded with a view of Haverstraw Bay. Interpretive signs inside the park document the battle, and staff members occasionally dress up in colonial costumes to set the mood. There are two

entrances to the park from Route 9W: a historic marker indicates the southern turnoff, while the northern one is more difficult to spot.

THE RAMAPO MOUNTAINS

Rockland's greatest outdoor treasure is an enormous green space that straddles the border with Orange County, running southwest from the Bear Mountain Bridge almost to the New Jersey state line. Thanks in part to families like the Rockefellers, Vanderbilts, and Harrimans, more than 50,000 rugged acres are divided into two adjoining state parks: Harriman (46,000 acres) and Bear Mountain (5,000 acres).

Harriman State Park

The first section of the Appalachian Trail was cleared here in 1923, and today, hikers can access 200 miles of trails and more than 30 lakes and reservoirs inside the second largest park in the New York state system. Seven Lakes Drive runs the length of Harriman State Park (Rte. 9W, Bear Mountain, 845/786-2701; admission $7) and provides access to the main recreation areas, including Lake Sebago, Lake Welch, Lake Tioran, and the Anthony Wayne Recreation Area.

Camping, swimming, and picnics are permitted. Wilderness accommodations include shelters, cabins, and campsites. There are two entrances to the park: from Route 17 in Sloatsburg or from the Palisades Parkway near West Haverstraw. Park only in designated areas. The park often fills to capacity on busy holiday weekends; a midweek visit affords more tranquility, but if you do arrive with the masses, you can quickly escape by heading into the backcountry.

Bear Mountain State Park

Formed in 1910 as a reaction against the proposed relocation of Sing Sing prison from Ossining, the smaller but well-developed **Bear Mountain** (Rte. 9W, Bear Mountain, 845/786-2701; admission $7) sees as many visitors per year as the most popular national parks. The sprawling parking lot gives an indication of how crowded the park can get on hot summer weekends.

Near the entrance, a stone lodge overlooking

Hessian Lake houses the **Bear Mountain Inn** (Bear Mountain, 845/786-2731, www.bearmountaininn.com; $89)—which was *the* place to stay in 1920s New York. Prospective guests had to complete an application and provide a personal recommendation for the privilege of spending the night. The price of $3.50 a day bought a room with all meals.

Inside the lodge, mounted moose and elk heads and a portrait of Rip Van Winkle stand guard above a great stone fireplace in the 2nd-floor lounge. Two spacious dining rooms seat dozens of guests for dinner, and guestrooms occupy the 3rd floor. The splendor of the old days has faded, however, and the lodge desperately needs attention. Efforts are under way to raise money for renovations, but it will be years before visitors see the results.

Behind the inn, Perkins Memorial Drive winds its way to the top of Bear Mountain and a commanding view of the highlands. Hikers can reach the summit in about three hours, starting at Hessian Lake. The **Bear Mountain Trailside Museum** entertains kids with exhibits on black bears, beavers, coyotes, and other animals. Additional activities include swimming, paddleboats, ice skating, and numerous seasonal festivals. Look for the entrance to Bear Mountain State Park on Route 9W, about half a mile from the traffic circle at the **Bear Mountain Bridge**.

Common wisdom said it would take the Bear Mountain Hudson River Bridge Company 30 years to build a span across the narrowest part of the Hudson—it would be the longest suspension bridge in its day. Engineers finished in 20 months, and the first crossing over the river opened to traffic in 1924. The Appalachian Trail crosses the river at this point, and many hikers stop to admire the views of the highlands from the span.

THE ROUTE 59 CORRIDOR

The old Nyack Turnpike, built to transport manufactured goods from the Ramapo Mountains to the Hudson River, is now a busy thoroughfare that connects the towns of Suffern, Spring Valley, and Nanuet to Nyack. Along Route 59 are several suburban communities with sprawling shopping centers.

On a more somber note, **The Holocaust Mu-**

Montgomery Place

seum and Study Center (17 South Madison Ave., Spring Valley, 845/356-2700, www.holocauststudies.org; Tues.–Thurs. noon–4 P.M. and occasionally Sun.; adults $5, students $3), in Spring Valley, displays documents, artifacts, and films as a powerful reminder of the tragedy. Particularly moving is the Children's Wall, built as a memorial to the youngest victims of the Holocaust.

Continuing along Route 59, you reach historic **Suffern** with a handful of shops and restaurants, as well as Rockland County's largest movie complex, the 1927 **Lafayette Theatre** (Rte. 59 & Washington Ave., Suffern, 845/369-8234). The **Suffern Railroad Museum** (Orange Ave., Suffern, 845/357-2600) is housed in the original Wells Fargo Express Mail Depot, which was restored in 1998. For a faster east-west route, take I-287, which runs parallel to Route 59.

SPORTS AND RECREATION

With two large state parks and several smaller green spaces, Rockland offers a surprising variety of possibilities for outdoor entertainment. You can do just about everything in Bear Mountain and Harriman State Parks: hike, bike, boat, camp, picnic, swim, fish, skate, ski, and play.

Winter Sports

When the Hudson ices over and snow blankets the highlands, cross-country skiers head to the two-mile trail at Nyack Beach State Park for a morning of exercise.

Hiking

Harriman State Park is a great place to hike in mid- to late-fall, since no hunting is allowed within its boundaries. A number of daylong routes, including the scenic Lichen Trail, lead to the summit of Surebridge Mountain. Claudius Smith's Den is another popular excursion into the wilderness. The hike begins at the Tuxedo train station (Orange County) along the red-dot trail and ends at the hideout of a Revolutionary War–era outlaw.

For an overnight hike, head to the Cornell trailhead near the Iona Island Bird Sanctuary off Route 9W, follow it to a ghost town called Doodletown, and camp at a shelter near Timp Brook.

Maps are available from the New York–New Jersey Trail Conference (156 Ramapo Valley Rd., Mahwah, NJ, 201/512-9348, www.nynjtc.org). Park only in designated lots for hikers and camp only in public camping areas.

Hook Mountain State Park (Rte. 9W, Nyack, 845/268-3020; admission $8) is well known as a place to watch hawks soar above the treetops. Enter through Rockland Lake State Park and follow signs to the executive golf course. As a courtesy, park away from the club house and look for a yellow mark on the curb next to the flag pole in the cul-de-sac. Proceed to the woods and follow the yellow-blazed trail to the blue blazed trail to the summit. Another entrance is found inside Nyack Beach State Park.

Mountain Biking and Road Riding

Piermont's scenic roads are popular with cyclists, but beware of the steep fine for riding double file. Stop in to chat with the crew at **Piermont Bicycle Connection** (215 Ash St., Piermont, 845/365-0900, www.piermontbike.com) and pick up maps and supplies before you ride. None of the shops in the area rent road bikes.

Golf

Spook Rock Golf Course (199 Spook Rock Rd., Ramapo, 845/357-6466; $55) has large, fast greens with tight fairways. The course consistently ranks in the top public courses in the state. **Rockland Lake State Park Golf Course** (Rte. 9W & Lake Rd, Congers, 845/268-3020; weekends $29, weekdays $24) is a 6,864-yard, par 72 course with 18 holes. A second nine-hole executive course has plenty of bunkers to keep golfers on their toes.

Swimming and Boating

Piermont Marsh is a unique aquatic habitat within walking distance of Piermont's shops and restaurants. The best way to explore it is by canoe or kayak, which you can rent from Captain Bill at **Paradise Boats** (845/359-0073). Look for a sign at the corner of Piermont and Paradise. September and October are the best months to go for a paddle.

Hudson Highland Cruises (Haverstraw Marina, West Haverstraw, 845/534-7245, www.hudsonhighlandcruises.com; adults $14, seniors and children $12) runs river tours out of West Haver-straw, with additional departures from West Point and Peekskill.

ACCOMMODATIONS

Accommodations with personality are surprisingly hard to come by in Rockland County. Like Westchester, Rockland has mostly conference centers and chains, from Marriott and Holiday Inn to Best Western and Super 8. Travelers will be better off continuing on to Orange County to settle down for the night.

Under $100

An alternative to the aging Bear Mountain Inn is **Overlook Lodge** (Bear Mountain, 845/786-2731, www.bearmountaininn.com; $99), on the other side of Hessian Lake. Motel-style rooms are simply furnished with two double beds and private baths, and you can't beat the price.

FOOD
Along the River—Route 9W

You can't go wrong in Nyack when it comes to finding good food. **Lu Shane's** (8 N. Broadway, Nyack, 845/358-5556, www.lushanes.com; mains $20–27) is a relative newcomer, with a raw bar and loud weekend jazz. **Hunters** (162 Main St., Nyack, 845/358-0055), run by the same owner, prepares Caesar salads at the table, and portions are large. **The King & I** (93 Main St., Nyack, 845/358-8588; Mon.–Thurs. and Sun. noon–10 P.M., Fri.–Sat. noon–11 P.M.; mains $7–10) has been serving curries and other specialties to locals for years. Grab an ice cream (or a frozen yogurt that tastes like the real thing) at **Emack and Bolios** (102 Main St., Nyack; $4–5), across the street.

In Piermont, **Pasta Amore** (200 Ash St., Piermont, 845/365-1911; Sun.–Thurs. noon–10 P.M., Fri.–Sat. till 11 P.M.; mains $10–16) does pasta right, with river views and patio seating. **Romolo's** (77 Rte. 303, Congers, 845/268-3770, www.dineromolos.com; closed Mon., lunch on weekdays only; mains $13–28) gets high marks for classic Italian cuisine. Serving tavern cuisine,

including a variety of steaks and seafood and even a chicken pot pie, **The Old '76 House** (110 Main St., Tappan, 845/359-5476, www.76house.com; mains $17–26) also has jazz on Saturday nights and a popular Sunday brunch.

The Ramapo Mountains

Just before the New Jersey state line, the **Mount Fuji Steakhouse** (296 Rte. 17, Hillburn, 845/357-4270, www.mtfujirestaurants.com; mains $20–45) is perched on a hilltop above Route 17. Seating around a private hibachi station and servers tossing cleavers in the air make it the perfect venue to celebrate a birthday or a family reunion. You'll likely wait for a table, even with a reservation. Arrive in daylight to catch the mountain views.

At the southern end of Harriman State Park, the town of Sloatsburg has a handful of casual dining options. Conveniently located on the main route through Harriman State Park, **Miele's Deli & Restaurant** (23 Seven Lakes Dr., Sloatsburg, 845/753-2662; mains $3–10) makes hot and cold sandwiches, as well as burgers and fried shellfish. **The Glenwood** (94 Orange Tpke., Sloatsburg, 845/753-5200; mains $16–30) prepares a comprehensive American menu of steaks, seafood, and chicken entrées.

In a pinch, you can also grab a quick bite to eat at the concession stand at Lake Welch State Beach in Harriman State Park. For a greater variety of dining options, Suffern, at the southern edge of the park along Route 59, is the next closest town.

The Route 59 Corridor

For a traditional Indian lunch buffet, try **Priya** (36 Lafayette Ave., Suffern, 845/357-5700, www.priyaindiancuisineny.com; Tues.–Sun. for lunch and dinner, buffet lunch Tues.–Fri.; mains $13–23).

Marcello's Ristorante of Suffern (21 Lafayette Ave., Suffern, 845/357-9108, www.marcellosgroup.com; Mon.–Sat. noon–2:30 P.M. and 5–9:30 P.M., Sun. 3–8:30 P.M.; mains $17–30) is a white linen affair with a menu of true Italian specialties. Look for the burgundy awning. Across the street, **Caffe Dolce** (24 Lafayette Ave., Suffern, 845/357-2066; Mon.–Fri. 11 A.M.–11 P.M., Sat. noon–11 P.M.) serves a more casual menu in a coffee and wine bar setting.

Pasta Cucina, (www.pastacucina.com; Mon.–Thurs. noon–10 P.M., Fri. noon–11 P.M., Sat. 5–11 P.M., Sun. 4:15–9 P.M.; mains $10–16) offers great value on family-style dining in three Rockland County locations: Suffern (8 Airmont Rd., Suffern, 845/369-1313), New City (261 S. Little Tor Rd., New City, 845/638-4729), and Stony Point (32 S. Liberty Dr., Stony Point, 845/786-6060).

ENTERTAINMENT AND EVENTS
Performing Arts
One of the most popular theater venues in Rockland County is Nyack's **Helen Hayes Theatre Company** (123 Main St., Nyack, 845/358-6333, www.hhtco.org). Performances include musicals, symphony, orchestra, and opera. Its Main Street location is close to a number of restaurants for pretheater dining. **Rockland Center for the Arts** (27 South Greenbush Rd., West Nyack, 845/358-0877, www.rocklandartcenter.org) holds classes, weekend performances, and interviews with performers.

Bars and Nightlife
Turning Point (468 Piermont Ave., Piermont, 845/359-1089, www.turningpointcafe.com) lures acclaimed jazz performers to a cozy space in Piermont Village. You can have dinner on the porch before the show. Alternatively, the art deco **Freelance Café and Wine Bar** (506 Piermont Ave., Piermont, 845/365-3250, www.xaviars.com; lunch and dinner Tues.–Sun.; small plates $6–15, large plates $18–24), next door to Xaviar's and owned by the same group, is the place to meet a friend for drinks. You'll have to wait for a table, because the café does not take reservations. **Hudson House of Nyack** (134 Main St., 845/353-1355; mains $14–19) also plays jazz on Thursday nights to accompany its New American menu.

Enjoy an evening of rarely shown documentaries at **Reality Bites** (100 Main St., Nyack, 845/358-8800, www.realitybites.net; daily 11:30 A.M.–10 P.M., till midnight on weekends), the newest hotspot in Nyack. Comic documentary filmmaker Steven M. Manin opened the theater and eatery in June 2004 to show documentaries,

unreleased films, and comic outtakes on three large plasma screens. Order "bites" for $1, or salads, sandwiches, and tapas for $7–10 while you watch. Check the website for a daily schedule of films.

Festivals
Suffern produces the **Native American Festival** (845/786-2701) at Harriman State Park each August. More than 1,000 artists, performers, and educators participate. The event culminates in a dance competition that draws competitors from across North and South America. The New York City Triathlon Club also runs a summer race series at Harriman.

Bear Mountain State Park puts on a festive **Octoberfest** (845/786-2701), with music and dancing in the crisp fall air. The Rockland Audubon Society (www.rocklandaudubon.org) runs field trips for wildlife observation.

SHOPPING
Farm Stands
The weekly **Nyack Farmers Market** (845/353-2221; Thurs. 8:30 A.M.–2 P.M.), at the corner of Main and Cedar Streets, is not to be missed. You can buy 20 different types of mushrooms from a single grower, plus the usual assortment of locally grown fruits and vegetables. Suffern, Spring Valley, and Haverstraw each have their own farmers markets during the growing season.

Antiques and Galleries
Art galleries and antique shops abound in Nyack and Piermont. In addition, the **Nyack Tobacco Company** (140 Main St., Nyack, 845/358-9300) carries one of the best selections of handmade cigars outside of New York City. Its cigars are stored in a digitally controlled humidor. Meanwhile, booklovers will find titles piled floor to ceiling in the **Pickwick Bookshop** (8 S. Broadway, Nyack, 845/358-9126).

On the Route 59 corridor, the **Palisades Center** (1000 Palisade Center Dr., West Nyack, 845/348-1000) opened in 1998 as a four-level megamall with 250 stores, anchored by Lord & Taylor, Filene's, Target, H&M, and Williams-Sonoma.

INFORMATION AND SERVICES

The **Rockland County Office of Tourism** (18 New Hempstead Rd., New City, 845/708-7300 or 800/295-5723) is headquartered in New City. In Nyack, look for a visitor information booth by the Clock Tower at Main and Cedar.

GETTING THERE AND AROUND

By Bus

Several companies run buses in Rockland County: Transit of Rockland (845/364-3333) and the Spring Valley Jitney (845/573-5800) provide local service, while Shortline Bus and Adirondack Trailways connect to parts north.

By Train

Metro-North (800/638-7646) and New Jersey Transit (201/762-5100) offer rail service to Rockland County. A ferry runs between Haverstraw and the Hudson line station in Ossining (800/53-FERRY or 800/533-3779), and cabs are readily available in major towns, including Nyack. Stewart Airport is the best place to rent a car.

By Car

The Palisades Interstate Parkway (Exits 4–15) connects Rockland County to the George Washington Bridge, and the Garden State Parkway heads to New Jersey. I-287 crosses the Tappan Zee Bridge to Westchester County. You can get frequent metropolitan area traffic reports on the radio at AM 880 and AM 1010.

The Hudson Highlands

Between the towns of Peekskill in Westchester County and Beacon in Dutchess County—a 15-mile stretch—a solid granite mountain range called the Appalachian Plateau crosses the Hudson. Here, the river has carved a narrow and deep path through the range to form the Hudson Highlands, a dramatic landscape that resembles the signature banks of the Rhine. Storm King Mountain and Breakneck Mountain rise up on opposite shores near Cold Spring, giving Or-ange and Putnam Counties some of the most beautiful vistas in the region.

PLANNING YOUR TIME

Few travelers attempt to see the entire Hudson Highlands area in one trip. Weekend itineraries are best limited to one section. For example, tar-get several sights along the river, or plan to visit one of the expansive state parks. West Point, the

Must-Sees

The Hudson Highlands

view of the Hudson from West Point

© PAUL ITOI

◫ **West Point:** This goldmine of American military history sits in one the most beautiful spots along the Hudson (page 50).

◫ **Storm King Art Center:** This unique outdoor sculpture museum features works from well-known American and British artists (page 52).

◫ **Greenwood Lake:** There's plenty of summer fun at this lake large enough for sailing and waterskiing (page 53).

◫ **Woodbury Common Premium Outlets:** This sprawling complex of designer outlets draws shoppers from miles around (page 59).

◫ **Boscobel Restoration:** The home of the annual Hudson Valley Shakespeare Festival is a restored neoclassical mansion called Boscobel (Beautiful Wood). From the wood-carved drapery on the balcony to the 18th century silver, china, and glassware within, this historic site is a cultural treasure (page 61).

◫ **Cold Spring Village:** The antique shops and restaurants in this town are conveniently located on the Metro-North commuter line (page 63).

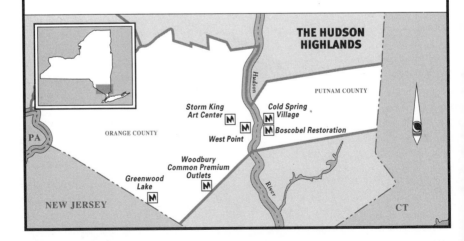

THE HUDSON HIGHLANDS

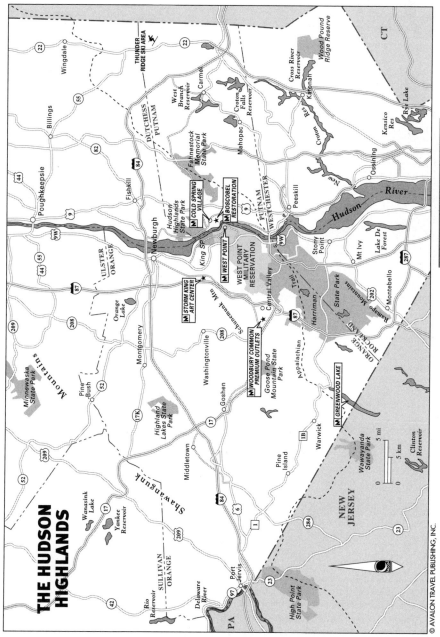

THE HUDSON HIGHLANDS

THUNDER RIDGE SKI AREA

Wingdale

Billings

West Branch Reservoir

Carmel

Croton Falls Reservoir

Wood Pound Ridge Reserve

CT

Cross River Reservoir

Katonah

Croton Res.

Rye Lake

Kensico Res

DUTCHESS
PUTNAM

Fahnstock Memorial State Park

Mahopac

Ossining

Poughkeepsie

Fishkill

Hudson Highlands State Park

M COLD SPRING VILLAGE

M BOSCOBEL RESTORATION

New

Peekskill

Hudson River

Newburgh

King Sp.

M WEST POINT

WEST POINT MILITARY RESERVATION

Stony Point

Lake De Forest

Mt Ivy

ULSTER
ORANGE

M STORM KING ART CENTER

Schunnemunk Mtn

Central Valley

Trail

State Park

Montebello

Ramapo Mountains

Orange Lake

Harriman

ORANGE
ROCKLAND

Montgomery

M WOODBURY COMMON PREMIUM OUTLETS

Washingtonville

Goose Pond Mountain State Park

Appalachian

Minnewaska State Park

Pine Bush

Highland Lakes State Park

Goshen

M GREENWOOD LAKE

Wawayanda State Park

Clinton Reservoir

Middletown

Warwick

Shawangunk

Pine Island

NEW JERSEY

Mountains

Wanasink Lake

Yankee Reservoir

0   5 mi

0   5 km

SULLIVAN
ORANGE

Rio Reservoir

Port Jervis

Delaware River

PA

High Point State Park

© AVALON TRAVEL PUBLISHING, INC.

The Hudson Highlands

Storm King Art Center, and Cold Spring Village are major destinations that can take from a few hours to a full day to explore. In summer, a day at Greenwood Lake followed by an evening of shopping and fine dining in Warwick make a good combination. Route 17 through western Orange County is a major access route to Sullivan County and the Catskill region.

Putnam County measures less than 20 miles north to south and is well-worth a full day's visit. Cold Spring is the county's most popular destination, and a day passes quickly in and around the riverside town. With an early start at the Bear Mountain Bridge, you'll have time for brief stops at Manitoga, Boscobel Restoration, and Constitution Marsh Wildlife Preserve, followed by a

walk and a meal along Cold Spring's Main Street. Serious antique shoppers will need more time, as will anyone who plans to hike the Hudson Highlands or paddle the river.

To add Clarence Fahnestock Memorial State Park and eastern Putnam County to the itinerary, follow Route 301 west out of Cold Spring through the towns of Kent, Carmel, and Brewster.

Scenic Drives

Route 9D in Putnam County, from Beacon to the Bear Mountain Bridge, winds its way through the dramatic Hudson Highlands. On the other side of the Hudson, Route 218 takes you over Storm King Mountain, with spectacular views of West Point and the Bear Mountain Bridge.

Orange County

New York's Orange County is everything that Southern California's "OC" is not: From Washington's Headquarters to the annual Renaissance Faire in Sterling Forest, this Orange County takes its historical sites and traditions seriously. It is the home of the prestigious U.S. Military Academy at West Point and several related attractions, which draw some three million visitors a year.

The only county in the Hudson Valley region with frontage on both the Hudson and Delaware Rivers begins 50 miles north and across the river from New York City, encompassing 816 square miles of fertile fields, rolling hills, and quiet suburban communities. Orange County's largest commercial centers are Newburgh, Middletown, and Port Jervis. Goshen is the county seat.

ALONG THE RIVER—ROUTE 9W

Orange and Rockland Counties share a border at the Bear Mountain Bridge on the west side of the Hudson River. Several thoroughfares meet here in a traffic circle at the approach to the bridge: Route 9W runs along the riverbank, the Palisades Parkway heads south toward New Jersey, and Route 6 runs west to join Route 17 (The Quickway). Appalachian Trail hikers also pass through on their way to or from Harriman State

Park. (The AT crosses the Hudson at the Bear Mountain Bridge.)

West Point

A few miles north of the bridge, the Hudson flows through its narrowest and deepest stretch (more than 200 feet), creating the strategic military position of West Point. In revolutionary times, American forces strung a 40-ton chain 500 yards across the river to keep the British at bay. After the colonial victory, President Thomas Jefferson believed the young nation needed to build its own military capability and wean itself from dependence on foreign expertise. He signed the United States Military Academy into law in 1802.

The academy's first curriculum produced civil engineers, who went on to build much of the nation's transportation infrastructure. West Point established its reputation for military excellence during the Civil War, when graduates including Robert E. Lee and Ulysses S. Grant fought against each other during almost every battle. Superintendents during the 20th century broadened the program to include academic, physical, and military education, and the first woman graduated from the academy in 1980.

Times have changed at West Point since 2001. Visitors no longer have open access to tour the

COURTESY OF ORANGE COUNTY TOURISM

aerial view of West Point

campus the way they once did. As an alternative, the academy runs guided bus tours daily, except on football Saturdays and holidays and during graduation week. The one-hour tour, led by **West Point Tours** (845/446-4724, Highland Falls), begins at the visitors center, off the West Point Highway, where you can view a model cadet barracks room and gather information about the academy.

Behind the visitors center stands the **West Point Museum** (www.usma.edu/museum; daily 10:30 A.M.–4:15 P.M.), which houses four floors of warfare exhibits covering every military conflict in the history of the United States (all 135 of them), from the Revolutionary War to Vietnam. A large weapons display in the basement has a World War I tank, while the small weapons include axes, clubs, and swords that date all the way back to the Stone Age. Tours often stop at **Fort Putnam,** a key position in defending the fortress, with panoramic views of the river and campus. **Trophy Point** offers a postcard-perfect view of the Hudson Highlands.

Familiar names grace the monuments across the central part of the campus: Patton, Marshall, MacArthur, Eisenhower, Schwarzkopf. More than 2,000 names are inscribed on the massive granite shaft of the striking **Battle Monument** (1897), designed by Sanford White, who also built and furnished the opulent Vanderbilt Estate in Hyde Park (see the *Mid-Hudson* chapter). Nearby, the **Old Cadet Chapel** (1836) is one of the oldest buildings still used on campus.

Extended two-hour tours, offered twice daily June–October, include a stop at the **West Point Cemetery,** which holds graves that date back to

1782 and represent casualties of almost every war the academy's graduates have fought.

The Gothic **Thayer Hotel** (674 Thayer Rd., West Point, 845/446-4731, www.thethayerhotel.com; $175), built in 1926, overlooks the Hudson at the south entrance to West Point. It was named for Colonel Sylvanius Thayer, superintendent of West Point from 1817 to 1833. A $26 million facelift in 1996 restored the hotel to its former glory. Portraits of military leaders decorate the walls in the formal dining room, which is popular for holiday gatherings.

Call before you intend to arrive at West Point, because the visitors center may cancel tours at any time. Photo identification is required for entry. Exit the New York Thruway at Exit 16.

From the back lawn of the hotel, you can see **Constitution Island,** the first place George Washington chose to fortify at West Point. Unfortunately, the British had the same idea and established a stronghold in 1777; the Americans won it back a year later. By the 1830s, the island

COURTESY OF ORANGE COUNTY TOURISM

a woman in traditional clothes, Constitution Island

fell into private hands. Henry Warner and his two daughters built a family estate, and for years the daughters invited cadets to the island to study the Bible. The Warners donated their house and gardens to the academy in 1908. Today's cadets complete many of their training exercises here.

Visitors must make a reservation to tour the 180-acre island. Boats depart from the South Dock inside West Point, past the Thayer Hotel. The nonprofit Constitution Island Association runs a shuttle from the Cold Spring rail station on select Saturdays during the summer.

Cornwall-on-Hudson

After West Point, Route 9W winds its way north to the base of Storm King Mountain and the quiet hamlet of Cornwall-on-Hudson. Alternatively, follow Route 218 north for a spectacular drive over Storm King Mountain, with gorgeous views of the fjordlike highlands. The **Museum of the Hudson Highlands** (The Boulevard, Cornwall-on-Hudson, 845/534-7781; Sat.–Sun. noon–4 P.M.), in Cornwall, hosts a variety of art and nature exhibits that explore the cultural and natural heritage of the area. The museum occupies two locations: At the Boulevard location near the river are the Ogden Gallery featuring local artists whose work focuses on the natural world, a gift shop, and occasional live animal exhibits. A mile and a half away on Route 9W is the 177-acre Kenridge Farm, an outdoor classroom of native flora and fauna.

Storm King Art Center

The Quaker Avenue exit off Route 9W leads to the expansive sculpture gardens of the Storm King Art Center (Old Pleasant Hill Rd., Mountainville, 845/534-3115, www.skac.org; Wed.–Sun. 11 A.M.–5:30 P.M.; adults $10). In this unique outdoor museum, you can walk along tree-lined paths and view larger-than-life sculptures against the dramatic landscape and everchanging light of the Hudson Highlands. The collection represents British and American artists, both postwar and contemporary. Some of the sculptures were designed expressly for their sites in the 500-acre park. *The Arch,* one of Alexander Calder's "stabiles," measures 56-feet high. In 2003, a monumental piece by Mark di Suvero called the *Joy of Life* was installed, weighing 20 tons and standing 70 feet tall. Storm King is a popular place for organized singles' outings from New York City. The center offers guided, self-guided, and audio tours, and picnics are highly encouraged.

Newburgh

Farther up the river at the intersection of Route 9W and I-84 lies Newburgh, a city that—like Poughkeepsie to the north—has struggled with its legacy as a manufacturing center. Jobs remain scarce, and many of the old buildings are run-down, but underneath the layers of industrial age, the city retains a deep sense of history. George Washington established Revolutionary War headquarters in a fieldstone fortress on a hill overlooking the river, and the building (84 Liberty St., Newburgh, 845/562-1195; Apr.–Oct. Wed.–Sat. 10 A.M.–5 P.M., Sun. 1–5 P.M.; adults $4, children $3) has been a national historic site since 1850. His army stayed nearby at the **New Windsor Cantonment State Historic Site** (Temple Hill Rd., Vails Gate, 845/561-1765), which offers musket and artillery demonstrations.

The 1839 **Crawford House** (189 Montgomery St., Newburgh, 845/561-2585), once the residence of a shipping merchant, houses the Historical Society of Newburgh Bay and the Highlands. On display inside the classic revival building are 19th-century antiques and paintings.

In addition to many private restorations under way, Newburgh has revived a section of its waterfront by turning several abandoned factories into an attractive boardwalk with a handful of upscale restaurants and shops. People now arrive at **Newburgh Landing** by the boatful on summer weekends, where a variety of cuisines and trendy bars are just steps away from a slip in the marina. Partygoers often sleep on their boats after a night of revelry at one of the nearby clubs.

From the water's edge, you can see the beginning of the narrow Hudson Highlands to the south. Several river cruises depart from the landing. To reach the landing, exit I-84 at Route 9W and turn left at the second light onto North Plank Road.

If you continue on Route 9W instead of heading to the landing, you'll soon reach the intersec-

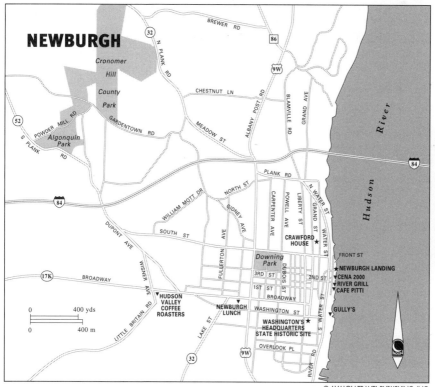

© AVALON TRAVEL PUBLISHING, INC.

tion of South Street and the edge of Newburgh's onetime gem of a green space: 35-acre **Downing Park** (Rte. 9W and 3rd St., Newburgh, 845/565-5559), named for architect Andrew Jackson Downing and designed by the same Frederick Law Olmstead and Calvert Vaux who created Central Park in New York City. The resemblance is striking, except that this park is now surrounded by low-income housing instead of multimillion dollar high rises. The restored Downing Park Shelter House serves as the city's visitors center.

CENTRAL ORANGE COUNTY—ALONG ROUTE 17
Greenwood Lake

The Appalachian Trail enters New York State from New Jersey at Greenwood Lake, a long, narrow body of water that joins the two states. Surrounded by dense forest and mountains, the natural lake is shallow with a maximum depth of 57 feet and wetlands at each end. Visibility is generally good, except after heavy storms. A narrow local road hugs the eastern shore of the lake, and busy Route 210 heads into New Jersey on the western side.

The Erie Railroad brought the first wave of visitors to the lake in the 1870s, and Babe Ruth was a frequent vacationer. Year-round residences crowd the shoreline today, but several access areas are open to the public for swimming and boating.

From Greenwood Lake, Route 17A climbs over Sterling Mountain to the east, winding through a 19,000-acre state park that is the site of a small ski resort and the annual Renaissance Faire before meeting up with Route 17 and the New York Thruway at the town of Tuxedo.

wakeboarder on Greenwood Lake

Fifties-era billboards and diners like the battered Red Apple Rest line this stretch of Route 17. During the peak of the summer resorts, traffic leaving New York City poured through town en route to the western Catskills. Look for the entrance to **Harriman State Park** (Rte. 9W, Bear Mountain, 845/786-2701; admission $7) on the east side of the highway. A much larger neighbor to Bear Mountain State Park at the Rockland County line, Harriman boasts the oldest stretch of the Appalachian Trail, which was cleared in 1923 (see the *Lower Hudson* chapter).

Warwick

In the opposite direction from Sterling Mountain on 17A—just minutes from the New Jersey state line—lies Warwick, one of the most charming Victorian villages in Orange County. A handful of art galleries, antique shops, and gourmet restaurants line Main Street in a scaled-down but convincing imitation of New York City's SoHo district. The fun begins at **Port of Call** (40 Main St., 845/986-9500, www.portofcall.net), a 3,500-square-foot gallery that repre-

sents fine art, photography, and sculpture from local, national, and international artists.

From May through December, the surrounding farmland produces a constant supply of freshly harvested treats: vegetables and berries in summer; pears, apples, and pumpkins in fall; evergreen Christmas trees in winter. Not surprisingly, the town features one of the best farmers markets around. Nightlife is lively, especially in summer when several local cafés and galleries play live music. Parking will challenge even the most seasoned urbanites on weekends.

Black Dirt Region

The township of Warwick encompasses much of the 14,000-acre Black Dirt region, an agricultural anomaly formed by glacial activity some 12,000 years ago. Polish and German immigrants cleared fields in present-day Pine Island and Florida by hand in the 1880s and discovered that the soil was well suited to growing onions. The region still produces about a quarter of all the onions consumed in the U.S. During the August harvest season, the sweet aroma seeps into the car the moment you enter the region.

To reach the Black Dirt region from Warwick, follow the Pine Island Turnpike (Rte. 1B) west to Pine Island, or Route 17A north to Florida.

Monroe

Back on Route 17, school children have been visiting the historic **Museum Village of Old Smith's Clove** (1010 Rte. 17M, Monroe, 845/782-8247, www.museumvillage.org; Jun.–Nov. Wed.–Sun. 11 A.M.–4 P.M.; adults $10, seniors $6, youth $5) in Monroe since the 1940s to learn about the wonders of colonial life, such as making wagons and candles. Walk from the red barn to the firehouse, weaver, and blacksmith in the shade of stately sugar maples. The museum is located behind a park-and-ride lot off Exit 129. Turns are well marked from the exit ramp.

Farther west, off Route 17M, is the craft village of **Sugar Loaf** (www.sugarloafartsvillage.com; Wed.–Sun. 11 A.M.–5 P.M.), a collection of boutique shops selling handmade goods including ceramics, clothes, and soaps.

Harness racing fans head to Goshen for a tour of

the sport's hall of fame. Housed in a 1913 Tudor stable, the **Harness Racing Museum & Hall of Fame** (240 Main St., Goshen, 845/294-6330, www.harnessmuseum.com; daily 10 A.M.–6 P.M.; admission $7.50) contains an extensive collection of Currier & Ives trotting prints, as well as photographs, trophies, and memorabilia. Interactive exhibits include a 3-D simulator and theaters.

WESTERN ORANGE COUNTY— I-84 TO THE DELAWARE RIVER

From the intersection with Route 17, I-84 heads southwest toward Middletown and Port Jervis at the southern end of the Shawangunk Mountains. The Neversink and Delaware rivers meet here, a stone's throw from both New Jersey and Pennsylvania.

A one-time hub for road, rail, and canal transportation, Port Jervis was named for John Bloomfield Jervis, an engineer who built the D&H Canal and Croton Aqueduct. Although the name suggests a major shipping port, the river is better suited to canoes than freighters. Today, a population of 10,000 supports several small to mid-sized industrial businesses, and Port Jervis serves as a gateway to the Upper Delaware River in Sullivan and Delaware Counties. Beginning in the town of Sparrowbush, about five miles outside of Port Jervis, Route 97 twists and turns and climbs over the **Hawk's Nest** to present breathtaking views of New York, Pennsylvania, and the Delaware River in between. At a height of 150 feet above the river, the road has several lookouts, called bay windows, that were built into the original design. BMW, Saab, Honda, and other car companies have filmed commercials along this stretch of winding road.

SPORTS AND RECREATION

Although more developed than the Upper Hudson Valley, Orange County has preserved a number of open spaces that are ideal for a surprising variety of mountain and aquatic adventures.

Winter Sports

Orange County enjoys a mild climate compared to other parts of the Hudson Valley, receiving only a foot of snow on average each winter. But the Hudson Highlands and Ramapo Mountains create ideal terrain for beginner skiers, and several local ski areas offer weekend and evening entertainment for families. One of the four chairlifts at the **Sterling Forest Ski Area** (581 Rte. 17A West, Tuxedo, 845/351-2163, www.skisterlingforest.com; Jan.–Feb. Mon.–Fri. 10 A.M.–5 P.M., Sat.–Sun. 9 A.M.–5 P.M., night skiing and riding till 10 P.M.; adults $39, juniors $29) crosses right over Route 17A. To the west of Greenwood Lake, also on Route 17A, is the smaller **Mount Peter Ski Area** (Rte. 17A, Warwick, 845/986-4940, www.mtpeter.com; adults $33, juniors $25), with three lifts.

Hiking

Backpackers can follow the **Appalachian Trail** from the New Jersey state line at Greenwood Lake (Orange County) across the Bear Mountain Bridge to the Dutchess County line near Kent (Putnam County). Along the way, is the oldest section of the AT, completed in 1923 in Harriman State Park. Moderate elevation changes provide valley and lake views.

In the western part of Sterling Forest above Greenwood Lake, the 5.3-mile Sterling Ridge Trail leads to views of Sterling Lake and the Sterling Fire Tower, while the four-mile Indian Loop Trail, an offshoot of the AT, climbs to views of Route 17 and the surrounding valley.

Birdwatchers have several good choices to explore in Orange County: The **Bashakill Wildlife Management Area** (Rte. 209 South, Westbrookville) is a bird sanctuary on 2,000 acres of state-owned wetlands, forests, fields, and abandoned orchards. And the **Eagle Institute** (Barryville, www.eagleinstitute.org, 845/557-6162) conservation group offers guided tours of bald eagle habitats along the Delaware and Hudson Rivers. The Orange County Audubon Society maintains another 62-acre sanctuary near the Heritage Trail, **6-1/2 Station Road Sanctuary** (6-1/2 Station Rd., Goshen).

Mountain Biking and Road Riding

On the access road to Museum Village is a treasure of a bikeway, the 15-mile Heritage Trail, which follows the bed of the old Erie Railroad, connecting Monroe to Goshen. You can rent bikes (or snowshoes in winter) at **Bryan's Bikes** (240 Main St., Cornwall, 845/534-5230).

Skateboarders will want to check out **Knoll Skatepark** (3142 Rte. 207, Campbell Hall, 845/254-6964; Tues. & Thurs. 5–9 P.M., Sat. 1–9 P.M., Sun. noon–4 P.M.), an indoor skateboard park featuring a ramp that measures six feet high and 32 feet wide with a 12-foot wall ride. An outdoor BMX course follows a series of jumps and trails.

Golf

A round of golf at the **Mansion Ridge Golf Club** (1292 Orange Turnpike, Monroe, 845/782-7888; $80–124) begins in the stone barn clubhouse and meanders through forest and across hills, with incredible views of the countryside. The championship course is the only Jack Nicklaus Signature Design course in New York State that's open to the public. Another good option is the **Central Valley Golf Club** (206 Smith Clove Rd., Central Valley, 845/928-6924; Apr.–Nov. daily dawn–dusk; $26–36), where golfers play with the Ramapo Mountains as a scenic backdrop.

In western Orange County, head to **Eddy Farm Golf Course** (Rtes. 42 & 97, Sparrowbush, 845/858-4333; Mar.–Nov. daily 7 A.M.–8 P.M.; $18), an 18-hole course featuring spectacular views of both the Catskill Mountains and Delaware River. The entrance is conveniently located five miles from I-84 near Port Jervis.

Swimming and Boating

Orange County offers easy access to a host of aquatic activities. On the Delaware River, **Silver Canoe Raft Rentals** (37 South Maple Ave., Port Jervis, 800/724-8342, www.silvercanoe.com; Apr.–Sep. daily 8 A.M.–7 P.M.) has canoes and kayaks for rent. Rates include transport and pickup. (See *Sullivan County* for additional canoe and kayak outfitters in the area.)

Adventurous scuba divers may consider an eddy dive in the Delaware River. Visibility is generally poor, but the sensation of drifting in a circle is something you won't experience when diving in the tropics.

Sailing and waterskiing are summer pastimes on Greenwood Lake. There are four marinas on the lake, and you can rent powerboats and personal watercraft at Long Pond Marina. A new public beach opened in 2004 on Windermere Avenue on the east shore. The **Greenwood Lake Triathlon,** held each year in mid-September, has become a popular race, drawing athletes from across the state.

Several marinas along the Hudson have boat ramps and services: **Highland Falls Marina** (72 Station Hill, Highland Falls, 845/446-2402; May–Oct. daily 9 A.M.–9 P.M.), within walking distance to West Point, has 44 clips and five moorings. In Newburgh, **Front Street Marina** (40 Front St., Newburgh, 845/661-4914) puts you at the doorstep of all the new restaurants and shops on the Newburgh waterfront. This is a state-of-the-art marina with all the amenities but no fuel.

Fishing and Hunting

Largemouth bass, chain pickerel, and panfish are the most popular catches in Orange County's lakes and ponds. The **Bait Bucket** (313 Rte. 211 West, Middletown, 845/361-4774; daily 6 A.M.–7 P.M.) sells bait, equipment, and licenses and will happily point you to the best access points. **O&H Bait Shop** (48 Main St., Chester, 845/469-2566; daily 6 A.M.–6 P.M.) is another option for fishing supplies.

For a guided trip on the Delaware, contact **Reel 'Em In Guide Service** (13 Fall St., Port Jervis, 845/856-3009; reservations required) to book a half-day trip for one or two people on a custom-made driftboat. Ice-fishing trips are an option in January and February.

To stock up on gear, visit the newest and largest branch of **Gander Mountain** (Crystal Run Plaza, 100 N. Galleria Dr., Middletown, 845/692-5600; Mon.–Fri. 9 A.M.–9 P.M., Sat. 8 A.M.–9 P.M., Sun. 9 A.M.– 7 P.M.), a sprawling destination store for gear-hungry outdoors lovers.

Aviation

For a romantic morning adventure, take a hot air balloon flight with **Above the Clouds** (Middletown, 845/692-2556, www.my-balloon.com;

May–Oct., reservations required). Flights with **Fantasy Balloon Flights** (2 Evergreen Lane, Port Jervis, 845/856-7103, www.fantasyfliers.com) depart from Randall Airport and include a glass of champagne. Private pilots can rent planes at **Freedom Air** (550 Dunn Lane, Montgomery, 845/457-3595; daily 9 A.M.–5 P.M.).

Horseback Riding

Horseback riding and lessons are available at the 230-acre **Borderland Farm** (340 South Rte. 94, Warwick, 845/986-1704, www.wolfsbane.com/borderland) or **Celtic Pines Farms** (135 Crawford St., Pine Bush, 845/361-3076, www.celticpines.com), which also has a B&B on the premises. **Juckas Stables** (Rtes. 302 & 17, Bullville, 845/361-1429, www.juckasstables.com) has 117 acres of trails and English and Western lessons. Camping is available.

ACCOMMODATIONS

The best places to stay in Orange County are clustered near Greenwood Lake and Warwick, and along the river between West Point and Cornwall. Small bed-and-breakfast inns are by far the most common, with an assortment of chain hotels located along I-84.

Under $100

The **New Continental Hotel** (15 Leo Court, Greenwood Lake, 845/477-2456, www.newcontinentalhotel.com; $85–130) is a comfortable and affordable lakeside option. Its rooms have tiled private baths and lake views. Twin and double beds are available.

$100–150

Four-poster or sleigh beds, fresh flowers, and bathrobes are among the special touches at **M The Inn at Stony Creek** (34 Spanktown Rd., Warwick, 845/986-3660, www.innstonycreek.com; $115–135). Canopy beds and working fireplaces set an elegant mood at the **Peach Grove Inn** (205 Rte. 17A, Warwick, 845/986-7411, www.peachgroveinn.net; $130–150). Its four rooms occupy an 1850 Greek Revival building furnished with 19th-century antiques throughout.

$150–200

Storm King Lodge (100 Pleasant Hill Rd., Mountainville, 845/534-9421, www.stormkinglodge.com; $150–175) offers four cozy rooms in a 19th-century lodge near Storm King Mountain. The Lavender and Pine rooms have fireplaces. Call ahead to schedule a masseuse appointment during your stay.

A piano room, library, and outdoor hot tub set the mood at the **The Glenwood House** (49 Glenwood Rd., Pine Island, 845/258-5066, www.glenwoodbb.com; $110–295). Its five comfortable rooms, with modern whirlpool baths, are set in an 1855 Victorian farmhouse.

West Point's **Thayer Hotel** (674 Thayer Rd., West Point, 845/446-4731, www.thethayerhotel.com; $175) has 151 modern but cozy rooms decorated in 19th-century Americana style. Guestrooms and suites inside the imposing granite building offer campus, river, or mountain views. Amenities include cable TV, high-speed Internet access, and a fitness center.

Over $200

A stay at the ultraromantic **M Cromwell Manor** (174 Angola Rd., Cornwall, 845/534-7136, www.cromwellmanor.com; $165–370) includes a gourmet breakfast and afternoon tea. Its 1764 cottage delights with a collection of antiques. Internet access is a plus for travelers who need to stay in touch with the real world.

Campgrounds

Oakland Valley Campground (399 Oakland Valley Rd., Cuddebackville, 845/754-8732; May–Oct.; $25–40) has large wooded sites for tents, trailers, and motorhomes. Amenities include water and electric hook-ups, flush toilets, firewood, cable TV, swimming pool, and free hot showers. **Otisville Campground** (298 Grange Rd., Otisville, 845/386-5104; open year-round) has tent sites next to a small pond, with wooded trails, telephone hookups, hot showers, and a laundry.

FOOD

Along the River–Route 9W

Centrally located **Painter's** (266 Hudson St.,

Cornwall-on-Hudson, 845/534-2109, www .painters-restaurant.com; lunch and dinner Tues.–Sun., Sun. brunch till 3 P.M.; mains $10–23) is a favorite eatery for summer dining from a menu with a mix of American, Mexican, Japanese, and Italian entrées. Save room for dessert. At West Point, the buffet-style champagne brunch in the Thayer Hotel is a memorable experience for a special occasion (Sun. 10 A.M.–2 P.M.).

In Newburgh, early risers head to **Hudson Valley Coffee Roasters** (639 Broadway, Newburgh, 888/822-6333, www.hudsonvalleyroasters.com) in an old factory on Broadway for a brew with more character than any Starbucks blend. Also on Broadway, enjoy the infamous hotdogs at **Newburgh Lunch** (348 Broadway, Newburgh, 845/562-9660), but the chef will turn you down if you dare ask for the recipe.

A trio of related Italian restaurants serve Tuscan specialities in the Newburgh area: **Cena 2000** (50 Front St., Newburgh, 845/561-7676) offers river views to match the cuisine. Neighboring **Café Pitti** (40 Front St., Newburgh, 845/565-1444; opens daily 11:30 A.M., Mon.–Thurs. till 10 P.M., Fri.–Sat. till 11 P.M., Sun. till 9 P.M.; mains $9–12) serves antipasti, panini, and pizzettes under a bright yellow awning. And the upscale **Il Cenacolo** (228 S. Plank Rd., Newburgh, 845/564-4494) gets high marks for its ever-changing antipasti platters.

River Grill (40 Front St., Newburgh, 845/561-9444, www.therivergrill.com; lunch Mon.–Fri. 11:30 A.M.–3 P.M., dinner daily 5–9:30 P.M., Fri.–Sat. till 10 P.M.; mains $20–27) offers surf and turf, including a seafood paella special, in a dining room with picture windows facing the Hudson. And just when you think you've reached the end of the road at Newburgh Landing, you reach a large dirt parking lot and **Gully's** (2 Washington St., Newburgh, 845/565-0077; Sun.–Thurs. 11:30 A.M.–10 P.M., Fri.–Sat. till 11 P.M.; mains $14–25), a two-story bar and restaurant on an old barge. The atmosphere is super casual, and the floor slopes with the tide. This is the place to order a bowl of steamers or a plate of surf and turf. On weekend nights, the upstairs bar stays open until the wee hours of the morning.

Central Orange County–Along Route 17

Locals pile in at ◪ **Ye Jolly Onion** (Rte. 517, Pine Island, 845/258-4277, www.yejollyonioninn.com; Wed.–Thurs. 5–9 P.M., Fri.–Sat. till 10 P.M., Sun. noon–7:30 P.M.; mains $15–20), a Pine Island tradition, to sample a variety of dishes made from the local bounty. Vegetarians can enjoy the healthy fare at **Pure City Restaurant** (100 Main St., Pine Bush, 845/744-8888).

New restaurants are opening at a fast clip in the Warwick area. But **The Landmark Inn** (Rte. 94, North Warwick, 845/986-5444, www.landmarkinnonline.com; dinner Tues.–Sun., lunch Tues.–Sat.; mains $18–24) remains a local favorite for casual American cuisine and evening cocktails. Out-of-towners head to the fancier **Chateau Hathorn** (33 Hathorn Rd., Warwick, 845/986-6099; Wed.–Sat. 5–10 P.M., Sun. 3–8 P.M.) for French cuisine in an 18th-century mansion. **Ten Railroad Avenue** (10 Railroad Ave., Warwick, 845/986-1509; Wed.–Sun.) serves a blend of Spanish and Italian cuisine and occasionally hosts live music performances. For another taste of Europe, visit neighboring **La Petite Cuisine** (20 Railroad Ave., Warwick, 845/988-0988; Tues.–Sun. 10 A.M.–4 P.M.).

At Greenwood Lake, the most popular choices for lakeside dining are **Emerald Point** (40 Sterling Rd., Greenwood Lake, 845/477-2275) and the **Breezy Point Inn** (620 Jersey Ave., Greenwood Lake, 845/477-8100, www.breezypointinn.com; open daily for lunch and dinner; mains $15–25), with a raw bar and German-influenced menu.

Near the New Jersey state line, away from the village bustle, **P&J Steak House** (40 Jersey Ave., Greenwood Lake, 845/477-0711, www.pandjsteakhouse.com; Mon., Wed., Thurs. 5–10 P.M. and bar till midnight, Fri.–Sat. 5–10 P.M. and bar till 1 A.M., Sun. 4–10 P.M. and bar till midnight; mains $14–35) prepares just about every cut of beef imaginable, from rib eye and filet mignon to Porterhouse and Chateaubriand. A few pasta and seafood entrées and a decent selection of reasonably priced wines complete the menu.

ENTERTAINMENT AND EVENTS

Performing Arts

West Point's **Eisenhower Hall Theatre** (www
.eisenhowerhall.com) is a top-notch venue for a
range of performances, from *The Full Monty* musical to the Vienna Boys Choir around the holidays.

Bars and Nightlife

These days, Newburgh Landing gets high marks
for a lively—and sometimes downright rowdy—
nightlife. **Blue Martini** (50 Front St., Newburgh,
845/562-7111) prepares more than 20 variations
on the theme, with happy hour specials. The
Front Street (26 Front St., Newburgh, 845/569-
8035; Sun.–Thurs. 11:30 A.M.–9 P.M., Fri.–Sat. till
4 A.M.; $5 cover), at the south end of Front Street,
gets particularly wild on weekend nights. For a
more mellow scene, Warwick locals gather at the
bar inside the **Landmark Inn**. Keep an eye out for
live music performance at Warwick's wineries and
cafés. **Applewood Winery** (82 Four Corners Rd.,
Warwick, 845/988-9292, www.applewoodor-
chardsandwinery.com; Fri. noon–5 P.M., Sat.–Sun.
11 A.M.–5 P.M.) produces chardonnay, cabernet
franc, and hard cider. And **Warwick Valley
Winery & Distillery** (114 Little York Rd., Warwick, 845/258-4858, www.wvwinery.com; daily
11 A.M.–6 P.M.) makes Riesling and pinot noir
wines, as well as apple and pear ciders and a variety of baked goods.

The family-owned, 1950s-era **Warwick Drive-
In Theater** (Rte. 94, 845/986-4440; adults $7,
children $4, under 4 free) is also packed on sum-
mer nights.

Festivals

Nothing quite tops the spirited rivalry of an
Army vs. Navy football game at West Point. West
Point Football Saturdays take place at Michie
Stadium, with a parade, cannon salute, and cadet
review to kick off the event. Ferry service is avail-
able from Tarrytown.

Cars line the sides of Route 17A over Sterling
Mountain during the popular **Renaissance Faire**
(Sterling Forest, Tuxedo, 845/351-5174; Aug.–
Sept. Sat.–Sun.; admission $19) each year. The
Orange County Fair (100 Carpenter Ave., Mid-

COURTESY OF ORANGE COUNTY TOURISM

Renaissance Faire Couple in traditional clothes

dletown, 845/343-4826, www.orangecounty-
fair.com) takes place in Middletown each July.

SHOPPING

Orange County has everything a shopper could
desire, from megachains and discount outlets to
one-of-a-kind boutiques. One of the county's
unique finds is Sugar Loaf, a small village of artisans who craft handmade ceramics, soaps, and
other goods.

N Woodbury Common Premium Outlets

Bargain hunters flock to the Woodbury Common Premium Outlets (498 Red Apple Court,
Rte. 32, Central Valley, 845/928-4000, www.pre-
miumoutlets.com; daily 10 A.M.–9 P.M.), at the
edge of Harriman State Park (Exit 16 off I-87).
Dozens of stores are arranged in a campuslike
setting, making it less-than-ideal for rainy-day
retail therapy. Look for significant discounts on

The Hudson Highlands

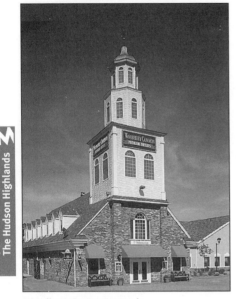

Woodbury Common steeple

name brands from Coach and Fendi to Banana Republic and Gap. Calvin Klein, Diesel, Max-Studio, and Ecco are among the newest additions to the complex. Beware, the long list of stores and often-deep discounts draw crowds on holiday weekends throughout the year. Shortline Bus offers daily service to the outlets, and several local hotels offer "shop and stay" packages.

Farm Stands

Orange County made national TV in February 2004 when the Food Network produced a Hudson Valley episode of *Food Nation with Bobby Flay,* featuring several local eateries. Among them was the **Quaker Creek Store** (757 Pulaski Highway, Goshen, 845/258-4570, www.quakercreekstore.com; Mon.–Fri. 7 A.M.– 7 P.M., Sat. 7 A.M.–6 P.M.) in Pine Island, a must-try for homemade sausages and smoked meats made by a third-generation owner and CIA graduate. The family-run business has evolved from a 1940s sandwich shop to a gourmet treasure. Onion rings are made from the bounty that makes the region famous.

Chances are, you'll have to wait for a parking space at the **Warwick Valley Farmers Market** (South St. parking lot off Main St., Warwick; Sun. 9 A.M.–2 P.M.) Local businesses sell homemade pies and candies, as well as fresh-picked produce. The entire town of Warwick shuts down for the wildly popular **Applefest** every September.

Antiques, Galleries, and Boutiques

Main Street in Warwick has a wide range of antique dealers selling everything old, from toys to rugs to lace, as well as several contemporary boutiques. Most stores close by 6 P.M., although some stay open until 8 P.M. on Fridays.

Victorian Treasures (21 Main St., Warwick, 845/986-7616, www.victoriantreasuresonline.com) specializes in Winnie-the-Pooh and other collectibles. And **The Eclectic Eye** (Railroad Ave., 845/986-5520) has furniture, rugs, and items the owner simply calls "worthies."

One of Warwick's top boutiques is **Frazzleberries** (16 Railroad Ave., Warwick, 845/987-8027, www.frazzleberries.com), known for cute country furnishings and festive seasonal displays. Another tempting store is **Newhards** (39 Main St., Warwick, 914/986-4544), which stocks upscale kitchen equipment and supplies, including pottery and cookbooks. On Railroad Avenue, three-year-old **Sweetbriar's** (26 Railroad Ave., Warwick, 845/986-5700, www.sweetbriars.com) makes designer candies, chocolates, and truffles.

INFORMATION AND SERVICES

A network of 10 tourist information centers serve Orange County visitors; several of them open seasonally. The **Orange County Tourism** (30 Matthews St, Goshen, 845/291-2136, www.orangetourism.org; Mon.–Fri. 9 A.M.–5 P.M.) office in Goshen can provide a wealth of information before or during a visit. The **Palisades Parkway Tourist Information Center** (between Exits 16 & 17, Palisades Interstate Parkway, 845/786-5003) stocks a variety of trail guides and road maps. This is also the place to pick up your New York State fishing license.

GETTING THERE AND AROUND

By Bus

Adirondack Trailways stops in Newburgh, while Shortline Bus stops include Monroe, Middletown, Newburgh, Goshen, Chester, and Central Valley. Main Line Trolley Bus offers local service to Chester, Goshen, Harriman, Middletown, Monroe, and Woodbury Common. New Jersey Transit also runs bus service to Greenwood Lake and Warwick.

By Train

The Metro-North Port Jervis Line stops in western Orange County between Port Jervis and Suffern, with connecting service to Newark International Airport in New Jersey and Penn Station in New York City. Alternatively, Beacon station along the Hudson Line is a short cab or shuttle ride across the river from Newburgh. The Newburgh Beacon Shuttle bus connects the Beacon station, downtown Newburgh, and Stewart International Airport.

By Car

In the eastern part of Orange County, Route 17, I-87, and I-84 form a triangle that encloses many of the most popular attractions in the area. More than a dozen taxi services cover Orange County, including West Point, Monroe, Warwick, and Greenwood Lake. Car rentals are available at Stewart International Airport.

Putnam County

Squeezed between the large and densely populated counties of Westchester to the south and Dutchess to the north are 231 square miles of the most dramatic landscape along the Hudson. On overcast days, a dreamy mist clings to the jagged ridgeline of the Hudson Highlands, producing a landscape reminiscent of a tale from the Brothers Grimm. Just 50 miles from Manhattan and easily accessible by rail, romantic Putnam County features two Victorian-era towns along the river, two large state parks, and hundreds of miles of wilderness trails. The county's many lakes and streams provide a vital source of freshwater for the New York City reservoir system.

Putnam does not have a Hudson River crossing of its own—its borders extend from just above the Bear Mountain Bridge to a point south of the Newburg/Beacon Bridge—however, two Metro-North rail lines make Putnam an easy day trip from New York City. The Hudson Line stops in Garrison and Cold Spring along the river, while the Harlem line stops in Brewster. From Brewster, it's about a 90-minute ride to Grand Central.

In addition to the train tracks, a 20-mile stretch of the Appalachian Trail crosses diagonally through Putnam County, from the Bear Mountain Bridge and **Hudson Highlands State Park** in the southwest to Clarence Fahnestock Memorial State Park and the Dutchess County line in the northeast.

Anthony's Nose at the Bear Mountain Bridge makes a logical starting point for a Putnam County tour. Follow Route 9D north from Westchester County or Route 301 east from I-84.

ALONG THE RIVER—ROUTE 9D

ⓜ Boscobel Restoration

Two rows of apple trees frame the view of the Hudson from the entrance to Boscobel (Beautiful Wood), a restored neoclassical mansion dating back to the 19th century. Named after an English manor, the home belonged to colonial loyalist States Morris Dyckman, a contemporary of Chancellor Robert Livingston.

The building originally sat on a 250-acre farm in Montrose, about 15 miles south of its present-day location. It was nearly lost to history when the federal government sold it to a demolition contractor in the 1950's for $35. Fortunately, a group of private citizens came to the rescue and moved the building, piece by piece, to a scenic bluff in Garrison.

The structure and details of the home create a light and airy feel that is unique among the Hudson Valley's riverside mansions. On the outside,

© PAUL ITOI

the Hudson on a foggy day

wood-carved drapery, complete with bowties and tassels, decorates the space between columns on the 2nd-floor balcony. Inside, Dyckman furnished Boscobel with exquisite silver, china, and glassware that he purchased in London in the late 18th century.

Home to a number of cultural events throughout the year, Boscobel Restoration (Rte. 9D, Garrison, 845/265-3638, info@boscobel.org, www .boscobel.org; Apr.–Oct. Wed.–Mon. 9:30 A.M.– 5 P.M., Nov.–Dec. Wed.–Mon. 9:30 A.M.–4 P.M.; adults $10, seniors $9, children $7, grounds only $7) hosts the annual Hudson Valley Shakespeare Festival. The museum runs a free shuttle from the Cold Spring Metro-North station on designated weekends. Call for exact dates. Visitors must pay an entrance fee to wander the formal gardens and the mile-long Woodland Trail, but the variety of roses (more than 150 types) and the views of West Point across the river are well worth the donation.

Directly below Boscobel, the National Audubon Society operates the **Constitution Marsh Wildlife Sanctuary** (Indian Brook Rd., Garrison, 914/265-2601). A short but steep and rocky path leads from the parking lot to a nature center and boardwalk that spans a large sec-

tion of tidal marsh—an ideal setting for birdwatchers. The center offers guided canoe trips in summer months. The parking lot off Route 9D can accommodate only eight cars at a time, so be prepared to change plans if the sign says "Full."

To the east of Route 9D in Garrison, Manitoga ("Place of the Great Spirit of Algonquin") and the Russel Wright Design Center are a one-of-a-kind nature retreat and residence created by nationally acclaimed designer Russel Wright. With his unique and practical designs for the home, Wright championed easier living and pioneered lifestyle marketing. Beginning in 1942, he transformed an abandoned quarry and lumberyard in Garrison into a 75-acre masterpiece of ecological design, featuring native plants, stones, and streams. Dragon Rock, his experimental home, sits on a rock ledge, surrounded by four miles of trails that connect to the Appalachian Trail. Visitors can tour the home and grounds daily beginning at 11 A.M. (Rte. 9D, Garrison, 845/424-3812, info@russelwrightcenter.org, www.russelwright-center.org; Mon.–Fri. 9 A.M.–5 P.M.; adults $15, children $5).

Another place to stroll in Garrison is the **Graymoor Spiritual Life Center** (Rte. 9, Garrison,

845/424-3671), the headquarters of the Franciscan Friars of the Atonement. Open to the public, the grounds offer a serene vantage for scenic river views.

Cold Spring Village

The timeless village of Cold Spring lies in the shadow of Storm King Mountain, which rises 1,000 feet across the Hudson at the narrowest and deepest stretch of the river. A haven for antique-lovers, Cold Spring's Main Street is divided into upper and lower sections that slope downhill toward an inviting gazebo at the river's edge—the site of many a marriage proposal. Pedestrians can cross the tracks via an underpass, but drivers must take a detour to the south to reach lower Main Street and the riverfront. An easy day trip for city dwellers, Cold Spring lures shoppers and diners by the trainful. Treasures from vintage toys to designer jewelry await within walking distance of the station.

Nearby, the **Putnam County Historical Society** and **Foundry School Museum** (63 Chestnut St., Cold Spring, 845/265-4010, www.pchs-fsm .org; Tues. & Thurs. 10 A.M.–4 P.M., Sat.–Sun.

2–5 P.M.) is a popular fieldtrip for area schoolchildren. Built in 1817 when America was reeling from the War of 1812 and the realization that it needed a domestic source of iron to defend its borders, the building contains a collection of tools, letters, blueprints, and decorative ironworks, such as the ornate Washington Irving Bench. Other highlights include a famous painting by John Ferguson Weir called *The Gun Foundry* and the Civil War–era *Parrot Gun.*

Outdoor activities are readily accessible from Cold Spring: The most popular pastimes include paddling the river and the Constitution Marsh Wildlife Preservation and hiking trails in the 4,200-acre Hudson Highlands State Park.

Hudson Highlands State Park

Extending the length of Putnam County, from Westchester to Dutchess, Hudson Highlands State Park offers 25 miles of hiking trails that meander along the ridgeline of the Hudson Highland range. Views of the river here are among the best anywhere in the region (Rte. 9D, Beacon, 845/225-7207).

Birdwatchers frequent 900-foot-high Anthony's Nose at the Westchester County line to watch hawks, eagles, and vultures hover over the Bear Mountain Bridge. A route to the summit of South Beacon Mountain, six miles round-trip, brings hikers to the highest point along the range. Look for the trailhead on Route 9D, four miles north of Cold Spring. For a more challenging hike (5.5 miles roundtrip), try the Breakneck Ridge Trail, which begins north of the tunnel on Route 9D, two miles north of Cold Spring. This trail covers some of the steepest terrain and most striking views in the park; however, it can be dangerous during inclement weather. Choose a different route in wet or windy conditions.

As a symbol of its commitment to preserving open space

COLD SPRING

To Hudson Highlands State Park

RIVER RD
RIVERVIEW RESTAURANT
NORTHERN AVE
GARDEN ST
FAIR ST
HIGH ST
CHURCH ST
MORRIS AVE
301
CHESTNUT ST
SANTA FE
MAIN ST
MARION AVE
STONE ST
LE BOUCHON
CATHRYN'S TUSCAN GRILL
COLD SPRING DEPOT
DEPOT SQ
PIG HILL INN B&B
HUDSON VALLEY OUTFITTERS
FOUNDRY CAFÉ
KEMBLE AVE
NORTH ST
FISH ST
LUNN TERR
HUDSON HOUSE RIVER INN
MAIN ST
WEST ST
NEW ST
CONSTITUTION DR

Hudson River

0   200 yds
0   200 m

© AVALON TRAVEL PUBLISHING, INC.

The Hudson Highlands

along the river, the New York State government added 240 acres to this park in 2002. Camping, campfires, bikes, and motorized vehicles are not permitted within the park. Fishing and boating is, however, permitted along the shoreline.

CENTRAL PUTNAM COUNTY— ALONG THE TACONIC STATE PARKWAY
Clarence Fahnestock Memorial State Park

The white sand beach at Lake Canopus in central Putnam County arrived by truck from Long Island in the late 1970s. Today, the completed waterfront complex has everything beach-goers need, save the salty air. A concession stand sells burgers and hot dogs, and there are showers, picnic tables, a boat launch, and campsites.

The beach sits within Putnam County's second state park, **Clarence Fahnestock Memorial State Park** (Rte. 301, Carmel, 845/255-7207), which covers 10,000 acres extending from a few miles east of Cold Spring to beyond the Taconic State Parkway. Several lakes and ponds are suitable for boating and fishing.

Hikes on 42 miles of wooded trails range from easy to moderately strenuous. The Three Lakes Loop is a popular route that follows the bed of an old railroad line and meets up with the Appalachian Trail at the end. Along the way, hikers meander through forest, wetlands, and dense patches of mountain laurel (3.2 or 5.9 miles, depending on shortcuts). Mountain bikers and horseback riders have access to additional trails and bridle paths. Access the park from Route 301, which connects Route 9 along the Hudson River to the Taconic State Parkway.

In addition to the beach, the park features the **Taconic Outdoor Education Center** (755 Mountain Laurel Rd., Cold Spring, 845/265-3773), which runs geology, aquatic ecology, astronomy, and outdoor skills programs for groups only. Guests stay in nine heated log cabins. In winter, the center has 15 kilometers of groomed cross-country ski trails, along with equipment rentals and lessons.

EASTERN PUTNAM COUNTY— ALONG I-84
Brewster

Named for a local contractor, Walter Brewster, who built a station for the Harlem Line Railroad in the 1850s, this village thrived as an early thoroughfare between New York City and Danbury, Connecticut. Today, however, the town is a mixed bag of 19th-century homes and run-down storefronts.

Unique among regional museums, Brewster's **Southeast Museum** (67 Main St., Brewster, 845/279-7500, www.southeastmuseum.org; Tues.–Sat. 10 A.M.–4 P.M.; admission free) documents a number of seemingly unrelated developments—from the arrival of the early American circus and the Borden Condensed Milk factory to the engineering of the Harlem Line Railroad and the Croton Reservoir—that took place in and around the town of Southeast. Located in a historic building in downtown Brewster, the museum also displays a collection of antique farm equipment, quilts, and other Americana in rotating exhibits throughout the year.

Carmel and Mahopac

On the shores of a small lake at the intersection of Route 6 and Route 301, Carmel (CAR-mel) has been the Putnam County seat since 1812. It is home to the second-oldest courthouse in New York State, a Greek Revival structure built in 1814.

Suburban Mahopac sits on the shores of Lake Mahopac, once a large resort community. Today, local residents water ski, sail, and fish the lake during summer months. The town has two marinas for launching and servicing powerboats.

Nearby in Kent is a more unusual sight: the peaceful **Chuang Yen Monastery** (Rte. 301, Kent, 845/225-1819), a Dharma education center featuring the largest Buddha statue in the Western hemisphere. The 37-foot Buddha Vairocana towers over thousands of smaller statues inside the Great Buddha Hall, a pagodalike structure that was built around the giant statue in the style of the Tang Dynasty era (A.D. 618–917). The Woo-Ju Memorial Library on the premises contains 70,0000 Buddhist reference texts in many different languages. A pleasant reading room faces Seven Jewels Lake and is open to the public.

SPORTS AND RECREATION

Putnam County offers a remarkable variety of outdoor activities, given its proximity to the urban sprawl of New York City. Much of the county's land and water is protected from development by the state park system. Trails are well maintained, and rental gear and professional instruction are readily available for a range of sports, including hiking, skiing, paddling, and horseback riding.

Winter Sports

In winter, Clarence Fahnestock Memorial Park becomes a playground for Nordic skiing, snowshoeing, ice skating, ice fishing, and snowmobiling. **Thunder Ridge Ski Area** (Rte. 22, Patterson, 845/878-4100, www.thunderridgeski.com; Mon.–Fri. 10 A.M.–9 P.M., Sat.–Sun. 9 A.M.–10 P.M.; adults $35, juniors $22) is a family-run business with easy slopes that are ideal for beginners. The mountain runs a free shuttle from the Patterson train station during the peak season.

Hiking

Both Hudson Highlands and Clarence Fahnestock State Parks maintain extensive trail systems for hikers, including well-traveled stretches of the Appalachian Trail. Water found on the trails within these parks is not safe to drink. Bring your own. Except for the designated camping area at Lake Canapus, camping and campfires are not permitted with the parks.

The **Putnam Trailway** follows the route of the old New York Central Railroad, connecting Mahopac to Carmel and Brewster. From 1881 until 1958, the Old Put ushered passengers between the Bronx and Brewster. Today, the tracks are a paved bike- and footpath. Many sections are still under construction.

Mountain Biking and Road Riding

Putnam's annual **Tour de Putnam Cycling & Mountain Biking Festival** (845/225-0381) takes place in late August. The races (15–100 miles)

start and finish in Kent, covering miles of Putnam's pretty countryside.

Golf

Golfers can choose from four public golf courses in Garrison, Mahopac, and Carmel. The **Highlands Golf Club** (Rte. 9D, Garrison, 845/424-3727; Mon.–Fri.; $17) has river views.

Swimming and Boating

Putnam County offers aquatic activities on the Hudson and in several natural lakes located in its two state parks. For a sandy beach, head to Lake Canopus in Clarence Fahnestock State Park.

Hudson Valley Outfitters (63 Main St., Cold Spring, 845/265-0221, www.hudsonvalleyoutfitters.com; Mon.–Wed. 11 A.M.–5 P.M., Thurs.–Fri. till 6 P.M., Sat. 9 A.M.–6 P.M., Sun. till 5 P.M.) runs beginner- to advanced-level kayak trips on the Hudson to Constitution Marsh, Bannerman Castle, and overnight destinations, as well guided hikes through the Hudson Highlands. The Constitution Marsh Wildlife Preserve offers guided canoe trips in summer months.

COURTESY OF ORANGE COUNTY TOURISM

paddlers float on the Hudson

The Hudson Highlands

Fishing and Hunting

Anglers head to the lakes to catch bass, perch, pickerel, and trout. Stillwater Lake in Fahnestock State Park is stocked with rainbow and brook trout each spring. Brown trout are common in the streams that feed the New York City Watershed. Thirteen miles of water are open to the public, and the season typically runs April 1–September 30. Regulations vary by location and are more protective in Putnam County than elsewhere in New York State. In designated areas, size limits may be higher, daily limits may be lower, and artificial lures may be required. Bow hunting for deer and wild turkey hunting are permitted in both states parks during limited seasons.

Horseback Riding

There are bridle paths in Clarence Fahnestock Memorial State Park, and **Hollow Brook Riding Academy** (Peekskill Hollow Rd., Putnam Valley, 845/526-8357, www.hollowbrookriding.com) offers lessons to new and experienced riders.

ACCOMMODATIONS

Putnam County accommodations range from historic inns along the river to budget motels and chains closer to the interstate.

Under $100

Heidi's Inn (Rte. 22, Brewster, 845/279-8011, www.heidisinn.com; $75–90), located between Brewster and Pawling, is a good choice for an affordable overnight stay. Some rooms include full kitchens. Country breakfast is a highlight at the two-room **Mallard Manor** (345 Lakeview Dr., Mahopac, 845/628-3595).

$150–200

At the bottom of Cold Spring's Main Street, the 1832 **Hudson House River Inn** (2 Main St., Cold Spring, 845/265-9355, www.hudsonhouse-inn.com; $155–225) has 11 well-appointed guestrooms with private baths, television, and breakfast included. Some rooms have balconies with views of the Hudson River.

Centrally located in Putnam County, **The Country House Inn** (1457 Peekskill Hollow Rd.,

Kent, 845/228-5838, www.countryhouseinn.com; $180–200) is the place to curl up in a rocker with a good book and enjoy the breeze that blows off Boyd's Reservoir. Part of the building dates to 1780, and during a 1997–1998 renovation, the owners restored four suites to their original size.

Formerly the home of a Marquise, the timeless **Plumbush Inn** (1656 Rte. 9D, Cold Spring, 845/265-3904; $165–185) has several stylish rooms and an adjoining gourmet restaurant. This 1867 Victorian is showing its age on the outside, but the interior country decor is still cozy and inviting.

Over $200

The lobby of the **Pig Hill Inn B&B** (73 Main St., Cold Spring, 845/265-9247, www.pighillinn.com; $150–220) doubles as an antique shop, and just about everything you see is for sale. Several rooms are individually decorated with poster beds and fireplaces. Breakfast is served in a lovely atrium in the back of the inn.

Garrison's romantic **Bird and Bottle Inn** (1123 Old Albany Post Rd., Garrison, 845/424-3000 or 800/782-6837) began as a restaurant in a 1761 farmhouse and then expanded into a four-room inn as well. Fireplaces, four-poster beds, and antique furnishings set the mood.

Campgrounds

The best place to pitch a tent in Putnam County is the shores of Lake Canopus in Clarence Fahnestock Memorial State Park.

FOOD

Putnam County restaurants excel in blending farm-fresh ingredients with international cuisine to please the cosmopolitan palette.

Along the River–Route 9D

Kick off a day of antiquing with a fresh-baked scone at the **Foundry Café** (55 Main St., Cold Spring, 845/265-4504; mains $5–10). At the intersection of Route 9W and Main Street in Cold Spring, **Santa Fe** serves reputable southwestern fare. Continuing down Main, **Cathryn's Tuscan Grill** (91 Main St., Cold Spring, 845/265-5582, www.tuscangrill.com; open daily for lunch and dinner; mains $12–24) is another longtime favorite for an upscale Italian lunch or dinner. **Brasserie Le Bouchon** (76 Main St., Cold Spring, 845/265-7676; Wed.-Sun. noon–10 P.M.) is a relatively new bistro with garden seating in warm weather.

The **Cold Spring Depot** (1 Main St., Cold Spring, 845/265-5000, www.coldspringdepot.com; open daily for lunch and dinner; mains $15–20), at the foot of Main, draws a crowd for its patio seating and separate clam bar. A Dixieland band plays live music on weekends. As the name implies, **Riverview** (45 Fair St., Cold Spring, 845/265-4778, www.riverdining.com; Tues.–Sun. for lunch and dinner; mains $8–20, cash only) features a terrace overlooking the Hudson and a simple Italian menu, including a variety of individual pizzas.

During the summer Shakespeare festival at Boscobel, the **Plumbush Inn** (1656 Rte. 9D, Cold Spring, 845/265-3904; Wed.–Sat. noon–2 P.M. & 5–9 P.M., Sun. noon–8 P.M.) is popular with theatergoers. The inn is known for its Continental menu, outstanding desserts, and formal and attentive service. Enjoy two intimate dining rooms with fireplaces in winter or a table on the porch in summer. Reservations are required.

Hudson House River Inn (2 Main St., Cold Spring, 845/265-9355, www.hudsonhouseinn.com; mains $17–28) is the place for an old-world dining experience. Executive chef Lukas E. Wagner hails from the Culinary Institute and serves a varied menu, from jambalaya pasta to New Zealand rack of lamb. The restaurant is affiliated with two Dutchess County eateries: Hudson's Ribs & Fish and Union House, both in Fishkill. A prix fixe Sunday brunch begins with a bloody Mary or mimosa and costs $23.

Another CIA-trained chef reigns at **Valley Restaurant at The Garrison** (2015 Rte. 9 at Snake Hill Rd., Garrison, 845/424-2339, www.thegarrison.com; Mon.–Sat. lunch & Thurs.–Sat. dinner, Sun. brunch & dinner), a golf and spa resort nestled among the Hudson Highlands. The American and Continental menu at the **Bird & Bottle Inn** has been a Garrison mainstay for years.

For a satisfying Mexican fix, sample the Yucatecan specialties at **Café Maya** (3182 Rte. 9 between Old Albany Post Rd. & Walmer Lane, Cold Spring, 845/265-4636). The best margaritas around are to be found at **🗹 Guadalajara** (2 Union St., Briarcliff Manor, 914/944-4380, guadalajara@mxr.com; mains $13–22) in a mustard yellow stucco building. Tile floors and bright colors complete the ambience inside. On the menu are tempting chiles rellenos, taquitos al carbon, tostadas, and bistec. Servers prepare guacamole at the table. Enjoy live music on Fridays and Saturdays.

Eastern Putnam County–Along I-84

A relative newcomer to Putnam County's restaurant scene, **Stoneleigh Creek** (166 Stoneleigh Ave., 845/276-0000, www.stoneleighcreek.com; Tues.–Sun. noon–2 P.M. & 5 P.M. till close, Mon. 5 P.M. till close; mains $18–28) opened in 2000 to serve the fly fishers who frequent a nearby stretch of the Croton River. Given its out-of-the-way location at the Westchester County line, this country bistro surprises first-time guests with starters of fried oysters and grilled quail, and mains that include rib eye, duck breast, and an unusual seafood cassoulet. Reservations are recommended on weekends.

Locals swear by Brewster's **🗹 Red Rooster Drive-In** (Rte. 22, Brewster, 845/279-8046) for burgers, fries, shakes, and ice cream. For an evening of house-cured gravlax, grilled antelope medallions, or roasted baby pheasant, head to **The Arch** (Rte. 22N, Brewster, 845/279-5011, www.archrestaurant.com; $64 prix fixe dinner, $35 brunch). For spicier fare, try **Jaipore Royal Indian Cuisine** (280 Rte. 22, Brewster, 845/277-3549, www.fineindiandining.com; daily noon–3 P.M. and 5–10 P.M.; mains $5–12), located in an 1856 mansion that was once a speakeasy. Known locally for its lunch buffet, the restaurant has several dining rooms, including an outdoor porch and patio.

ENTERTAINMENT AND EVENTS
Performing Arts
The theater event of the summer in Putnam County is the **Hudson Valley Shakespeare Festival** (845/265-9575, www.hvshakespeare.org).

Performances take place under a tent at Boscobel Restoration. Locals also adore the **Philipstown Depot Theatre** (Lower Station Rd., Garrison, 845/424-3900, www.philipstowndepottheatre .org) at Garrison Landing.

Festivals

Dozens of dealers participate in the **Cold Spring Antiques Show** (845/265-4414, www.cold-springantiquesshow.com) held each June in Mayor's Park on Fair Street.

Bars

Sports fans can view 22 TVs and a most impressive collection of memorabilia at **The Stadium** (1308 Rte. 9, Garrison, 845/734-4000, www.sta-diumbarrest.com). Unique treasures represent the essential all-American pastimes: football, baseball, basketball, and hockey, including two Heisman trophies, Mickey Mantle's Triple Crown award, and more. The restaurant serves pub fare 11:30 A.M.–10 P.M., and the bar stays open late with 16 beers on tap.

SHOPPING

Farm Stands

The Hudson Valley's orchards aren't far away from Putnam County. Brewster (municipal parking lot at Rte. 22 & Rte. 6; Sat. 10 A.M.–2 P.M.) and Cold Spring (former hospital lot, 845/265-3611; May–Oct. Sat. 7:30 A.M.–2 P.M.) host two of the most popular farmer's markets around.

Antiques and Galleries

Antique shoppers must head to Cold Spring for a day of retail adventure. Several blocks of shops line Main Street, with window displays of vintage toys, coins, jewelry, and home furnishings. Among them, **Serious Toyz** (82 Main St., Cold Spring, 845/265-6543. www.serioustoyz.com; Thurs.–Mon. noon–6 P.M.) buys and sells an assortment of collectible toys, including tin, pressed steel, die cast, plastic, and character toys. **Joseph's Fine Jewelry** (171 Main St., Cold Spring, 845/265-2323) handles coins and currency, as well as antiques and jewelry. Most stores close by 6 P.M., with some open later on weekend evenings.

Mahopac's **Kitch 'n' Kaffe** (985 Rte. 6, Mahopac, 845/621-3535, www.kitch-n-kaffe.com; Mon.–Fri. 9 A.M.–8 P.M., Sat. 9 A.M.–6 P.M., Sun. 10 A.M.–6 P.M.) sells high-end cooking equipment and ingredients, in addition to offering cooking classes for home chefs. In Carmel, watch glassmaker **John Burchetta** at work in his 100-year old barn (Burchetta Glass Studio & Gallery, 1544 Rte. 6, Carmel, 845/225-1430, www .burchetta.com; Sat.–Sun. 10 A.M.–5 P.M.).

INFORMATION AND SERVICES

The **Putnam Visitors Bureau** (110 Old Rte. 6, Bldg. 3, Carmel, 800/470-4854, www.visitput-nam.org) is headquartered in Carmel, and its website contains detailed information on major destinations and sights in the county. The **Brewster Chamber of Commerce** (31 Main Street, 845/279-2477) is located near the Southeast Museum.

GETTING THERE AND AROUND

By Bus

Putnam Area Rapid Transit covers major towns throughout the county with five lines (845/878-RIDE or 845/878-7433; $1.25 one-way), but the Metro-North lines are a more reliable way to get around.

By Train

Two Metro-North rail lines serve Putnam County: the Hudson Line stops in Garrison and Cold Spring along the river, while the Harlem Line runs to Brewster on its way from Grand Central Station to Dover Plains in Dutchess County. Taxis are generally available from the stations. Alamo Rent A Car (845/567-9847) has a rental office in Newburgh.

By Car

The easiest way to see Putnam County is by car, and the fastest routes are I-84 and the Taconic State Parkway. Public transportation is not out of the question, however, particularly if you plan to visit and stay in one of the towns along the Metro-North train lines, such as Garrison, Cold Spring, or Newburgh.

The Mid-Hudson

Above the Hudson Highlands, the river widens once again, and the surrounding terrain forms rolling hills, babbling brooks, and expansive orchards. Dutchess and Ulster Counties share 40 miles of coastline along this stretch of the Hudson, with three points of connection: the Newburgh-Beacon, Mid-Hudson, and Kingston-Rhinecliff Bridges. A strong focus on the arts, abundant gourmet dining opportunities, and a variety of outdoor attractions draw visitors for weekend and longer stays.

Cultural highlights in the Mid-Hudson region include the Frances Lehman Loeb Art Center, the new Dia:Beacon Museum, and the prestigious Culinary Institute of America. To complement the gourmet cuisine, a handful of wineries on both sides of the river produce award-winning chardonnay, pinot noir, merlot, and cabernet franc wines.

Several large state parks, including the southern region of the Catskill Preserve, offer leaf peepers a prime setting for viewing the spectacular display of fall colors. If you aren't afraid of heights, head to the Shawangunk Ridge in Ulster County for a day of rock climbing. And if you are inclined to stay at sea level, there are miles of country roads to explore by bicycle and numerous streams and creeks that offer prime conditions for fly-fishing.

PLANNING YOUR TIME

By far the most popular destination in the region is the bustling college town of New Paltz and the surrounding countryside. You can walk the town center in a few hours, but to absorb the alternative vibe, you'll want at least a couple of days. Plan a hike or a bike ride and then enjoy a

Must-Sees

⋈ **Dia:Beacon Museum:** Dutchess County's newest contemporary art museum draws art aficionados out of New York City for a refreshing change of pace. Expansive single-artist galleries flooded with natural light hold paintings, sculptures, and installations from the 1960s to the present (page 72).

⋈ **Vanderbilt Estate:** The 50-room home of Frederick and Louise Vanderbilt exhibits a variety of interior design influences, from renaissance to rococo. A carved wooden ceiling in the formal dining room is one of many European antiques found by designer Stanford White (page 76).

⋈ **Culinary Institute of America:** Set on a picturesque riverside campus, the CIA trains aspiring professionals and enthusiasts in the art of fine cuisine. Tour the grounds at sunset before eating in one of the five public restaurants on campus (page 77).

⋈ **Rhinebeck:** Rhinebeck stands out as an upscale enclave in an otherwise rural county. Victorian, Colonial, and Greek Revival buildings line several

Huguenot Street, New Paltz

blocks of boutique stores, country inns, and gourmet restaurants (page 78).

⋈ **Huguenot Street:** Named for the French Huguenots who came to America to escape persecution, Huguenot Street in New Paltz features a block of stone dwellings that are now more than 300 years old (page 94).

⋈ **Minnewaska State Park Preserve:** Ulster County's gem of a park covers 12,000 acres of the Shawangunk ridge with a sparkling glacial lake (page 96).

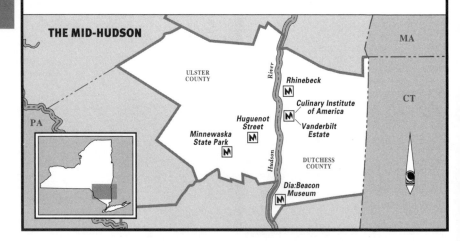

THE MID-HUDSON

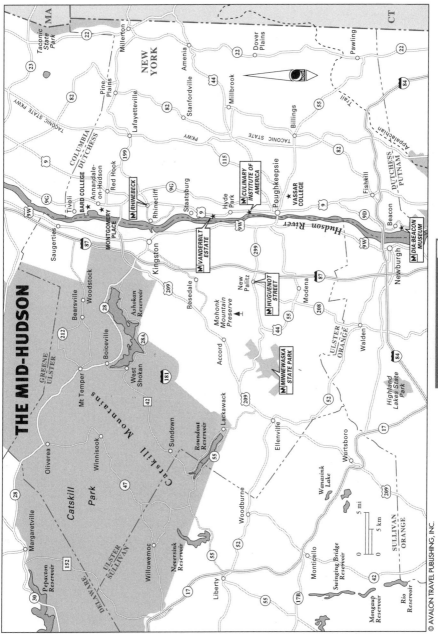

© AVALON TRAVEL PUBLISHING, INC.

meal at one of the area's outstanding eateries. Climbers will want to spend the week.

Poughkeepsie and Kingston, the largest cities in the area, are not destinations per se; however, you won't be wasting your time if you stop to stroll or dine along their historic waterfronts. History buffs may want to make a special trip to tour the many preserved sites.

In northern Dutchess County, a 60-mile loop begins at the train station in Poughkeepsie and follows Route 44 east to Millbook, then Route 22 north to Millerton, and Route 199 west to the Hudson River. From there, Route 9 hugs the riverbank back to Poughkeepsie. The drive should take two to three hours, depending on stops.

Ulster is a large county, and there are several options for scenic driving routes. One approach is to begin at the Mid-Hudson Bridge and follow Route 9D north to Kingston. Then take Route 28 west to Mount Tremper. A short loop along Route 212 heading northeast takes you through Woodstock and Saugerties and eventually back to Route 9W. Or you can continue along Route 28 to Belleayre Mountain and Delaware County beyond. Closer to Kingston, Route 209 south off Route 28 goes to New Paltz and Minnewaska State Park. Allow about half an hour to drive from New Paltz to Kingston on local roads, and an hour to cross the county from east to west.

Dutchess County

Scenic Dutchess County offers a telling mix of restored historic landmarks and nearly deserted manufacturing centers, bedroom communities, and progressive towns that attract weekenders by the thousands. A sampling of its historic riverside mansions should anchor every first-time visitor's itinerary. The county seat, Poughkeepsie, was designated the New York State capital in 1777 for about a decade. IBM set up shop in the 1950s, and despite the massive layoffs of the early 1990s, the company remains the county's dominant employer.

Poughkeepsie and Dover Plains mark the northern ends of the Metro-North commuter lines. But while the southern half of Dutchess County has succumbed to the congestion of suburban sprawl, the northern part retains an idyllic charm.

ALONG THE RIVER—ROUTE 9
Dia:Beacon Museum

A flight along the Hudson in search of a new museum space resulted in the creation of Dutchess County's newest cultural attraction: Dia:Beacon Museum (3 Beekman St., Beacon, 845/440-0100, www.diabeacon.org; Apr.–Oct. Thurs.–Mon. 11 A.M.–6 P.M., limited winter hours; adults $10, students $7).

Michael Govan, director of New York City–

based Dia Center for the Arts, reportedly spotted the 75-year-old printing plant from the air and immediately chose the site to house the museum's permanent collection. The result is an enormous contemporary art museum that draws art aficionados out of New York City for a refreshing change of pace. Spacious single-artist galleries flooded with natural light hold paintings, sculptures, and installations from the 1960s to the present. Don't miss Richard Serra's *Torqued Ellipses* on the lower level. The towering pieces look especially dramatic at sunset, when they catch the light streaming in through frosted-glass windows. Outside, the West Garden presents sweeping river views.

Beacon

The Dia museum is located outside the small city of Beacon, which began to show the early signs of revival in the 1990s with the restoration of a stretch of East Main Street, now the city's antique district. Its 16,000 residents are nestled between Mount Beacon, a recent extension of the Hudson Highlands State Park, and the eastern bank of the Hudson. A handful of major renovations are under way to draw overnight visitors to its historic buildings and waterfront—including a project to reopen the famed Incline Railway to the top of Mount Beacon—but for now, the town still reflects the wear and tear of its industrial days.

One sight that has been maintained over the years is the 1709 **Madame Brett Homestead** (50 Van Nydeck Ave., Beacon, 845/896-6897 or 845/831-6533; 1–4 P.M., by appointment), another George Washington haunt and Dutchess County's oldest dwelling. Visitors can tour 17 rooms filled with antiques, artwork, and seven generations' worth of Brett family memorabilia.

Farther north on Route 9D, the **Mount Gulian Historic Site** (145 Lamplight St., Beacon, 845/831-8172; Wed.–Sun. 1–5 P.M.) appears at the end of a row of modern townhouses. The 18th-century Dutch stone barn and 44 acres of gardens descending to the riverbank belonged to the Verplanck family and served as the headquarters of influential Revolutionary War General Friedrich Wilhelm Augustus von Steuben, a German volunteer who led the Americans to a critical victory at Freehold, New Jersey in 1778.

Fishkill and Wappingers Falls

Two miles east of Beacon, the signature steeple of the **First Reformed Church** (55 Main St., Fishkill) marks the village center of Fishkill (Fisherman's Creek), a major hub of wartime activity during the American Revolution. The church dates to 1731 and served as both a New York State government meeting place and a prison. Today, the town primarily hosts business travelers en route to IBM.

One mile south of town at the freeway interchange of I-84 and Route 9, the **Van Wyck Homestead Museum** (Rtes. 9 & I-84, Fishkill, 845/896-9560; Sat.–Sun. 1–4 P.M.) stands out among the surrounding group of chain hotels. Army officers and heads of state convened here during the American Revolution. The barracks and blacksmith shop that once surrounded the home are lost to history, but the town historical society continues to restore the inside with original documents and period furnishings. Visitors are welcome.

Stony Kill Farm Environmental Center (Rte. 9D, Wappingers Falls, 845/831-8780; Mon.–Fri. 8:30 A.M.–4:45 P.M., Sat. 9:30 A.M.–12:30 P.M., Sun. 1 –4 P.M.), run by the New York

Department of Environmental Conservation, is a good place to stop for a picnic and a refresher in environmental science. Look for one of two entrances off Route 9D (Exit 11 from I-84). A tree-lined driveway leads to the Manor House and surrounding gardens. Inside, a visitors center houses an extensive library with titles on a wide variety of nature topics, including acid rain, wildlife management, and environmental literature.

Visit the Common Ground Farm on the property to learn about the model of Community-Supported Agriculture (CSA). Historic buildings associated with the farm include a 19th-century barn and farmhouse and an 18th-century Dutch stone house.

Several interpretive trails, ranging from .5 to 2.5 miles long, lead walkers though evergreen and hardwood forests, across fields, and around ponds. Brochures for self-guided tours are available at each trailhead. The center holds special events throughout the year, including maple sugaring demonstrations, wildflower walks, and programs for children.

Poughkeepsie

Poughkeepsie has suffered the fate of postindustrial contraction worse than most. In a textbook case of urban decay, the majority of the city's middle class residents fled the city center for the suburbs during the late 20th century, leaving once-beautiful homes boarded up and constructing a six-lane arterial in their wake. When IBM slashed its workforce by two-thirds in the early 1990s, scores of small businesses went under, and the local economy never fully recovered. Though this city of 30,000 has a few historical gems, well-meaning locals continue to steer travelers north to Rhinebeck for a decent night's sleep.

That said, there are signs a long overdue recovery may be in the works: riverfront festivals are drawing crowds again, and new eateries are breathing life into the city, one renovation at a time. Poughkeepsie has reopened its Main Street to car traffic to draw retail businesses back. The old Poughkeepsie Railroad Bridge is undergoing a transformation into a pedestrian bikeway. And the Bardavon 1869 Opera House continues to stage first-rate theater performances. With the

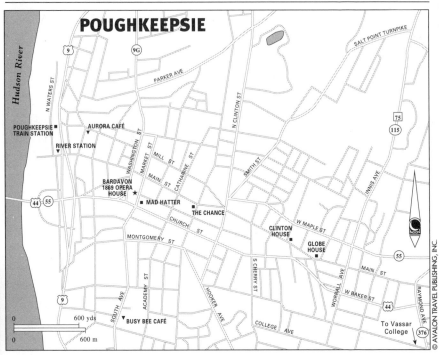

POUGHKEEPSIE

SALT POINT TURNPIKE

Hudson River

PARKER AVE

POUGHKEEPSIE
TRAIN STATION ■
AURORA CAFÉ

RIVER STATION ▼

BARDAVON
1869 OPERA
HOUSE ★

■ MAD HATTER

THE CHANCE ■

CLINTON
HOUSE ■

GLOBE
HOUSE ■

MONTGOMERY ST

CHURCH ST

W MAPLE ST

MAIN ST

W BAKER ST

■ BUSY BEE CAFÉ

COLLEGE AVE

To Vassar
College

0   600 yds
0   600 m

© AVALON TRAVEL PUBLISHING, INC.

The Mid-Hudson

influence of Vassar College, New York City commuters, and the Culinary Institute of America, Poughkeepsie has an appealing mix of culture and diversity. Like Newburgh to the south and Kingston to the north, its recovery hinges on making the waterfront an attractive place for residents and visitors alike.

Poughkeepsie's Main Street begins at Waryas Park under the Mid-Hudson Bridge and runs east-west between the two legs of the arterial (Rte. 44/55) until it reaches the town of Arlington. The Hudson River Sloop *Clearwater* and its sister vessel, Mystic Whaler, dock here when they are in the area, as Poughkeepsie is the headquarters for the nonprofit organization that runs them.

Modeled after the Dutch vessels that sailed the Hudson in the 18th century, *Clearwater* was conceived in the 1960s as a call to action to clean up the river before it was too late. In a unique onboard classroom setting, *Clearwater* volunteers educate local residents about the importance of environmental awareness and conservation. Since

1966, the watchdog organization has battled GE on the dumping of PCBs into the river, prosecuted Clean Water Act offenders, and pioneered the model of encouraging environmental advocacy through a hands-on sailing experience.

Moving away from the riverfront, a number of historic sites are clustered in the downtown area near Academy Street. The **Clinton House** (549 Main St., Poughkeepsie, 845/471-1630; Tues.–Fri. 10 A.M.–3 P.M.) holds the offices and library of the Dutchess County Historical Society. This stone building hosted the New York State government briefly in 1777 and was rebuilt after a fire in 1783. The society also runs neighboring **Glebe House** (635 Main St., Poughkeepsie, 845/454-0605, www.theglebehouse.org; Wed.–Sun. 1–4 P.M.; adults $5) a restored home dating back to 1767.

The **Bardavon 1869 Opera House** (35 Market St., Poughkeepsie, 845/473-5288, box office 845/473-2072, www.bardavon.org) escaped demolition in the mid-'70s to become listed on the

National Historic Register. With its original pipe organ (a 1928 Wurlitzer Theatre Organ), and an interior dome that dates to 1920, the Bardavon is one of the oldest surviving theaters in the U.S. Legendary performers from Mark Twain to Frank Sinatra have appeared on its stage. Today, the theater hosts the Hudson Valley Philharmonic and a full schedule of musical, dance, film, and theater productions by contemporary artists.

Samuel B. Morse became a household name in the 1840s when he developed the first commercial telegraph, sending the famous words "What hath God wrought" across the line. With money earned from the venture, Morse bought **Locust Grove** (2683 South Rd., Poughkeepsie, 845/454-4500; daily 10 A.M.–3 P.M.; adults $6, children $3), a 100-acre property south of the Mid-Hudson Bridge that is now a National Historic Landmark. The Italian villa houses an informative exhibit on telegraph technology, as well as American and European furniture and many of Morse's own paintings. The surrounding woods and gardens are open to the public year-round.

Vassar College

Between downtown Poughkeepsie and Arlington is the ivory tower of Vassar College, a top-ranked liberal-arts school that draws students from across the country and around the world. Vassar's attractive campus is spread over 1,000 acres with some 200 varieties of trees interspersed among inviting lawns. English brewer Matthew Vassar founded the college in 1861 in an effort to provide young women with courses in science, math, art history, and music that rivaled the best men's schools in the country. Vassar remained single-sex until 1969, when the first coed class was admitted.

Vassar prides itself on being first among U.S. colleges to have established its own art gallery. Today, the **Frances Lehman Loeb Art Center** (124 Raymond Ave., Poughkeepsie, 845/437-7745, fllac.vassar.edu; Tues.–Sat. 10 A.M.–5 P.M., Sun. 1–5 P.M.; free admission) holds a varied permanent collection, from ancient Egyptian sculptures of marble and red granite to contemporary American paintings. Enter the gallery near the main gate on Raymond Avenue.

Back at the river's edge, Matthew Vassar's former home is now the **Springside National Historic Site** (185 Academy St., Poughkeepsie), preserved as the last standing design of landscape architect Andrew Jackson Downing. Most of the estate's 44-acres belong to a private condominium complex now, but visitors can view the restored gatehouse and wander along old carriage roads. Look for the entrance on Academy Street, on the west side of Route 9.

East of Vassar College, where Route 55 meets the Taconic State Parkway, is **James Baird State Park,** with an 18-hole golf course, tennis courts, picnic areas, and hiking trails. Its wooded trails are popular with local runners, while families attend programs at the nature center.

Hyde Park

Hyde Park offers a strong lineup for students of history and fine cuisine. For starters, the **Franklin D. Roosevelt Home National Historic Site** (4097 Albany Post Rd., Hyde Park, 845/229-2501 or 845/229-9115, www.nps.gov/hofr; daily 9 A.M.–5 P.M.; admission $14), where the four-term president lived all his life, houses FDR's presidential library and museum. Exhibits inside chronicle the president's and first lady's achievements. Visitors can also tour **Top Cottage** (7097 Albany Post Rd. Rte 9, Hyde Park, www.nps.gov/hofr; Thurs.–Mon. 10 A.M.–5 P.M.), the hilltop retreat where FDR met with international heads of state. Trails on 300 acres lead to the river's edge.

Eleanor Roosevelt spent many quiet years at the unassuming Val-Kill Cottage after FDR's death. Today, the **Eleanor Roosevelt National Historic Site—Val-Kill** (Rte. 9G, Hyde Park, 845/229-9115, www.nps.gov/elro; admission $8) welcomes visitors with guided home tours and 180 acres of beautifully landscaped grounds.

Between Hyde Park and Rhinebeck along Route 9 stands a tribute to the Gilded Age: the former residence of Ogden Mills—a financier and philanthropist—and Ruth Livingston Mills, a descendant of the Livingston family that first settled much of Columbia

County. The home began as a 25-room Greek Revival in 1832. Subsequent renovations by the same architectural firm that built the Vanderbilt estate turned it into a massive 65-room estate adorned with exquisite furnishings from Europe, Greece, and Asia. The property was handed over to the State of New York in 1938 to become the **Staatsburg State Historic Site** (Old Post Rd., Staatsburg, 845/889-8851; Wed.–Sat. 10 A.M.–5 P.M., Sun. noon–5 P.M.) Renovations were under way in mid-2004.

If trains are your guilty pleasure, save time to visit the **Hyde Park Railroad Station** (34 River Rd., Hyde Park, 845/229-2338; adults $5, children $4) before leaving the area. Built in 1914, the station was restored by the Hudson Valley Railroad Society and holds a treasured place on the National Register of Historic Places.

Vanderbilt Estate

A tour inside the Vanderbilt Estate (Rte. 9, Hyde Park, 845/229-9115, www.nps.gov/vama; daily 9 A.M.–5 P.M.; admission $8) will also send you straight back to the days of robber barons, railroad monopolies, and American capitalism run amuck. A fine product of the Gilded Age, the 50-room home of Frederick and Louise Vanderbilt exhibits a variety of interior design influences, from renaissance to rococo. A carved wooden ceiling in the formal dining room is

CIA RESTAURANTS

G raduates of the Culinary Institute of America often settle close to their alma mater. More than a dozen restaurants in Dutchess County are owned and operated by CIA alumni.

Allyn's Restaurant
4258 Rte. 44
Millbrook, NY
845/677-5888
www.allyns.com
Alumnus: Allan Steven Katz, 1977
approximate distance from CIA: 16 miles

Calico Restaurant & Patisserie
9 Mill St.
Rhinebeck, NY
845/876-2749
www.calicorhinebeck.com
Alumnus: Anthony Richard Balassone, 1981
approximate distance from CIA: 13 miles

Emerick House (Bed & Breakfast)
44 Partition St.
Saugerties, NY
845/247-9601
www.emerickhouse.com
Alumnus: John Grandin Dragun, 1992
approximate distance from CIA: 39 miles

Gersky's Restaurant and Catering
898 Rte. 6
Mahopac, NY
845/621-0696
www.gerskys.com
Alumnus: Joel M. Comiskey, 1980
approximate distance from CIA: 40 miles

The Haymaker
718 Dutchess Turnpike
Poughkeepsie, NY
845/486-9454
www.thehaymaker.com
Alumnus: Scott Holtzhouser, 2000
approximate distance from CIA: 6 miles

Hillside Manor Restaurant & Caterers
240 Blvd. Rte. 32
Kingston, NY
845/331-4386
Alumnus: Deno M. Demosthenes, 1980
approximate distance from CIA: 31 miles

one of many European antiques found by designer Stanford White.

Though they only spent a few weeks a year at the estate, the Vanderbilts enjoyed entertaining guests, who arrived by boat, rail, or private car. Thirteen rooms on the 3rd floor were reserved as quarters for the maids of lady visitors. Outside, the property remains as beautiful today as it did a century ago. Local residents meet here on weekends to play Frisbee and picnic on the lawn. Contemporary artists often set up canvases to paint the river and surrounding landscape. The Hyde Park Trail system connects the Roosevelt and Vanderbilt estates along the river. Inquire at any of the homes for a trail map. If you plan to

visit more than one of these historic homes, consider a combination ticket for $22.

Culinary Institute of America

Since 1970, Hyde Park has been home to the oldest culinary college in the U.S., the prestigious Culinary Institute of America (Rte. 9, Hyde Park, 845/452-9600, www.ciachef.edu). Set on a picturesque riverside campus, formerly the site of a Jesuit seminary, the CIA trains aspiring professionals and enthusiasts in the art of fine cuisine. Its facilities include 41 kitchens and the largest collection of culinary books and reference materials of any library in the country. Among the school's best-known graduates is Anthony Bourdain, author

Inn at Osborne Hill
150 Osborne Hill Rd.
Fishkill, NY
845/897-3055
www.osbornehill.com
Alumni: Janine and Todd Gray, 1996
approximate distance from CIA: 14 miles

John's Harvest Inn
633 Rte. 17M
Middletown, NY
845/343-6676
Alumnus: John Patrick Botti, 1982
approximate distance from CIA: 46 miles

Marcel's
Rte. 9W
West Park, NY
845/384-6700
Alumnus: Michael James Hoysradt, 1978
approximate distance from CIA: 30 miles

Mina
29 W. Market St.
Red Hook, NY
845/758-5992
www.minarestaurant.com
Alumni: Natalie Steward, 1998, and John DiBenedetto, 2000
approximate distance from CIA: 16 miles

Pippy's at the Square
2 Delafield St. (at Mt. Carmel Square)
Poughkeepsie, NY
845/483-7239
Alumnus: Lou Fusaro, 1997
approximate distance from CIA: 5 miles

The Postage Inn
838 Rte. 32
Tillson, NY
845/658-3434
www.thepostageinn.com
Alumnus: James Gerard Jerkowski, C.E.C., 1986
approximate distance from CIA: 20 miles

Umberto's of Mamma Marisa
2245 South Rd. (Rte. 9)
Poughkeepsie, NY
845/462-5117
www.umbertos.org
Alumnus: Alberto Annunziata, 1991
approximate distance from CIA: 10 miles

Xe Sogni
Rte. 44
Amenia, NY
845/373-7755
www.xesogni.com
Alumnus: Jason Thomas, 1993
approximate distance from CIA: 24 miles

of the bestseller *Kitchen Confidential* and executive chef of Les Halles in New York City.

Tour the grounds at sunset before dining in one of the five public restaurants on campus. Better yet, enroll in one of the CIA's Boot Camp programs, which are multiday intensive courses geared toward cooking enthusiasts. Classes cover a variety of rotating topics, such as French cuisine, baking, and healthy cooking. Tuition is steep at $1,500.

Rhinebeck

Continuing north on Route 9, Rhinebeck stands out as an upscale enclave in an otherwise rural region. Victorian, Colonial, and Greek Revival buildings line several blocks of boutique stores, country inns, and gourmet restaurants expanding out from the intersection of Routes 9 and 308. (Route 9 is called Mill Street south of Route 308, and Montgomery Street north of Route 308; Route 308 is also called Market Street.)

At the center of all the activity is the **1766 Beekman Arms** (Rte. 9, Rhinebeck, 845/876-7077, www.beekmanarms.com), reportedly the oldest continuously operating inn in the U.S. Indeed, colonial history and political intrigue ooze from every creak in the floorboards. George Washington, Philip Schuyler, Benedict Arnold, and Alexander Hamilton are among the most famous overnight guests. Local townspeople gathered inside for safety while the British burned Kingston to the ground across the Hudson.

As Rhinebeck grew into a commercial crossroads, the inn became a popular venue for political and cultural discussion. FDR even delivered several victory speeches from the front porch. The inn has expanded over the years, but much of the original building remains in tact, including the oak beams and pine plank floor. The place is worth a peek, whether or not you plan to stay the night.

Next door to the Beekman Arms, FDR oversaw construction of the **Rhinebeck Post Office** (6383 Mill St.) through the Works Progress Administration (WPA). The building was designed to commemorate the first house in Rhinebeck. Inside, a series of murals chronicle the town's history. The **Dutch Reformed Church,** across Route 9 from the post office, was built in 1808.

© THOMAS GOTH

Main Street in Rhinebeck

Surrounding the town of Rhinebeck are idyllic family farms and grand country estates. **Wilderstein** (330 Morton Rd., Rhinebeck, 845/876-4818, www.wilderstein.org; Thurs.–Sun. noon–4 P.M., Sat.–Sun. 1–4 P.M.), a riverside mansion located south of town on Route 9, has a five-story round tower that juts upward from its center, offering views of an equally dramatic landscape. With ties to the prominent Beekman and Livingston families, this fanciful Queen Anne country home began as an Italian villa in the mid-19th century. Carefully planned trails, vistas, and lawns around the property reflect the Romantic Era aesthetic.

North of town, the Dutchess County Fairgrounds holds antique car shows and the annual Dutchess County Fair. Amtrak services the train station in Rhinecliff, three miles to the west.

Red Hook

The sleepy town of Red Hook received its name when early Dutch explorers ventured up the Hudson to find red sumac and Virginia creeper in full bloom. The Dutch called it Red Hoek (Red Peninsula), and the name has stuck ever since. A modern-day bedroom community, Red Hook encompasses the Village of Tivoli and hamlet of Annandale-on-Hudson on the banks of the river, as well as Bard College and the Village of Red Hook to the east.

At **Alison Wines & Vineyards** (231 Pitcher La., Red Hook, 845/758-6335, www.alison-wines.com; Aug. daily 11 A.M.–5 P.M., Sept.–Oct. Thurs.–Mon. 11 A.M.–5 P.M., Dec. 1–24 Fri.–Sun. 11 A.M.–5 P.M.), winemaker Rick Lewitt makes a point of demystifying the wine-tasting experience. He greets nearly every visitor who walks in the door, offering tastings and informative barrel tours.

Lewitt is a Westchester County native and a Bard College graduate who left a career in journalism to pursue a passion for wine. With Long Island already crowded and expensive, and the Finger Lakes too far away from New York City, he settled on the Hudson Valley. He apprenticed in Oregon to learn pinot noir, and locally at Millbrook Winery, before setting up shop in a dairy barn on the old Grieg Farm in Red Hook. Alison Vineyards specializes in pinot noir and hopes to harvest grapes from two unusual varietals in the near future: Aligote, from France, and Dornfelder, from Germany's Ahr Valley.

A rocker on the North Porch is the best seat in the house at **Montgomery Place** (River Rd., Annandale-on-Hudson, 845/758-5461, www.hudsonvalley.org; Apr.–Oct. Wed.–Mon. 10 A.M.–5 P.M., Nov.–mid-Dec. weekends only; adults $7, seniors $6, children $4, grounds only $4). Nestled among 434 acres of woodlands with views of the Catskill Mountains across the Hudson, Montgomery Place is a stunning riverside estate conceived in the Federal style. Located in Annandale-on-Hudson, the home has been restored with period furnishings and enchanting gardens.

Many of the undergraduate students at **Bard College** (Rte. 9G, Annandale, 845/758-6822, www.bard.edu) have views of the Hudson and Catskill Mountains from their dorms. An affiliate of Columbia University, the liberal-arts school is set on 500 acres of lawns and woodlands. A variety of music and performing arts programs are open to the public year-round.

CENTRAL DUTCHESS COUNTY — ROUTES 44 AND 22
Millbrook

A number of New York City residents call upscale Millbrook their home away from home. Set on a hillside at the gateway to the Dutchess Wine Trail, the town supports a handful of top-notch restaurants. An exclusive Orvis hunting club and nearby boarding school draw repeat visitors. **Innisfree Gardens** (Tyrrell Rd., Millbrook, 845/677-8000; Sat.–Sun. 11 A.M.–5 P.M., Wed.–Fri. 10 A.M.–4 P.M.; admission $7) is popular with locals and visitors alike.

Petronella Collins, president of the Innisfree Foundation, has called the park "a textbook of tips for the home gardener." Inspired by ancient Chinese gardens, the 200-acre property applies Chinese ideas of design and motion to a decidedly American landscape. The result is a spectacular display of flora ranging from lotus blossoms to daffodils. Visitors can picnic on the

© THOMAS GOTH

Millbrook countryside

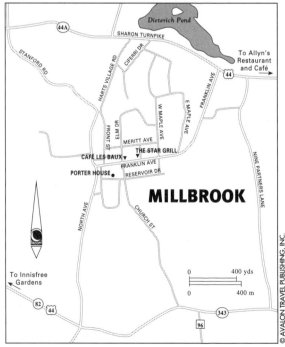

© AVALON TRAVEL PUBLISHING, INC.

grounds, walk the trails, or simply find a secluded place to while away the afternoon.

The scenic rural roads that surround Millbrook's town center are ideal for running and cycling. A popular route is to follow the Dutchess Wine Trail, which isn't exactly a trail, but a joint marketing effort of several local vineyards, located on different roads in different towns. While it's a far cry from the Silverado Trail in California's Napa Valley, the roads connecting Alison Wines, Clinton Vineyards, and Millbrook Winery & Vineyards cover miles of pretty countryside. Meanwhile, the wineries themselves produce some of the highest-quality labels in New York State.

Millbrook Winery & Vineyards (26 Wing Rd., Millbrook, 800/662-9463, www.millbrookwine.com; daily 11 A.M.–6 P.M.)

© THOMAS GOTH

Main Street in Millbrook

introduced French hybrid grapes to the region and makes an outstanding chardonnay. A few miles away, **Clinton Vineyards** (212 Shultzville Rd., Clinton Corners, 845/266-5372, www.clintonvineyards.com; Fri.–Sun. 11 A.M.–5:30 P.M.) is known for its seyval blanc.

On a hilltop overlooking Millbrook Winery & Vineyards stands **Wing's Castle** (717 Bangall Rd., Millbrook, 845/677-9085; May 31–Sept. 1. Wed.–Sun. 10 A.M.–5 P.M., Sept.–Dec. 20 weekends only), the kind of place one might expect to find in Baja California. Made of stones and pipes and salvaged appliances—materials too solid and functional to be thrown away—this private home gets high marks for resourceful and eclectic design. Owners Peter and Toni Wing invite visitors from Memorial Day to Christmas.

The Harlem Valley

Continuing northeast from Millbrook, Route 44 enters the scenic Harlem Valley, which follows the west side of the Taconic Range and the Connecticut border from Pawling to Pine Plains. The land here is sparsely populated, with only a few thousand residents per town, and much of it is permanently protected from development. Taconic State Park, Stissing Mountain Forest, and the Harlem Valley Rail Trail are a few of the outdoor attractions.

Route 44 meets Route 22 at the rural town of Amenia and the **Troutbeck Inn and Conference Center** (Leedsville Rd., Amenia, 845/373-9681, www.troutbeck.com). Named in 1765 for its counterpart in England, Troutbeck was founded by literary-minded farmers who knew the likes of Emerson and Thoreau. The original stone house is surrounded by sycamore trees and flower gardens. In the early 20th century, Sinclair Lewis, Earnest Hemingway, and Theodore Roosevelt were frequent guests of Troutbeck's second owners, Joel and Amy Spingarn. Joel Spingarn was instrumental in the founding of the NAACP and served as the organization's second president. Although the inn no longer attracts the same kind of movers and shakers—today's guests are primarily conference and wedding attendees—it still offers fine cuisine and quaint accommodations in a tranquil setting.

HUDSON VALLEY WINERIES

Enterprising Hudson Valley farmers planted the first French American hybrid grapes in the 1970s, and the quality and popularity of their wines have been rising steadily ever since to meet the demands of increasingly sophisticated local consumers. Today, the Hudson Valley is the smallest of four major wine regions in New York State, with about 20 producers. (The others are Long Island, the Finger Lakes, and Great Lakes regions.) Among the newcomers is Dutchess County's Alison Wines & Vineyards.

According to Alison Wines & Vineyards winemaker Rick Lewitt, site selection is key to producing wines in this region. His winery is at the top of the commuter belt, where grape growers have to compete with real estate developers who will offer farmers $15,000 an acre for their apple orchards.

Unlike the hot, dry climate that nurtures California zinfandel, merlot, and cabernet sauvignon grapes, cooler temperatures in the Hudson Valley are well suited for growing the types of grapes you find in Burgundy, Germany, and northern Italy: chardonnay, aligote, dornfelder, and pinot noir. The resulting wines are earthy, crisp, and clean with a moderate alcohol content.

Grape	European Growing Region	Hudson Valley Wineries
Dornfelder	Rhinehessen and Pfalz (Germany)	Alison Wines (planted)
Pinot noir	Burgundy (France)	Alison Wines, Millbrook Winery
Aligote	Burgundy (France)	Alison Wines (planted)
Seyval blanc	French-American hybrid	Clinton Vineyards
Tocai friulano	Friuli (Northern Italy)	Millbrook Winery

© PAUL ITOI

Millbrook Winery & Vineyards

South of Amenia on Route 22 is Wassaic and the terminus for the Harlem Valley Line of the Metro-North commuter rail. The ride to Grand Central Station takes about two hours, with a transfer in Southeast.

Next stop is the **Webatuck Craft Village** (Rte. 55, Wingdale, 845/832-6601), on Route 55 off Route 22 near Wingdale, where resident artists work in copper, tin, clay, glass, and wood. The village consists of half a dozen buildings, and visitors shop here for one-of-a-kind handmade items, from furniture and stained-glass windows to ceramics and vintage toys.

Routes 22 and 55 meet at Pawling, in the southeastern corner of Dutchess County. Named after Colonel Henry Beekman's daughter, Catherine Pawling, the town has been a crossroads of commercial activity since colonial days. Pawling's early settlers were Quakers, as documented by the display of artifacts in the **Quaker Museum, Akin Free Library** (2nd Fl., Quaker Hill, Pawling, 845/855-9316, www.pawhistory.com; Sat.–Sun. 2–4 P.M.). The 1764 Oblong Friends Meeting House served as a temporary hospital for George Washington's troops in 1778. And Washington set up headquarters in the John Kane House. Inside is a replica of the village from the year 1948, complete with moving trains.

Today, Pawling attracts New York City commuters, Appalachian Trail hikers, and celebrities seeking privacy. Keep an eye out for permanent resident James Earl Jones if you pass through town.

SPORTS AND RECREATION
Winter Sports
Cross-country skiing is permitted on the golf course at Baird Park and along the Harlem Valley Rail Trail. The **McCann Ice Arena** (Mid-Hudson Civic Center, 14 Civic Center Plaza, Poughkeepsie, 845/454-5800, www.midhudsonciviccenter.com) offers public skating session year-round.

Hiking
A 30-mile stretch of the Appalachian Trail passes through the hills of Dutchess County, connecting the towns of East Fishkill, Dover Plains, Beekman, and Pawling along the way. Several well-marked access areas have trailside parking. In Stormville, find one on Route 52, three miles east of the Taconic State Parkway. In Poughquag, the area is at the intersection of Routes 55 and 216 or Depot Hill Road, off Route 216. In Pawling, it's on Route 22, north of town. Note that mountain bikes are not allowed on the trail.

Additional areas for hiking include the **Pawling Nature Preserve** (Quaker Lake Rd., Pawling), on 1,000 acres, and Poughkeepsie's **Bowdoin State Park** (Sheafe Rd., Poughkeepsie, 845/298-4600), on 300 acres near the riverfront.

Mountain Biking and Road Riding
Whether you are riding off-road or on, Dutchess County offers terrain to suit all levels, from casual to aggressive. The scenery alternates between rolling hills, charming villages, and Hudson River views. The **Mid-Hudson Bicycle Club** (www.midhudsonbicycle.org) organizes area rides through the summer and fall. And coming soon: a Hudson River crossing, just for bikes. The old Poughkeepsie Railroad Bridge, closed since 1974, is scheduled to open to foot and bike traffic within a couple of years.

A section of the scenic **Harlem Valley Rail Trail** begins in Amenia. The path follows the tracks of the old New York and Harlem Railroad and is paved for foot and bike traffic. Also in Amenia, the **Wassaic State Forest** on Route 22 is another tranquil place to get away from it all.

Golf
Golfers have a dozen or more courses to choose from in Dutchess County. Foremost among them is the swanky **Branton Woods Golf Course** (178 Stormville Rd., Hopewell Junction, 845/223-1600; $90–130), a semiprivate course located in Hopewell Junction. But the best course for the money in Dutchess County is **The Links at Union Vale** (153 N. Parliman Rd., Union Vale, 845/223-1000, thelinksatunionvale.com; daily 6:30 A.M.–dark; Mon.–Thurs. $38, Fri.–Sun. $52, cart rental $13 per player). Another good option is the **Beekman Country Club** (11 Country Club Rd., Hopewell Junction, 845/226-7700,

beekmancountryclub.com; Sat.–Sun. 6 A.M., Mon.–Fri. 7 A.M.; weekends $65, weekdays $46, seniors $36).

Swimming and Boating

Kids love to slip and slide down the tubes at **Splash Down Park** (2200 Rte. 9, Fishkill, 845/896-6606, www.splashdownpark.com; May–Sept. daily 10 A.M.–7 P.M.; admission $21).

Fishing and Hunting

Anglers have a number of streams, lakes, and ponds to choose from, as well as the Hudson River itself. Outside of Millbrook, **Orvis Sandanona** (Rte. 44A, Stone Ridge, 845/677-9701, www.orvis.com/sandanona; Apr.–Oct.) offers fly-fishing lessons and instruction in the English Churchill method of shooting clays. The club hosts a September Vintager's Side by Side Championship.

Aviation

Aviators must plan a weekend visit to the **Old Rhinebeck Aerodrome** (Stone Church Rd., Rhinebeck, 845/758-8610, www.oldrhinebeck .org; mid-Jun.–mid-Oct.; adults $15, children $5), which hosts weekend air shows during summer and fall, complete with vintage fashion shows. The museum's collection of antique aircraft includes working models dating back to the early 20th century.

Blue Sky Balloons (19 Teller Ave., Beacon, 888/999-2461, www.blueskyballoons.com; daily sunrise–sunset; $175 per person) offers morning and evening tours.

ACCOMMODATIONS

Business travelers congregate around corporate headquarters in southern Dutchess County, while the more unique inns are found in the northeastern part of the county. Book early around major events. Hotels are known to fill up as far as a year in advance.

$100–150

Millbrook's **Porter House** (17 Washington Ave., Millbrook, 845/677-3057, www.porterhouse-

bandb.com; $115–175) is popular with members of the Orvis fly-fishing center and parents of boarding school students. It has three cozy suites and two rooms in a beautiful 1920 stone house. Another midpriced option that's close to area wineries is the six-room **Red Hook Inn** (7460 S. Broadway, Red Hook, 845/758-8445, www.theredhookinn.com, $125), built in 1824. Lace curtains let in plenty of natural light. Hardwood floors, antique furnishings, and floral bedspreads complete the decor.

$150–200

A bevy of famous people have stayed at the modern **Inn at the Falls** (50 Red Oaks Mill Rd., Poughkeepsie, 845/462-5770, innatfalls@aol.com, www.innatthefalls.com; $170), as evidenced by the wall of signed photographs in the lobby. Built at the edge of Wappingers Creek, the inn caters primarily to business travelers. A sunny atrium and porch for breakfast compensate for rooms that are on the dark side.

You won't forget an overnight stay at the über-historic **⚑ 1766 Beekman Arms** (Rte. 9, Rhinebeck, 845/876-7077, www.beekmandelamaterinn.com; $140–300). Ask for a room in the main house, where the ceilings are low and the floors creak with every step. Forget about getting a reservation when the auto shows come to town. Repeat visitors reserve every room on the premises more than a year in advance.

Marble baths, French antiques, and ornate silk fabrics set the Gilded Age tone at **Belvedere Mansion** (10 Old Rte. 9, Stattsburg, 845/889-8000, www.belvederemansion.com), a riverside getaway located between Hyde Park and Rhinebeck. Rooms in the neoclassical mansion, restored in 1993, run $275. Individually decorated rooms in the Carriage House have king-sized beds for $150–175. Smaller rooms, called Cozies ($75–95), are a good way to get affordable lodging at an upscale venue. Suites in the new Hunting Lodge cost $250–450.

Over $200

If your ideal weekend getaway is all about the room and board, Dover Plains has the romantic **Old Drovers Inn** (Rte. 22, Dover Plains, 845/

832-9311, www.olddroversinn.com), with weekend rates of $350–475. There is a two-night minimum, but the cost includes dinner for two and full breakfast. A Relais & Chateaux property, the restaurant and four guestrooms are set on 12 acres in an early 18th-century home. An international clientele has replaced the cattle drovers of the early days, but the traditional American cuisine is every bit as hearty (mains $20–39).

Le Chambord (2073 Rte. 52, Hopewell Junction, www.lechambord.com) has been a longtime favorite for elegant affairs. Set in an 1863 mansion, the inn has nine beautifully decorated rooms in the main building, and 16 more in a newer wing.

Campgrounds

Ideal for a family car-camping trip, **Wilcox Memorial Park** (Rte. 199, Stanfordville, 845/758-6100; $20–25 for nonresidents) has two small lakes with fishing, boat rentals, and swimming, Memorial Day–Labor Day. Kids can safely explore miles of trails by foot or on bikes.

FOOD

Dutchess County eateries range from classic diners and contemporary American bistros to game-inspired, farm-fresh menus, and the occasional international treat.

Along the River–Route 9

Ask a group of locals to name the best diner in town and you'll spark a heated debate. **The Palace Diner** (294 Washington St., Poughkeepsie, 854/473-1576, www.thepalacediner.com; daily 24 hours; mains $16–19) gets the best marks for food. The **Arlington Diner** (251 Dutchess Tpke, Poughkeepsie, 845/452-1554) is a convenient standby that closes at midnight, while the **Acropolis Diner** (829 Main St., Poughkeepsie, 845/452-6255) gets bonus points for serving around the clock. The **Daily Planet** (1202 Rte. 55, La-Grangeville, 845/452-0110; mains $11), near Arlington High School, is a relative newcomer that has been slowly stealing market share.

The best international foods in Dutchess County hide out near the Vassar College campus. **Miss Saigon Restaurant** (25 LaGrange Ave.,

Poughkeepsie, 845/485-9706; Sun.–Sat.; mains $12) serves a reliable bowl of Vietnamese pho. Nearby, the **Beech Tree Grill** (1–3 Collegeview Ave., Poughkeepsie, 845/471-7279; Mon. 5–11 P.M., Tues.–Sat. 11:30 A.M.–11:30 P.M., Sun. 11:30 A.M.–10 P.M.; mains $13–17) has a decent wine and beer list, with an inviting bar and a dinner menu of hearty pub fare.

In Fishkill, **Union House** (1108 Main St., Fishkill, 845/896-6129; Mon.–Sat. 5–10 P.M., Sun. 4–9 P.M.; mains $13–23) opened in 2001 in a handsome brick building with slate-blue shutters. Dark wood, gold mirrors, and a domed ceiling produce a sophisticated air. On the menu are market fresh fish, steak, and ribs. Entrées at **Hudson's Ribs and Fish** (1099 Rt. 9, Fishkill, 845/297-5002, www.hudsonsribsandfish.com; Mon.–Sat. 4–10 P.M., Sat.–Sun. 2–9 P.M.; mains $16–28) come with a piping hot popover on the side.

Il Barilotto (1113 Main St., Fishkill, 845/897-4300; Mon.–Sat. 11 A.M.–2:30 P.M. and 5–10 P.M., Fri.–Sat. till 11 P.M.) has a broad selection of wines by the glass to accompany its reliable Italian menu. **Aroma Osteria** (114 Old Post Rd., Wappingers Falls, 845/298-6790; Tues.–Sat. 11:30 A.M.–2:30 P.M. and 5–10 P.M., Fri.–Sat. till 11 P.M., Sun. 4–9 P.M.; mains $15–24), run by the same owners, ranks among the best Italian eateries in the region. A renovation in 2004 upgraded the setting to match the cuisine.

In between gallery visits in Beacon, grab a table for a Victorian tea at the **Cup and Saucer Tea Room** (165 Main St., Beacon, 845/831-6287, www.cupandsaucertearoom.com; mains $7–10). The restaurant serves high tea Sundays 4–6 P.M. for $37.50 per person.

Near the Poughkeepsie train station, the **River Station** (25 Main St. or 1 Water St., Poughkeepsie, 845/452-9207; $16–24) serves dependable surf and turf on a pleasant outdoor terrace that overlooks the Hudson. A few blocks away, **Aurora Café** (145 Mill St., Poughkeepsie, 845/454-1900) serves delicious Italian pastries made on the premises. And **Busy Bee Café** (138 South Ave., Poughkeepsie, 845/452-6800; Mon.–Fri. lunch, Tues.–Sat. dinner) draws lunch and dinner crowds for creative New American fare.

The incredibly popular Adams Fairacre Farms

on Route 44 has lured a handful of new restaurants to the neighborhood. In a plaza across from the market, **The Haymaker** (Rte. 44, Poughkeepsie, 845/486-9454; $9–22), run by a CIA graduate, serves American food with an Asian flare. Next door to Adams, **Bourbon Street Grill** (779 Dutchess Tpke./Rte. 44, Poughkeepsie, 845/485-1672, www.811BourbonSt.com; lunch and dinner daily; mains $13–25) opened in late 2003 with a menu of Cajun specialties, including jambalaya, gumbo, and shrimp Newburg.

In a bold suburban move, **Isabella** (308 Titusville Rd., btw. Rte. 55 and Noxon Rd., Poughkeepsie, 845/485-9999; lunch Tues.–Fri. noon–3 P.M., dinner Mon.–Sat. 5–10 P.M., Sun. 4–9 P.M.; mains $9–24) has brought New York City style to a strip mall outside of Poughkeepsie. Owner Vincent Cappelletti opened the restaurant in April 2003 as a Mediterranean bistro that could lure residents on their way to evening events at Vassar College, the Bardavon, or the Mid-Hudson Civic Center. Inside, the atmosphere is contemporary, with an inviting bar on the right and a cozy dining room on the left. Entrées range from lasagna to filet mignon. So far, the gamble has paid off—reservations are essential on weekends and even recommended midweek.

Down the hill, the daughter of LaGrange's longtime butcher, Melissa Wade Haras, has opened **P.C.'s Paddock** (273 Titusville Rd., Poughkeepsie; 845/454-4930; Tues.–Thurs. 11:30 A.M.–9 P.M., Fri. 11:30 A.M.–10 P.M., Sat. 5–10 P.M.; $11–18). This family knows meat, and The Hunt portion of the menu features London broil, rack of lamb, and steak au poivre, along with lighter fare. Call for reservations—locals fill the dining room to enjoy a hearty meal in the company of a family that has been in the area for seven generations.

CIA sophomores run the kitchens in five campus restaurants (Culinary Institute of America, 1946 Campus Dr., Hyde Park, www.ciachef.edu). Main dishes at **American Bounty** (845/471-6608; Tues.–Sat. 11:30 A.M.–1 P.M. and 6–8:30 P.M.; mains $21–27) feature regional cuisine such as grilled filet mignon, roasted pork tenderloin, and a New England Seafood Sampler. The reasonably priced **M Apple Pie Bakery Café** (Roth Hall,

845/905-4500; Mon.–Fri. 8 A.M.–6:30 P.M.; mains $2–7) is a favorite among local residents. Also at the casual end of the scale is **St. Andrews Café** (Mon.–Fri. for lunch and dinner; mains $17–20) for contemporary American fare. The Asian-influenced menu includes Korean-style short ribs and grilled marinated tuna with soba noodles.

The elegant **Ristorante Caterina de Medici** (Colavita Center for Italian Food and Wine; Mon.–Fri. for lunch and dinner; mains $15–24) serves Italian specialties under a Venetian chandelier. For a more casual dining experience, ask to be seated in the Al Forno Dining Room. Finally, **Escoffier Restaurant** (Roth Hall, 845/471-6608, lunch mains $18–25, dinner mains $25–32) excels in classic French cuisine, from Provencal to Parisian delights. The à la carte menu, inspired by the late chef Auguste Escoffier, features entrées such as braised veal cheeks, monkish tournedos, and poached chicken breast with truffle consommé. When making reservations, note that CIA restaurants are only open when the school is in session.

Catch sunset over the river from the 100-seat dining room of **Belvedere Mansion** (Thurs.–Sun. 5:30–8:30 P.M.), serving a menu of New American cuisine in a formal setting. This cigar-friendly restaurant takes pride in its selection of after-dinner drinks, which include single malt scotches, brandies, ports, and dessert wines.

In Rhinebeck, start the day with a mouthwatering French pastry at **Calico Restaurant** (6384 Mill St., Rhinebeck, 845/876-2749, www.calicorhinebeck.com; Wed.–Sat. bakery opens at 8 A.M., lunch 11 A.M.–2:30 p.m., dinner from 5 P.M., Sun. brunch 11 A.M.–2:30 P.M.; pastries $4, lunch mains $8–10, dinner mains $17–21), or enjoy a full meal later in the day.

M Terrapin (37 Montgomery St., Rhinebeck, 845/876-3330, www.terrapinrestaurant.com; Tues.–Sun. 5–10 P.M., Fri.–Sat. till 11 P.M.; $18–28) is a hotspot for creative New American cuisine, including a grilled double-thick pork chop with rhubarb demi-glace, rack of spring lamb, Peking duck, and several vegetarian entrées. Its sister establishment, Terrapin Red, is a cozy bar and bistro that's open daily for lunch and dinner.

Two-story **40 West** (40 W. Market St., Rhinebeck, 845/876-2214; Thurs.–Mon. 5–9:30 P.M., weekends till 10 P.M.) is another Rhinebeck stand-out, with live acoustic guitar music on weekends. Outside of town, **Diaspora** (1094 Rte. 308, Rhinebeck, 845/758-9601; Wed.–Sun. 5–10 P.M., Fri.–Sat. till 11 P.M.; mains $14–20) gets high marks for Greek cuisine, including seafood and lamb dishes.

Also in Rhinebeck, **Le Chambord** (mains $14–35) prepares classic French dishes in a formal setting. Tournedos, chateaubriand, venison, and sea scallops anchor the menu. At the Beekman Arms, **Traphagen** (6387 Mill St., Rhinebeck, 845/876-1766; Mon.–Thur. 11:30 A.M.–9 P.M., Fri.–Sat. till 10 P.M., Sun. 10 A.M.–9 P.M.; mains $13–25) offers a cozy and historic atmosphere for enjoying American favorites like turkey pot pie, pork tenderloin, and brook trout. One of the dining rooms is a greenhouse addition to the original 18th-century building.

Central Dutchess County–Routes 44 and 22

Taking a page from the Chez Panisse book, Millbrook's **The Star Grill** (3299 Franklin Ave., Millbrook, 845/677-5600; dinner Thur.–Mon.; mains $20) prepares a seasonal New American menu based on Hudson Valley produce. **Café Les Baux** (152 Church St., Millbrook, 845/677-8166; Wed.–Mon. noon–3 P.M. & 5–9 P.M., Fri.–Sat. till 10 P.M.; mains $7–23) is the place for a croque monsieur and a slice of tarte Tatin. Open since 2002, the French bistro serves lunch and dinner in a warm and cozy dining room located in the center of town. Just outside of town is another classic Millbrook eatery, **Allyn's Restaurant and Café** (4258 Rte. 44, Millbrook, 845/677-5888, www.allyns.com; mains $17–24), serving new American fare in a converted 200-year-old church.

Continuing up the Taconic State Parkway, the **Fireside Bar and Grill** (1920 Salt Point Turnpike, Salt Point, 845/266-3440; mains $9–22) serves 25-ounce beers in frosted mugs. It's been around for generations and has a friendly staff that serves tasty baby back ribs, barbecue, tri-tip, and prime rib on weekends. There's more barbecue to be found at **Max's Memphis Barbecue** (136 S. Broadway/Rte. 9, Red Hook, 845/758-6297). Nearby, **Mina** (29 W. Market St., Red Hook, 845/758-5992, www.minarestaurant.com; $18–26) prepares a delicious menu of lamb chops, prosciutto-wrapped cod, or whole roasted trout.

ENTERTAINMENT AND EVENTS
Performing Arts

The 1869 **Bardavon Opera House** (35 Market St., Poughkeepsie, 845/473-2072, www.bardavon.org) is one of the top performing-arts venues in Dutchess County. It hosts the Hudson Valley Philharmonic and a full schedule of musical, dance, film, and theater productions by contemporary artists.

At the other end of the architectural spectrum, the **Fisher Center for the Performing Arts** (Rte. 9G, Annandale, 845/758-7900, fishercenter.bard.edu) is housed in a modern, stainless-steel building on the Bard College campus. Its innovative shows include orchestra, chamber, and jazz music, as well as modern theater, dance, and opera. The **Bard Music Festival** (Rte. 9G Bard College, Annandale-on-Hudson, summerscape.bard.edu) focuses on a single composer each year. The **Manor House Café,** just steps away from the theater, offers a $35 prix fixe dinner on performance nights.

The Rhinebeck Theatre Society and other local groups perform at the **Center for the Performing Arts at Rhinebeck** (Rte. 308, Rhinebeck, 845/876-3080, www.centerforperformingarts.org). Also in Rhinebeck, **Upstate Films** (6415 Montgomery St., Rte. 9, Rhinebeck, 845/876-2515, www.upstatefilms.org) has been showing indie films since 1972. Regulars can't resist the homemade treats at the candy counter.

Bars and Nightlife

Poughkeepsie's proximity to New York City means that well-known performers come to town on a fairly regular basis. Most popular among the city's nightclubs is **The Chance** (6 Crannell St., Poughkeepsie, 845/471-1966, www.thechancecomplex.com), which plays live music. The Chance is part of an entertainment complex that includes four different clubs all in one building. The others

The Mid-Hudson

are Club Crannel Street, The Loft (for DJ music), and the Platinum Lounge.

Next to the Bardavon, the Victorian **Mad Hatter** (51 Market St., Poughkeepsie, 845/454-7400) is an indoor and outdoor bar with a gold-leaf ceiling, DJ music, and no cover charge. The owners have been steadily upgrading the venue in recent years. The latest enhancement is a late-night bar menu. **Bananas Comedy Club** (Best Western Inn, 2170 Rte. 9, Poughkeepsie, 845/462-3333, www.bananascomedyclub.com; admission $10) is the place to go for a good laugh. At 10:30 P.M., Fishkill's Il Barilotto restaurant transforms into a Manhattan-style night club called **IB Notte** and stays open till 2 A.M.

Festivals

Summer in Dutchess County brings one food, wine, auto, and art festival after another. The **Hudson Valley Food & Wine Festival** takes place at Montgomery Place in June. Kids get excited when the **Dutchess County Fair** (Rte. 9, Dutchess County Fairgrounds, Rhinebeck, 845/876-4001) comes to town in July. Two of the largest antique car shows in the northeast are also held at the fairgrounds: The **Hudson River Valley Antique Auto Association's Annual Car Show & Swap Meet** arrives in May, and the **Good Guys Classic Rods Auto Show** (Rte. 9, Dutchess County Fairgrounds, Rhinebeck, www.good-guys.com) takes place in September.

Wineries from the Hudson Valley and across New York State gather at Grieg Farm each September for the **Hudson Valley Wine Fest** (www.hudsonvalleywinefest.com, $18)—a weekend of gourmet food, crafts, wine seminars, cooking demos, and live music.

The town of Beacon has begun a series of art exhibits called **Second Saturday Beacon** (845/838-4243; noon–9 P.M.), for which galleries, shops, and restaurants stay open late to host openings and performances.

Spectator Sports

For an evening of all-American fun, head to **Dutchess Stadium** (Rte. 9D, Wappingers Falls, 845/838-0094; admission $4.75–12.50) to watch

the Hudson Valley Renegades play minor league baseball. Tickets are easy to come by, and the games are often followed by fireworks.

SHOPPING

A busy commercial zone crowds Route 9 from Fishkill to Hyde Park, with one shopping mall after another. Head for the hills to avoid the chains. **La Vie en Rose** (7376 S. Broadway, Red Hook, 845/758-4211) sells vintage clothing from the 1800s to the 1960s.

Farm Stands

The after-work stop for fresh veggies at a local farm stand is a way of life for Dutchess County residents. True connoisseurs can tell from the first bite if their corn was picked in the morning or afternoon. You can often find these stands at major local intersections, such as at Routes 9 and 9G near Rhinebeck. If you have more time on your hands, pick your own produce at an orchard like **Fishkill Farms** (222 E. Hook Cross Rd., Hopewell Junction, 845/897-4377), which has been growing apples for 75 years. At **Montgomery Place Orchards** (Back River Rd., Annandale-on-Hudson, 845/758-6338), you can combine your picking with a tour of the historic Montgomery Place mansion.

Family-run **Adams Fairacre Farms** (765 Dutchess Turnpike, Poughkeepsie, 845/454-4330, www.adamsfarms.com; Mon.–Fri. 8 A.M.–9 P.M., Sat.–Sun. 8 A.M.–7 P.M.) began as a roadside stand in 1932, selling homegrown fruits and vegetables to Poughkeepsie residents. Today, the company is a local phenomenon with 650 employees operating three large retail spaces in Poughkeepsie, Kingston, and Newburgh. In addition to fresh produce, Adams sells gourmet cheese, breads, coffee, and meats, including many locally made products. Expect long lines on weekends. **Greig Farm** (223 Pitcher La., Red Hook, (845)758-6561, www.greigfarm.com) has evolved from a standard apple-picking operation to a year-round marketplace and bakery.

Antiques and Galleries

Every town in Dutchess County has its share of

antique finds. Twenty-five of them are found under one art deco roof at Red Hook's **Annex Antiques Center** (23 E. Market St., Red Hook, 845/758-2843, www.annexantiquecenter.com; daily 11 A.M.–5 P.M.) Watch artisans at work in half a dozen shops along the Ten Mile River at the **Webatuck Craft Village** (Rte. 55, Wingdale, www.huntcountryfurniture.com/webatuck). Handmade crafts include blown glass, pottery, and objects made of copper, tin, and wood. Most of the shops are open 10 A.M.–5 P.M. daily except Tuesday.

Bookstores

Booklovers will find both big chains and independent treasure chests across the county. For example, **Merritt Bookstore** (Millbrook, 845/677-5857, www.merrittbooks.com; Mon.–Sat. 9 A.M.–6 P.M., Sun. 10 A.M.–5 P.M.) sells new fiction and nonfiction, with additional locations in Red Hook and Cold Springs.

INFORMATION AND SERVICES

The **Dutchess County Tourism Promotion Agency** (3 Neptune Rd., Suite M-17, Poughkeepsie, 845/463-4000, www.dutchesstourism .com) can provide a wealth of information on places to see across the county. Several of the smaller towns have visitor centers as well: **Rhinebeck Chamber of Commerce** (19 Mill St., Rhinebeck, 845/876-5904, rhinebeckchamber.com) and **Red Hook Area Chamber of Commerce** (P.O. Box 254, Red Hook, 845/758-0824, www.redhookchamber.org).

GETTING THERE AND AROUND

By Bus

Shortline Bus provides daily service to Poughkeepsie, Hyde Park, and Rhinebeck from New York City, Long Island, and New Jersey. Adirondack Trailways also runs buses between Poughkeepsie and New York City. The Dutchess County Loop Bus System (14 Commerce St., Poughkeepsie, 845/485-4690) covers major destinations, including Dutchess County Community College, Marist College, and the Poughkeepsie Train Station. In Poughkeepsie, a city bus system with six lines services all parts of the city.

By Train

Amtrak and Metro-North offer frequent connections to the Poughkeepsie Train Station, and taxis are usually waiting. On weekdays, the parking lot overflows with commuter vehicles. Amtrak also stops in Rhinecliff to the north. And the Metro-North Hudson Line stops in Beacon to the south, while the Harlem Line services Pawling, Dover Plains, and Wassaic.

By Car

The most direct routes through Dutchess County are the Taconic State Parkway and Route 22. Route 9 follows the Hudson River through the most densely populated areas of the county. I-84 runs east-west, connecting motorists to I-87, the New York State Thruway. Avis and Hertz have rental car offices off Route 9, near the IBM complex in Poughkeepsie. Budget, Enterprise, and Sears also have rental facilities in the area. Each major town in the county has at least one taxi service.

The Mid-Hudson

Ulster County

The Esopus Indians were the first people to settle mountainous Ulster County. European invasion began with a Dutch trading post in 1614, and a series of battles with the Native American population ensued for the next few decades. A group of French Huguenots arrived in 1663, fleeing religious persecution on the continent. One hundred years later came the British, who would burn Kingston—the county seat—to the ground during the Revolutionary War.

Ulster's early industries were the production of cement and bluestone; its communities also prospered as the terminus for the Delaware & Ulster Canal, which delivered coal from mines in Pennsylvania to the Eastern Seaboard.

Covering more than a thousand square miles of riverfront, foothills, and two distinct mountain ranges, modern-day Ulster County is a haven for rock climbers and general outdoor enthusiasts. The state university at New Paltz and nearby Minnewaska State Park attract a young and active crowd that supports an abundance of cafés, bookstores, restaurants, and gear shops. Farther west lie Woodstock, the Esopus River for tubing, and a few of the summer boarding houses that were popular in the 1960s.

Ulster boasts the highest peak in the Catskills: Slide Mountain, which rises 4,180 feet above the town of Oliverea. The Ashokan Reservoir, completed in 1917 in a major engineering feat, supplies more than half of New York City's water.

ALONG THE RIVER—ROUTE 9W

One of the oldest and prettiest spans across the Hudson, the Mid-Hudson Bridge, connects southern Ulster County to downtown Poughkeepsie. Since 1999, pedestrians have been allowed to cross it on foot, bicycle, or in-line skates. To get to the walkway, follow Havelin Drive off Route 9W to a small park that connects to the bridge.

Ten miles south of the Mid-Hudson Bridge, **Gomez Mill House** (11 Millhouse Rd., Marlboro, 845/236-3126, www.gomez.org; Wed.–Sun. 10 A.M.–4 P.M.; adults $7.50, seniors $5, students

$2) boasts a multicultural past that reaches all the way back to the time of the Spanish Inquisition. Luis Moses Gomez, a Sephardi or descendant of the Jews who settled Spain and Portugal in the Middle Ages, fled persecution in the early 18th century and built a trading post in Marlboro in 1714. Subsequent owners of the fieldstone home were Patriots of the American Revolution, farmers, writers, artisans, and environmentalists. Today, the building is the oldest surviving Jewish homestead in North America. Tours of the inside are available, and the museum holds cultural events and lectures through the summer season.

Slabsides Burroughs Sanctuary

Naturalist John Burroughs wrote hundreds of essays over the span of his career, many of them from a log cabin tucked away in the woods near present-day West Park. A student of Whitman and Thoreau, Burroughs treasured the simple things in life: books, friends, and above all, nature. Of a summer hike in the southern Catskills, he wrote, "An ideal trout brook was this, now hurrying, now loitering, now deepening around a great boulder, now gliding evenly over a pavement of green-gray stone and pebbles; no sediment or stain of any kind, but white and sparkling as snow-water, and nearly as cool."

A visit to the Burroughs retreat, called **Slabsides** (Burroughs Dr., West Park, 845/384-6320), will bring out the nature writer in any traveler. The John Burroughs Association, formed soon after Burroughs died in 1921, maintains the grounds of the 180-acre Slabsides Burroughs Sanctuary and opens the 1895 cabin to the public twice each year, on the third Saturday in May and the first Saturday in October. Allow about 20 minutes to walk from the parking lot to the cabin.

Kingston

As the third most important Dutch trading post (after New Amsterdam/Manhattan and Fort Orange/Albany), Kingston played a pivotal role in the establishment of New York State. But early

© PAUL ITOI

A future bikeway connects Dutchess and Ulster Counties.

settlers paid dearly for their independence: during the American Revolution, the British retaliated against the colonists by burning the city to the ground. The tragedy left its mark, and no story is repeated more often as one tours the Hudson Valley's historic sights.

Like Saugerties to its north, Kingston developed around a strategic watershed: where the Rondout Creek meets the Hudson River. Settlers traded cement, bricks, and bluestone, and Kingston served as a transportation hub during the steam and rail eras. Today, greater Kingston is a sea of mega retail stores with some interesting pockets of culture and history. A variety of architectural styles have been preserved, from Federal, Georgian, and Greek Revival to Romanesque, Italianate, neoclassical, and art deco. Two areas are of interest to the traveler: the Stockade Historic District and the revitalized Rondout Village.

Colorful brick facades of mauve, orange, and lima-bean green line Wall Street inside the old stockade, originally built to keep Native Americans out. Many of the homes in this district are private residences, but a few are open to the public. A gorgeous Federal home at the corner of Main and Wall Streets was saved in the late '30s

by Fred J. Johnston, an antique and restoration specialist. Johnston deeded the home and collection of 18th- and 19th-century furnishings to a local nonprofit organization, and the building is open to the public.

Up the street stands the Old Dutch Church, dating back to the 18th century. George Clinton, the first governor of New York and vice president to Jefferson and Madison, is buried here. Hoffman House, at the north end of Front Street, is a Dutch colonial structure dating back to 1679. A pair of entrepreneurs renovated the building in the mid-'70s and turned it into a restaurant.

In 1777, a group of local political leaders gathered in Kingston to draft the New York State constitution. The first senate convened at 312 Fair Street, now the **Senate House State Historic Site** (296 Fair St., Kingston, 845/338-2786; Mon., Wed., Sat. 10 A.M.–5 P.M., Sun. 11 A.M.–5 P.M.; adults $4, children $1). A historical exhibit contains paintings by Kingston's own John Vanderlyn.

For a guided tour of the Stockade District homes and the Senate House, contact 1658 Stockade District Walking Tours (63 Main St.,

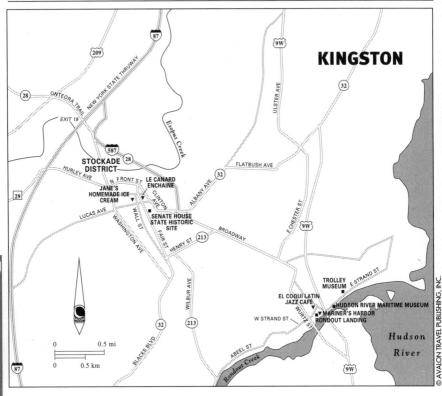

KINGSTON

© AVALON TRAVEL PUBLISHING, INC.

Kingston, 845/339-0720; adults $3, children $2). Tours are offered the first Saturday of the month May–October starting at 2 P.M., or by special appointment. Stop by the Tourism Information Caboose on Washington Avenue (800/331-1518) to pick up a self-guided brochure. Take New York Thruway Exit 19 to reach downtown Kingston.

When you leave the Stockade District, follow Broadway to its end at the edge of the Rondout Creek, where a handful of upscale restaurants, including the new Mariner's Harbor, have revitalized Rondout Village, a cluster of restored brick buildings near the Route 9W crossing. In summer, you can dine in one of the landing's trendy eateries and finish the evening with a stroll along the waterfront.

The **Hudson River Maritime Museum** (50 Rondout Landing, Kingston, 845/338-0071,

www.ulster.net/~hrmm; May–October Fri.–Mon. 11 A.M.–4 P.M.; adults $5, seniors and children $4) opens here each spring with the annual Kingston Shad Festival. A restored 1898 steam tug named Mathilda takes up most of the museum's yard. Inside are a 100-year-old shad boat and a number of model ships. A collection of paintings, prints, photos, blueprints, and artifacts document the maritime history of the river—from sloops and ice boats to steam engines and tugs—and the industries it has supported throughout the years.

A short boat ride across the creek will get you to the **Rondout Lighthouse,** which dates to 1913 and is the largest on the river. Period furnishings and memorabilia trace the history of the lighthouse and its keepers. A $10 fee for adults includes admission to the museum.

For a taste of life during the railroad era, visit

COURTESY OF ULSTER COUNTY TOURISM

Rondout Lighthouse

the **Trolley Museum** (89 E. Strand St., Kingston, 845/331-3399, www.tmny.org; Memorial Day–Columbus Day Sat.–Sun. noon–5 P.M.) at Rondout Landing and take a short ride along the original tracks of the Delaware and Ulster Railroad. The trolley stops at Kingston Point Park on the Hudson River. Exhibits inside the museum trace the history of rail transportation, and visitors can watch restorations in progress in the workshop below.

Saugerties

The Esopus Creek empties into the Hudson at Saugerties. Water rushing out of the mountains once powered a mill that led the town to the forefront of the paper industry. Recognition on the National Register of Historic Places has put Saugerties on the map once again, with an eight-block stretch of 18th- and 19th-century homes, antique shops, and top-notch restaurants that draw a growing number of travelers.

The restored **Saugerties Lighthouse** (off Mynderse St., 845/247-0656, www.sauger-

tieslighthouse.com), built in 1869, is a half-mile walk from the town center along a nature path that can be flooded at high tide. Now a two-room bed-and-breakfast, the house is furnished in 1920s-era style. Guided tours are available Memorial Day–Labor Day 2–5 P.M. ($3 donation).

Plan to arrive on a weekend afternoon, with time to browse the **Hope Farm Press and Bookshop** (252 Main St., Saugerties, 845/246-3522, www.hopefarmbooks.com; Mon.–Sat. 10 A.M.–6 P.M., Sun. noon–4 P.M.) before catching some live music at the **Chowhound Café** (112 Partition St., Saugerties, 845/246-5158, www.thechowhoundcafe.com).

Tucked away on a narrow country lane between Saugerties and Woodstock is a vestige of the bluestone era. Over four decades, sculpture artist Harvey Fite turned an abandoned quarry behind his house and studio into a six-acre sculpture garden that's open to the public on weekends throughout the summer. A small gallery onsite holds a collection of quarryman's tools. Look for

The Mid-Hudson

The Mid-Hudson

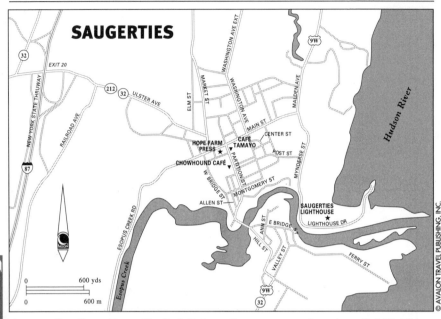

© AVALON TRAVEL PUBLISHING, INC.

the turnoff to Opus One at The Red Onion restaurant on Route 212.

Modern-day flower children gathered at nearby **Winston Farm** in July of 1999 to recreate the good times of the original Woodstock Music Festival (held not in Woodstock, but in nearby Delaware County). The property is privately owned, and you must ask permission to pay a visit.

NEW PALTZ AND SURROUNDINGS

More than any other community in the Hudson Valley, New Paltz offers travelers a healthy dose of alternative culture. In early 2004, Mayor Jason West brought the town to the center of a national debate when he began marrying same-sex couples on the heels of the highly publicized unions in San Francisco. Within walking distance from the town center, the SUNY New Paltz campus fosters a vibrant student community.

New Paltz has deep roots in protecting groups who face discrimination. The town owes its name to a group of French Huguenots from Mannheim, Germany—part of a region called Die Pfalz—who came to the New World in 1677 to escape religious persecution. These early settlers built homes above the Wallkill River on present-day Huguenot Street.

A short walk uphill from Huguenot Street puts you on Main Street in striking distance of most of the shops and restaurants in town. The **Wallkill Valley Rail Trail** crosses Main Street just below Route 32, making this an ideal stopover for walkers or cyclists following the length of the trail from Wallkill to Rosendale. Drivers should take Exit 18 from the New York Thruway to reach New Paltz. Expect traffic jams and difficult parking on summer weekends.

Huguenot Street

Several of the six original stone buildings on this street have survived more than three centuries of evolution in the community. The original structures of the Bevier-Elting, Jean Hasbrouck, and Abraham Hasbrouck Houses were built in the 1680s, and these homes are preserved as they would have looked in the 18th century. The 1799 LeFevre House was built in the federal style, and

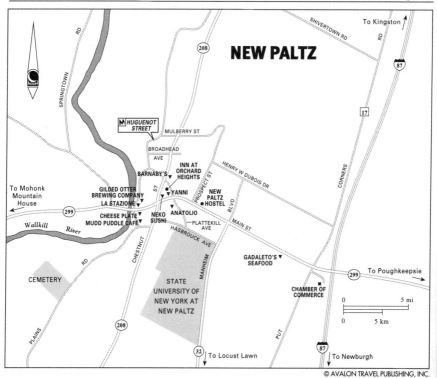

© AVALON TRAVEL PUBLISHING, INC.

the museum has furnished it with 19th-century accoutrements. The Deyo House is designed to portray an 1890s aesthetic, while the colonial Freer House was remodeled in the 1940s.

The Huguenot Historical Society runs guided tours from its visitor center in the DuBois Fort (18 Broadhead Ave., New Paltz, 845/255-1660, www.hhs-newpaltz.org; Tues.–Sun. 10 A.M.–4 P.M.) Tours run 50 or 90 minutes and cost $10 for adults, $9 for seniors and students, and $5 for children, with reduced rates for the abbreviated tour.

The organization also maintains **Locust Lawn** (Rte. 32, Gardiner, 845/255-1660; Wed.–Sun. 9:30 A.M.–4 P.M.), an 1814 Federal mansion that belonged to the prominent Hasbrouck family. A collection of family memorabilia is on display inside. The home was closed for renovations in 2004.

The Shawangunk Ridge

Between New Paltz and the Catskill Mountains lies another mountain range with its own geologic history, the Shawangunk Ridge. The result of a continental collision, the exposed sedimentary rock of the Shawangunks offers amateur and professional geologists an accessible, living laboratory to study the formation of the Appalachian Mountains—an eroded range that once stretched as high as the Himalayas.

The Shawangunk Ridge runs from the town of Rosendale all the way to New Jersey and Pennsylvania. From the spotted salamander to the black bear, it supports a delicate habitat for dozens of endangered plants and animals, among them the dwarf pitch pine, which grows on bedrock, and the peregrine falcon. Shale cliffs and dramatic overhangs also form ideal pitches for serious rock climbers, who know the area affectionately as The Gunks. Indeed, they arrive by the hundreds on clear summer days, with ropes, harnesses, and chalk in tow.

Three protected wilderness areas cover a large portion of the Shawangunk Ridge: Minnewaska State Park Preserve, the Monhonk Preserve, and Sam's Point Preserve.

M Minnewaska State Park Preserve

Acquired by New York State in 1987, **Minnewaska State Park Preserve** (Rte. 44/55, New Paltz, 845/255-0753, www.nysparks.com; open year-round for day-use; $7 per vehicle) encompasses 12,000 acres with a main entrance at Lake Minnewaska, off Route 44/55. Though the elevation here is about 2,000 feet, the scrubby pines, precipitous cliffs, and sparkling water might trick you into thinking you are above 10,000.

Hikers have a full menu of options within Minnewaska, from easy 2-mile routes to challenging 10-mile loops. You can actually follow the ridgeline by foot from the Appalachian Trail at the New Jersey state line all the way to Wurtsboro and the Bashakill Preserve, in Sullivan County. Climbers will want to head to the Peter's Kill Escarpment, a good alternative to the crowds at the Mohonk Preserve. Bicycles are allowed on the carriage paths only, not on the trails.

In addition to the Lake Minnewaska parking lot, Minnewaska has parking and trailheads at Peter's Kill to the east and Awosting to the west. A word of caution: to protect the fragile ecosystem, the park service limits the number of visitors allowed in Minnewaska at once. On summer weekends, the lots often fill immediately after opening. It's a good idea to arrive with a backup plan in mind, such as exploring the Wallkill Valley Rail Trail. Note that Minnewaska is a day-use park only; there are no overnight accommodations, and visitors must pack out all trash.

Outside of Minnewaska on Route 44/55 is the unassuming town of Gardiner, which finds itself at the center of a crossfire between real estate developers and environmentalists. The private owners of 2,600 acres that make up the Awosting Reserve next to Minnewaska mean to build a community of 350 luxury homes, complete with a new golf course and sewage treatment plant. Conservationists argue the development would threaten the habitat of some two dozen endangered species, while obstructing the views from trails in the adjoining state parks. But for now, the plans are stalled in a sea of red tape, and the Shawangunk Trail remains unharmed.

Mohonk Preserve

Adjoining Minnewaska to the north is the **Mohonk Mountain Preserve** (1000 Mountain Rest Rd., New Paltz, 845/255-1000, www.mohonk .com), set aside by the environmentally conscious Smiley family. Climbers flock here to choose from 1,000 different routes through world-class crags and crevices. Hikers have another 65 miles of trails to explore. Follow Route 199 from New Paltz to find the Mohonk visitor center. Climbers will want to continue past the center to the West Trapps trailhead. Parking lots fill quickly on weekend mornings. Entrance fees are $8 for hikers and $10 for climbers and cyclists.

At the intersection of Minnewaska and Mohonk lies the **Mohonk Mountain House** (1000 Mountain Rest Rd., New Paltz, 845/255-1000, www.mohonk.com), whose story begins with 280 acres of land, a 10-room inn, and a pair of Quaker twins. In the late 19th century, Albert and Alfred Smiley built rival country inns on the ridgeline, which grew to accommodate hundreds of guests at a time. A network of carriage paths connected the properties and provided the ideal setting for quiet contemplation. One of the original buildings burned down, but to this day, the historic Mohonk Mountain House, on the shores of Lake Mohonk, is owned and run by descendants of the Smiley family.

In its heyday, this sprawling hotel entertained a slew of famous guests, among them John Burroughs, Andrew Carnegie, and Theodore Roosevelt. Mohonk is no longer the remote and elegant wilderness getaway it was in the 19th century, but the property remains as beautiful as ever and continues to draw a steady crowd of tourists. Today, it serves as a popular venue for weddings and corporate events.

South of Minnewaska is the 4,600-acre **Sam's Point Preserve,** created in 1997 to protect the rare ridgetop dwarf pine barrens that define the landscape. Trails lead to numerous valley vistas, and the moderately strenuous 7.6-mile hike to

Verkeerderkill Falls takes about five hours round-trip. Follow Route 52 to Cragsmoor.

Rosendale

Surrounding New Paltz are several smaller but equally charming towns: Route 32 north takes you to Rosendale, home of the internationally acclaimed Rosendale Cement Company, whose "natural cement" limestone was used in nearly every major construction project undertaken in the 19th century: Rosendale cement found its way into the Brooklyn Bridge, the wings of the U.S. Capitol, the pedestal of the Statue of Liberty, the Washington Monument, Grand Central Terminal, and even the Panama Canal.

Geologists head to Rosendale's abandoned mines for clues about the past. The **Widow Jane Mine,** run by the Century House Historical Society, is a rare horizontal mine that is open to the public. Since its operational days ended, the mine has been used to grow mushrooms and trout, and as a venue for musical performances.

The society also operates the former estate of farmer-turned-businessman A. J. Snyder, an 1809 home that's listed on the National Register of Historic Places. A tour of the **Snyder Estate** (668 Rte. 213, Rosendale, 845/658-9900, www.centuryhouse.org; May–October Wed., Sat., and Sun. 1–4 P.M., or by appointment; adults $3, children $1) covers the house and mine, as well as a visit to the Delaware & Hudson Canal and a look at the old cement kilns.

Still an industrial community at heart, Rosendale lures foodies out of New Paltz with the Rosendale Cement restaurant, which more than a few residents claim to be the best fine dining around.

High Falls

About 15 minutes from New Paltz by car, High Falls is the kind of place where locals give you funny looks when you try to get a cell phone signal. Tucked away in the Shawangunk Mountains, on the south shore of the swift-flowing Rondout Creek, High Falls has found a niche in accommodating the spillover of weekenders from New Paltz. Many residents here started as weekenders, evolved into part-time commuters, and eventually moved in for good. A two-block stretch of businesses includes a handful of charming stores and

Egg's Nest, High Falls main intersection

eateries, including the exclusive **Depuy Canal House** (Rte. 213, High Falls, 845/687-7700, www.depuycanalhouse.net; mains $32–44).

It was a cold January day in 1825 when the founders of the Delaware and Hudson Canal Company began their company's public offering with a show and tell on Wall Street: the burning of anthracite coal. In the midst of the War of 1812, the country faced its first energy crisis and needed an alternative to bituminous coal, which the British had been supplying. Pennsylvania coal offered an alternative; the challenge was getting it from inland hills to coastal settlements.

The offering succeeded and thus began the construction of the Delaware and Hudson Canal. Built by Irish immigrants on the heels of the Erie Canal (by the same architect), it measured 108 miles long, 4 feet deep, and 32 feet wide. Along the way, the canal passed through 108 locks and crossed 137 bridges. At its terminus, it had to drop 70 feet to sea level in Rondout Creek—a series of five locks did the trick.

Today, the **D&H Canal Museum** (Mohonk Rd., High Falls, 845/687-9311, www.canal-museum.org; Mon. 11 A.M.–5 P.M., Thurs.–Sat. 11 A.M.–5 P.M., Sun. 1–5 P.M.; adults $3, children $1, families $7), housed in the former St. John's Episcopal Church, is a National Historic Landmark with lock demonstrations and a collection of documents and artifacts that trace the history of canal and railroad transportation.

Traveling Route 209 from High Falls toward Kingston, you pass through Marbletown, where the Ulster County Historical Society maintains a stone farmhouse with an exhibit of 18th- and 19th-century furniture and farming tools (2682 Rte. 209, Marbletown, 845/338-5614; June–Sept. Wed.–Sun. 1–5 P.M.). Five generations of Davenports have farmed the land in neighboring Stone Ridge. Today, the family's farm market, greenhouse, and pick-your-own services are a favorite local destination.

Hurley

The next town on Route 209 is Hurley, settled in 1661. When the British set Kingston in flames in November 1777, settlers fled here for safety. The township lost several of its original villages to the flooding of the Ashokan Reservoir in 1907.

Hurley's Main Street features a cluster of privately owned stone houses built during the 17th, 18th, and early 19th centuries. The **Hurley Heritage Society Museum** (52 Main St., Hurley, 845/338-1661, www.hurleyheritagesociety.org; Sat. 10 A.M.–4 P.M., Sun. 1–4 P.M.; admission $3) can arrange a guided tour that begins with the 1853 Dutch Reformed Church and includes a burial ground with headstones dating back to 1715.

THE SOUTHERN CATSKILL MOUNTAINS—ROUTE 28

Ashokan Reservoir

Route 28 West out of Kingston leads to the Ashokan Reservoir, the southern Catskill Mountains, and many of the old resorts that made the region world famous. Completed in 1915, the second-oldest reservoir in the New York City watershed (Croton is the oldest) holds 123 billion gallons in a man-made lake that covers 253 square miles. Nine villages were flooded in its making, and an entire cemetery of revolutionary war graves were dug up and relocated.

Woodstock

Follow the turnoff for Route 375 to reach the bustling mountain town of Woodstock, a one-time artists' colony with deep roots in folk and rock music. (Bob Dylan was a longtime resident.) Unlike some of the Hudson Valley's river towns, Woodstock has not reinvented itself overnight to appeal to a new demographic. Its busy cafés and art galleries give the impression of a genuine place with a passion for the arts.

Present-day Woodstock attracts a creative and outdoor-oriented crowd, including many New York City escapees. Uma Thurman and David Bowie are occasionally seen around town. As the daughter of singer Levon Helm (The Band), blues singer Amy Helm has continued to uphold the town's musical tradition with Ollabelle, a new sextet whose contemporary music blends gospel, blues, bluegrass, and country styles. Woodstock is also one of the few towns in the region that has several inviting accommodations within walking distance of its shops and restaurants.

A popular day hike from Woodstock is the **Overlook Mountain Fire Tower** at 3,150 feet elevation. On clear days, the summit rewards hikers with a sweeping view of the Hudson River to the east. The trail (2.4 miles one-way) passes the remains of the Overlook Mountain House, another of the Catskills' 19th-century inns. Listen for the rattle of the endangered timber rattlesnake along the way. To reach the trailhead from Woodstock, follow Rock City Road from Route 212 and cross Route 33, where the name changes to Meads Mountain Road. The trailhead is about 1.5 miles up the mountain.

Across from the trailhead, one of Woodstock's old inns, the former Mead Mountain House, is now a Tibetan Buddhist monastery called the **Karma Triyana Dharmachakra** (352 Meads Mountain Rd., Woodstock, 518/679-5906, office@kagyu.org; Sat.–Sun. 1:30–3 P.M.). It may be the only monastery in the world located in a 19th-century farmhouse. Visitors can tour the main shrine room, which contains one of the largest Shakyamuni Buddha statues in North America. A library and bookstore are also open to the public.

After the Ashokan Reservoir and just minutes from Woodstock, a cluster of new buildings stand out on Route 28 like the set of a Hollywood film. Centered on a converted 1841 barn in the hamlet of Mount Tremper, they are the shops and restaurants of **Catskill Corners,** an upscale commercial plaza that seems out of place in the otherwise bohemian countryside. The main attraction for those passing through is a giant kaleidoscope.

Phoenicia

Further along Route 28 is Phoenicia and the Catskill Mountain Railroad, which offers rides along the Esopus Creek. A better way to tour the creek, however, is by inner tube. On hot summer days, visitors line up at several rental shops in town to rent tubes that will float them down the gentle creek.

Train aficionados will want to check out the **Empire State Railway Museum** (Ulster &

Delaware Railroad Station, Phoenicia, 845/688-7501; Memorial Day–Columbus Day Sat.–Sun. 11 A.M.–4 P.M.; admission by donation), which houses artifacts, photographs, and films that document the history of rail travel in the area.

Slide Mountain

A few miles past Phoenicia in the town of Shandaken, Route 42 turns north to Greene County. And soon after, in Big Indian, comes the turn for Route 47 or Oliverea Slide Mountain Road. This road leads to Frost Valley and the base of Slide Mountain, at 4,190 feet. It's an eight-mile drive along Route 47 to the Winnisook Club and the Slide Mountain parking lot.

Naturalist John Burroughs spent long hours contemplating the highest peak in the Catskills. In an essay about the southern Catskills, he wrote that the peak looked like the back and shoulders of a gigantic horse: "The horse has got his head down grazing; the shoulders are high, and the descent from them down his neck very steep; if he were to lift up his head, one sees that it would be carried far above all other peaks, and that the noble beast might gaze straight to his peers in the Adirondacks or the White Mountains."

Burroughs spent many years fishing the streams that drained the mountain and camping on all sides of the peak before he attempted a summit. On approaching Slide at last from a spruce grove on the north side, he wrote, "The mountain rose like a huge, rock-bound fortress from this plain-like expanse. It was ledge upon ledge, precipice upon precipice, up which and over which we made our way slowly and with great labor, now pulling ourselves up by our hands, then cautiously finding niches for our feet and zigzagging right and left from shelf to shelf."

It's much easier to access Slide Mountain today, but the hike remains one of the most difficult in the Catskill Preserve. A strenuous five-mile route from the parking lot leads to the top. There are no views from the summit proper, but from a ridge that connects Slide to neighboring Wittenberg, you can see all but one of the thirty-four Catskill peaks that rise above 3,500 feet (Thomas Cole peak is obscured by Hunter Mountain). Allow 4–5 hours to complete the hike.

Belleayre Ski Center

Past the turnoff for Oliverea, Route 28 begins to climb until it reaches the base of the **Belleayre Ski Center** (Rte. 28, Highmount, 845/254-5600, www.belleayre.com; daily 9 A.M.–4 P.M.) in Pine Hill. With ideal terrain for intermediate skiers, Belleayre is located within the "forever wild" Catskill Preserve. Skiers began carving turns down its slopes as early as the 1930s, and in 1949, the New York State Department of Environmental Conservation cleared a network of trails and opened the area to the public. Today, Belleayre sponsors outdoor and cultural programs year-round, including the renowned **Belleayre Music Festival** in summer.

SPORTS AND RECREATION
Winter Sports

With an annual base of 75 to 165 inches of snow and the highest skiable peak in the Catskills, Belleayre offers the most varied terrain for downhill skiers and snowboarders in Ulster County. It is especially popular with families. In addition, the mountain boasts the only snowcat skiing in the Catskills and grooms 9.2 kilometers of cross-country ski trails. Adult tickets cost $42 on weekends and $32 midweek, with multiday discounts. Lifts run 9 A.M.–4 P.M. daily.

Belleayre Mountain Statistics
Base: 2,025 feet
Summit: 3,429 feet
Vertical: 1,404 feet
Trails: 38
Lifts: 8
Skiable acres: 171
Snowmaking: 96 percent
Snow report: 800/942-6904

Beginners or families with young kids may prefer the considerably smaller **Sawkill Family Ski Center** (167 Hill Rd. off Sawkill & Jockey Hill Rd.; Kingston, 845/336-6977, www.sawkill-ski.com, late June–Labor Day, Sat.–Sun. and hol-

climbing area in Peter's Kill in Minnewaska State Park

© PAUL ITOI

idays 10 A.M.–4 P.M.; full day $20, half day $17, Fri. night $13, 1-hour tubing $10) or **Roamer Mountain Park** (355 Woodland Valley Rd., Phoenicia, 845/688-5553; Dec.–Mar. 10 A.M.–5 P.M.) for snow-tubing in Phoenicia.

The **Frost Valley YMCA** (Frost Valley Rd., Claryville, 845/985-2291, www.frostvalley.org) in the shadow of Slide Mountain, provides access to 35 kilometers of cross-country ski trails, including several cable bridge crossings. Strung high above a swift-flowing creek, these "bridges" are made of three single cables in an inverted triangle: one for your feet and the other two for your hands. Choose a different route if you are at all afraid of heights. Ideal for groups, Frost Valley has cabins on the premises with hot showers and flush toilets. Some are in better shape than others. Meals are included with your stay, and reservations are required.

For the most extensive network of cross-country ski trails, head to Minnewaska State Park. The Mohonk Preserve and Mohonk Mountain House also groom trails for skiers. Rent your gear on the way in at **Rock & Snow** (44 Main St., New Paltz, 845/255-1311, www.rocksnow.com).

Hiking

Hikers will find endless miles of beautiful terrain in the Shawangunks, at Minnewaska, Sam's Point, and Mohonk Preserve (65 miles of trails). Note, there is no camping in Minnewaska. And other than a hot dog stand that occasionally sets up at the top of the Minnewaska parking lot, food and water are not readily available near the trailheads. Stock up on supplies before you head into the park.

For a moderately challenging day hike near Woodstock, head to the base of Overlook Mountain, on Meads Mountain Road (www.catskilltowers.com). For a more strenuous route, head west to climb the highest peak in the range: Slide Mountain. John Burroughs called Slide a "shy mountain" because it was difficult to spot until he got very close, and even on the ascent, it was difficult to find the peak.

Mountain Biking and Road Riding

New Paltz is a mecca for avid cyclists. Surrounding country roads have terrain to match all levels: flat fields, rolling hills, and steep climbs. Stop by the **Bicycle Depot** (15 Main St., New Paltz, 845/255-3859, www.bicycledepot.com) at the bottom of Main Street for route advice. This is also one of the only shops in the area that rents decent road bikes. The gear is in good condition and prices are reasonable.

Mountain bikers can choose between gentle rail trails and more aggressive single track. Woodstock and New Paltz both have convenient access to trail heads. The **Wallkill Valley Rail Trail** (New Paltz, www.gorailtrail.org; dawn to dusk) is a favorite route for trail riding, jogging, and walking. This 12-mile trail connects the towns of New Paltz, Rosendale, and Gardiner. All trail signs have maps on the back.

Try **Overlook Mountain Bikes** (93 Tinker St., Woodstock, 845/679-2122) or **Catskill Mountain Bicycle** (3 Church St., New Paltz, 845/255-3859) for maps and gear. **Table Rock Tours and Bicycle Shop** (292 Main St., Rosendale, 845/658-7832, www.tablerocktours.com; Mon.–Wed. 10 A.M.–5 P.M., Thurs.–Sat. 10 A.M.–6 P.M., Sun. 10 A.M.–2 P.M.) offers one- and two-day bike tours of Ulster County.

Golf

More than a dozen golf courses are scattered along the base of the Shawangunks in Ulster County. One of the prettiest, **Apple Greens Golf** (161 South St., 845/883-5500, www.applegreens.com; $24), is set on an apple orchard. It also offers one of the best deals in the area for 18 holes. The **Shawangunk Country Club** (Leurnkill Rd., Ellenville, 845/647-6090) has nine holes on a hilly course that's built around a large pond.

Swimming and Boating

Ulster County offers access to several unusual water sports: For starters, a day of drifting along the Esopus Creek is practically a mandatory activity for anyone who lives within a day's drive of Phoenicia. Time your visit on the one day a month when the water is released, and you'll be in for a real adventure. **F-S Tube and Raft Rental** (Main St., Phoenicia, 845/688-7633) offers transportation and rentals. **Town Tinker Tube Rental** (Bridge St.,

The Mid-Hudson

COURTESY OF ULSTER COUNTY TOURISM

the sloop *Clearwater*

Phoenicia, 845/688-5553, www.towntinker.com; daily 9 A.M.–6 P.M.; $25/day full gear rental) offers tubing courses for beginners and experts. It takes about two hours to travel 2.5 miles along the river.

Planning a trip to the Caribbean and need to get certified to dive? Spend two weekends with **Deep-Six Underwater Systems** (14 Deerpath Drive, New Paltz, 845/255-7446, dsusdive@aol.com, www.deep-six.com; Mon.–Sat. 9 A.M.–5 P.M.) and you'll be good to go. Training dives take place at Diver's Cove in Lake Minnewaska, where the Mid-Hudson Diving Association has set up a bench and drying racks for fellow divers.

Lake Minnewaska is hands-down the most beautiful place to swim in Ulster County. In summer, the surface temperature climbs to a refreshing 75 degrees. Visibility is not as good as it once was (10–12 feet on average), but underwater cliffs and a maximum depth of 72 feet make for an interesting dive in a safe environment. Expect a thermocline at about 30 feet.

If you prefer to stay on top of the water, set sail for an evening of water, wine, and cheese with the **Great Hudson Sailing Center** (Dock St., Kingston, 845/429-1557, www.greathudsonsailing.com; daily 10 A.M.–5 P.M.). The center offers guided sails, lessons, sales, and rentals. A 16-hour sailing course on two consecutive weekends makes a great active getaway ($400 per person, $360 for a second person).

Two additional operations launch boats from Rondout Landing: **Hudson Rondout Cruises**

(Rondout Landing, Kingston, 845/338-6515) go from the Kingston Lighthouse south to the Esopus Meadows Lighthouse. Inquire about dinner and brunch cruises. **North River Cruises** (Rondout Landing, Kingston, 845/679-8205, www.northrivercruises.com) has a boat called *Teal* that is available for private charters.

Fishing and Hunting

Anglers primarily use nymphs and streamers to fish the lower Esopus, since it gets less water pressure than the Delaware, Willowemoc, and Beaverkill. As a tailwater, the Esopus offers the best conditions late in the season. Access the stream near Boiceville.

Fly-fishing with Bert (P.O. Box 153, Tillson, 845/658-9784, bdflycaster@aol.com) offers fly-fishing instruction and guide services on the Catskill's trout streams in May, June, and September. **Ed's Fly-Fishing & Guide Services** (69 Ridge Rd., Shokan, 845/657-6393, tailwaters@hvc.rr.com) is another option near the Ashokan Reservoir. **Osprey Marine** (12 Butterville Rd., New Paltz, 845/255-8737, captain@ospreymarine.com, www.ospreymarine.com; June–Oct.) runs fishing charters on the Hudson River out of Kingston when the striped bass run in spring.

Aviation

Learn to glide at the **Mountain Wings Hang Gliding Center** (150 Canal St., Ellenville, 845/647-3377, www.mtnwings.com), where an introductory program costs $140. The course is certified by USHGA (United States Hang Gliding Association) and includes one day of training with videos and a simulator, followed by supervised flights.

If you'd rather have someone else handle the controls, call **River Aviation** (1161 Flatbush Rd., Kingston, 845/336-8400) for an aerial tour of the river and dramatic views of the Shawangunks. Flights depart from the Kingston-Ulster airport.

You can jump from 13,500 feet and freefall to 6,000 with **Skydive the Ranch** (45 Sandhill Rd., Gardiner, 845/255-4033, www.skydivetheranch.com; $185 per jump including gear). Repeat visitors can complete all 13 levels of the Instructor Assisted Freefall (IAF) skydiver training program. Group rates are also available.

Rock Climbing

When the weather cooperates, climbers descend on the Mohonk Preserve (West Trapps trailhead; admission $10) to scale several of the 1,000 world-class pitches in the preserve. A good alternative to climbing in the Mohonk Preserve is the **Peter's Kill Area** (Rte. 44/55, New Paltz, 845/255-0752, www.nysparks.com; open daily at 9 A.M.; $5/day) in Minnewaska State Park. Located five miles west of the junction of Routes 299 and 44/55, and one mile east of the main park entrance, Peter's Kill boasts some of the best bouldering anywhere in the northeast. You'll climb on quartz conglomerate cliffs found a half-mile walk from the parking lot. A range of single-pitch climbs will suit various levels. The area has a daily limit of 70 climbers.

Before you go, pick up a helmet, shoes, chalk, and a climbing harness at **Rock & Snow** (44 Main St., New Paltz, 845/255-1311, www.rocksnow.com; Mon.–Fri. 9 A.M.–6 P.M., Sat. 8 A.M.–8 P.M., Sun. 8 A.M.–7 P.M.) Brush up on your skills at **The Inner Wall** (234 Main St., New Paltz, 845/255-ROCK or 845/255-7625, www.theinnerwall.com), an indoor climbing gym.

High Angle Adventures (178 Hardenburgh Rd., Ulster Park, 800/777-2546, www.highangle.com) offers a range of classes, including classes for women, lead training, and transition courses from indoor to outdoor environments. Locals also recommend **Mountain Skills** (Stone Ridge, 845/687-9643) for climbing instruction.

You can also rent climbing shoes and camping equipment at the **Eastern Mountain Sports** (EMS) store (4124 Rte. 44/55, Gardiner, 845/255-3280, www.emsclimb.com; Mon.–Sun. 8:30 A.M.–5 P.M.) at the intersection of Routes 299 and 44/55. Unlike other EMS locations, this one is a designated Climbing Specialty Store that offers classes, rental gear, and repair services. Note that the center does not rent harnesses, helmets, ropes, or protective gear.

ACCOMMODATIONS

Ulster accommodations conjure images of historic mountain houses, rustic country inns, and wooded campgrounds. There are surprisingly few places to stay in downtown New Paltz, but many quaint bed and breakfast inns dot the surrounding countryside.

Under $100

True to its reputation as a university town, New Paltz has one of the few hostel accommodations in the Hudson River Valley region. Stay from one night to two weeks at the **New Paltz Hostel** (145 Main St., New Paltz, 845/255-6676, www.newpaltzhostel.com), within walking distance to public transportation, university buildings, and stores and restaurants of downtown New Paltz. Shared rooms (up to six people) cost $24 per person per night, and private rooms run $61–77 for one or two people and $66–132 for larger groups. The hostel closes during the day between 10 A.M. and 4 P.M.

$100–150

Private porches and a central location are defining features of **The Inn at Orchard Heights** (20 Church St., New Paltz, 845/255-6792; $100–150). Owners Janet and Darryl Greene offer five rooms in their 1888 Queen Anne Victorian. Some are on the small side and not all have private baths, but you can't beat the location for convenience. **Evelyn's View** (12 Riverknoll Rd., Milton, 845/795-2376; $100–150) sits on a bluff overlooking the Hudson. Its four cozy rooms are decorated in a simple country style.

Another affordable option within walking distance to Rondout Landing is the **Rondout B&B** (88 West Chester St., Kingston, 845/331-8144, www.rondoutbandb.com; $100–115). Four well-kept guestrooms are in a turn-of-the-20th-century home. Two have private baths, and the other two share a bath and sitting room.

$150–200

A picturesque stream meanders through the property at **Captain Schoonmakers** (913 Rte. 213, High Falls, 945/687-7946, www.captainschoonmakers.com; $150–200). The inn is a 1760 stone house; rooms are located in the carriage house with private balconies and air conditioning. The owners are animal lovers, and a posse of cats and dogs roam the grounds at all times.

A hundred-year-old Bechstein grand piano

takes center stage at the **N** **Sparrow Hawk Bed and Breakfast** (4496 Rte. 209, Stone Ridge, 845/687-4492, www.sparrowhawkbandb.com; $139–195). Set among a stand of black locust trees just off busy Route 209, the inn is located 15 minutes from downtown New Paltz. Owners Betsy and Howard Mont have created a romantic escape in their 1770 brick colonial. Cozy guestrooms feature air conditioning and high-quality linens; a gourmet breakfast starts the day right.

Weekend reservations are difficult to secure at the two-room **Saugerties Lighthouse** (off Mynderse St., Saugerties, 845/247-0656, www.saugertieslighthouse.com; Apr.–Oct. $160, Nov.–Mar. $135, breakfast included). Accommodations are rustic, with a shared bath and limited electricity.

Over $200

One of the most inviting places to stay anywhere in the Hudson Valley sits at the edge of the Shawangunks with views of sheer cliff walls right outside the window. Built in 2001, the **N** **Minnewaska Lodge** (Rte. 44/55, Gardiner, 845/255-1110, www.minnewaskalodge.com; $200–220) has 26 modern but cozy rooms with a fitness center and a spacious, ground-floor breakfast room. Data ports are a plus for those traveling with a computer. Trails lead right from the back porch, and the restaurants and shops of New Paltz are just six miles away.

The historic **Mohonk Mountain House** (100 Mountain Rest Rd., New Paltz, 845/255-1000 or 800/772-6646; $179–735) is showing its age these days. Rates include buffet-style breakfast and lunch and a four-course dinner, as well as afternoon tea and cookies. Jackets are required for dinner service, and alcohol is only available at dinner or for private consumption in guestrooms at other times. Rooms, suites, and cottages represent a variety of styles. Some create the feeling of a cozy mountain lodge, while others feature elaborate Victorian fabrics. Optional extras include balconies, fireplaces, or views. Televisions are available in some public areas.

The Inn at Stone Ridge/Hasbrouck House (3805 Rte. 209, Stone Ridge, 845/687-0736, www.innatstoneridge.com; $195–425) has five suites in a handsome 18th-century Dutch Colonial that's set on 150 acres of woods and gardens between New Paltz and Kingston. Rooms are decorated in warm tones and country quilts.

Campgrounds

Campers have all kinds of options in Ulster County. **Yogi Bear's Jellystone Camp-Resort** (50 Bevier Rd., Gardiner, 848/255-5193, nyyogi@aol.com) is a large but well-run operation with two locations, Lazy River in Gardiner and Birchwood Acres in Woodridge. Amenities include canoe rentals, showers, and swimming pools.

FOOD

Ulster County holds some culinary surprises, as well as a number of mainstay establishments.

Along the River–Route 9W

By many accounts, the **Raccoon Saloon** (1330 Rte. 9W, Marlborough, 845/236-7872) serves the best burger in the region, if not more broadly speaking. Tucked away on a hill in a suburban neighborhood, **The Would** (120 North Rd., Highland, 845/691-9883, www.thewould.com; mains $18–26) occupies the site of a 1920s-era summer resort and is worth a special trip for a memorable New American meal.

Mariner's Harbor (1 Broadway, Kingston, 845/340-8051, www.marinersharbor.com; Mon. 4–10 P.M., Tues.–Sat. 11:30 A.M.–10 P.M., Sun. noon–9 P.M.; mains $15–28), a longtime standby for quality seafood, has moved from its former Highland location to Rondout Landing in Kingston. On the same block are several newer establishments: the **Downtown Café** (1 West Strand, Kingston, 845/331-5904; mains $16–25) has an extensive wine list and an open dining area with a vintage storefront exterior. **El Coqui Latin Jazz Café** (21 Broadway, Kingston, 845/340-1106) serves Puerto Rican specialties.

In Kingston's Stockade District, pop into **Jane's Homemade Ice Cream** (305 Wall St., Kingston, 845/338-8315) for a milkshake or quick lunch. For fine dining, **Le Canard Enchaine** (276 Fair St., Kingston, 845/339-2003, www.lecanard-enchaine.com; daily 5–10 P.M.; mains $17–25) is an authentic French bistro serving classics like cassoulet and reasonably priced wines.

Additional options for global cuisine include decent Tex-Mex at the **Armadillo Bar and Grill** (97 Abeel St., Kingston, 845/339-1550, www.armadillos.net; mains $12–17) and Chinese fusion at **China Rose** (608 Ulster Ave., Kingston, 845/338-7443), which has a sister restaurant across the river in Rhinecliff.

New Paltz and Surroundings

New Paltz has it all when it comes to food: sushi, Mediterranean, haute cuisine, and cheese. For breakfast or a quick bite to eat at lunchtime, head to **The Bakery** (13A N. Front St., New Paltz, 845/255-8840, www.ilovethebakery.com; daily 7 A.M.–6 P.M.; mains $4–8). Soups and sandwiches change daily, and there are a handful of tables in a courtyard outside. Service is slow, but the baked goods are worth the wait.

New York City chef Jaques Qualin and his wife Leslie Flam have turned an old German tavern into a slice of Paris at **The French Corner** (3407 Cooper St., Stone Ridge, 845/687-0810, www.frcorner.com; Tues.—Sun. from 5 P.M., Sunday brunch 11:30 A.M.–3 P.M.; mains $24–32). You might begin the evening with a champagne cocktail, move on to the veal chop, and finish with a tart featuring locally picked fruit.

At the end of Main Street in New Paltz is the **Gilded Otter Brewing Company** (3 Main St., Rte. 299, New Paltz, 845/256-1700, www.gildedotter.com; Mon.–Thurs. 11:30 A.M.–10 P.M., Fri.–Sat. till 10:30 P.M., Sun. 10 A.M.–8 P.M.; mains $14–21), with a good selection of wursts and schnitzels and freshly brewed beers to wash them down. The bar stays open till 2 A.M.

Gadaleto's Seafood (246 Main St., Cherry Hill shopping center, New Paltz, 845/255-1717; Sun.–Thurs. 11:30 A.M.–9 P.M., Fri.–Sat. 11:30 A.M.–10 P.M.; mains $8–18) is a local institution that supplies many area restaurants with their fresh catch. Consumers can sample the goodies at the raw bar or place an order for fish and chips or crab cakes. Be prepared to wait; the restaurant can get crowded, and service tends to be slow.

Closer to the center of town, one of New

Paltz's old movie theaters was converted into a giant pub-style restaurant in 2003. **Barnaby's** (Rte. 32/N. Chestnut St., New Paltz, 845/255-2433; mains $10–25) prepares hearty steaks, burgers, seafood, and salads.

Located just steps away from the Walkill Valley Rail Trail, the **Cheese Plate** (10 Main St., Suite 302, New Paltz, 845/255-2444) is the perfect place to stop for a picnic. The owner is a Dutchess County native and Manhattan escapee who offers an outstanding selection of local and imported cheeses, from Sprout Creek Farm across the river to the Pyrenees of Spain and France. Next door, the **Mudd Puddle Café** (10 Main St., New Paltz, 845/255-3536, www.muddpuddlecoffee.com; Wed. 9:30 A.M.–5 P.M., Thurs. 9:30 A.M.–6 P.M., Fri.–Sat. 9:30 A.M.–7 P.M., Sun.–Mon. 9:30 A.M.–5 P.M.; $5.45 "best deal" includes a cup of soup and half panini) roasts its own coffee and serves homemade soups and sandwiches. Also near the trail, **La Stazione** (5 Main St., New Paltz, 845/256-9447) takes its name from the train station it converted into an eatery. Student servers staff the dining room, and the menu consists of reasonably priced Italian dishes.

A landlocked location is no obstacle to culinary creativity at **Neko Sushi** (49 Main St., New Paltz, 845/255-0162), where the chef presents an artistic variety of raw fish and maki rolls each evening. Two doors up, **Yanni Restaurant & Café** (51 Main St., New Paltz, 845/256-0988, www.yannirestaurant.com; daily 11:30 A.M.–11 P.M.; mains $8–12) offers a late-night menu of gyros, Greek salad, spanikopita, and other specialties to a clientele of students and weekend tourists. Greek TV is an added highlight. The string of ethnic treats continues up the street at **Anatolio** (62 Main St., New Paltz, 845/255-3700; 11 A.M.–11 P.M.), a Turkish establishment run by a pair of twin brothers.

The Loft (46 Main St., New Paltz, 845/255-1426) serves American fish and meat dishes. Dine amidst the historic stone buildings of Huguenot Street at **Locust Tree** (215 Huguenot St., New Paltz, 845/255-7888), which serves northern European cuisine.

The good eats don't end at the New Paltz town line. Rosendale, the next town over, has one of the best kept secrets around: **M Rosendale Cement** (419 Main St., Rosendale, 845/658-3210, www.rosendalecement.com; Thurs.–Mon. 5:30–10 P.M., Fri.–Sat. dinner till 11 P.M., Sun. from 5 P.M., Sun. brunch 11 A.M.–3 P.M.; $15–22) is a chic Manhattan-style restaurant situated right on the bank of the Walkill River. Comfort food abounds at this eclectic locals favorite. Progressive dishes such as a prosciutto-wrapped cod fillet with lentils balance out comfort staples, including meatloaf and ribs. Behind the restaurant is a super-cool Airstream trailer that serves as a bar.

High Falls claims one of the region's most exclusive fine-dining establishments in the **Depuy Canal House** (Rte. 213, High Falls, 845/687-7700, www.depuycanalhouse.net; Thurs.–Sat. 5:30–9 P.M., Fri.–Sat. till 10 P.M., Sun. 4–9 P.M., Sun. brunch 11:30 A.M.–2 P.M.; mains $32–44; reservations required). Guests can choose a three-, four-, or seven-course menu ($75), which features game dishes, such as a rabbit hunter's soup or venison medallions served rare with a maitake-mushroom risotto. Head to the more casual **Chefs on Fire** (Rte. 213, High Falls, 845/687-7778; mains $6–12), downstairs, to refuel after climbing the Shawangunks.

If the southwestern food at **The Egg's Nest** (Rte. 213, High Falls, 845/687-7255, www.theeggsnest.com; daily 11:30 A.M.–11 P.M., Fri.–Sat. till midnight; mains $6–12) doesn't leave a memorable impression, the funky decor certainly will. Toasters hang from the ceiling, and tinfoil is stuck on the walls. Indeed, everything about the place is intentionally mismatched. Enjoy the huge portions, and save room for dessert.

Steaks anchor a menu that features local ingredients at the charming **Inn at Stone Ridge** (mains $17–30), which has both formal and casual dining options. Preparations include au poive, gorgonzola sauce, and braised mushrooms. For an unusual appetizer, consider the truffled Black Angus steak tartar with a fresh quail egg. The tavern menu includes panini, burgers, and quesadillas (mains $8–15).

Southern Catskill Mountains–Route 28

CIA graduates Rickie and James Tamayo opened **Café Tamayo** (89 Partition St., Saugerties, 845/ 246-9371, www.cafetamayo.com; Wed.–Sun. from 5 P.M.; mains $12–20) in 1987 to heartfelt applause. Antique fans, plaster on canvas ceilings, and a gorgeous hand-carved bar set the mood, while crispy duck confit tempts the palette.

Between Saugerties and Woodstock, a colorful decor and central bar complement a menu of Cajun jerk chicken, ahi tuna, Thai mussel stew, and churrasco-style grilled meats at **New World Home Cooking** (1411 Rte. 212, Saugerties, 845/246-0900, www.newworldhomecooking .com; Mon.–Sat. noon–3 P.M. & 5–11 P.M., Sun. 4–10 P.M.; mains $14–32).

Red Onion (1654 Rte. 212, Woodstock, 845/679-1223; Mon., Tues., Thurs. 5–10 P.M., Fri.–Sat. 5–10:30 P.M., Sun. 11 A.M.–3 P.M. and 5–9 P.M.; mains $9–23) is one of the newest eateries to open in progressive Woodstock. Located in an 1830s farmhouse, the restaurant serves international fare and a Sunday brunch at half a dozen tables arranged around a cozy bar.

For a casual meal and a memorable experience, try a homemade muffin at **M Bread Alone** (22 Mill Hill Rd., Woodstock, 845/679-2108, www.breadalone.com; daily 7 A.M.–6 P.M.), a European-style organic bakery and café with additional locations in Kingston, Rhinebeck, and Boiceville. The owner, Daniel Leader, is a CIA graduate who traveled from Paris to the Pyrenees to learn what gives European breads their hearty flavor. He now produces 15 tons of fresh bread per week from twin ovens that were custom-built by a Parisian oven mason. At headquarters in Boiceville, you can take an impromptu tour of the bakery while you sip a frothy cappuccino.

Another breakfast mainstay, famous for its variety of pancakes, lies farther west in Phoenicia. **Sweet Sue's** (Main St., Phoenicia, 845/688-7852; Thurs.–Mon. 7 A.M.–3 P.M.; mains $7–12) is the perfect place to start or end a day of tubing on the Esopus River.

Celebrity sightings are common among the trendsetters who dine creekside at **The Bear** (295 Tinker St./Rte. 212, Bearsville, 845/679-5555, www.bearcafe.com; Sun.–Thurs. 5–10 P.M., Fri.–Sat. 5–11 P.M.; mains $17–26). Entrées range from grilled tofu to filet mignon and from Caesar salad to a half-pound hamburger.

Across the parking lot is your best chance for good Chinese at **The Little Bear** (845/679-8899, mains $10–16, weekday lunch specials $5–6).

ENTERTAINMENT AND EVENTS

Performing Arts

Come summer, the **New Paltz Summer Repertory Theatre** (SUNY New Paltz Samuel Dorsky Museum of Art, Theatre, Music, Festivals; 75 S. Manheim, New Paltz, 845/257-3872) performs at the SUNY New Paltz campus. Its Shakespeare Under the Stars show is a popular feature every year.

In Woodstock, the **Colony Café** (22 Rock City Rd., Woodstock, 845/679-5342; Thurs.–Tues. from 7 P.M.) stages music concerts and poetry readings inside a historic dinner theater.

Bars and Nightlife

New Paltz and Kingston's Rondout Landing present the most options for nightlife. About a dozen bars line a short stretch of Main Street in New Paltz, a town that allows its watering holes to stay open until 4 A.M. Many, though by no means all, of them are student hangouts. Open-mic Wednesdays are a popular feature at **Oasis** (58 Main St., New Paltz, 845/255-2400). **Bacchus** (4 S. Chestnut St., New Paltz, 845/255-8636, www.bacchusnewpaltz.com), near the corner of Main and Chestnut, keeps 300 beers on hand to accompany a menu of Southwestern fare. Students and local residents alike enjoy the late-night appetizer menu Sunday–Wednesday until 11 P.M. and Thursday–Saturday until 1 A.M.

Buffalo wings and a dozen TVs are a hit at **McGillicuddy's Restaurant & Tap Room** (84 Main St., New Paltz, 845/256-9289; daily 11 A.M.–4 A.M.; Fri.–Sat. night cover $3), which also has a pool table and dance floor.

P&G's Restaurant (91 Main St., New Paltz, 845/255-6161, www.pandgs.com; Mon.–Sat. 8:30 P.M.–4 A.M., Sun. noon–4 A.M., Fri. happy hour 3–9 P.M.), affectionately known as "pigs," is a New Paltz institution among students and alumni. Nightly specials include $2 pitchers of Newcastle beer and a menu of casual pub fare.

The legendary **Country Inn** (1380 County Road 2, Krumville, 845/657-8956), in a southern Catskill hamlet, changed hands in 2003 when founder Larry Erenberg retired, but it's business-as-usual under new management. Choose from hundreds of beers among a crowd of locals and travelers.

Saugerties locals gather at the **Chowhound Café** (112 Partition St., Saugerties, 845/246-5158, www.thechowhoundcafe.com; Wed.–Sun. 11 A.M.–10 P.M., Sat. brunch 11 A.M.–3 P.M., Sun. brunch 10 A.M.–3 P.M.; mains $10–23) on weekend afternoons to down a burger and listen to live jazz in a super casual setting. Besides the reliable burger and Caesar salad, the menu features Latin American specialties, including a churrasco steak.

Festivals

The **Belleayre Music Festival** draws a large crowd of music lovers to the Catskills each summer. Popular with kids in October is the **Headless Horseman Hayride & Haunted House** (778 Broadway, Ulster Park, 845/339-2666, www.headlesshorseman.com) on Route 9W between Highland and Kingston. The attraction is open during the last two weekends in September and every weekend in October. Reservations are required.

The **Woodstock Film Festival** (www.woodstockfilmfestival.com) celebrated its fifth anniversary in October 2004. The festival draws a number of leading filmmakers and critics to watch a selection of the industry's newest and boldest independent films.

The hundred-year-old **Ulster County Fair** (Libertyville Rd., 845/255-1380, www.ulstercountyfair.com; $12 admission) takes places in August each year, with music, amusement rides, and fireworks. The fairgrounds are located two miles outside of New Paltz.

SHOPPING

Farm Stands

While in the Saugerties area, be sure to sample a taste of the hardneck garlic that grows nearby. Darker in color than the more common softneck garlic that grows in California's Gilroy, hardneck garlic is better suited to colder climates. July is the harvest season. And during the last weekend in September, **Gippert Farm** (266 Churchland Rd., Saugerties, 845/247-9479) hosts the annual Hudson Valley Garlic Festival (www.garlicgoddess.com), now in its 15th season. Hundreds attend to try the local variety. Some say it's more bitter than what you buy at the grocery store; others disagree. See for yourself.

Davenport Farms (3411 Rte. 209, Stone Ridge, 845/687-0051, www.davenportfarms.com) operates a popular farm market, greenhouse, and pick-your-own field on Route 209 in Stone Ridge. To pick your own strawberries, head to **Kelder's Farm** (5755 Rte. 209, Kerhonkson, 845/626-7137, www.kelderfarm.com) in early June.

Antiques and Galleries

There are literally dozens of antique shops and art galleries across Ulster County, many of them clustered around Saugerties and Rosendale. The **Woodstock School of Art** (2470 Rte. 212, Woodstock, 845/679-2388, wsart@ulster.net) holds auctions and exhibitions during summer months. The **Center for Photography at Woodstock** (59 Tinker St., Woodstock, 845/679-9957, info@cpw.org, Mar.–Dec. Wed.–Sun. noon–5 P.M.) shows contemporary works in a small gallery. It also runs workshops, auctions, and lectures.

A number of home furnishing stores have opened in High Falls and Stone Ridge, selling both new and old pieces. **Lounge Furniture** (8 2nd St., High Falls, 845/687-9463) has couches, area rugs, lighting, and other accents. **Four Winds** (Rte. 209 at Rte. 213, Stone Ridge, 845/687-4080, www.fourwindsathome.com; Mon. 10 A.M.–5 P.M., Tues. by appointment, Wed.–Thurs. 10 A.M.–5 P.M., Fri. and Sun. 10 A.M.–6 P.M., Sat. 10 A.M.–5 P.M.) specializes in southeast Asian decor.

Most of the 30 antique shops in Saugerties are located within the eight-block commercial area on Main, Market, and Partition streets. At **Saugerties Antiques Gallery** (104 Partition St., Saugerties, 845/246-2323), owner Pat Guariglia caters to other dealers with a two-floor showroom of European and American antiques. **Partition Street Antiques** (114 Partition St., Saugerties, 845/679-7561, www.partitionstreetantiques.com; Thurs.–Mon. 11 A.M.–5 p.m.) collects a range of American furniture styles, including rattan, bamboo, and Mission oak.

Bookstores

Anyone with more than a passing interest in New York State history should plan a visit to Saugerties to browse the extensive collection of titles in the **Hope Farm Press and Bookshop** (252 Main St., Saugerties, 845/246-3522, www.hopefarmbooks.com; Mon. 10 A.M.–6 P.M., Sun. noon–4 P.M.) The press was founded in 1959 by a retired director of the New York City Public Library. And current owner Richard Frisbie has carried on the tradition with equal passion. Look for the storefront on the south side of Main Street. Frisbie houses two sister bookshops in one location—the larger sign over the door says Booktrader, which is a general-interest bookstore, and a smaller sign in the window reads Hope Farm Press & Bookshop. Exit the New York Thruway at Exit 20. It's open daily 10 A.M.–6 P.M. Sundays and most holidays noon–4 P.M.

Though it seems a little out of place, the fanciest shopping in Ulster County is found at **Emporium at Emerson Place** (5340 Rte. 28 at Mt. Pleasant Rd., Mt. Tremper, 845/688-5800; daily 10 A.M.–7 P.M.). Gourmet foods, aromatherapy products, country furniture, and home decor are all on display.

Wineries

Like Dutchess County, Ulster has a handful of wineries producing a range of varietals. You can hit each of them by driving a 30-mile loop called the Shawangunk Wine Trail (845/255-2494, www.shawangunkwinetrail.com). Better yet, ride a bike. This group of nine family-owned wineries are scattered along the back roads connecting the New York State Thruway, I-84, and Highway 17 between New Paltz and Warwick in Orange County. A trail map is available online and at any of the member wineries. One of the closest stops to downtown New Paltz is **Rivendell Vineyards and Winery** (714 Albany Post Rd., New Paltz, 845/255-2494, finewine@aol.com; daily 10 A.M.–6 P.M.).

INFORMATION AND SERVICES

The Kingston Heritage Area Visitor Centers, located at 20 Broadway and 308 Clinton Avenue (845/331-7517 or 800/331-1518, www.ci.kingston.ny.us; Mon.–Fri. 9 A.M.–5 P.M., also May–Oct. weekends 11 A.M.–5 P.M.) can provide information about Kingston's past and present. This is the place to pick up brochures, maps, and schedules of events.

Alternatively, look for the Kingston Tourism Caboose in the traffic circle off I-87 Exit 19 (845/340-3766). In Saugerties, stop by the McDonald's on Route 212, I-87 Exit 20 (845/246-5816). A tourist information center at Belleayre Mountain also has a wealth of information for travelers (800/431-4555, www.belleayre.com).

GETTING THERE AND AROUND
By Bus

Ulster County Area Transit serves major towns and rural areas across the county (845/340-3333). Routes and schedules are available online at www.co.ulster.ny.us/ucat. In addition, Adirondack Trailways (800/858-8555) runs connector services to and from other destinations in the region.

Kingston has its own reliable public transportation system called CiTiBus (845/331-3725, www.ci.kingston.ny.us/CityGovt/Agencies.html#Citibus; $.75), with three city routes. The closest train station is at Rhinecliff directly across the Hudson River.

By Car

Car rentals can be found at the Stewart and Albany airports. Blue Mountain Limousine is another way to get to and from the airport (845/246-4404). Taxis are also available at the airports, bus terminals, and at the Rhinecliff train station. Kingston gets congested by Ulster County standards, and the narrow streets downtown can be disorienting. But with a little patience, it's easy enough to find your way around.

The Mid-Hudson

The Western Catskills

Health spas and yoga retreats have replaced yesterday's summer boarding houses in the western Catskill region. Although sleepy Sullivan and Delaware Counties do not directly border the Hudson River, they make a natural extension to many Hudson Valley itineraries. Here, the slopes of the Catskill Mountains fade into dairy farms, historic covered bridges, and newer second-home communities. Hundreds of lakes and streams entertain anglers and bird-watchers alike.

© PAUL ITOI

Must-Sees

Look for **M** to find the sights and activities you can't miss and **M** for the best dining and lodging.

M Sivananda Ashram Yoga Ranch: A retreat at this secluded country yoga center includes time for contemplation and relaxation, as well as daily yoga practice. Sign up for a single class, a weekend retreat, or a month-long teacher-training program. Nature trails meander across the wooded property, and meals come from an organic garden onsite (page 115).

angling outside the Catskill Fly Fishing Center

M Catskill Fly Fishing Center and Museum: Located in the heart of some of the country's best fly-fishing, the museum celebrates the art and sport of the catch (page 117).

M Roscoe: They call it Trout Town U.S.A. for a good reason. A haven for anglers and outdoor enthusiasts of all kinds, Roscoe lies at the junction of the Beaverkill and Willowemoc Rivers, on land that provoked many a battle between the Iroquois and Algonquin nations (page 117).

M Upper Delaware Scenic and Recreational River: This winding stretch of Route 97 begins near the Orange/Sullivan county line and leads to breathtaking views of New York, Pennsylvania, and the Delaware River (page 118).

M Andes: Northeast of the Peptacon Reservoir lies the upland village of Andes, where in 1845 Moses Earle and a group of local farmers refused to pay overdue rents to protest the feudal system of land ownership (page 127).

M Catskill Scenic Trail: This 19-mile rail trail begins in Grand Gorge off Route 23 and runs west to Bloomsville (page 128).

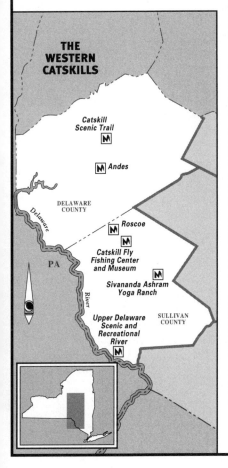

THE WESTERN CATSKILLS

Catskill Scenic Trail **M**

M Andes

DELAWARE COUNTY

M Roscoe
M
Catskill Fly Fishing Center and Museum

PA

M
Sivananda Ashram Yoga Ranch

Upper Delaware Scenic and Recreational River
M

SULLIVAN COUNTY

The Western Catskills

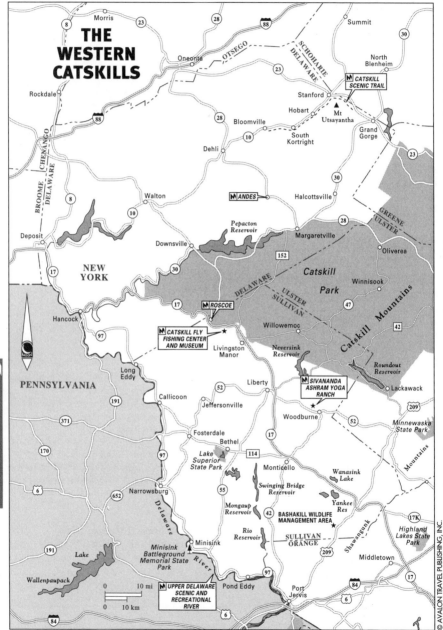

THE
WESTERN
CATSKILLS

Morris

Rockdale

Oneonta

Bloomville

Dehli

Walton

Downsville

NEW
YORK

Hancock

Deposit

PENNSYLVANIA

Long
Eddy

Callicoon

Jeffersonville

Fosterdale

Bethel

Narrowsburg

Minisink
Battleground
Memorial State
Park

Minisink

Wallenpaupack

Lake

Summit

North
Blenheim

Stanford

Hobart

South
Kortright

Mt
Utsayantha

Grand
Gorge

[M] CATSKILL
SCENIC TRAIL

[M] ANDES

Halcottsville

Pepacton
Reservoir

Margaretville

Oliverea

Catskill
Park

Winnisook

[M] ROSCOE

[M] CATSKILL FLY
FISHING CENTER
AND MUSEUM

Livingston
Manor

Willowemoc

Neversink
Reservoir

Roundout
Reservoir

Liberty

[M] SIVANANDA
ASHRAM YOGA
RANCH

Lackawack

Woodburne

Minnewaska
State Park

Monticello

Wanasink
Lake

Lake
Superior
State Park

Swinging Bridge
Reservoir

Yankee
Res

Mongaup
Reservoir

BASHAKILL WILDLIFE
MANAGEMENT AREA

Highland
Lakes State
Park

Rio
Reservoir

SULLIVAN
ORANGE

Middletown

Lake

Pond Eddy

Port
Jervis

[M] UPPER DELAWARE
SCENIC AND
RECREATIONAL
RIVER

Delaware River

BROOME
CHENANGO
DELAWARE

OTSEGO

SCHOHARIE
DELAWARE

DELAWARE

ULSTER
SULLIVAN

GREENE
ULSTER

Catskill Mountains

Mountains

Shawangunk

MOON

The Western Catskills

© AVALON TRAVEL PUBLISHING, INC.

0   10 mi

0   10 km

PLANNING YOUR TIME

The busiest seasons in the western Catskills correspond to peak fishing conditions: April–June and September–October. In July and August, many inns fill with parents visiting their children at local summer camps. Hunters arrive in November, and most towns are quiet January–March.

It takes less than an hour to drive the length of the Quickway (Route 17) from Wurtsboro to Rockland, but there are many back roads to explore along the way. A weekend stay allows time for both sightseeing and recreation. Most Sullivan County itineraries center on a specific activity, such as fishing, yoga, or antique shopping. Head here to enjoy the serenity of a quiet morning on the Beaverkill or to visit a selection of the three-dozen shops along the Sullivan County Antiques Trail.

Popular itineraries in Delaware County include self-guided barn and farm stand tours, day-long bike rides, and multiday hikes and canoe trips. No major highways cross the county, and it takes about three hours to drive the perimeter. Add a half-day stop to pick your own fresh berries or bid on rare antiques in a country auction.

Sullivan County

Home to many of the family resorts that made the Catskills famous during the early to mid-20th century, Sullivan County stretches from the Orange and Ulster county lines in the east to the Delaware River and state of Pennsylvania to the west, covering a total area of about 1,000 square miles. The northern part of Sullivan County lies within the Catskill Preserve, but the terrain is more hilly than mountainous, with many of the same exposed rock ledges that characterize other parts of the Catskill region.

With a low population density (though not as low as Delaware County), Sullivan County supports a diverse ecosystem, including a growing number of bald eagles that make an annual winter appearance. Abundant trout in two famous rivers, the Willowemoc and Beaverkill, attract diehard fly fishers, while two large reservoirs at Neversink and Rondout send freshwater to New York City, 90 miles to the southeast. Despite its outdoor treasures, Sullivan County is best known as the site of the original 1969 Woodstock Music Festival, a three-day extravaganza that took place in the town of Bethel.

Sullivan County separated from Ulster County in 1809, borrowing its name from the controversial Revolutionary War General John Sullivan. In 1779, Sullivan led a devastating attack against the remaining Native American settlements in New York and Pennsylvania. He later became the first governor of New Hampshire.

Early Dutch settlers in Sullivan County built tanneries, bluestone quarries, sawmills, and gristmills to compensate for the lack of arable land. Irish and German immigrants later arrived to build a canal and two railroads connecting Pennsylvania and its stores of natural resources to New York City. Novelist and local resident Stephen Crane popularized Sullivan County in the 1890s with a series of *Sullivan County Sketches*. Around 1900, the Jewish Agricultural Society began to encourage Jewish farmers to move to Sullivan County from New York City. But when the new residents found the land difficult to farm, they supplemented their income by turning their farmhouses into boarding houses. Thus began the Borsch Belt and its history of famous resort hotels, most of which have faded into history.

Today, Sullivan County consists of 15 townships and no large cities. Monticello is the county seat.

ALONG THE QUICKWAY

Wurtsboro

Real estate values are climbing here as people move in from suburban areas to the east and south, but Wurtsboro still moves at the comfortably slow pace of a rural community. A string of inviting shops and cafés lines a two-block stretch of Sullivan Street, off Route 209.

The Western Catskills

© PAUL ITOI

Wurtsboro Airport hangar

Aviation enthusiasts will want to meet the pilots at the family-run **Wurtsboro Airport** (Rte. 209, Wurtsboro, 845/888-2791; daily 9 A.M.–5 P.M.), one of the oldest soaring sites in the country. A low ridge of the Catskills passes through the town, creating the ideal updraft for flying sans motor. In fact, pilots have soared as far as Georgia in one day from this tiny airstrip. A sailplane ride begins with an exhilarating tow on the runway. Most flights pass over the **Bashakill Wildlife Management Area** (Rte. 209 South, Westbrookville) outside of town, a prime location for viewing bald eagles. The airport is located on Route 209, two miles north of town. Call to schedule a tour or lesson.

Monticello

Sullivan County's largest township and government headquarters, Monticello is the next major stop on the Quickway. Many of the storefronts along Broadway are showing signs of age and neglect, but the imposing **Sullivan County Court-** **house** (414 Broadway, Monticello), made of sandstone in 1909, is a notable exception. Aside from a handful of food and gas options, the only attractions that call for a longer stop are the **Monticello Raceway** (Rtes. 17 & 17B, Monticello, www.monticello-raceway.com) and the **Mighty M Gaming Casino** (204 Rte. 17B, Monticello, 866/777-GAME or 866/777-4263, www.monticelloraceway.com), which opened in June 2004. Its investors battled authorities for several decades to secure permission to open the casino. At launch time, local residents expected the casino to draw thousands of new visitors each day.

For rail travelers, Monticello is located a half hour from the Middletown train station on the Port Jervis Line. Several hotels provide transportation to the racetrack. Take Exit 104 off Route 17.

Kiamesha Lake and Fallsburg

Follow Route 42 northeast out of Monticello to reach Kiamesha Lake, a popular fishing destina-

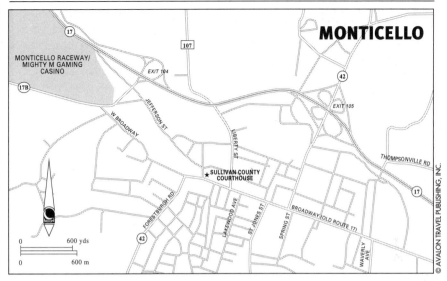

tion, where smallmouth bass, perch, and pan-fish are the most common catches. The lakeside **Concord Resort & Golf Club** (Concord Rd., Kiamesha Lake, 888/448-9686, www.concord-resort.com) is undergoing a $500 million facelift that began in 2000. The new property is de-signed to draw business conventions and full-time residents. In the meantime, golfers can stay in one of a few rooms that have been kept open.

At the **Shree Muktananda Ashram** (371 Brickman Rd., South Fallsburg, 845/434-2000, ext. 2202, www.siddhayoga.org/shree-muk-tananda-ashram.html; opens daily 9 A.M.), in the next town over, students of Siddha yoga con-gregate for a healthy dose of spiritual develop-ment and renewal. In recent decades, the center has turned three abandoned hotels into a vibrant community. Day visitors are welcome to partic-ipate in meditations, hatha yoga classes, and meals. A large temple dedicated to Bhagawan Nityananda, spiritual founder of the Siddha yoga discipline, is also open to the public. If you visit the grounds, respect the modest dress code and quiet atmosphere of the center.

Continuing along Route 42, the weathered buildings that line the streets of Fallsburg were once rows of pristine stucco hotels drawing visi-tors all the way from the Atlantic coast. Tough times have lingered in the area since the advent of air conditioning and airplane travel, and the largest employers are now three county prisons in neighboring Woodbourne. That said, local resi-dents are taking steps to revive their quiet town. The unsightly remains of hotels and bungalows abandoned long ago are gradually disappearing. And a new overlook at the Neversink River offers visitors a place to enjoy the falls that provided waterpower for the mills and tanneries that sus-tained the town in its earlier days.

Sivananda Ashram Yoga Ranch

Every Friday after work, a group of harried city dwellers gathers at a busy yoga center in Manhat-tan for a ride to a weekend escape at the Sivananda Ashram Yoga Ranch (Budd Rd., Woodbourne, 845/436-6492, www.sivananda.org/ranch) in northern Sullivan County. Unlike other adven-ture-filled vacations, a getaway here promises ample time for relaxing and rejuvenating.

Located 12 miles north of Monticello in Wood-bourne, the yoga center occupies 77 acres of se-cluded countryside. Wooded areas surround open lawns and a pond. Guests can participate in a single class, a weekend retreat, or a month-long

The Western Catskills

teacher-training program. The day begins with breathing and meditation exercises. Asana sessions take place at 8 A.M. and 4 P.M. daily. After yoga practice, guests can walk the nature trails or enjoy the wood-fired sauna. Volunteers prepare meals from a large organic garden and greenhouse. Accommodations are shared rooms in either a turn-of-the-20th-century farmhouse or a 1920s-era hotel. Camping is also allowed. Call ahead for transportation from the bus terminal in Woodbourne. Rates are $65–70 per night, $50 full day, $25 half day, and $12 for one class.

Hurleyville

Route 104 out of Monticello leads to Hurleyville, where you can take a walk through history at the **Sullivan County Historical Society Museum** (265 Main St., Hurleyville, 845/434-8044; Sat. 10 A.M.–4:30 P.M., Sun. 1–4:30 P.M.) Built in 1912, the building housed the Hurleyville Schoolhouse until 1945. Exhibits include a vintage general store and post office, as well as a collection of textiles from the turn of the 20th century.

Route 17B to Bethel

Dairy farmer Max Yasgur put the unassuming town of Bethel in the global spotlight when he agreed to host the 1969 Woodstock Music Festival—a soggy, three-day extravaganza that turned green pastures to slop, private homes into soup kitchens, and schools into makeshift hospitals.

The idea for a rock concert near Bob Dylan's home in Woodstock began as a late-night conversation in a Manhattan apartment and became within a few short months the largest music event in history. Hundreds of thousands attended, among them Ken Kesey and the Merry Pranksters from California. They grooved to the hottest sounds of the day, including Jefferson Airplane, Credence Clearwater Revival, The Who, The Grateful Dead, and the closing act, Jimi Hendrix. Cars en route to Bethel jammed the New York Thruway and created a 10-mile backup a full day before the event began.

A simple stone marker on Hurd Road off Route 17B commemorates the event. Cable TV executive Alan Gerry purchased the former **Yasgur Farm** in the late '90s and announced plans to

invest $46 million to create the Bethel Woods Performing Art Center, featuring a 4,000-seat outdoor pavilion and 650-seat theater. After a long legal battle, the Gerry Foundation broke ground in the summer of 2004 and announced that the New York Philharmonic would open the inaugural season in 2006. Local residents speculate that Bethel Woods may become the philharmonic's permanent summer home, cementing its name in the music hall of fame.

Liberty to Livingston Manor

Back on the Quickway, Liberty's town center has a few antique shops and a Greek Revival Methodist church. To the east, the **Neversink Reservoir** (Neversink, 845/985-2524), completed in 1953, holds 34.9 billion gallons of water and covers 93 square miles in the northeastern corner of Sullivan County. Its northern section lies within the Catskill State Park. The reservoir is open to fishing for brown trout, smallmouth bass, pickerel, panfish, and landlocked salmon. Follow Route 16 east from the Quickway.

Beyond Neversink, the privately owned **Grahamsville Historic District** (Rte. 55, Grahamsville) on State Route 55 consists of six Gothic Revival, Italianate, and Greek Revival structures on 200 acres. Outside of town, the **Kalonymus Escarpment,** a National Natural Landmark created by glacial activity, may pique the interest of amateur geologists. The **Rondout Reservoir** in Grahamsville is an observation point for bald eagles.

East of the Quickway along Route 82 lies the hamlet of DeBruce, where New York State operates one of its 12 fish hatcheries. The **Catskill Hatchery** specializes in raising brown trout. Some 115,000 pounds of fingerlings and yearlings leave the hatchery each year, from a base of two million eggs. The state places the trout in rivers, streams, lakes, and ponds to support recreational fishing and to restore native species to damaged environments.

Aside from the flurry of renovations under way in its town center, Livingston Manor might still be the kind of place where the milk arrives daily at your doorstep. During the railroad era, the town once known as Purvis had the only Y-

THE NEW YORK CITY WATERSHED

New York City consumes 1.3 billion gallons of water a day, and most of it comes from reservoirs in the Catskill Region. The massive watershed is the largest unfiltered surface water supply anywhere in the world.

Reservoir	Capacity (billion gallons)
Croton System (1842)	86.6
Ashokan Reservoir (1915)	22.9
Schoharie Reservoir (1928)	17.6
Rondout Reservoir (1950)	9.6
Neversink Reservoir (1954)	34.9
Pepacton Reservoir (1955)	140.2
Cannonsville Reservoir (1964)	95.7

Reservoir permits are free but required in order to fish. Rowboats are allowed, but motorboats are not. Camping is also not allowed.

shaped track in the area for turning trains around. The town became a transportation hub as a result. A pair of wagon wheels marks the beginning of Main Street, and the swift-flowing Willowemoc Creek runs parallel to it, with an attractive schoolhouse on the opposite shore. Fly-fishing conditions are just about ideal here, and every other storefront sells fishing gear.

These days, Livingston Manor is a town in transition. A group of progressive investors out of New York City recently purchased several buildings in an effort to turn the town into a vibrant community for the arts. Although the investment brings the prospect of new jobs, some locals bristle at the threat of change.

Catskill Fly Fishing Center and Museum

A few miles farther up the Willowemoc is the Catskill Fly Fishing Center and Museum (1031 Old Rte. 17, Livingston Manor, 845/439-4810, flyfish@catskill.net, www.cffcm.org; Sat.–Mon. 10 A.M.–4 P.M., Tues.–Fri. 10 A.M.–1 P.M.), a beautiful facility on 55 acres. A one-lane wooden bridge leads to the parking lot, and

you can often see fly fishers casting right in front of the museum.

These waters were the stomping ground of the late Lee Wulff, celebrated angler, conservationist, and writer. His words appear on a plaque inside the museum: "Over my many years of fishing, I have learned that angling's problems are never solved. They rise anew with each new pool and each new day. Fishing, especially fly fishing, has problems, solutions, challenges and rewards, which have always captured my imagination and stimulated my creativity." His wife, Joan Wulff, continues to run the **Wulff School of Fly Fishing** (Lewbeach, 800/328-3638, www.royalwulff.com) nearby in Roscoe.

The exhibits in this well-funded museum will interest most outdoor enthusiasts, whether or not they care to learn how to tie a fly. Vintage rods and reels depict the sport in its early days. A wall of materials used in tying flies includes fox hair and a rare feather that comes from specially bred chickens. An old fashioned Cortland line-braiding machine in the back corner still works.

Watch the pros tie their delicate flies on Saturdays April–October. The center offers courses on stream ecology and angling, fly tying, and rod building. A blue sign on the west side of Old Route 17 marks the entrance to the center.

Covered Bridges

Most visitors enjoy crossing Sullivan County's rivers, even if they don't want to catch the fish that live in them. Early settlers in the area constructed bridges over the Beaverkill and Willowemoc using native hemlock trees, and three historic covered bridges have survived to the present day: **Covered Bridge State Park** (Livingston Manor) outside of Livingston Manor, **Beaverkill State Park** in Lewbeach (Route 154), and Willowemoc (Route 84). When he wasn't performing in New York City, composer Irving Berlin lived and wrote music in the hamlet of Lewbeach, beginning in 1938. Former CBS anchorman Dan Rather reportedly owns property in Beaverkill.

Roscoe

The land around Roscoe, at the western edge of Sullivan County, once marked the disputed border between the Iroquois and Algonquin nations. Today the town is better known as a haven for anglers and outdoor enthusiasts, and store owners kindly ask patrons to leave their studded wading shoes at the door. The Beaverkill and Willowemoc Rivers meet in Roscoe, a.k.a. Trout Town U.S.A., at a place called Junction Pool, which is recognized as the birthplace of dry fly casting. Opening day of trout season (April 1) draws a crowd of fishing enthusiasts each year, from distinguished instructors and fly tyers to renowned New York City chefs.

More developed than the surrounding hamlets, Roscoe has a number of reputable tackle shops, inns, and restaurants, most of them in a row along Stewart Street. Shortline Bus offers weekend packages to Roscoe from Port Authority in New York City.

If you go, check out the **Roscoe Ontario & Western Railway Museum** (Roscoe, 607/498-4346, www.nyow.org/museum.html), which features a restored red caboose, the town's original trout weathervane and train signal, and the Cooks Falls and Roscoe watchman's shanties. The museum facade is built of materials from a local station. Inside is an impressive collection of railroad and fly-fishing memorabilia.

ALONG THE DELAWARE— ROUTE 97

Upper Delaware Scenic and Recreational River

Exit 53 off I-84 puts you at the intersection of Route 97 and the start of the Upper Delaware Scenic and Recreational River (www.upper-delaware.com), a national park that extends 73 miles from the New York/New Jersey state line through Sullivan County and into the southern part of Delaware County. It takes about three hours to drive the length of the park.

Conceived in the early 1930s as a scenic and commercial route, Route 97 connects Port Jervis in Orange County to Hancock in Delaware County, with the majority of the highway running through Sullivan County. This winding road is New York's equivalent to the West Coast's Highway 1. It climbs over hills and crosses ravines, featuring many turnouts and picnic areas

along the way. Route 97 enters Sullivan County at Mongaup, just after the Hawk's Nest section of the road in Orange County. Brown Scenic Byway signs, depicting a river and road with green on both sides, were installed in 2004.

At 410 miles in length, the Delaware is the longest free-flowing river in the northeast. Its East Branch originates in the natural springs of the Catskills, while the West Branch begins in Schoharie County, near Pennsylvania. The rocky terrain of the western Catskills forms Class I and Class II rapids along some stretches. Before the era of rail travel, the Delaware and Hudson Canal served as a vital connection between the two commercial rivers. For anglers, the Delaware is home to scores of trout, bass, walleye, eel, and shad.

Take a detour from Route 97 at the town of Pond Eddy (Route 41), about five miles past the Hawk's Nest, to head north to Glen Spey and the **St. Volodymyr Ukrainian Church** (Glen Spey, 845/856-5500). Like its counterpart in Greene County, this architectural wonder was built without a single nail.

Minisink Ford

Sullivan County's only Revolutionary War skirmish took place at Minisink Ford in July of 1779, when a group of 120 colonists were defeated by a combined force of Native American and Tory soldiers. Today, the site is listed on the National Register of Historic Places. **Minisink Battleground Memorial State Park** (County Rd. 168, Minisink Ford; opens daily 8 A.M.) encompasses 57 acres of woodlands, with walking trails and an interpretive center that recounts both the political and the natural history of the site.

Also at Minisink Ford is the oldest suspension bridge in the U.S., the Delaware Aqueduct or **Roebling Bridge**. Built by John A. Roebling, the same engineer who designed the Brooklyn Bridge, this historic bridge dates back to 1848, when it was constructed to support the Delaware and Hudson Canal. Though the bridge has been converted to carry cars instead of coal, the original cables still hold it in place.

The Eagle Institute

Although winter is not the most popular season

to visit the Delaware River, it is the best time to catch once-endangered bald eagles in action. A small group of eagles are year-round residents along the Delaware, while a larger population migrates from Canada, spending mid-December through mid-March in the warmer climate.

The nonprofit **Eagle Institute** (Rte. 97, Barryville, 845/557-6162, www.eagleinstitute.org), based in Barryville, runs guided field trips and other educational programs. Popular observation points include: **Mongaup Falls Reservoir** (Forestburgh), off Route 42 (not to be confused with Mongaup Pond in northeastern Sullivan County) and **Rio Reservoir** in Forestburgh. Novelist Stephen Crane reportedly penned *The Red Badge of Courage* from his cabin in nearby Forestburg.

Narrowsburg

The Delaware River reaches its deepest point, 113 feet, at Narrowsburg, where the earliest colonial settlers arrived in the 1770s, during the French and Indian War. The **Fort Delaware Museum of Colonial History** (Rte. 97, Forestburgh, 845/252-6660; Sat.–Sun. 10 A.M.–5:30 P.M.), run by the New York State Department of Education, recreates the pioneers' way of life and is a popular destination for local school children. Over the years, Narrowsburg has developed a vibrant community of artists and a number of cultural attractions. Several art galleries and theaters draw year-round visitors.

From Narrowsburgh, Route 52 leads away from the river toward Cocheton Center, Kenoza Lake, Jeffersonville, and eventually Liberty. Along the way is a historic bridge that's made of stone instead of timber. While many covered bridges have been preserved, the only original stone bridge with three arches remaining in the U.S. crosses the Callicoon Creek in the town of Kenoza Lake. It was built in 1872 and is now known as **Stone Arch Bridge Historic Park** (Rtes. 52 & 52A, Kenoza Lake).

Hanging geraniums and crisp new American flags greet visitors on Main Street in Jeffersonville, the next town along Route 52. Settlement here coincided with the arrival of the New York and Erie Railroad in the 1830s, but a fire destroyed most of the original buildings in 1918. A

number of Victorians have been recently restored, including one that houses the **The Blue Victorian** (4874 Main St., Jeffersonville, 845/482-5544, www.thebluevictorian.com; Fri.–Mon. 10 A.M.–5 P.M.) art gallery at the intersection of Route 52 and Maple Avenue. The heiress of the Hearst family fortune, Patty Hearst, spent part of her famous 1974 captivity in the Jeffersonville home of Symbionese Liberation Army accomplice Nicki Scott.

Callicoon

If you stay on Route 97 and continue north toward Delaware County, you'll reach the hamlet of Callicoon (Wild Turkey), where the only remaining single-screen movie theater in Sullivan County, built in 1948, is still open for business. Although it was first settled in the 1600s, no building here is older than 1888 because of a fire that leveled the town.

SPORTS AND RECREATION
Winter Sports

Sullivan County has one small downhill ski area that's ideal for youngsters, or anyone who's just starting to get the hang of the sport. **Holiday Mountain** (99 Holiday Mountain Rd., Monticello, 845/796-3161, www.holidaymtn.com) in Monticello has snowmaking facilities to cover all 14 of its trails.

For Nordic skiers, many of Sullivan County's hotels and inns maintain their own trails. The towns of Fallsburg, Liberty, and Thompson open trails to the public. Ice fishing and snowmobiling are also popular winter activities.

Hiking

For many years, the 108-mile-long D&H Canal carried coal, cement, bluestone, and other industrial materials from Pennsylvania to New York City. Built by Irish and German immigrants over the course of three years, the canal played an instrumental role in the growth and development of the Atlantic seaboard. The advent of the railroad retired the canal from service, but today you can walk, bike, or ski some 20 miles of it. The restored sections, however, are not yet all connected.

Willowemoc Wild Forest, in the southwest

corner of the Catskill Preserve, is another good place to get away from it all. Located 18 miles north of Liberty and nine miles northeast of Livingston Manor, its 14,800 "forever wild" acres include trails maintained for hiking, skiing, biking, and snowmobiling. About 15 miles of paths are reserved for hikers only. The terrain is gentle, with rolling hills instead of tall peaks. Four trailheads departing from Neversink and Rockland have parking nearby. Campfires and primitive camping are allowed, but there are no facilities.

Privately run **Eldred Preserve** (1040 Rte. 55, Eldred, 845/557-8316, www.eldredpreserve.com) is a year-round fishing and hunting resort on 3,000 acres off Route 55. Facilities include three stocked fishing ponds and a sporting-clay range, and the resort runs fishing tournaments in summer. Services include guided trips, corporate events, a pro shop, and motel-style accommodations in log-cabin buildings.

The National Park Service maintains the challenging three-mile **Tusten Mountain Trail,** near the Ten Mile River, off Route 97 between Barryville and Narrowsburg. The route reaches 1,100 feet at its highest point.

Mountain Biking and Road Riding

The **Bicycle Club of Sullivan County** (845/794-3000, ext. 5010) and **Mike Fraysee's Sports Resort** (573 High Rd., Eldred, 800/994-3335, www.mikefrayssesports.com) offer guided cycling tours.

Golf

Sullivan County offers several championship golf courses with moderate green fees and inspiring views of the Catskills. The 7,650-yard, world-class course at the Concord Golf Resort ranks among the best courses in the country, according to Golf Digest (Concord Rd., Kiamesha Lake, 888/448-9686, www.concordresort.com; weekends $65, weekdays $45).

Swimming and Boating

Mongaup Pond is actually a 12-acre lake, the largest body of water inside the Catskill State Park that is not a New York City reservoir. A variety of fish live in the lake, and visitors can swim,

fish, and paddle in its refreshing waters. Boat rentals are available through the Mongaup Pond State Campground (Exit 96 off Rte. 17, DeBruce, 845/439-4233; daily fee $14). Camping is permitted mid-May–Columbus Day.

For a day at the beach, head to 1,400-acre **Lake Superior State Park** (Rte. 55, Bethel).

Several outfitters run trips along the Delaware: **Kittatinny Canoes** (Rte. 97, Barryville, 800/FLOAT-KC or 800/356-2852, www.kittatinny.com; daily 8 A.M.–5 P.M.) has canoes, rafts, kayaks, and tubes for trips ranging from calm to white water. **Whitewater Willie's** (Rte. 97, Pond Eddy, 800/233-RAFT or 800/233-7238, www.whitewaterwillies.com; Apr.–Sept. 30) is another reputable operation with reasonable prices.

Fishing and Hunting

Fly-fishing was first introduced to the U.S. in Sullivan County, and the tradition draws a majority of Sullivan County visitors today. You can learn to tie flies at one of several area schools, such as the renowned Wulff School of Fly Fishing. Or drop in for a workshop at the Catskill Museum of Fly Fishing. Trout season opens April 1, and the shad run peaks in May on the Delaware River. In addition, the county and state stock hundreds of lakes and streams. The **Beaverkill Angler** (Main St., Roscoe, daily 8:30 A.M.–5 P.M.) has everything you need for a day of casting in the river. Leave your studded shoes at the door.

Guides and gear are available at a number of additional operations in Trout Town U.S.A.: **Catskill Flies Fly Shop & Fishing Adventures** (6 Stewart Ave., Roscoe, 607/498-6146) leads trips and rents equipment. You can sleep and fish with **Baxter House B&B and River Outfitters** (Old Rte. 17, Roscoe, 607/498-5811, www.baxterhouse.net). A half day of wade fishing runs $175 for one or two people, full day $245. Driftboat trips are $200 half day and $295 full day. Modest accommodations are available in six recently renovated rooms ($45–125).

Local fisherman Anthony Ritter runs driftboat trips along the Upper Delaware River through **Gone Fishing Guide Service** (20 Lake St., Narrowsburg, 845/252-3657, www.gonefishing-gs

© PAUL ITOI

river view outside the Catskill Fly Fishing Museum

.com; Apr.–Nov. daily). Catches include shad, trout, smallmouth bass, and walleye.

Aviation
Learn to fly (with or without an engine), or just take an aerial tour at the private **Wurtsboro Airport** (Rte. 209, Wurtsboro, 845/888-2791; daily 9 A.M.–5 P.M.). There are grass and paved runways. A taxi service is available for rides into town. Other local facilities include Monticello Airport and Sullivan County International Airport.

ACCOMMODATIONS
Under $100
N The Reynolds House (1934 Old Rte. 17, Roscoe, 607/498-4422, www.reynoldshouse-inn.com; $75) is an excellent value option for cozy accommodations in a central location. Each room in this three-story inn has a private bath with a very small shower. Dark wood and floral prints define the look and feel. The breakfast room has a fireplace and kitchenette. The inn

caters to hunters and fishers, as well as parents of children at local summer camps.

Just off Route 97, near an eddy in the Delaware River, the **Narrowsburg Inn** (182 Bridge St., Narrowsburg, 845/252-7247, www.narrows-burginn.com; $65–135) has been in business since 1840. Current owners Tom and Rose Prendergast took over in 1996. Seven basic guestrooms share three baths, and one suite has a private bath.

The five-acre meadow surrounding the **Old House on a Hill** (295 Lt. Brender Hwy., Ferndale, 845/292-3554, www.oldhouseonahill.com; $75–105) invites guests to read a book and enjoy the summer breeze from a weathered Adirondack chair. Once the servants' quarters for a large hotel complex, the 1860 farmhouse has been restored as a B&B that serves a European-style breakfast. Original wainscoting from floor to ceiling makes the four guestrooms dark, but light-colored linens help to compensate.

$100–150
As a hundred-year-old boarding house, **Sunrise**

The Western Catskills

House B&B (193 North Branch Rd., Jefferson-ville, 845/482-3778, www.sunrisehousebandb .com; Apr.–Dec.; $125) has four comfortable rooms on a 45-acre property.

$150–200
Another Jeffersonville option is **Griffin House** (178 Maple Ave., Jeffersonville, 845/482-3371, www.griffin-house.com; $139–159) in a large Victorian. A six-course gourmet dinner is available with advance reservation.

Villa Roma (356 Villa Roma Rd., Callicoon, 845/887-4880 or 800/533-6767, www.vil-laroma.com; Apr. 1–Jan. 1), a resort and conference center, manages to blend some of the old-fashioned Catskill resort flavor with a host of modern amenities. A variety of vacation packages include meals and entertainment as well as accommodations.

Over $200
Enjoy a peaceful getaway beside a private lake at the **Inn at Lake Joseph** (400 Saint Joseph Rd., Forestburgh, 845/791-9506, www.lake-joseph.com; up to $310). Its gorgeous Redwood room has 18-foot ceilings, and the newly completed Tudor room has high ceilings and a deck with over 700 square feet of living space.

Campgrounds
Beaverkill Campground (Berrybrook Rd., Roscoe, 845/439-4281; mid-May–Labor Day; $15) has 108 sites along the Beaverkill with hot showers. On the Delaware, **Indianhead Campground** (Barryville, 800/874-2628, www.indi-anheadcanoes.com; $11 per person) has wooded campsites with fire rings, right next to the river.

FOOD
While not as sophisticated as the cuisine found closer to the Hudson, Sullivan County has a few good standbys for hearty country cooking.

Along the Quickway
Catch a Willowemoc trout and have it prepared at **Ianine's** (982 DeBruce Rd., DeBruce, 845/439-3900, www.debrucecountryinn.com;

The Potager, Wurtsboro

daily 8 A.M.–10 A.M.; 7–10 P.M.) inside the De-Bruce Country Inn.

Wurtsboro has several tempting places for nourishment. The friendly ⚑ **Uncommon Grounds** café (108 Sullivan St., Wurtsboro, 845/888-2121, www.ugcoffee.com) makes a legitimate iced coffee and features evening jazz for a $5 cover. A few doors up the street, **The Potager** (116 Sullivan St., Wurtsboro, 845/888-4086, www.thepotager.com) is a bright yellow Victorian set back from the road. Inside are a large garden center and café.

In Livingston Manor, **Papa Tony's Tree Hut** (Old Rte. 17, Livingston Manor, 845/439-4611) will treat you right with a hearty meatball sub or slice of pizza. And **Bel Villaggio** (64 Stewart Ave, Roscoe, 607/498-9920, www.belvillaggio.com; opens Wed.–Mon. 11 A.M.) ranks as one of the finest eateries in Roscoe. Tables are set with a bottle of wine in true northern Italian style. Outdoor seating is a plus.

Along the Delaware—Route 97
Order breakfast all day at the **Whistle Stop Café**

(119 Kirk Rd., Narrowsburg, 845/252-3355; Sun.–Thurs. 6:30 A.M.–8 P.M., Fri.–Sat. 6:30 A.M.–9 P.M.). The dining room at family-oriented **Lander's River Café** (A. Dorrer Dr., Narrowsburg, 845/887-6800; daily 7 A.M.–9 P.M.) overlooks the Delaware River. Next to the Landers Motel, **Fandrews Restaurant** (Rte. 97, Narrowsburg, 845/252-3566; daily 11 A.M.–10 P.M.) has a menu of burgers, soups, and salads.

The Narrowsburg Inn (182 Bridge St., Narrowsburg, 845/252-7247, www.narrowsburginn.com; summer Wed.–Sun., spring and fall Sat.–Sun.) offers a menu of tavern staples.

Chef Michael Werneke cooks New American fare at **Michael's Delaware Valley Grill** (Glen Spey, 845/856-6900; Mon.–Thurs. 5:30–10 P.M., Fri.–Sat. 5–11 P.M., Sun. 4–9 P.M.).

Callicoon boasts the most upscale dining in Sullivan County. Filet mignon with bourbon sauce and blackened yellowfin tuna anchor a menu of country-style entrees at **The 1906 Restaurant** (41 Lower Main St., Callicoon, 845/887-1906, www.1906restaurant.com; daily 5–10 P.M.; mains $14–27). Booth seating and a notable wine list complete the dining experience. **The Club at Villa Roma** (356 Villa Roma Rd., Callicoon, 845/887-4880 or 800/533-6767, www.villaroma.com; Apr. 1–Jan. 1) serves Italian American cuisine in a pleasant dining room with views of the resort's golf course. And **Matthew's on Main** (19 Lower Main St., Callicoon, 845/887-5636; summer daily 11 A.M.–10 P.M.; winter, spring, fall Thurs.–Tues. 11 A.M.–10 P.M.) has outdoor tables with a view of the Delaware River.

River views are a draw at **Eagle's Nest Restaurant** (58 Eagle's Nest Rd., Bloomingburg, 845/733-4561; Apr.–Dec. Wed., Thurs., Sun. 5:30–9 P.M.). **Grech's Millbrook Inn** (1774 Rte. 97, North Pond Eddy, 845/856-7778) is known for German specialties. Healthy foods abound at the **East Ridge Organic Diner & Country Store** (10770 Rte. 97, Hankins, 845/887-5751; daily 7 A.M.–9 P.M.).

Stella's (4879 Main St., Jeffersonville, 845/482-9532; lunch Wed.–Fri. 11:30 A.M.–2:30 P.M., Sat.–Sun. 11:30 A.M.–2 P.M.; dinner Wed., Thurs., Sun. 5 P.M.–9 P.M., Fri.–Sat.) opened for business in 2004 with a menu that features regional cuisine made of foods from local farms. The setting is a restored building that overlooks the Callicoon Creek.

ENTERTAINMENT AND EVENTS
Bars and Nightlife
The newest attraction in Sullivan County is the **Mighty M Gaming Casino** (204 Rte. 17B, Monticello, 866/777-4263, www.monticelloraceway.com), which opened in June 2004 at the Monticello Raceway.

Festivals
The ultimate place to celebrate opening day of the trout season is the Junction Pool in Roscoe. Crowds of locals and fly-fishing enthusiasts gather on the often icy rocks to watch celebrity "first casters" kick off the season. The annual Two-Headed Trout Dinner is held Saturday night at the Rockland House. Another annual outdoor event is **Eaglefest** (School Auditorium, Narrowsburg, 845/252-7409, www.narrowsburg.org), timed to coincide with the bald eagle migration from Canada in January.

SHOPPING
Sullivan County shops carry antiques and a wide variety of handmade country goods, from marmalade to greeting cards. **Canal Towne Emporium** (107 Sullivan St., Wurtsboro, 800/882-6552, www.canaltowne.com; daily 10 A.M.–5 P.M.) is a cavernous gift shop filled with gourmet foods (some locally produced and some from afar), as well as candles, bath products, and other country accents for the home.

Antiques
Start a hunt for treasured antiques at **Ferndale Antiques** (52 Ferndale Rd., Ferndale, 845/292-8701; July–Aug. daily 10 A.M.–5 P.M., Mon. holidays and Sept.–June Thurs.–Sun. 10 A.M.–5 P.M.), among the largest shops in the county, with 13 rooms on four floors of an 1894 mansion. Specialties include Depression-era glassware, as well as furniture, paintings, toys, kitchenware, lighting, and accessories. Take Exit 101 off Route 17. At the

store, pick up a free copy of the **Sullivan County Antiques Trail** map, which began with 21 participating shops across the county and was scheduled to double in size in 2004.

The summer flea market at the Monticello Raceway is another popular venue for finding old-fashioned treasures. Farther along Route 17, **Liberty Antique Warehouse Auctions** (Rte. 17 Quickway, Liberty, 914/292-7450, www.libauction.com) holds regular auction events.

One of Wurtsboro's oldest homes—an 1825 canal house—is the storefront for **Hamill's Antiques** (81 Sullivan St., Wurtsboro, 845/888-5356, daily 11:30 A.M.–5 P.M.). Shop for antique paintings, sculptures, jewelry, and chandeliers. On summer weekends, cars jam the roadside parking lot of **Memories** (Rte. 17, Parksville, 845/292-4270 or 800/222-8463, www.memoriesantiques.com; daily 10 A.M.–5 P.M.), between Exits 97 and 98 on Route 17. Six showrooms with thousands of home furnishings, lighting, and other antiques are the draw.

In addition to a full array of antiques wares, **The Blue Victorian** (4874 Main St., Jeffersonville, 845/482-5544, www.thebluevictorian.com; Apr.–Dec. Thurs.–Mon. 10:30 A.M.–6 P.M., Jan.–Mar. Fri.–Sun. 11 A.M.–5 P.M.) has dedicated a gallery to the work of local artists. The shop occupies a beautifully restored Victorian that was once the home of the town physician.

Browse collections of clothing, pottery, Depression-era glass, prints, mirrors, and more at the **Antique Center of Callicoon** (26 Upper Main St., Callicoon, 845/887-5918; Jul.–Aug. Thurs., Fri., Mon. 11 A.M.–4 P.M.; Sat. 10 A.M.–4 P.M.; Sun. 11 A.M.–3 P.M.; Sept.–Jun. Sat. 10 A.M.–4 P.M.; Sun. 11A.M.–3 P.M.).

Farm Stands

In this land of dairy farms and boutique growers, it's difficult to narrow the list of farm stands to manageable length. Callicoon's **Apple Pond Farming Center** (Hahn Rd., Callicoon Center, 845/482-4764) is one of the standouts. **Silver Heights Farm** (275 Eggler Rd., Jeffersonville, 845/482-3572) grows heirloom vegetables, herbs, and flowering plants. The **Sullivan County Area Farmers Market** (845/292-6180) takes place in four locations: Callicoon, Liberty, Monticello, and Roscoe. Hours vary by location.

Knaub's Farm Antiques & Gifts (1168 County Rte. 23, Narrowsburg, 845/252-3781; May–Dec. Sat. 9:30 A.M.–7 P.M., Sun. 10 A.M.–4 P.M.) is a combination antique shop, gift shop, and roadside farm stand.

INFORMATION AND SERVICES

The Sullivan County Visitors Association (www.svca.net) operates information booths at Rock Hill, Livingston Manor, and Roscoe during the busy fishing season. Look for the red caboose off Route 17 at DeBruce Road.

GETTING THERE AND AROUND

Sullivan County is easily accessible from Stewart International Airport and New York City transportation hubs. Shortline Bus (800/631-8405) provides service from Port Authority in New York City to Monticello, with frequent express service and connections to smaller towns like Roscoe. Many resorts provide shuttle transportation from Monticello. Car rentals are available through independent companies (no major chains) in Fosterdale and Monticello: **Fosterdale Rent-a-Car** (Rtes. 17B & 52, Fosterdale, 845/932-8538, www.17bcars.com; Mon.–Sat. 8:30 A.M.–8:30 P.M., Sun. till 2 P.M.; $29–52 per day) and **Marty's** (4461 Rte. 42, Monticello, 845/794-5025; daily 8 A.M.–9 P.M.).

Taxi services in Monticello and Bloomingburg serve all major airports. Note that Route 17 is becoming an interstate, I-86.

Delaware County

It's hard to imagine two worlds more opposed than the exclusive Hamptons of Long Island and the fertile hills of rural Delaware County. And yet, scores of former beachgoers are trading their ocean view for a fixer-upper and a pair of cross-country skis.

The reason? Property that's beautiful, affordable, and within a two-hour drive of New York City. Roughly the size of Rhode Island, Delaware County is the third-largest county in New York State and has the lowest population density (33.2 persons per square mile) of any county in the Hudson Valley and Catskill region—a figure that almost triples in summer. Encompassing the headwaters of the Delaware River, the area is known for an abundance of freshwater and unparalleled hunting and fishing.

Early European settlers arrived in present-day Delaware County in the 1780s by traveling the Catskill Turnpike. This first route to the western frontier was a dirt road with periodic tollgates that connected the Village of Catskill in Greene County to the Susquehanna River in Unadilla.

New York State recognized Delaware County as a separate county in 1797. Lumbering and stone cutting sustained the local economy at first, followed by agriculture. In the 1840s, Delaware County became a focal point of the Anti-Rent Wars, during which poor farmers across the country began to protest the feudal system that prevented them from owning the land they farmed.

Holstein and Jersey cows still graze the hillsides here, and you'll find a sampling of barns in every shape, style, and condition—from those that are barely still standing, to others that have been restored as inviting markets, homes, and bookstores.

ALONG ROUTE 28

Fleischmanns

A 40-mile drive from Kingston along Route 28 leads to Fleischmanns, at the eastern edge of Delaware County. Initially known as Griffin Corners in the early 19th century, the town is named for Charles F. Fleischmann (think yeast and whiskey). Fleishmann had emigrated from Austria-Hungary to Cincinnati in the 1860s and started the Vienna Bakery that would make him world famous. Already a successful businessman, he bought property in Delaware County in 1883 and began spending summers in the mountain air.

Soon an entire community of summer residents, mostly well-to-do families, were building lavish Victorian homes along Wagner Avenue, many of which are standing today. Dozens of resorts opened in the surrounding area, but only a handful remain in business: the old Fleischmanns Hotel, for example, is now home to **Roberts' Auction** (see *Shopping*).

At the center of Main Street stands the handsome **Skene Memorial Library** (1017 Main St., Fleischmanns, 845/254-4581, www.skenelib.org; Wed.–Sat. 11 A.M.–5 P.M.), founded with a $5,000 grant from Andrew Carnegie and completed in 1901. An old carriage barn behind the library houses the **Fleischmanns Museum of Memories,** with exhibits that document the town's history as a thriving summer resort.

Arkville

One of the most scenic railroad lines in the east connected Kingston on the Hudson to Oneonta at the western boundary of Delaware County. Over the course of its hundred-year history, the Delaware & Ulster Railroad transported lumber, bluestone, livestock, produce, coal, and tourists across 107 miles of mountains and valleys. To date, three stretches of the original route have been restored for visitor enjoyment: the New York State Trolley Museum Kingston, the Catskill Mountain Railroad in Phoenicia, and the **Delaware & Ulster Railride** (Rte. 28, Arkville, 800/225-4132, www.durr.org; call for schedule; adults $10, children $6) in Arkville.

The depot is the most visible attraction around as you enter Arkville on Route 28 (south side of the street). Tours leave twice daily on weekends, May–October, and also on Wednesday–Friday in the months of July and August. A round-trip

© PAUL ITOI

Delaware & Ulster Railroad engine

tour to Roxbury takes less than two hours (one hour round-trip to Halcottsville). Dogs are welcome aboard the D&U.

Next to the Arkville Fire House, on the north side of Route 28, is the **Erpf House Gallery** (Rte. 28, Arkville, 845/586-2611; Mon.–Fri. 10 A.M.–4 P.M., Sat. noon–4 P.M.), featuring artwork that explores themes of nature and captures the history of the Catskill region. Rotating exhibits include paintings, photography, sculpture, installation art, and crafts. The gallery also hosts periodic lectures, workshops, and an artist-in-residence program.

Margaretville and the Pepacton Reservoir

Delaware County sustained $20 million in flood damage when the Blizzard of '96 was followed by unseasonably warm temperatures and heavy rains. Margaretville's Bridge Street, along the banks of the East Branch of the Delaware, suffered some of

the most severe damage from the disaster, and nine buildings were ultimately condemned.

In the years since, town officials have succeeded in turning the natural disaster into an economic opportunity. With a sizable disaster-relief grant from New York State, Margaretville has constructed a new waterfront park and river walk, along with new sidewalks and landscaping along Main Street. The result is a charming downtown, with several restaurants, shops, and inns—all of which are conveniently close to endless open space for fishing, hiking, and cycling.

A scenic detour from Route 28 leads to the **Pepacton Reservoir,** formed by a dam at the beginning of the East Branch of the Delaware River. The reservoir is named for one of the four towns it flooded when construction was completed in 1955, and one gets the feeling that more than a few locals are still bitter over the loss.

With a capacity of 140.2 billion gallons of water, the Pepacton is the largest reservoir in the

The Western Catskills

New York City Watershed and provides about 25 percent of the total supply. The man-made lake covers 15 miles and 7,500 acres, supporting a healthy population of brown trout. Fish taken from these waters average about five pounds, with record-setters exceeding 20 pounds. Fishing and rowboats are allowed with a free permit. Several outfitters supply gear and lead trips on the reservoir. No swimming or motorboats are allowed.

At the western end of the reservoir on Route 30 is the village of Downsville and the Downsville Covered Bridge, at the intersection of Route 206. This 174-foot bridge still carries one lane of traffic at a time (maximum height six feet) across the East Branch of the Delaware River.

Andes

Northeast of the Peptacon Reservoir lies the upland village of Andes (www.andesny.org), where in 1845 Moses Earle and a group of local farmers refused to pay overdue rents to protest the feudal system of land ownership. Sheriff Osman Steele intervened in the dispute and was killed by the protesters, drawing national attention to the issue. President Abraham Lincoln signed the National Homestead Act into law 15 years later, in 1862, distributing hundreds of millions of acres of land into private hands.

One of the oldest buildings in town is the 1800 **Hunting Tavern Museum** (Rte. 28, Andes, 845/676-3747; call before visiting), named for its first proprietor, Ephraim Hunting. Sheriff Steele reportedly downed his last drink here and uttered the now-famous words, "Lead cannot penetrate Steele," shortly before he was shot. Today, the tavern hosts local art exhibits, dance performances, and period dinners.

Proximity to the reservoir and a handful of hotels and restaurants make Andes a popular stop in Delaware County. Galleries and antique shops invite visitors to explore its Main Street. In winter, snowmobilers gather at Hogans General Store on Main Street to refuel.

Andes is getting a facelift in 2005 with new sidewalks and store entrances, and the local train station is destined to be converted into a visitor center and museum. The Trailways Bus Line passes through town.

Bovina and Roxbury

Scenic Route 6 connects Margaretville to Bovina, where actors Brad Pitt and Jennifer Aniston had become the newest residents until their split in 2005. An alternative drive from Margaretville follows Route 30 north to Halcottsville and then Roxbury. In an unlikely pairing, financier Jay Gould and naturalist John Burroughs share the town of Roxbury as their birthplace and family homestead. When Gould left home to invest in railroads, Burroughs remained in the Catskills writing volumes about the natural wonders around him.

A line from "In the Southern Catskills" captures Burroughs' worldview: "Only the sea and the mountain forest brook are pure; all between is contaminated more or less by the work of man." **Woodchuck Lodge** (607/326-7908, www.roxburyny.org), the Burroughs family farmhouse, is now a National Historic Landmark.

The Gould family left behind a legacy of architectural splendor. St. Lawrence marble and Tiffany stained-glass windows adorn the **Jay Gould Reformed Church** (Main St., Roxbury). Helen Gould Shephard, daughter of Jay Gould, built the 1911 classic Greek Revival building that has housed the **Roxbury Arts & Cultural Center** (Vega Mountain Rd., Roxbury, 607/326-7908) since 1988. Recently restored **Kirkside Park** (Rte. 30, Main St., Roxbury, 607/326-3392, www.roxburyny.com) and the **Shephard Hills Golf Course** (Golf Course Rd. off Bridge St., Roxbury, 607/326-7121, www.shephardhills.com) were also part of her original estate. Today, Roxbury is an attractive town of 2,500 residents, many of them retirees and second-home owners who enjoy the variety of outdoor activities within reach.

Delhi

In the center of Delaware County, where Route 10 meets Route 28, is Delhi (DEL-high), the largest and most commercially developed municipality in the region. As the county seat, this town of 50,000 holds the **Delaware County Courthouse,** as well as the headquarters for several regional newspapers and radio stations. The **Delaware County Historical Association** (NYS Rte. 10, Delhi, 607/746-3849, www.dcha-ny.org;

Tues.–Sun. 11 A.M.–4 P.M., Memorial Day–Oct. 15; adults $5) maintains seven historic buildings on a property located 2.5 miles north of Delhi on Route 10. Among the restored buildings are a tollgate house from the Catskill Turnpike and the 1797 Frisbee House and barn. The museum displays rotating exhibits in its two galleries, from war memorabilia to quilt shows.

Route 10 heads south from Delhi along the West Branch of the Delaware River, passing through the quiet towns of Hamden, Walton, and Deposit along the way.

ALONG ROUTE 23

M Catskill Scenic Trail

If you follow Route 23 west from Greene County, you'll reach the town of Grand Gorge just over the Delaware county line. The East Branch of the Delaware River begins here, and you can pick up the Catskill Scenic Trail (Rte. 23, Grande Gorge, 607/652-2821), which sits on top of the old railroad tracks of the Ulster & Delaware Railroad and runs 19 miles to Bloomville. The hard-packed trail is well suited for biking, jogging, horseback riding, and cross-country skiing, and it offers access to several fishing along the river. The railroad track foundation keeps the trail at a gentle grade, so visitors of all ages and physical conditioning can enjoy the hike. The trail may be accessed from many towns along the way; parking lots are available in Bloomville at Route 10 and Route 33. No overnight camping is available.

At the intersection of Routes 23 and 10 lies Stamford and Mount Utsayantha (Beautiful Spring). The West Branch of the Delaware originates at this 3,214-foot peak, and it's one of the few Catskill summits that you can reach by car. A one-mile gravel road leads to the top and a view of four states on clear days. On the way to the summit is the recognized gravesite of a Mohawk princess who drowned herself in a nearby lake in grief over the loss of her son.

Stamford evolved from a distribution center for butter to a thriving resort town at the turn of the 20th century, and its 20-acre mountaintop park lured visitors from across the country. Today, the walking paths are overgrown and the abandoned observation tower shows signs of neglect. But in 2004, town officials secured a grant to restore the park to its former glory. In the meantime, the Utsayantha Flyers Organization has built several launch ramps for hang gliders and keeps a watchful eye on the property.

Turn off Route 23 onto Route 12 to reach East Meredith and the working saw and gristmill at the **Hanford Mills Museum** (County Rtes. 10 & 12, East Meredith, 800/295-4992, www.hanfordmills.org; daily 10 A.M.–5 P.M.).

SPORTS AND RECREATION

Winter Sports

You have to be one of the first 2,000 skiers to get fresh tracks at **Ski Plattekill** (Plattekill Mountain Rd., Roxbury, 607/326-3500, www.plattekill.com; Fri.–Sun. 8:45 A.M.–4:15 P.M.; $38) on a powder day. Normally open three days a week, the mom-and-pop mountain sells $25 tickets and runs the T-bar to expert terrain on days of 12-inches or more. But the owners stop selling tickets when they reach the 2,000 mark.

Plattekill gets upwards of 200 inches of snow a year—more natural snow than even the Catskill High Peaks typically get.

Ski Plattekill Statistics
Base: 2,150 feet
Summit: 3,500 feet
Vertical: 1,100 feet
Trails: 35
Lifts: 4
Skiable acres: 75
Snowmaking: 75 percent
Snow report: 607/326-3500

The considerably smaller **Bobcat Ski Center** (Rte. 28, Andes, 845/676-3143, www.skibobcat.com; Dec.–Mar. Fri.–Sun. and holidays 9 A.M.–4 P.M.; adults $25, students $12) recently added snowboard rentals to its list of services.

Bobcat Ski Center Statistics
Base: 1,050 feet
Summit: 3,345 feet
Vertical: 1,050 feet

Trails: 18
Lifts: 2
Skiable acres: 80
Snowmaking: 20 percent
Snow report: 845/676-3143

The **Delhi College Golf Course** (Rte. 28, Delhi, 607/746-4000) is open to the public all winter long for cross-country skiing and snowshoeing. Snowmobilers congregate in the town of Andes, often to refuel at Hogans General Store (Main St., Andes, 8 A.M.–8 P.M.) and lunch at the Andes Hotel (Main St., Andes, 845/676-4408, daily lunch and dinner, Sun. brunch).

Hiking

The Catskill Preserve and **Utsayantha Trail System** (Stamford, 607/652-7581) offer miles of wilderness for day hikes or overnight trips. A stretch of the 552-mile Finger Lakes Trail System crosses Delaware County with several good places to camp overnight, including Beale Pond at Oquaga Creek State Park (Rte. 20, Masonville, 607/467-4160). Contact the Delaware County Chamber of Commerce or write to the Finger Lakes Trail Conference Service Center (P.O. Box 18048, Rochester, NY 14618), for a current trail map. Visit www.delawarecounty.org/hiking for information about access points and routes.

Mountain Biking and Road Riding

Whether you want to log 15 miles or a century, Delaware County has some of the best terrain around for cycling. Plan a route to tour the county's covered bridges. In summer, Plattekill opens its lifts for mountain biking.

A Bike Peddler Corp. (41 Stewart Ave., Roscoe, 607/498-4188; daily 8 A.M.–4 P.M.) rents bikes and sells maps and gear.

Barryville-based Lander's River Trips (see *Swimming and Boating*) recently added new Fuji mountain bikes to its list of rental services (full day $28, half day $16). **Pearson Park** (Liberty, 845/292-7690), on Walnut Mountain, features 265 acres of novice to expert terrain, including challenging single-track riding. For road riders, the Bicycle Club of Sullivan County (845/794-3000, ext. 5010) leads tours April–October.

Golf

Hanah Country Inn & Resort (576 West Hubbell Hill Rd., Margaretville, 800/752-6494, www.hanahcountryclub.com; $150–275) has a U.S.G.A.-rated course that's known as the Terminator. Inquire about combined room and greens fee packages. **French Woods Golf & Country Club** (Hancock, 845/887-4595, basslumber@hancock.net) is an 18-hole, 6,000-yard, par 72 course with woods and pond views.

Swimming and Boating

Paddlers head for the Delaware and Susquehanna Rivers for adventure. Mongaup Pond has a swimming beach with lifeguard supervision. Rowboats and canoes are allowed on the lake (rentals available), but not motorboats.

Lander's River Trips (5666 Rte. 97, Narrowsburg, 800/252-3925, www.landersrivertrips.com; rentals $19–37), family-run since 1954, runs 10 bases along the Upper Delaware River, with rafts, canoes, and kayaks for rent. Camping and packages are available.

Located near the Pepacton Reservoir, **Al's Sport Store** (Rtes. 30 & 206, Downsville, 607/363-7740, www.alssportstore.com; Mon.–Fri. 5:30 A.M.–6 P.M., Sat.–Sun. 5 A.M.–7 P.M.) offers day or overnight camping trips on the Delaware River. Shuttle service is available. **Smith's Canoe & Drift Boat Rental** (Rte. 97, Hancock, 607/637-2989) has drift boats and canoes for rent with access directly on the Delaware River.

Fishing and Hunting

Delaware County offers hundreds of miles of some of the top fishing streams, rivers, and reservoirs in the country. The season begins each April with the hatching of the blue-winged olive fly. For freestone stream fishing, the Willowemoc and Beaver Kill are legendary. The Pepacton reservoir offers still-water anglers plentiful opportunities for catching bass and occasionally huge browns.

ACCOMMODATIONS

Accommodations are hit or miss in rural Delaware County. Small country inns range from musty and neglected to positively charming. The good news is that even the best are relatively affordable.

Under $100

Located between Downsville and Delhi, **M Octagon Farm Bed & Breakfast** (34055 State Highway 10, Walton, 607/865-7416; $80–120) offers comfortable accommodations in a unique 1850s building. The main house has five guestrooms with one shared bath. A cottage has two additional bedrooms, plus a full kitchen. And the Creekside House has three bedrooms and a private outdoor space, available for $350–375 per couple. The surrounding property was once a dairy farm, and today the owners grow produce for sale at the Octagon Farm Market onsite.

Down comforters are a bonus in three guestrooms at the **M Country House Bed and Breakfast** (257 East Bramley Mountain Rd., Bovina Center, 607/832-4371, www.country-housebandb.com; $85–90). In addition, the 1840 farmhouse features pine floors, private baths, and tasteful, old-world furnishings, making it a solid deal all-around. Best of all, the inn is set on a 300-acre cattle farm, which means all-natural beef on your breakfast table.

For a motel with a twist, try the **The Roxbury** (2258 County Hwy. 41, Roxbury, 607/326-7200, www.theroxburymotel.com; $95). Its simple rooms combine cheerful colors and the convenience of in-room kitchenettes.

One of the best-known places in Margaretville is the **Margaretville Mountain Inn** (1478 Margaretville Mountain Rd., Margaretville, 845/586-3933, www.margaretvilleinn.com; $100). Set in an aging Victorian on a hill above the town, the B&B has several floral rooms with brass bed frames. Some rooms share a bath. For more modern accommodations and a more convenient location, request a room in the newer building in town.

$100–150

Near Belleayre Ski Resort, **The Highlands Inn** (923 Main St., Fleischmanns, 845/254-5650, www.thehighlandsinn.com; $135) surprises with wireless Internet access in a large Victorian. The downside: only three of the seven rooms have private baths, and there is a two-night minimum.

$150–200

Hanah Country Inn & Resort (576 West Hubbell Hill Rd., Margaretville, 800/752-6494, www.hanahcountryclub.com; $150–275) provides standard chain hotel–style accommodations, but the resort offers enough activities to keep you out and about the entire day. Take the free shuttle to Plattekill Mountain for some downhill mountain biking, or head out to face the Terminator golf course. A golf school onsite will help tune up your game. The resort offers numerous golf, ski, and mountain biking packages.

Over $200

Vacation homes are another option for weekend or extended stays. For example, **Catskill Getaway,** (155 Main St., Andes, 631/751-5221, www.catskillgetaway.com; $500/weekend or $1,000/week) is a four-bedroom country home that's centrally located in Andes and available for rent year-round.

Campgrounds

Peaceful Valley Campground (Rte. 30, Shinhopple, 607/363-2211) is the place to pitch your tent. Canoe rentals are available by the day or by the week. An alternative is the **Little Pond Campground** (Barkaboom Rd., Margaretville, 845/439-5480). From Route 30 in Margaretville, go south about six miles to New York City Road and then to Barkaboom Road, and the campground will be on the right.

FOOD

Along Route 28

Margaretville has a handful of decent eateries, including **Café on Main** (Main St., Margaretville, 845/586-2343; mains $9–20), serving Italian classics such as chicken cacciatore, several pasta dishes, and flank steak. Stop in for lunch while you browse the shops.

For a taste of the gourmet, head to **That Certain Something** (496 Main St., Fleischmanns, 845/254-5155), a popular spot among weekenders that's run by Toni Perretta, a former cosmetics executive.

The unfortunately named town of Downsville hosts the upscale **Old Schoolhouse Inn** (Upper Main St., Downsville, 607/363-7814; Tues.–Thurs. 5–9 P.M.; Fri.–Sat. 5–10 P.M.; Sun. 10 A.M.–9 P.M.; mains $14–26). The menu includes lobster, prime rib and trout dishes, and you'll dine under a large collection of stuffed hunting trophies.

Get your blueberry pancakes at **Cassies Kitchen** (Main St., Andes, 845/676-4500; Thurs.–Tues. breakfast and lunch). **The Andes Hotel** (Main St., Andes, 845/676-4408; daily lunch and dinner, Sun. brunch) serves hearty fare, especially in winter when the snowmobilers ski into town. Smokey guacamole and outstanding margaritas are to be found at **Cantina** (corner of Main St. and Delaware Ave., Andes, 845/676-4444; Wed.–Mon. lunch and dinner).

Along Route 23

Roxbury's **Taste Buds Country Store and Restaurant** (Main St., Roxbury, 607/326-3663) is a classic: an old-fashioned soda fountain located conveniently close to Plattekill. In South Kortright, **The Hidden Inn** (Main St., South Kortright, 607/538-9259, www.thehiddeninn.com; Tues.–Sat. 5–9 P.M., Sun. noon–7 P.M. mains $12–18) offers a long menu of surf-and-turf standards alongside more exotic offerings such as frog legs and escargot. The prime rib is a popular order and the restaurant is well known for its duck à l'orange.

ENTERTAINMENT AND EVENTS
Performing Arts

The **West Kortright Centre** (Turnpike Rd., West Kortright, 607/278-5454, www.westkc.org) is one of the premier performance venues in Delaware County. Housed in a restored church on Turnpike Road in West Kortright, it offers an array of musical performances throughout the summer season, as well as gallery exhibits.

Set in a historic building in downtown Franklin, the **Franklin Stage Company at Chapel Hall** (Franklin, 607/829-3700, www.franklinstagecompany.org) produces a mix of modern and classical theater. The company's free

admission policy sets a fun and irreverent tone. The **Open Eye Theatre Company** (1000 Main St., Margaretville, 845/586-1660, www.theopeneye.org) recently moved into a permanent theater on Main Street.

Bars and Nightlife

The Red Barn (18 Kelsey Rd., Deposit, 877/560-2276, www.nyredbarn.com) is a bar, restaurant, and dance hall with live music and dinner theater in a restored barn. Catch the Folk Music Festival in late July.

Festivals

Set on a 500-acre farm and year-round campground, the **Peaceful Valley Bluegrass Festival** (Downsville, 800/467-3109) takes place in July. RV hookups and a swimming pool help beat the heat during the day, but nights can be chilly.

Listen to classical music performances at the **Honest Brook Music Festival** (Meredith, 607/746-3770, www.hbmf.org) or try your hand at the two-man saw during the annual **Lumberjack Festival** (Riverside Park, Deposit, 607/278-5744, www.hanfordmills.org).

SHOPPING

If you love to buy and sell goods on eBay, try the offline equivalent at one of Delaware County's professional auction houses. At **McIntosh Auction Service** (Rte. 28, Margaretville, 607/832-4829, www.mcintoshauction.com), Chuck McIntosh has been in the business for 30 years. You can bid on antiques, machinery, or even a farm estate. Another reputable operation is **Roberts' Auction** (820 Main St., Fleischmanns, 845/254-4490, www.roberts-auction.com). After you've bought the farm, you can sample the local bounty at the **Pakatakan Farmers Market** (Kelly Round Barn, Rte. 30, Halcottsville, 914/254-4290; Sat. 9 A.M.–3 P.M.) or the Octagon Farm Market (34055 State Highway 10, Walton, 607/865-7416).

Pick your own blueberries about 10 miles outside of Delhi at **Windy Knob Farm** (6657 Turnpike Rd., Meredith, 607/746-2991; daily July–Oct. sunrise–sunset). Alpacas and llamas graze the pastures at **Eastbrook Farms** (2410 Dunk Hill Rd., Walton, 607/746-3849, www .eastbrookfarms.com), where you can buy woven and knitted scarves, shawls, and baby blankets. A restored carriage house holds a collection of rare and used books at **Bibliobarn** (Roses Brook Rd., South Kortright, 607/538-1555; daily 9 A.M.–6 P.M.).

Blink Gallery (454 Lower Main St., Andes, 845/676-3900, www.blinkgallery.net; Apr.–Dec.) features contemporary artists in a wide variety of mediums including ceramics, glass, and paintings. At the other end of Main, **Paisley's Country Gallery** (75 Main St., Andes, 845/676-3533; Apr.–Feb. Thurs.–Sun. 10 A.M.–5 P.M.) is also worth a look for antiques and gifts.

INFORMATION AND SERVICES

The **Delaware County Chamber of Commerce** (114 Main St., Delhi, 607/746-2281, info@ delawarecounty.org, www.delawarecounty.org) is located in Delhi and maintains an informative website.

GETTING THERE AND AROUND

It's easier to rent a canoe than a car in outdoor-oriented Delaware, but you'll need wheels to get around this rural county, as public transportation is virtually nonexistent. Albany International Airport is your best bet for a rental. Adirondack Trailways (800/225-6815) offers bus service to Delhi.

The Upper Hudson

The Catskill and Berkshire Mountains frame the upper section of the Hudson River Valley. In between, small lakes and dense hardwood forests alternate with rolling hills and cultivated fields. Rural communities dot the landscape, welcoming visitors with historic sites, antique shops, and the promise of outdoor adventure.

Striking in any season, the Upper Hudson Valley makes an exceptionally enjoyable winter getaway, when every inn has a wood fire burning and hearty meals warm you from the inside out.

Greene and Columbia Counties succeed in creating that cozy feeling the Austrians call *gemütlichkeit.* Cross-country skiers can explore varied terrain on private and public lands, while downhill skiers and riders can find steeps and parks for all levels. And for those who don't measure fun in vertical feet, snowmobiles, snowshoes, and ice skates provide a few more alternatives.

If you're the kind of person who travels to eat, not the other way around, the Upper Hudson Valley also holds a few hidden gems. The

Must-Sees

Look for **M** to find the sights and activities you can't miss and **M̲** for the best dining and lodging.

M Kaaterskill Falls: An hour-long walk on a well-marked, but strenuous, trail leads to the base of the 180-foot falls that inspired many a Hudson River School painter. With the old tanneries and hotels long gone, the falls are actually more pristine today than they were 100 years ago (page 140).

M The Escarpment Trail: Near the town of Haines Falls, a 1,500-foot plateau marks the site of the old Catskill Mountain House, one of America's first resort hotels. The five-state view from the edge of the escarpment makes the park one of the most popular in the Catskill region today (page 141).

M Tannersville: This mountaintop town bustles with activity year-round. A row of colorful Victorians on Main Street holds restaurants, cafés, bars, and shops, while the Mountaintop Arboretum grows native and exotic trees and shrubs on seven acres of land (page 141).

M Clermont State Historic Site: The classical Clermont estate on the Hudson River north of Germantown belonged to the high-society Livingston family (page 155).

M Olana State Historic Site: The Persian-style Olana mansion, near the Rip Van Winkle Bridge,

© PAUL ITOI

the Taconic State Parkway in Columbia County

was the brainchild of Hudson River School painter Frederic Church (page 155).

M Shaker Museum and Library: This remarkable collection of artifacts offers an informative introduction to the Shaker way of life (page 159).

M Taconic State Park: This expansive green space encompasses 5,000 acres at the base of the Taconic Range, near the Massachusetts and Connecticut state lines (page 159).

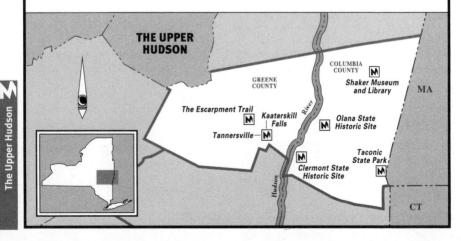

THE UPPER HUDSON

GREENE COUNTY

COLUMBIA COUNTY

M Shaker Museum and Library

MA

The Escarpment Trail **M**

Kaaterskill Falls

Tannersville—**M**

River

M Olana State Historic Site

Taconic State Park **M**

M Clermont State Historic Site

Hudson

CT

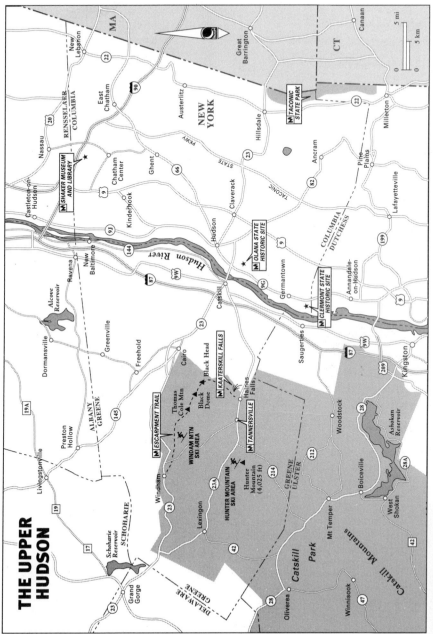

© AVALON TRAVEL PUBLISHING, INC.

French-inspired country cuisine at Aubergine, the newly restored art deco Ruby's Hotel in Freehold, and the multicourse contemporary American tasting menu at the Basement Bistro should top any gourmet's must-dine list.

PLANNING YOUR TIME

With a selective itinerary, you can easily tour Greene or Columbia in a day of scenic driving. (It takes less than an hour to drive the length of either one.) But you'll need a long weekend to sample the range of historic sites and outdoor activities these counties offer. Allow an hour for the round-trip hike to Kaaterskill Falls or a day to summit one of the High Peaks. Tours of the Clermont and Olana historic homes last about an hour, plus time walk the grounds and contemplate the views. Serious antique shoppers can spend a full day or more in downtown Hudson.

Many visitors to the upper Hudson plan weekend getaways around an outdoor activity or a charming inn. Others choose to take in a quick sight or memorable meal en route between New York City and New England or western New York State. Historic homes and local festivals can make good day trips, depending on your starting point.

In Greene County, the loop along Routes 23 and 23A covers about 40 miles and takes less than an hour to complete by car with no stops. An out-and-back excursion to Coxsackie along Route 385 and the Hudson River adds another hour round-trip. Columbia County has three parallel routes running north to south: Route 9G follows the river's edge, the Taconic State Parkway is the fastest, and Route 22 runs along the foot of the Taconic Hills.

Starting at the southern border with Dutchess County, a good loop is to follow Route 9G about a half-hour north to the city of Hudson, then meander on local roads up to Kinderhook and Chatham. From there, you can zip back to your starting point along the Taconic, or continue east and take Route 22 south through Hillsdale and Copake. The entire loop should take about two to three hours with no stops.

Greene County

If you had the means to vacation in remote Greene County during the early to mid-19th century, you might have stayed at the world-famous Catskill Mountain House—along with Alexander Graham Bell, Henry James, Oscar Wilde, Ulysses S. Grant, Mark Twain, and their contemporaries. A one-day journey from New York City began with a steamboat ride to Catskill Landing and concluded with a harrowing 12-mile, four-hour stagecoach ride to the eastern edge of the High Peaks region.

Between the Kaaterskill Creek and Sleepy Hollow, a steep and narrow road climbed to the top of a rocky plateau called Pine Orchard. Here, the classical Mountain House stood with its 13 Corinthian columns, painted stark white against a backdrop of hemlock and white pines and surrounded by hundreds of square miles of untamed forest. In the words of author Roland Van Zandt, the hotel offered the "ideal combination of wilderness and luxury" and symbolized "a nation's young wealth, leisure, and cultural attainments."

Modern rail and jet travel changed Greene County forever, sending would-be visitors to more exotic destinations. In 1963, the New York State Department of Conservation declared the long-abandoned hotel a danger to hikers and burned what remained of the building to the ground one winter morning. Visitors today can only imagine the imposing white structure and the famous people who stayed in it, but the setting remains as enchanting as two centuries ago.

Located on the west side of the Hudson, with Albany County to the north and Ulster County to the south, Greene County features 20 miles of riverfront, several charming valley and mountain towns, and Kaaterskill Falls—at 260 feet, the highest waterfall in the east. The magical surroundings inspired American literary master Washington Irving to write the tale of Rip Van Winkle, the hen-pecked husband who wandered into the mountains and fell into a 20-year sleep.

Named after Revolutionary War General Nathanael Greene of Rhode Island, the original Greene County consisted of four towns: Catskill and Coxsackie on the river, Freehold in the valley, and Windham on the mountaintop. Agriculture, forestry, and a few dozen tanneries drove the local economy in the early days. But the opening of the Erie Canal in 1825 diverted ships and manufactured goods from Catskill to Troy, sending the once-prosperous county into a tailspin—until a group of Romantic Era writers and painters, including Thomas Cole, popularized the region for its scenic beauty.

Dairy farms and orchards came next, along with German and Irish immigrants and summer residents. From the polka dancers at the Mountain Brauhaus to the International Celtic Festival at Hunter Mountain, the county retains much of its immigrant influence today.

After a steady decline during the mid-20th century, Greene County is quietly capturing the imagination of travelers, writers, and outdoor enthusiasts again. Author Allegra Goodman chose

the valley as the setting for her first novel, *Kaaterskill Falls* (Delta, 1999), which intertwines the stories of three Orthodox Jewish families from New York City who spend summers in the area. On the mountaintop, an effort is under way to revive Hunter Village with a focus on art and cultural events.

Members of the Catskill 3500 Club visit Greene County to climb many of the highest peaks in the range, including Blackhead, Black Dome, and Thomas Cole Mountain. The county also supports three winter ski resorts—Hunter Mountain, Cortina Mountain, and Windham Mountain—which offer city dwellers a convenient alternative to driving four hours to New England resorts or traveling by plane to the Rockies.

Note that the weather is often cooler, windier, and wetter on the mountaintop than at the river's edge. Bring layers in any season.

ALONG THE RIVER—ROUTE 385
Rip Van Winkle Bridge
The Rip Van Winkle Bridge spans the Hudson at mile 112, counting from the south. If you approach the crossing from Routes 9G or 82,

© GARY GOTH

The Upper Hudson

a winter view from the Rip Van Winkle Bridge

both in Columbia County, the first sight of the Catskill's purple-gray peaks will catch you off guard. For generations, the bridge has stood as a divider between civilization and wilderness, or what many locals call "up country." The range's cluster of High Peaks rises to 4,000 feet, just 12 miles west of the sea-level river.

Begin your tour of Greene County with a walk across the mile-long span of the bridge. Built during the Great Depression at a cost of $2.4 million and opened in 1935, the bridge connects the small cities of Catskill and Hudson, ushering visitors into the forever-wild lands of the Catskill Preserve. (Car toll $1, eastbound only.) The New York State Bridge Authority has preserved the look of the original Dutch colonial toll plaza so as not to alter the view from the Olana State Historic Site directly across the river.

Park in a lot near the toll plaza on the Catskill side of the bridge. (Pedestrians only on the sidewalk. Bikes must use the narrow traffic lanes.) Pause at the middle of the span to take in the 360-degree views. The river below is tidal freshwater. To the north, Stockport Middle Ground Island is one of four sites belonging to the National Estuarine Research Reserve. The Hudson Athens Lighthouse, on a smaller island to the Northwest, was established in 1874 and had a live-in keeper until 1949. The gentle hills of Columbia County rise in the east behind the waterfront city of Hudson. And the clay-tiled rooftop of Olana, the Persian-style castle of painter Frederic Church, stands above the trees to the southeast. Turn back west, and the Catskill Mountains beckon.

Catskill

Historian Henry Brace wrote in 1876 that early Dutch settlers purchased the village of Catskill in 1684 for "a gun, two shirts, a kettle, two kegs of beer, and, as usual, a little rum." For more than two centuries, the village thrived as an agricultural crossroads and a gateway to the mountains. But the building of the Rip Van Winkle Bridge marked the beginning of a long decline. These days, the town is dreadfully quiet in winter, but come summer, the waterfront

awakens with boating, outdoor dining, and an open-air market.

Catskill's Main Street runs parallel to Catskill Creek, which widens and empties into the Hudson just past the center of town. (There is a municipal parking lot off Main.) Two-story row houses line both sides of the street, many of them housing attorneys' offices, as Catskill is the county seat. The **Greene County Courthouse,** at the intersection of Main and Bridge (also Rte. 385), is a white, neoclassical structure that towers over its neighbors. Behind the **Catskill Public Library** (1 Franklin St., 518/943-4230, catskill@francomm.com, http:// catskill.lib.ny.us; Mon.–Wed. noon–8 P.M., Fri. 10 A.M.–5 P.M., Sat. 10 A.M.–2 P.M.), in another neoclassical building. The library has a local history collection with many books about the steamboats of the Hudson.

Main Street takes a sharp turn to the left as you approach the mouth of the Catskill Creek. Follow West Main to its end to reach Catskill Point, Dutchman's Landing, and Mariner's Point Restaurant. Many community activities take place here during the summer months.

Ramshorn-Livingston Sanctuary (Grandview Ave., 845/473-4440, ext. 270, landpres@ scenichudson.org, www.scenichudson.org/parks/ shparks/ramshorn), is the largest tidal swamp forest along the Hudson. Paddlers can rent boats and explore some 480 acres via 3.5 miles of waterways that lead out to the river itself. Heron, waterfowl, and other birds feed here, and American shad and bass come in spring to spawn. Open dawn to dusk year-round, the sanctuary is jointly owned and operated by the Scenic Hudson Land Trust and the National Audubon Society (P.O. Box 1, Craryville, 518/325-5203, ny.audubon .org/ramshorn.htm).

North of Catskill proper, the **Catskill Game Farm** (400 Game Farm Rd., 518/678-9595, www.catshillgamefarm.com; May 1–Oct. 31 daily 9 A.M.–5 P.M., July–Aug. daily 9 A.M.–6 P.M.; adults $16.95, children 4–11 $12.95, under 3 free) runs a petting zoo that dates back to 1933. Some of the animals are native to the area—like the American elk and mountain lion—but many others come from distant lands.

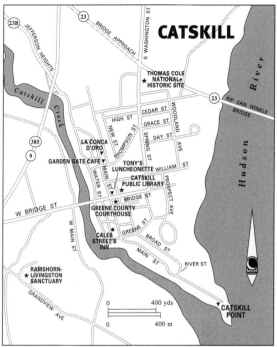

CATSKILL

© AVALON TRAVEL PUBLISHING, INC.

Today, the pale yellow house sits on the outskirts of town, ironically close to a busy traffic light and a Mobil gas station. Despite the encroaching surroundings, the views continue to inspire awe. On display inside the house and studios are a few of Cole's paintings, as well as furniture and family memorabilia. A $1 million restoration of the main house was completed in 2003. Phase 1 of the restoration of Cole's studio began in 2004.

Athens

Head north on County Route 385 (Spring Street) from Catskill about four miles, and you'll come to the much smaller village of Athens. The Dutch arrived here in 1686, and the town was a landing point for the Athens-Hudson ferry service, which dates back to the late 1770s. Built into a hillside, with a splash of color on some of its old Victorian homes, the town hints of San Francisco, except for the two industrial plants that frame its borders.

Several blocks of river views and a few restaurants greet travelers right at the water's edge—though you have to look hard to find them. Second Street, off Route 385, leads you to the striking **Stewart House Restaurant and Bed and Breakfast** (Second St., 518/945-1357, info@stewarthouse.com, www.stewarthouse.com), a historic inn that catered to visitors who arrived by ferry in the 1880s but fell out of favor when trains and bridges replaced steamboat travel. In 2000, New York City–based editor Owen Lipstein breathed new life into the Victorian era venue. It's worth a peek inside to the see the original tin ceiling and inlaid marble fireplace in the formal dining room, even if you don't plan to stay for dinner.

It's rare to find many cars in the **Cohotate Preserve** (Rte. 385, www.troop45.com/cohotate/cohotate.htm), south of town, but the site is worth a visit for its river views and environmental information. The parking lot is well marked

Cedar Grove

Around the time that the Romantic Era began to take hold in America, a young artist named Thomas Cole ventured up the river from New York City in search of inspiration for a series of sketches. The canvases and exhibition that followed put him in the national spotlight and helped to make the Catskills world-famous.

Cole spent most of his adult years at Cedar Grove in the town of Catskill, now the **Thomas Cole National Historic Site** (218 Spring St., Catskill, 518/943-7465, info@thomascole.org, www.thomascole.org; May–Oct. Fri.–Sat. 10 A.M.–4 P.M., Sun. 1 P.M.–5 P.M.; admission $5). He painted landscapes and taught students like Frederic E. Church, who later established his own residence on a hillside across the river. With a shared interest in painting mountain peaks and waterfalls instead of portraits, Cole and his students became known collectively as the Hudson River School of Art.

The Upper Hudson

with a large sign on Route 385. A gravel road leads to the river, and from there, an interpretive trail describes the habitats of local plants, animals, and fish, leading to spectacular river views. The Greene County Environmental Education Center recently added a pond to attract and support a greater variety of wildlife for nature walkers. Students of Columbia-Greene County College take environmental classes in a new lab on the premises. For those who want to get on the water, there is a well-maintained boat ramp with parking for 25 cars just north of town.

Coxsackie

Continuing north along Route 385 brings you to Coxsackie (cook-SAK-ee), borrowed from an Algonquin Indian expression meaning "owl hoot" or "place of wild geese." Reed's Landing was once a busy center for shipbuilding and transportation, and today the town retains an industrial feel. The remains of a Hudson River freighter called the *Storm King* rest in shallow water near the town's River Park.

When the icehouses of the Hudson became irrelevant, creative entrepreneurs discovered they were ideal for growing mushrooms. The Greene County Historical Society has estimated that by the late 1930s, Coxsackie-based Knaust Brothers controlled about 85 percent of the country's mushroom business as a supplier to companies like Heinz and Campbells.

One mile south of the Coxsackie boat launch is the **Hudson River Islands State Park,** (1 Hailes Cave Rd., Voorheesville, 518/872-1237), on the islands of Gay's Point and Stockton Middle Ground. Accessible only by boat, the park protects many rare and endangered species and allows picnics, fishing, and camping Memorial Day–Columbus Day.

Moving away from the river, the main attraction in Coxsackie is the oldest surviving dwelling in upstate New York, a 1663 stone house now known as the **Bronck Museum** (90 County Rte. 42, 518/731-6490, www.gchistory.org/bronck .html; Memorial Day weekend–Oct. 15 Wed.– Fri. noon–4 P.M., Sat. 10 A.M.–4 P.M., Sun. and holidays 1–4 P.M.; adults $4, youth 12–15 $2, children 5–11 $1.50, under 5 free). In 1662,

Pieter Bronck, a Dutchman who lived in Albany, received a land patent from the British government to settle in modern-day Coxsackie. He built a one-room structure in 1663 and expanded it 20 years later to include a loft with an Indian lookout. In 1738, Bronck's grandson added a new brick house to the property.

The museum consists of these two homes—furnished with period art, linens, ceramics, and silver—and several Dutch colonial barns. The Victorian Horse Barn contains a model of the famous Catskill Mountain House and other Greene County memorabilia. A single, center pole supports the roof of the Thirteen-Sided Barn. And the Dutch Barn has its original wood floor, made of pegged oak planks three-inches thick. The Greene County Historical Association runs the museum and holds special events throughout the year. Check www.gchistory.org/calendar.html for a current calendar.

Unless you are continuing on to Albany via Route 9W or the New York State Thruway, now is a good time to retrace your steps to Catskill and head west on Routes 23 or 23A toward the mountaintop.

ALONG ROUTE 23A
Ⓜ Kaaterskill Falls

Asher B. Durand, another of the Hudson River painters, spent many summers in Palenville and established one of America's first artist colonies here in the 1840s. This quiet town sits at the base of the High Peaks and the edge of Catskill Park. Washington Irving's Rip Van Winkle fell into his 20-year slumber above Palenville in the Kaaterskill Clove.

Leaving town, you enter Catskill Park, and the road becomes narrow and steep with retaining walls and hairpin turns. Ice-climbers scale the frozen waterfalls in winter, while hikers take to the trails in spring, summer, and fall. Look for the trailhead to Kaaterskill Falls about a mile into the ascent. Thomas Cole wrote of the falls:

> *There is a deep gorge at the midst of the loftiest Catskills, which, at its upper end, is*

*terminated by a mighty wall of rock; as the
spectator approaches from below, he sees its
craggy and impending front rising to the
height of three hundred feet. This huge
rampart is semi-circular. From the centre of
the more distant or central part of the semi-
circle, like a gush of living light from
Heaven, the cataract leaps, and foaming
into feathery spray, descends into a rocky
basin one hundred and eight feet below.*

"The Falls of Kaaterskill in Winter," from the
New York Evening Post, *March 29, 1843*

With the old tanneries and hotels long gone,
the falls are actually more pristine today than
they were a hundred years ago. An hour-long
walk (2.7 miles) on a well-marked but strenuous
trail brings you to the base of the falls and back.
(It is also possible to reach the top from the
North Lake Public Campground; however, the
descent along the waterfall is extremely dangerous and not advised.)

The Escarpment Trail

The first town you reach on the mountaintop,
driving west on Route 23A, is Haines Falls, at
2,200 feet elevation. A small green hut before
the turn-off to North Lake has visitor information. Gas, groceries, and banking services are all
located along Main Street (Route 23A), and several places in town rent snowmobiles and mountain bikes. Turn right on County Route 18
(North Lake Road) to reach North Lake Public
Campground and trails leading to the Escarpment, a 1,500-foot plateau upon which the
sprawling Catskill Mountain House once rested.
Poet and journalist William Cullen Bryant described the site like this:

*On that point, scarce visible on the breast
of the mountain, the beautiful and the gay
are met, and the sounds of mirth and music
arise, while for leagues around the mountain torrents are dashing, and the eagle is
uttering his shriek, unheard by human ear.*

as quoted in The Catskill Mountain House,
by Roland Van Zandt

By virtue of its remote setting within a day's journey from thriving New York City, the antebellum
Catskill Mountain House became one of America's first luxury resorts. Under the direction of
Charles L. Beach, son of a stagecoach operator,
the inn drew influential artists, designers, busi-
nessmen, and politicians from the entire Atlantic
corridor for a period of more than 50 years. Some
guests stayed a week, while others spent the full
summer in the cool mountain air. Beach expanded the original Greek-style building rapidly
to keep up with demand, growing from 10 rooms
in 1824 to more than 300 by the 1880s.

The Catskill Mountain House remained a
focal point of the American Romantic Movement until the advent of modern rail and auto
transportation diverted visitors away from the
region. By 1950, the building stood in ruins.
Today, it is lost to history. The view, however,
continues to astound first-time visitors. On a
clear day, you can see five states from the edge of
the escarpment, making the park one of the most
popular in the Catskills.

Tannersville

Tannersville bears the responsibility of reminding
locals and visitors of an unfortunate episode in
Catskill history. Around the turn of the 19th
century, the business of manufacturing leather
became lucrative for those who were willing to
endure the labor-intensive process. When mountaintop tanners discovered that hemlock bark
served as an effective tanning agent, they began to
strip the virgin forest of its trees, peeling the bark
away and leaving the trunks to rot on the forest
floor. By 1855, the forest had been stripped of almost every hemlock tree, and the mountaintop
had to reinvent itself.

Tannersville didn't actually incorporate until
after the tannery boom had passed, but the centrally located **Mountain Top Arboretum** (Rte.
23C, 518/589-3903, www.mtarbor.org; open
year-round) seems to make amends for the past.
Stop by for a lesson in native and exotic trees
and shrubs. You can wander across seven acres in
a guided or self-led tour, or join one of its many
horticultural education programs.

Extending in both directions from the

The Upper Hudson

AMERICAN GINSENG

The Chinese weren't the only ones to discover the healthful side effects of wild ginseng. Native Americans discovered the plant in the Catskills long before the Dutch settlers arrived, and local residents have been consuming it in teas, lotions, and tonics ever since.

In Chinese medicine, ginseng roots are believed to energize and rejuvenate the body and enhance immunity. Although most of the world's supply is now cultivated in China and Korea, the highest-quality ginseng grows wild under the shade of deciduous trees like the sugar maple.

In the mid-1990s, Bob Beyfuss at the Cornell Cooperative Extension of Green County began an experiment—to teach local farmers how to simulate the wild growth of ginseng in their own backyards, the Catskill Mountains. Earning a price of $500 or more per pound, the root offered struggling farmers a way to supplement their meager income.

Wild ginseng is difficult to find and identify. Few know it well are willing to share their secrets. But those who care to sustain its presence in the Catskills spread the seeds of a plant before they harvest its root. The plant is protected by law in New York State and may only be picked September 1–November 30.

The most inviting building in town is an enormous red barn that serves as headquarters for the Catskill Mountain Foundation (CMF), a nonprofit dedicated to revitalizing the mountaintop with cultural events and programs. It publishes the free *Catskill Mountain Guide* with a detailed calendar of events. Across Main Street from the red barn are two renovated buildings that house the **CMF Theater, Bookstore, and Gallery** (Rte. 23A, 518/263-5157, http://bookstore.catskillmtn.org; Mon.–Thurs. 11 A.M.–5 P.M., Fri. 10 A.M.–8 P.M., Sat. 10 A.M.–10 P.M., Sun. 11 A.M.–5 P.M.).

Leaving Hunter on Route 23A, you pass Route 296, a shortcut to Windham. An alternative and more scenic route, however, is to continue west until County Route 17, the turnoff to Jewett, which winds its way though orchards and historic homes up to Maplecrest, just outside of Windham.

If you skip the scenic drive and head toward Lexington, you'll soon pass the Baroque-style lanterns of the **St. John the Baptist Ukrainian Catholic Church** (518/263-3862, www.brama.com/stjohn/shop.html; daily 9 A.M. mass, additional service Sun. 10 A.M.; store hours Tues.–Fri. noon–4 P.M., Sat. 10 A.M.–2 P.M., and 6–8 P.M., Sun. 11:30 A.M.–2 P.M.) Built of cedar logs imported from British Columbia, the church serves as a spiritual and cultural center for Ukrainians living in the U.S. and represents the traditional architecture and wood-carvings of the Carpathian highland people. The church hosts art exhibits and a folk art store in a separate community center.

arboretum, Main Street is sporting a new look: charming Victorians freshly painted in purples, reds, and yellows give the place an updated, yet old western feel.

Hunter Mountain

As soon as temperatures dip below freezing, the 1,100 snow guns at Hunter Mountain (Rte. 23A, 800/FOR-SNOW or 800/367-7669, www.huntermtn.com; daily 8:30 A.M.–4 P.M.) begin to paint the mountain white. A winter destination since 1960, Hunter still attracts diehard skiers from the Tri-State Area.

You can walk to the sleepy town of Hunter from the parking lot, as long as you aren't wearing ski boots. Many of the buildings on Main Street have experienced a recent makeover; however, many more could use still some extra attention.

Prattsville

Route 23A meets up with Route 23 out of Windham in an open field at the Batavia Kill crossing. From there, it is a mile into Prattsville, another mountaintop village. You can't drive through Prattsville without learning a thing or two about its founder, the eccentric Colonel Zadock Pratt. For some 13 years in the early 19th century, Pratt ran one of the world's largest and most successful tanneries, and he used the profits to build present-day Prattsville. According to local lore, he completed the building of a new tannery dam in

FORTY TO ONE

W hile McDonalds is trying to win your breakfast dollars with the McGriddle—featuring maple-flavored sugar crystals that are baked into your pancakes—a handful of Hudson Valley farmers continue to produce real maple syrup the old-fashioned way. They drill holes in hard maple trees, collect the sap that drips out, and boil excess water away in a wood-fired evaporator. The end result is Grade A maple syrup that turns a quick breakfast into a gourmet brunch.

Once an off-season income supplement for dairy farms, maple sugarhouses today draw late-season skiers and other visitors for a lesson in culinary science. The process begins in late February or early March, when temperatures climb into the 40s during the day and return to the low 20s at night. For about four to six weeks, the fluctuating temperatures move tree sap from roots to leaves and back again, allowing the farmer to catch some of the flow without harming the tree. The most authentic sugarhouses hang aluminum buckets on each trunk to collect the sap, although larger operations have upgraded to plastic pipes in order to speed up the process.

Straight out of the tree, sap runs clear, with just a hint of sweetness. Back in the sugarhouse, the farmer boils the frothy liquid in the long flutes of a steel evaporator, staying up all night long when necessary to finish the day's harvest. An instrument called a hydrometer measures the specific gravity of the liquid and tells the boiler when the sap has officially reached the distinctive amber color and thickness we associate with the real stuff. It's a precise and labor-intensive operation—for every 40 gallons of raw sap, a sugarhouse will produce approximately 1 gallon of syrup.

Most tours begin with collecting sap from the sugar bush and then return to the sugarhouse to see the evaporator in action. Adults will savor the rich and steamy aroma inside the sugarhouse, while youngsters will enjoy romping around in the snow and mud outside. If you have the time, stay long enough to watch your host finish a batch of syrup—that's when the real culinary skill comes into play.

SUGARHOUSES IN THE HUDSON VALLEY

Ulster County
Lyonsville Sugarhouse & Farm
591 County Road 2/Krumville Rd., Kripplebush
845/687-2518

Mountain Dew Maple Products
351 Samsonville Rd., Kerhonkson
845/626-3466

Greene County
Maple Glen Farm
Scribner Hollow Rd., East Jewett
518/589-5319

Maple Hill Farms
107 C. Crapser Rd., Cobleskill
518/234-4858 or 866/291-8100
www.maplehillfarms.biz

Sullivan County
Andersen's Maple Farm
534 Andersen Rd., Long Eddy
845/887-4238

Muthig Farm
1036 Muthig Rd., Parksville
845/292-7838

Delaware County
Catskill Mountain Maple
65 Charlie Wood Rd., De Lancey
607/746-6215

Shaver-Hill Farm
Shaver Rd., Harpersfield
607/652-6792

The Upper Hudson

November 1824, as the first layer of ice was forming on the Schoharie Creek, and then celebrated by swimming the length of the dam.

Despite his role in destroying a large chunk of the Catskill forest, Zadock was well liked by his community, as his generosity far outweighed his shameless self-promotion. His life's achievements are depicted in a bas-relief sculpture on a large, flat rock at the outskirts of town. Called Pratt Rock, the stone carving includes the tannery, a hemlock tree, and many of Pratt's family members.

In the center of town, Pratt's former residence is now the **Zadock Pratt Museum** (518/299-3369, prattmuseum@hotmail.com, www.prattmuseum.com; Memorial Day–Columbus Day Thurs.–Mon. 1–4:30 P.M.). It contains period furnishings, a Steinway piano, photographs of Pratt, and a model of his tannery.

ALONG ROUTE 23
Windham Mountain

From the intersection of Routes 23 and 23A, it is a nine-mile drive along the Batavia Kill to Greene County's other downhill ski resort, **Windham Mountain** (Rte. 23, Windham, 800/754-9463, www.skiwindham.com), a smaller but more upscale version of nearby Hunter. With a base elevation of 1,500 feet and a summit of 3,100 feet, Windham attracts New York City day-trippers by the busload. Mogul experts head for the bumps on Wheelchair and Wedel, while speed demons let loose on Wolverine. Intermediate skiers enjoy the two-mile-long Wrap Around trail, and a run through the terrain park ends with an enormous gap jump at the bottom.

Windham Village is about a mile from the ski resort parking lot, too far to walk in winter weather. Along Main Street, contemporary art galleries alternate with skier-friendly eateries. A few of the ski shops rent mountain bikes in summer. **Windham Fine Arts** (5380 Main St., 518/734-6850, info@windhamfinearts.com, www.windhamfinearts.com) rotates shows every four to six weeks and has information about other galleries and cultural events in the area.

From Windham, the Mohican Trail (Route 23) begins to descend back down to the valley

floor, and the peaks of Blackhead and Black Dome come into view. A local artist runs a creative firewood stand by sculpting split wood into a new design each winter—for example, a barn or a railroad train. The western trailhead for the Escarpment Trail begins here as well. On the clearest of days, the Point Lookout Inn offers a spectacular five-state view to the northeast, with the peak of New Hampshire's Mount Washington visible in the distance.

East Durham

Irish immigrants were among the first settlers on the north side of Route 23. Stone walls mark old boundaries along County Route 31, and every sign in Durham and East Durham has a shamrock, or at least green lettering. A visit to **Guaranteed Irish** (2220 Rte. 145, East Durham, 518/634-2392, www.guarateedirishshop.com; July–Aug. daily 9 A.M.–9 P.M., Sept.–June 9 A.M.–6 P.M.), at the corner of County Routes 31 and 145, will put you in the proper frame of mind to enjoy this town. An enormous retail space has an overwhelming selection of Irish-made goods.

Next door is Darby's Irish Pub and Restaurant, the local watering hole. (Route 145 between them goes to Freehold.) The **Zoom Flume Water Park** (Shady Glen Rd. off Rte. 145, 800/888-3586, www.zoomflume.com; June–Sept. 10 A.M.–6 P.M. and some weekends until 7 P.M.; admission $18.95 adult, $15.95 kids) is a popular summertime attraction for kids. On the same road, **Hull-O-Farms** (10 Cochrane Rd., Durham, 518/239-6950, www.hull-o.com), founded in 1779, is a working dairy farm that allows overnight guests to participate in everyday farm activities.

Freehold and Greenville

There are two reasons to divert to Freehold when traveling along Route 23: to take an aerial tour in a classic J-3 Cub or to savor the French-inspired menu at the recently opened Ruby's Hotel. The **Freehold Airport** (Rte. 67, Freehold, 518/634-7626, www.cdrpc.org/Air_Freehold.html; Apr.–Dec. daily 9 A.M.–6:30 P.M.) offers daily scenic rides (weather permitting), a ground and flight school, and general aviation services. It is privately owned and operated by Clements J. Hoovler Jr. of the Catskill Valley Flying Service. The restaurant is about a 10-minute walk from the runway.

A few miles up the road from Freehold on Route 32, William Vanderbilt constructed a Queen Anne-style home in 1889. Today, the white, two-story building is a county inn set on six acres of manicured lawns and decorated in Victorian and country accents. In summer, the **Greenville Arms 1889 Inn** (South St., 518/966-5219 or 888/665-0044, www.greenevillearms .com) hosts a series of Hudson River Valley Art Workshops in its Carriage House Studio.

Cairo
Once the center of a booming Greene County poultry business and a major producer of fresh fruits, Cairo (CARE-o) is a good place to stop for services. You'll find groceries at the Great American, gas at Cumberland Farm, a True Value hardware store, and a standby for locals. A new set of decorative streetlights and real concrete sidewalks line Main Street, but the town is still lacking in restaurants.

The primary colors of the **Mahayana Buddhist Temple** (700 Ira Vail Rd., 518/622-3619; daily 7 A.M.–7 P.M.; donations accepted) look oddly out of place in South Cairo, 2.5 miles from Route 23B. Members of the New York City–based Eastern States Buddhist Temple of America retreat to the woods here for quiet contemplation. A red and yellow arch leads the way down a steep driveway to the temple, set on two small ponds. Visitors are welcome to explore the site.

Don't leave Cairo without wandering through the hamlets of Purling and Round Top. Newly built log cabins alternate here with 150-year-old farmhouses, and fields have grown up around abandoned farm equipment. Leaving Cairo on Mountain Avenue (County Rte. 24), you'll pass the Purling post office, Shinglekill Falls, and a roller rink that has been open more or less continuously since the 1950s. Gino Altimari at the **Round Top Raptor Center** (733 Bald Hill Rd. N., 518/622-0118, www.caironychamber.com/ rountoprapce.html; Memorial Day–Columbus

Day Tues.–Sun. 1–4 P.M.; adults $7, children $2) teaches visitors about falcons, hawks, and other local birds of prey.

SPORTS AND RECREATION
Downhill Skiing and Snowboarding
You haven't skied the northeast until you've endured subzero temperatures, frostbite warnings, and the wet blast of artificial snow in your face. The après-ski whirlpool tub (there are many options) becomes an all-important finish to the day. **Hunter Mountain** (Rte. 23A, Hunter, 800/367-7669, www.huntermtn.com; $51 weekend/holiday, $41 midweek) has three mountains that can handle 15,000 skiers per hour, but lift lines can still run up to an hour on busy weekends.

Hunter Mountain Statistics
Base: 1,600 feet
Summit: 3,200 feet
Vertical drop: 1,600 feet
Trails: 53
Lifts: 11
Skiable acres: 240
Snowmaking: 100 percent of terrain
Snow report: 800/486-8376

Windham Mountain (Rte. 23, Windham, 800/754-9463, www.skiwindham; $50 weekend/holiday, $40 midweek) is open mid-November through mid-April 8 A.M.–4 P.M. weekends and 9 A.M.–4 P.M. midweek, as long as the weather cooperates. You can also ski at night Thursday through Saturday and some holidays 4–10 P.M. from December until March. Adult lift tickets cost $40 nonholiday, with discounts for students and multiday day tickets. For an additional $15, you can sign up for First Tracks to get on the slopes an hour before the lifts open to the masses. Pick up Route 23 West at New York State Thruway Exit 21. Windham maintains a useful website through which you can book lift tickets and rental equipment, or listen to the snow report updated daily by Darrell, the mountain's head snow-maker.

Windham Mountain Statistics
Base: 1,500 feet
Summit: 3,100 feet
Vertical: 1,600 feet
Trails: 39
Lifts: 7
Skiable acres: 242
Snowmaking: 97 percent of terrain
Snow report: 800/729-4766

A left turn off Route 23A before Selena's Diner in Tannersville leads to a hemlock-lined road and the entrance to **Cortina Mountain** (Clum Hill Rd., 866/926-7846, www.cortinamountain.com; adults Sat. $18, Sun. $16). Under new management since 2002, Cortina maintains a tubing run, terrain park, and paint ball facility. The owners are remodeling the resort with the upscale Hotel Scribner Hollow as a model. When the lifts start running, the tiny hill may once again become a fine place for kids to learn to ski or snowboard. With a base elevation of 2,200 feet, Cortina has the highest base of any ski areas in Catskills; however, lifts were not running in winter 2003–2004.

Cortina Mountain Statistics
Base: 1,925 feet
Summit: 2,650 feet
Vertical: 725 feet
Trails: 10
Lifts: 4
Skiable acres: 87
Snowmaking: 100 percent
Snow report: 866/926-7846

Bob Hostetter, a ski patroller at Hunter Mountain and licensed rock-climbing guide, shares his knowledge and experience of the Catskills' backcountry ski secrets through **Catskill Backcountry Ski Tours** (P.O. Box 712, Hunter, 518/589-6989, www.catskill-bcski.com).

Nordic Skiing

Several areas on the mountaintop offer varied terrain for Nordic skiers: **White Birches Ski Area** (Nauvoo Rd., Windham, 518/734-3266) maintains 35 kilometers of groomed trails for novice to expert skiers. A cozy lodge onsite has a fireplace and snack bar. **Villaggio Resort Cross Country Skiing Area** (Haines Falls, 518/589-5000) has 300 acres and 14 kilometers of marked, groomed trails suitable for beginner and intermediate skiers. And the **Mountain Trails Cross Country Ski Center** (Rte. 23A, Tannersville, 518/589-5316, info@mtntrails.com, www.mtntrails.com; adult full-day $13, $10 after 2 P.M., teens $10, junior $8; full-day rental $15) has another 35 kilometers of groomed, patrolled trails with rentals, sales, a lodge, lessons, and a snack bar onsite. Daily hours vary according to snow conditions. Note: the summer Escarpment Trail is not safe for cross-country skiing.

In the valley, the **Winter Clove Inn Nordic Skiing Area** (Winter Clove Rd., Round Top, 518/622-3267, www.winterclove.com) opens 400 acres to public, with rentals available. Expert trails climb into the hills, while the easier trails follow a streambed.

Snowshoeing, Tubing, and Snowmobiles

Snowshoeing is one of the fastest-growing sports in America, and Greene County offers plenty of great trails. **Mountain Trails Cross Country Ski Center** (Rte. 23A, Tannersville, 518/589-5316, info@mtntrails.com, www.mtntrails.com) offers trails of varying grades that traverse bridges and wind through conifers. Ski patrol monitors the trails for safety. **North Lake Public Campground** (County Rte. 18, Haines Falls, 518/589-5058) has trails along wooded areas and up to the site of the Catskill Mountain House with stunning views of the Hudson River Valley. Rent equipment in nearby Hunter. The trails at **Colgate Lake** (off Rte. 78, East Jewett) run through an open meadow with great views of the Blackhead Mountain Range. Take Route 23A to Tannersville, and turn onto Route 23C, and then right onto Route 78 by the post office.

Cortina, Hunter, and Windham all have 8- to 12-lane snow tubing runs with lift access. Tickets range from $18 all day at Cortina to $25 at Windham and Hunter. Hunter also has the

Bear Creek Landing (Rtes. 214 & 23A, Hunter, 518/263-3839) ice rink.

Several outfitters run guided snowmobile trips: **Rip Van Winkle Ranch** (Rte. 23A, Haines Falls, 800/804-5799) has snowmobile and ATV rentals for use on mountain trails. **Ponderosa Fun Park** (4620 Rte. 32, Catskill, 518/678-9206) rents snowmobiles for use on private land.

Hiking

Hikers can't get enough of the northern Catskills in summer and fall. They hit the trails in search of tasty wild blueberries, wild ginseng, geological wonders, or a simply a view and a breath of fresh air. Trailhead parking lots fill early on sunny weekends, but with a little determination, it's still possible to escape the crowds. Although the most popular trails are well maintained, it's not uncommon to encounter some bushwhacking on many hikes. It's a good idea to carry water, topographical maps, and a compass or GPS, no matter how far you plan to go. *Catskill Trails: A Ranger's Guide to the High Peaks, Book One*, by Edward G. Henry, (Black Dome Press, 2000), covers more than 20 hikes in the area, including the trails to Kaaterskill Falls and the Escarpment.

Major trailheads are clustered around the towns of Hunter, Jewett, and Prattsville. From Route 23A in Hunter, you can access the Escarpment and the vista from the site of the old Catskill Mountain House, as well as Roundtop and Twin Mountains. The Big Hollow Road in Jewett leads to trails that summit the High Peaks of Blackhead, Black Dome, and Thomas Cole. Further West, near Prattsville, you can reach trails to Westkill, Huntersfield, and Bearpen Mountains.

To see what inspired the romantic landscapes of the Hudson River School painters, hike a portion of the 24-mile-long Escarpment Trail, which connects Route 23 in East Windham with the North Lake Public Campground to the south. A three-day out-and-back hike with loops at each end traverses 30 miles of thick hardwood forests and hemlock groves, allowing time for diversions to the summits of Windham High Peak, Acra Point, and Blackhead Mountain along the way.

Dramatic elevation changes make for challenging terrain, so plan to take it slow. Camping is not restricted below 3,500 feet, but conservationists encourage hikers to set up camp in designated areas to minimize the impact on the forest. You can fill water bottles at numerous natural springs along the trail.

For a guided hike, the **Mountaintop Historical Society** (www.mths.org) leads summer and fall trips. There is no charge to join, but the organization asks participants to complete a registration form in advance. The site links to online versions of area topographical maps on maptech.com

Back at the river's edge, the Scenic Hudson Land Trust has rescued a seven-acre stretch of shoreline from development and created **Four-Mile Point Preserve,** a nature trail that leads to an overlook 60 feet above the river. From the Rip Van Winkle Bridge, follow Route 385 almost eight miles north to Four-Mile Point Road.

For an unusual adventure, mushroom expert John Boyle of **Home and Forest** (South St., Durham, 518/239-8039) leads identification workshops and foraging trips. He also sells growing kits.

Mountain Biking and Road Riding

Cyclists in Greene County can find miles of traffic-free roads to pedal, but be prepared to climb. Many old logging roads offer scenic and challenging mountain biking terrain. And when the snow melts away, Hunter opens part of its trail system to mountain bikers who want to start at the top. Hikers may try to tell you otherwise, but bikes are allowed on most of the trails in the area; take caution, however, when considering a loop on the ridge trail. The terrain is steep and rocky, making much of it unsuitable for riding.

Several shops on the mountaintop offer rentals and trail maps: **Hunter Mountain Biking** (Rte. 23A, Hunter, 888/HunterMtn or 888/486-8376, www.huntermtn.com; July–Oct. weekends) has trails at the base and summit of the mountain, with lift access. **The Bike Shop at Windham Mountain Outfitters** (Rte. 296 & South St., Windham, 518/734-4700, www.windhamoutfitters.com) rents bikes and leads trips for all levels. And **White Birches Mountain Biking** (Navoo Rd., Windham, 518/734-3266) has 15 miles of trails with single and double track, but no rentals.

Golf

Green County has 10 golf courses with scenic views of the surrounding countryside. Most are open April through November. The **Blackhead Mountain Lodge & Country Club** (Blackhead Mountain Rd., 888/382-7474, www.blackheadmountaingolf.com) maintains a challenging 18-hole par 72 course with stunning views of the High Peaks. Newly opened in 2003, **Christman's Windham House Country Inn and Golf Resort** (5742 Rte. 23, Windham, 518/734-4230 or 888/294-4053, www.windhamhouse.com) operates two courses—an 18-hole and a 9-hole—with four sets of tees. Tannersville has two 9-hole par 35 courses that are open to the public: **Colonial Golf Club** (Main St., Tannersville, 518/589-9807) and the **Rip Van Winkle Country Club** (3200 Rte. 23A, Tannersville, 518/678-9779).

Swimming and Boating

A dip in a mountain lake or a paddle along the river are the water sports of choice in Greene County. North Lake offers swimming and non-motorized boating, and lifeguards are on duty Memorial Day through Labor Day. Farther west, **Dolan's Lake** (Ski Bowl Rd., Hunter, 518/263-4020) has a picnic area and lifeguard on duty in summer months.

Several marinas offer boaters convenient access to the Hudson. Part of the New York State Park System, the **Athens Boat Launch** (Rte. 385, Athens, 518/945-1551) has a hard surface ramp and parking for 25 cars. The **Coxsackie Boat Launch** (Reed St., Coxsackie, 518/731-2718), also a state facility, has a hard surface ramp and parking for 36 cars and trailers. **Hagar's Harbor** (off Rte. 385, Athens, 518/945-1858; May–Oct.) has floating docks, showers, and a riverside restaurant with a raw bar on the patio.

In Catskill, turn right at the bend in Main Street onto Greene Street to get to the full-service **Catskill Marina** (Greene St., 518/943-4170 or 800/747-2720), which has gasoline, 20 boat slips (150 feet maximum), showers, restrooms, laundry, and even a heated pool. Two other marinas, Hop-O-Nose and Riverview Marine Services, are located farther out on West Main. Riverview

rents kayaks, rowboats, and canoes. **Dutchman's Landing** (Lower Main St., 518/943-3830) has four boat ramps, picnic tables, and barbecues. The **Hudson River Water Trail Association** (www.hrwa.org) sponsors numerous outings and operates facilities for river-goers. The group is lobbying to develop a water trail from the mouth of the Hudson to the Great Lakes.

Fishing and Hunting

Whether you want to catch shad, bass, or trout, **River Basin Sport Shop** (66 W. Bridge St., Catskill, 518/943-2111) will provide all the tackle and advice you need for fishing in the area. When the ice melts, **Bear Creek Landing** (Rtes. 214 & 23A, Hunter, 518/263-3839, www.bearcreeklanding.com; Mon.–Thurs. 10 A.M.–10 P.M., Fri. 10 A.M.–11 P.M., Sat. 9 A.M.–11 P.M., Sun. 9 A.M.–10 P.M.) opens a trout-fishing preserve on 80 mountaintop acres. Around the same time, the Batavia Kill near Prattsville becomes a mecca for fly fishers. Bass season begins on the third Saturday in June and runs through October.

Licensed hunters may take grouse, pheasant, turkey, deer, black bear, and small game from public wilderness areas or private clubs during specified seasons. See the *Know* chapter for New York State Department of Environmental Conservation regulations. Upland bird hunters should head to the pheasant preserve at the **Friar Tuck Resort** (4858 Rte. 32, Catskill, 800/832-7600).

Aviation

The **Freehold Airport** (Rte. 67, Freehold, 518/634-7626, www.cdrpc.org/Air_Freehold.html; Apr.–Dec. daily 9 A.M.–6:30 P.M.) offers daily scenic rides (weather permitting), a ground and flight school, and general aviation services.

ACCOMMODATIONS

Country inns with a colonial ambience are the theme for places to stay in Greene County. You can find a few modern hotels near the ski resorts and budget motels along the highways, but the most charming accommodations include a country breakfast and a friendly chat with the innkeeper.

Under $100

A mile from the slopes, on the road that connects Windham to Hunter, is the modern ℕ **Hotel Vienna** (107 Rte. 296, Windham, 518/734-5300, www.thehotelvienna.com; $85–115 nonholiday). Straight out of the Austrian alps, rooms have beamed ceilings, cherry furniture, lace curtains, and tiled balconies. Amenities include cable TV, phones, and air-conditioning, as well as an indoor pool and Jacuzzi. For those returning from the slopes, the innkeeper serves afternoon cookies and tea by the breakfast room fireplace. Midweek specials and ski packages are available.

$100–150

The beautifully restored **Stewart House Restaurant and Bed and Breakfast** (Second St., Athens, 518/945-1357, info@stewarthouse.com, www.stewarthouse.com; $110 with continental breakfast) attracts Shakespeare enthusiasts and city dwellers in search of a romantic weekend getaway. Five immaculate guestrooms on the 2nd floor are decorated with cheerful colors and antique furnishings. Every room has a private bath, a couple have river views, and No. 7 has a fireplace. Hollywood trivia gurus should request No. 8, which not only overlooks the river but is the place where actress Meryl Streep dies in the 1987 film *Ironweed*.

One place in Catskill Village is worth an overnight visit: **Caleb Street's Inn** (251 Main St., Catskill, 518/943-0246, calebstreetsinn@hotmail.com, www.mhonline.net/~calebinn; $100–160), at the corner of Greene and Main, just above the Catskill Marina. A white 1790 house with black shutters, the inn has a veranda that overlooks Catskill Creek. Its bright guestrooms feature hardwood floors, large windows, and antique beds and dressers.

Linda and Hugh are your friendly hosts at the creekside **Tumblin' Falls House** (Mountain Ave., Purling, 800/473-0519, tfallsbb@francomm.com, www.tumblinfalls.com; $85–165). The inn accommodates 8–10 guests in a pale yellow Victorian that's set back from the road. All four rooms have mountain views, and a large, terraced deck and hot tub overlook the 30-foot falls. The Falls View Suite has the best view.

The Eggery Inn (County Rte. 16, Tannersville, 800/785-5364, www.eggeryinn.com; $115–145), on the mountaintop, is popular with international guests. Its 15 cozy rooms have comfortable beds, as well as cable TV, air-conditioning, and in-room phones. Owners Julie and Abe will make you feel right at home. The inn has a view of Hunter Mountain from the bar and dining room. And with a pair of binoculars, you can tell how long the lift lines are.

The ℕ **Redcoat's Country Inn & Restaurant** (50 Dale Lane, 518/589-9858, info@redcoatsonline.com, www.redcoatsonline.com; $95–175, with a full county breakfast) is worth a look, even if you aren't going to dine or stay the night in one of its cozy rooms. A large stone fireplace heats the lounge and dark-wood bar. And from a black wicker rocking chair on the sloping front porch, the mountains look close enough to touch. Guestrooms are decorated in muted rose and blue tones and simply furnished with brass bed frames and antique dressers. From the traffic light in Tannersville, turn left and follow Elka Park Road to Dale Lane.

$150–200

The ℕ **Winter Clove Inn** (Winter Clove Rd., Round Top, 518/622-3267, www.winterclove.com; $80–90 per person per night, including all meals) rests on 400 acres at the base of North Mountain, bordering "forever wild" state land. A creek meanders through the property, and when the winter storms roll in, guests can ski on 15 kilometers of marked cross-country trails. Inside, guestrooms feature a colonial decor, with hardwood floors, four-poster beds, and lacy white linens. The hotel attracts more suburban families than city folk. Its amenities include heated indoor and outdoor swimming pools and a nine-hole golf course. The old carriage house was converted into a bowling alley and soda fountain in the 1950s. Repeat visitors to the bowling alley quickly learn to use the warp in the floor to their advantage.

Winwood Mountain Inn (Main St., Windham, 518/734-3000, info@winwoodinn.com, www.winwoodinn.com; $135–205), previously the Windham Arms, offers free transportation to Windham from the train station in Hudson, 40 minutes away. Its 55 modern rooms are painted in earthy tones and are minimally furnished. Ask for a mountain view, or you may end up facing the courtyard instead. Amenities include an indoor fitness center and movie theater.

Many repeat visitors at the **Greene Mountain View Inn** (S. Main St., Tannersville, 518/589-9886 or 877/489-9963, www.greenemountain-viewinn.com; $125–175 weekends) come to attend services at the 100-year-old synagogue located four doors down the street. A 1981 Ms. Pacman machine and big screen TV in the lounge area complement the antique jukebox and mirror in the breakfast room. Rooms are small but clean, with natural wood accents and sloping roofs on the top floor; some have more recently updated bathrooms than others. No. 19, the newest guest room, is a miniloft with four steps leading from the bed area up to a small sink and shower. The room has mountain views on two sides, and many guests request it in advance, despite its small size.

The expansive **Scribner Hollow Lodge** (Rte. 23A, Hunter, 518/263-4211 or 800/395-4683, www.scribnerhollow.com; $135–165) is a rustic mountain chalet with modern amenities, including an underground pool and spa called the Grotto. Deluxe rooms are decorated in a southwest, hunting lodge, or country motif. The Prospect Restaurant on the premises stocks an impressive wine cellar to accompany entrees like locally smoked Catskill rainbow trout, Hudson Valley lamb sausage, and cider-glazed breast of Long Island duckling. Mains are $21–28.

Half of the guestrooms at the **Point Lookout Inn** (Rte. 23, East Windham, 518/734-338, www.pointlookoutinn.com; $150–165) feature the property's stunning five-state view of the Hudson River Valley and beyond. (Be sure to request the valley view.) Located a short distance from Windham, the recently renovated inn maintains a country feel. Guests are invited to help themselves to anything in the inn's refrigerator for breakfast.

The combination of antique furnishings and original, contemporary art at the **Greeneville Arms 1889 Inn** (South St., Greeneville, 518/966-5219, www.greenevillearms.com; $115–195) gives the place a unique feel. Some rooms in the main house of this country inn feature canopied or four-poster beds and private porches or balconies. Owners Eliot and Letitia Dalton recently added two rooms in a new Victorian cottage on the grounds.

Sunny Hill Resort & Golf Course (518/634-7642, www.sunnyhill.com; $280–350, including all meals) is popular with golfers and families. The resort has 100 basic motel-style rooms in seven different buildings gathered around the 18-hole golf course. Some rooms have balconies and mountain views.

Campgrounds

Greene County has two state campgrounds and more than a dozen private campgrounds to choose from. **North Lake Public Campground** (North Lake Rd., Haines Falls; early May–Oct.) has 200 tent and RV sites, plus picnic areas, hot showers, flush toilets, and a boat launch. **Devil's Tombstone State Campground** (Rte. 214, Hunter, 800/688-2267; May 16–Sept. 1) has 24 sites, picnic tables, and a playground.

Next door to the Catskill Game Farm, **Catskill Campground** (79 Castle Rd., Catskill, 518/678-5873, catskillcamptv@cisbec.net, May 15–Columbus Day) has 50 sites for tents and RVs. You can also pop your tent at Whip-O-Will, (County Rte. 31, Round Top, 518/622-3277 or 800/969-2267; Apr.–Oct. 15.).

FOOD
Along the River—Route 385

For seafood in summer, head to **Catskill Point** (7 Main St., Catskill, 518/943-5352; mains $20–30), which features a large outdoor patio with a white picket fence and a tempting raw bar. **Tony's Luncheonette** (325 Main St., Catskill, 518/943-1076, Mon.–Fri. 6:30 A.M.–5 P.M., Sat. 7 A.M.–2 P.M., Sun. 7 A.M.–noon; mains $4–7) boasts the best burgers and egg sandwiches in town. And the **Garden Gate Café** (424 Main St., Catskill, 518/943-1994; average main dish $5) serves breakfast and lunch with a menu covering everything from omelets to burgers.

La Conca D'Oro (440 Main St., Catskill, 518/943-3549) serves reliable Italian fare to a local clientele. Another local favorite for hearty French fare is **La Rive Restaurant Francais** (141 Dedrick Rd. off Old Kings Rd., Catskill, 518/943-4888), which opens at 6 P.M. Monday through Saturday May–October, and at 2:30 P.M. on Sundays.

Stewart House Restaurant and Bed and Breakfast (2nd St., Athens, 518/945-1357, info@stewarthouse.com, www.stewarthouse.com; Wed.–Sun.; average main dish $15) has a formal dining room and a casual bistro and serves standard pub fare, as well as local specialties like Black Angus beef, grilled rainbow trout, and littleneck steamers.

Turn right at the end of 2nd Street in Athens to find **Ⓜ Ursula's Riverside Diner** (6 S. Water St., Athens, 518/945-2107; daily 6 A.M.–10 P.M.), located across the street from a riverfront park. With a nautical theme and inviting home-cooked food, Ursula's fills up for Sunday brunch, even in the dead of winter. The service is friendly and attentive. On the menu are omelets and pancakes for breakfast; hot and cold sandwiches for lunch; Italian, seafood, and hearty meat dishes for dinner. Breakfast mains average $5, lunch $7, and dinner $12.

One of the Hudson Valley's culinary gems is found on a country road a few miles west of Coxsackie. Owner and chef Damon Baehrel established **Ⓜ The Basement Bistro** (776 Rte. 45, Earlton, 518/634-2338, www.sagecrestcatering.com/bistro.asp) in 1990 as a showcase for his catering business, Sagecrest Catering. He built and landscaped the property by hand to create a warm and elegant restaurant setting. A 2002 renovation added more elbow room and a wine cellar. Baehrel has mastered the element of surprise in fine dining. His initial a la carte menu has evolved into two prix fixe menus featuring locally grown ingredients. For example, a December menu might feature first-of-the-season winter truffles. The bistro offers two seatings per night Thursday–Saturday at 5 P.M. (Sunday at 4 P.M.) and 8:15 P.M. A Chef's Tasting includes 5–7 courses ($45–50 per person), and the Grand Tasting includes 12–15 courses ($50–55 per person)—many of which arrive at the table unannounced. Both options are not always available, and prices vary, depending on the ingredients. Call up to four weeks in advance for reservations

(required), and follow the instructions on the machine to be sure you are confirmed. Turn your cell phone off at the door to get off to a good start with the chef.

Along Route 23A

In winter, **Jam's Café** (Rte. 23A, Haines Falls, 518/589-6481) packs hungry skiers in for brunch. **Romito's Pizza** (Rte. 296, Windham, 518/734-3511), serves a Wednesday night special: a large cheese pizza for $6.50.

Maggie's Krooked Café (Main St., Tannersville, 518/589-6101; opens 7 A.M.; mains $8–12) is known for a reliable cup of coffee, delicious homemade muffins, and hearty breakfast fare. Locals say the prices are high, but where else are you going to get an icy fruit smoothie? **Poncho Villa's** (6037 Rte. 23A, Tannersville, 518/589-3154; Mon.–Thurs. 4–10 P.M., Fri.–Sat. noon–11 P.M., Sun. noon–9 P.M.; average main dish $13) will satisfy a craving for south-of-the-border cuisine.

The cozy **Mountain Brook Dining and Spirits** (Main St., Hunter, 518/263-5351, mains $15–30) has an island bar in the middle of the main dining room and an inviting sofa near the door. Rack of lamb and yellowfin tuna are two standout dishes on the continental menu.

Along Route 23

A 10-minute walk from the Freehold airstrip is **Ⓜ Ruby's Hotel** (3689 Rte. 67, Freehold, 518/634-7790; Thurs.–Sun. dinner only; mains $18–25), in a restored art deco building that dates back to the 1800s. New York City chef Ana Sporer serves French-influenced cuisine, including duck confit and coq au vin, as well as steaks, and seafood. The restaurant has a bar and soda fountain in the front and a formal dining room in the back. Outdoor seating is available in the summer.

Farther up the street, the **Freehold Country Inn** (Rtes. 32 & 67, Freehold, 518/634-2705, www.freeholdcountryinn.net; Mon.–Sat. 4–9 P.M., Sun. noon–9 P.M.; mains $20–35) serves hearty American fare in a relatively formal setting.

The stately **Ⓜ Bavarian Manor** (866 Mountain Rd., Round Top, 518/622-3261, www.bavarianmanor.com; mains $15–25) sits on 100 acres of prime Catskill forest in Purling. The business has hosted German Americans (and those who wish they were) since 1865. A decidedly Old World German restaurant serves all the requisite dishes—schnitzel, sauerbraten, spaetzle, rouladen, and bratwurst—as well as seafood and wild game. The kitchen is a designated training facility for students of the Culinary Institute of America. Upstairs, 19 rooms have private bath, TV, fireplace, Jacuzzi, and air-conditioning.

Hartmann's Kaffeehaus (County Rte. 39, Round Top, 518/622-3820; Easter–Christmas) is the real deal: sinfully delicious Viennese pastries, and the only place around to get a decent cup of coffee. Look for a large, white building with bright blue trim, next to the firehouse.

Maassmann's Restaurant (Blackhead Mountain Rd., Round Top, 888/382-7474, www.blackheadmountaingolf.com), at the Blackhead Mountain Golf Course, is popular with locals for special occasions like Easter dinner. On the menu are American and German dishes. Call ahead to reserve the Stammtisch Corner, which seats five to seven people. Maassmann's serves dinner Friday–Saturday in winter, Thursday–Sunday in spring and fall, and daily in summer. Mains range $12–20.

The Alpine Pork Store (Rte. 23B, South Cairo, 518/622-3056; Thurs.–Fri. 9 A.M.–5 P.M., Sat. 9 A.M.–3 P.M.), in South Cairo, sells German-style sausages or wursts, as well as a full menu of fresh meats cut-to-order. This is a good place to stop on the way to a ski condo at Windham Mountain.

Lunch is the time to dine at **The Victorian Rose at Point Lookout Inn** (Rte. 23, East Windham, 518/734-3381, www.pointlookoutinn.com; mains $15–32), preferably on a clear day, when the view stretches all the way to New Hampshire, 180 miles to the north. Reserve early for a fireside table.

Zerega's (Main St., Windham, 518/734-4655; mains $10–15) makes New York–style pizza by the slice or the pie. Order at the take-out window on the right side for slices, the dining room is for people ordering whole pies.

The popular **La Griglia Restaurante** (Rte. 23, Ashland, 518/734-4499) has moved west of Windham to the neighboring town of Ashland.

The menu consists of tempting northern Italian dishes like osso bucco, roast duck, and of course, pasta. The chef also runs a bakery and café in town, just off Main Street (La Griglia Café, Church St., Windham, 518/734-6100).

ENTERTAINMENT AND EVENTS

Performing Arts

Stewart House owner Owen Lipstein founded the **Shakespeare on the Hudson Theatre Company** (2 N. Water St., 518/731-8030, info@shakespeareonthehudson.com, www.shakespeareonthehudson.com) a few years before buying the old hotel. Summer performances begin at 8 P.M. Thursday–Saturday.

Bars and Nightlife

The German theme continues all year long in Round Top, where the **Mountain Brauhaus** (430 Winter Clove Rd., Round Top, 800/999-7376, www.mountainbrauhaus.com) pours Dinkelacker beer by the stein. Polka dancers take the floor on weekend nights. Young people congregate at **Slopes Bar** (242 Main St., Tannersville, 518/589-5006, www.slopesniteclub.com) in Tannersville for après ski refreshments and late-night entertainment. The **Friar Tuck Resort** (4858 Rte. 32, Catskill, 800/832-7600) hosts occasional country-and-western music concerts. Keep an eye out for the Elvis impersonator at **Nick's** (Rte. 32, Cairo, 518/622-9468). He also makes the rounds to other local bars and clubs.

Festivals

Bass tournaments draw large crowds to Catskill in Spring, when the striped bass are running. Anglers should head to **River Basin Sports** (66 W. Bridge St., Catskill, 518/943-2111; Tues.–Sat. 8:30 A.M.–5 P.M.) for dates and details. For longtime Catskill residents, the run of the American shad heralds the arrival of summer. **The Hudson River Shad Festival** (Main St., Catskill, 518/828-3375) takes place in May or June with shad tasting, music, theater programs, and even a lecture on harvesting ice from the Hudson.

At the annual **Catskill Ginseng Festival,**

(Catskill Point, Lower Main St., Catskill, 518/ 943 6612; 10 A.M.–5 P.M.; admission $4), you can taste freshly harvested ginseng, sample ginseng foods and beverages, view wild ginseng roots that are more than 100 years old, and purchase some of the highest-quality wild ginseng roots available in the U.S.

For 27 years, the Michael J. Quill Irish Cultural & Sports Centre (2119 Rte. 145, 518/634-2286 or 800/434-FEST, www.east-durham.org) has hosted the **East Durham Irish Festival,** drawing participants from across the Hudson Valley with Irish music performances and a one-acre "map" of Ireland, bordered with flags of the country's provinces and counties.

The Catskill Mountain Foundation theater shows a mix of independent and Hollywood films. In summer, a series of Hunter Mountain Festivals draws large crowds, with the **International Celtic Festival** and **Oktoberfest** among the most popular events. A calendar is available at www.huntermtn.com/calendar.htm.

In summer, beginner and experienced artists can enroll in a series of **Hudson River Valley Art Workshops** (South St., Greenville, 518/966-5219, info@artworkshops.com, www.artworkshops.com) at the Greenville Arms 1889 Inn. Weekend and weeklong programs cover watercolor, oil, acrylic, pastel, drawing, or collage. Tuition costs $300 for a weekend course and $475 for a weeklong course. A package with accommodations and dinners is $600 for three nights and $960 for six nights.

SHOPPING

Antiques, crafts, and locally made foods are among the best finds in Greene County.

Farm Stands

Local farmers bring produce to the **Riverside Market** (Dutchman's Landing, Catskill, 518/622-9820) on Saturday mornings June through October. Pop into **Traphagen's Honey and Gourmet Shop** (Rte. 23A, Hunter, 518/ 263-4150; Thurs.–Mon. 9 A.M.–5 P.M.) on the way out of Hunter to satisfy a craving for sugar. **Maple Hill Farm** (Route 23A, Lexington,

518/299-3195), just up the road, sells locally made maple syrup and deerskin products.

The Catskill Mountain Foundation shares its space with the **CMF Farm Market** (Rte. 23A, Main St., 518/263-4908, ext. 204, www.catskill-mtn.org; Sun.–Wed. 11 A.M.–5 P.M., Thurs.–Fri. 11 A.M.–6 P.M., Sat. 10 A.M.–6 P.M.), which stocks organic produce and locally made goods. Check the fridge for outstanding Camembert and ricotta cheeses made by the Old Chatham Sheepherding Company across the river in Columbia County. The CMF bookstore across the street carries a wide range of local interest titles.

In summer, stop by **Black Horse Farms** (Rte. 9W, Athens, 518/943-9324, www.blackhorse-farms.com; daily 9 A.M.–6 P.M.) for fresh-picked corn on the cob and other seasonal produce. The family-run store also sells baked goods, plants, maple syrup and honey.

Galleries

The hand-painted chandeliers of contemporary artist Ulla Darni are on display at **The Blue Pearl** (7551 Rte. 23, East Windham, 518/734-6525, bluepearl@mhonline.net; Mon.–Fri. 11 A.M.–4 P.M., Sat.–Sun. 11 A.M.–6 P.M.), located on Route 23, just below the Point Lookout Inn. Gallery owner Paula Cirnigliaro also maintains three floors of antiques, including Mexican and Spanish pottery, Indian and Tibetan tapestries, silver tea sets, and decorative ironwork. The store has its own café on the ground floor.

Although it's not exactly a gallery, **Guaranteed Irish** (2220 Rte. 145, East Durham, 518/634-2392, www.guaranteedirishshop.com; July–Aug. daily 9 A.M.–9 P.M., Sept.–June 9 A.M.–6 P.M.), at the corner of County Routes 31 and 145, contains a wide variety of Irish-made goods, including hand-crafted jewelry, tweed jackets, and Celtic music. With 5,000-square-feet of space, Guaranteed Irish bills itself as America's largest Irish import store.

Antiques

American Gothic Antiques (Rte. 23A, Hunter, 518/263-4836; Thurs.–Sun. 11 A.M.–5 P.M.) specializes in lamps from the 19th and 20th centuries. A few miles down the mountain at the eclectic **Last Chance Antiques and Cheese Café** (602 Main St., Tannersville, 518/589-6424, www.lastchanceonline.com; daily 11 A.M.–9 P.M.), a way of luring antique shoppers in the door has evolved into a full-fledged gourmet food store and restaurant. The store is covered floor to ceiling in antique instruments and Victorian-era accessories. Enjoy an unusual brew (there are 300 beers to choose from), a cheese platter, or a rich chocolate fondue.

Opera House Antiques Center (21 2nd St., Athens; Tues.–Sun. 11 A.M.–6 P.M.) represents multiple dealers selling furniture and other collectibles.

Books

If the mountain air catches you by surprise, **Rip Van Winkle Outfitters** (Main St., Tannersville, 518/589-5541) is the place to go for an extra layer of clothes. The store carries a wide selection of local interest books, in addition to fishing, hunting, and general outdoor gear.

INFORMATION AND SERVICES

Visitor information is available at Exit 21 of the New York State Thruway/I-87. The **Greene County Tourism Office** (P.O. Box 527, Catskill, 800/355-2287, tourism@discovergreene.com, www.greene-ny.com; year-round daily 9 A.M.–4 P.M., longer hours in summer) will answer questions through its website; by email, phone, and fax; or in person. After hours, an outdoor kiosk provides information on local sights and accommodations.

The Greene County Council on the Arts (398 Main St., Catskill, 518/943-3400, www.greenearts.org) keeps a calendar of countywide gallery exhibits, performances, lectures, and related events.

GETTING THERE AND AROUND

By Bus

Adirondack Trailways (800/858-8555, www.escapemaker.com/adirondacktrailways) offers daily service year-round from the Port Authority Terminal in New York City. Stops include Catskill, Palenville, Hunter, and Windham, and you can walk to town from the bus stops, or inquire about hotel and resort shuttles.

By Train

Greene County does not have its own rail service, but **Amtrak** (518/355-2287 or 800/872-7245, www.amtrak.com) stops in Hudson across the river, about eight miles from Catskill Village. You can get a taxi from the station, and some area hotels also run free shuttles. Enterprise Rent-a-Car (518/943-0028) has a location in Hudson.

By Car

The New York State Thruway (I-87) and Route 9W are the primary north-south arteries through Greene County. Exit the Thruway at Exit 21 for the most direct approach to the mountaintop. Routes 23 and 23A traverse the county from the Rip Van Winkle Bridge to the border with Delaware County.

Columbia County

Framed by the Hudson River to the west and the Berkshire Mountains to the east, the landscape of Columbia County features rolling hills, green pastures, and extensive woodlands. Many longtime farmers in Columbia County have converted their struggling dairy operations into niche organic businesses that cater to local restaurants and residents who join community-supported agriculture programs. The transition has allowed many local growers to keep their connection to the land while earning an almost satisfactory living.

The historic city of Hudson got its start as a center for whaling and shipping in the early 19th century and later became a center for iron-ore production. An industrial past continues to haunt the city. Unfortunately for weekenders and conservationists, the St. Lawrence Cement Company wants to move its plant from south of Catskill in Greene County to just outside of Hudson. At stake are 150 jobs—enough to make a real difference to a rural community. The controversy has enraged residents on both sides of the fence, and red "Stop the Plant" signs have appeared on every other lawn throughout Columbia County.

Named after Christopher Columbus, Columbia County's history is closely tied to that of the powerful Livingston family. In the late 17th century, Scottish entrepreneur Robert Livingston began buying land along both sides of the Hudson from Native American tribes. In the early 1700s, King George I deeded him a large tract of land covering most of present-day Columbia County. He became the first lord of Livingston Manor, which served as the county seat with its own representation in the New York State legislature. Six more generations of Livingstons held prominent political and economic positions in the area until the mid-20th century, when the family's riverside property, Clermont, was handed over to the state.

ALONG THE HUDSON— ROUTE 9G

ⓜ Clermont State Historic Site

Wild turkeys roam the grounds at Clermont ("clear mountain" in French), the former riverside estate of Robert Livingston Jr., who is also known as Robert of Clermont, or simply as the Chancellor. Robert Jr. served as New York State chancellor, signed the Declaration of Independence, and later became ambassador to France. In 1728, he inherited 13,000 acres of present-day Columbia County from his father, the first lord of Livingston Manor, and built a Georgian-style riverside home between 1730 and 1750. The house was designed to catch stunning views of the Catskill Mountains across the river.

The British burned this first home to the ground during the Revolutionary War, as punishment for Livingston's support of colonial independence. Margaret Beekman Livingston, who managed the estate during the war, escaped with a grandfather clock that remains in the foyer today. She promptly rebuilt the home in time to host George and Martha Washington in 1782. When he wasn't involved in national affairs,

Robert of Clermont turned his attention to entrepreneurial projects. For example, he introduced merino sheep from France and partnered with Robert Fulton to build the first steamship to cruise the Hudson.

Frozen in time since the start of the Great Depression, the manor reflects the tastes of the seven generations that lived in it. A crystal chandelier in the drawing room came from 19th-century France, and the library contains books from the 17th century. The dining room, newly restored in January 2004, has a marble fireplace mantel. And the original house telephone sits on a table outside the dining room. (The number was 3.) A frieze over the fireplace in the study depicts Alice Livingston and her two daughters, the last residents of the estate. Oddly, an entire room upstairs is dedicated to pets of the family.

Today, the beautifully landscaped grounds of the 500-acre **Clermont State Historic Site** (1 Clermont Ave., Germantown, 518/537-4240, fofc@valstar.net, www.friendsofclermont.org; Apr. 1–Oct. 31 Tues.–Sun. and Mon. holidays 2–5 P.M., Nov. 1–Mar. 31 Sat.–Sun. 11 A.M.–4 P.M.; $5 adults, $4 seniors/students, $1 children 5–12, children under 5 free) are open to the public year-round. A popular time to visit is mid-May, when the lilacs are in bloom.

The visitors center, located in the old carriage house, stocks a good selection of local interest books. And a reference library in the house is open by appointment. Nearby Germantown has gas, ATMs, and the obligatory Stewarts Shop.

ⓜ Olana State Historic Site

Ten miles north of Germantown stands another historic residence, in every way quite the opposite of Clermont. Landscape painter Frederic Edwin Church began his career in 1846 under the tutelage of Thomas Cole and went on to earn worldwide recognition. At age 24, he became the youngest artist ever elected to the National Academy of Design. As a painter who also grasped the power of marketing, Church learned how to generate hype and income for his paintings. He often showed a single painting at a time and charged admission for anyone who wished to view it.

Though he traveled extensively during his

lifetime, Church held a strong connection to the Hudson River Valley and chose to settle on 126 acres just south of the present-day Rip Van Winkle Bridge. Following a trip to the Middle East, he designed a sprawling Persian-style residence on top of a hill overlooking the Hudson and landscaped the grounds as if he were composing one of his romantic paintings. New York State rescued the home in 1966 from the nephew of Church's daughter-in-law, who intended to sell all of its furnishings in a Sotheby's auction. On display are a few of Church's own works, as well as many of the paintings, sculpture, and furnishings that he collected from his travels to South America and the Middle East.

Olana (5720 Rte. 9G, Hudson, 518/828-0135, www.olana.org; Apr.–Nov. Tues.–Sun. 10 A.M.– 5 P.M., Dec.–Apr. Sat.–Sun 11 A.M.–4 P.M.) is open with guided tours on the hour. Tours cost $7 for adults, $5 for students, $2 for kids; and there is a grounds fee of $5 on weekends and holidays 10 A.M.–7 P.M. Visitors are welcome to walk the trails in summer or cross-country ski in winter.

Hudson

If you looked down Hudson's Warren Street for the first time and thought you had landed in an Atlantic seaboard beach town, you wouldn't be far from the truth. The city still reflects its heritage as a whaling port in the early 19th century.

Fearing a British retaliation after the American Revolution, a group of Nantucket whalers moved inland to the Hudson River shoreline and incorporated a city in 1785. With a strategic location and carefully planned grid of streets, Claverack Landing, later renamed Hudson, became a center for shipbuilding and sperm-oil production. By the mid-19th century, the city was firmly established as the economic and political center of Columbia County.

As the city declined in the early 20th century, it earned a reputation for its active red light district. Author Bruce Hall revisits this aspect of Hudson's history in a book called *Diamond Street: The Story of the Little Town with the Big Red Light District* (Black Dome Press, 1994). Today, antique shops have replaced the brothels, but little else has changed. Rows of restored Greek Re-

vival and Federal townhouses line both sides of historic Warren Street for several blocks, extending from the town square to the river. New York City designers flock to more than 70 antique shops, which carry everything from Tibetan tapestries to Russian furniture.

In the 100 block is the **Robert Jenkins House & Museum** (113 Warren St., 518/828-9764; July–Aug. Sun.–Mon. 1–3 P.M., or by appointment), an 1811 Federal-style building with whaling and military exhibits that document the city's colorful past. A deserted promenade at the end of Warren Street offers river views, and the city is developing a new park south of the train station.

The Firemen's Association of the State of New York (FASNY) operates the **Museum of Firefighting** (117 Harry Howard Ave., Hudson, 877/347-3687, www.fasny.com; daily 9 A.M.– 4:30 P.M., closed holidays) in downtown Hudson. Two exhibit halls include paintings, photographs, and related memorabilia. The fire engines, pumps, and clothing on display date back to the 18th and 19th centuries. Residents of New York's Volunteer Fireman's Home, next door, staff the museum and happily answer questions about the history and current state of their profession.

Kinderhook

Kinderhook received its name, which is Dutch for "children's point," from Henry Hudson himself. The story goes that when he arrived in 1609, Hudson saw a group of Mohican children staring at the *Half Moon* and named the place Kinderhook Landing, now the town of Stuyvesant. Present-day Kinderhook lies several miles inland, on Kinderhook Creek. Numerous restored homes and historical sites make this town one of the most interesting destinations in northern Columbia County. The village hosted several notable guests during the Revolutionary War: Colonel Henry Knox passed though on his way to deliver a shipment of artillery from Fort Ticonderoga to Boston. And Colonel Benedict Arnold spent the night to recover after the victory of Bemis Heights.

Washington Irving reportedly wrote "Rip Van Winkle" during a stay in Kinderhook, and he based "The Legend of Sleepy Hollow" on local residents, though the story took place in

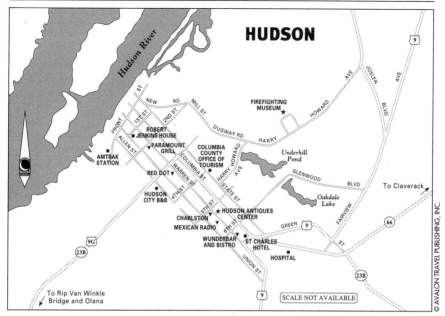

Tarrytown. The town of Kinderhook has published a detailed guide to its many private and public historic homes at www.kinderhookconnection.com/history2.htm. The walking tour begins at the Village Green, formed by the intersection of several streets that date back to the early 19th century: Albany Avenue, Broad Street, Hudson Street, and Chatham Street.

The **Columbia County Museum** (5 Albany Ave., 518/758-9265, www.cchsny.org; Memorial Day–Labor Day Mon.–Fri. 10 A.M.–4 P.M., call for occasional Sat. hours, Sept–May Mon., Wed., Fri. 10 A.M.–4 P.M., Sat. 1–4 P.M.), run by the Columbia County Historical Society, has extensive collections of paintings and artifacts from around the county.

Take a tour of a Federal-style mansion at the **James Vanderpoel House** (Board St., 518/758-9265; Memorial Day–Labor Day Thurs.–Sat. 11 A.M.–5 P.M., Sun. 1–4 P.M.; adults $3, students $2, members and children under 12 free, discounted combination tickets with the Lukyas Van Alen House available). This restored brick building is the former home of James Vanderpoel, a prominent lawyer and politician. Inside,

an elegant, curved staircase rises from a grand entryway. The home is decorated throughout with furnishings from the 1820s.

The **Luykas Van Alen House** (Rte. 9H, 518/758-9625; Memorial Day–Labor Day weekend Thurs.–Sat. 11 A.M.–5 P.M., Sun. 1–5 P.M.; adults $3, students $2, members and children under 12 free, discounted combination tickets with the James Vanderpoel House available) is a 1737 Dutch farmhouse with mid-18th century furnishings. The site appeared in Martin Scorsese's 1993 film *The Age of Innocence.* On the property is the white 1920 Ichabod Crane Schoolhouse, named after the teacher in Washington Irving's famous story "The Legend of Sleepy Hollow."

Located two miles outside of Kinderhook, the former home of Martin Van Buren, the eighth President of the United States, is now a historic site. The surrounding land was a working farm of over 200 acres. Built in 1797, the **Martin Van Buren National Historic Site** (1013 Old Post Rd., 518/758-9689, www.nps.gov/mava) is a Federal-style home that was remodeled in 1849, and Van Buren spared no expense: Brussels carpets and 51 elaborate wallpaper panels that form a hunting mural are on display inside.

The **Parker O'Malley Air Museum** (435 County Rte. 20, off Rte. 9H & Rte. 66, Ghent, 518/392-7200, www.parkeromalley.org; first Sat. of the month 10 A.M.–4 P.M., or by appointment) features civilian and military aircraft from the 1920s, '30s, and '40s. Most are maintained in flying condition, and there is a wind tunnel on site. Open cockpit airplane rides are available by appointment, starting at $75.

ALONG THE TACONIC STATE PARKWAY

Lake Taghkanic State Park

During sticky summer heat waves, **Lake Taghkanic State Park** (1528 Rte. 82, Taghkanic, 518/851-3631) is a popular day-trip for Mid-Hudson Valley residents. The clean and refreshing lake has two beaches with lifeguard supervision and a boat launch. Overnight accommodations include tent and RV campsites, as well as cabins and cottages (May–October only, reserve online through www.reserveamerica.com). The park service maintains trails for hiking and biking. In winter, it allows cross-country skiing, snowmobiles, ice skating, and ice fishing when the lake freezes. Hunters can take deer and turkey in season.

West Taghkanic

A large population of second-home owners have settled among the 19th-century schoolhouses in the hamlet of West Taghkanic. The name Taghkanic meant "water enough" or "full of timber" to the Algonquin Indians who once lived here. Today, the most notable building in town is the retro West Taghkanic Diner, at the intersection of Route 82 and the Taconic State Parkway.

Claverack

Continuing north on the Taconic State Parkway, you arrive at the intersection of Route 23, an old canon route that connects Hillsdale to Hudson. Equidistant between Hudson and the Taconic is the hamlet of Claverack, best known for its 1786 stone courthouse, where Alexander Hamilton tried a famous libel case involving a Hudson

newspaper publisher and President Thomas Jefferson. Today, Claverack is the center of an ongoing controversy over a proposed cement plant.

The name Claverack derives from the Dutch for clover field. Historians believe Henry Hudson chose the name for the fields of white clover he saw when he first arrived. The 1727 Reformed Protestant Dutch Church stands as a testament to the town's first settlers, and Dutch architecture populates this stretch of Route 23.

Several pick-your-own berry farms are nearby, including **Hotalings** (518/851-9864) for cherries, apples, and strawberries, and **Philip Orchards** (518/851-6351) for apples and pears. Contemporary writer Leila Philip wrote a memoir of her family's longstanding connection to Claverack entitled *A Family Place: A Hudson Valley Farm, Three Centuries, Five Wars, One Family* (Viking, 2001).

Chatham

Though it is technically part of Columbia County, Chatham marks the unofficial gateway to southern New England and the Berkshires. There are actually several Chathams: At the commercial center is the town of Chatham, Route 203 off the Taconic State Parkway. The Village of Chatham, founded in 1795, has dozens of historical markers and claims one of the country's last operational one-room schoolhouses, now home to the **Riders Mills Historical Association** (at the intersection of Riders Mills Road and Drowne Road, 518/794-7156). Quiet North Chatham lies on the Valatie Kill and the Rensselaer County line, while East Chatham offers a treasure trove for booklovers: Librarium Second Hand Books.

The **Old Chatham Sheepherding Company** (155 Shaker Museum Rd., 888/743-3760, www.blacksheepcheese.com) operates one of the largest sheep farms in the U.S. and makes a Camembert that aficionados claim to rival the best that France can produce. Many of the nation's top restaurants serve the award-winning cheese, including the French Laundry, in California's Napa Valley. Stop in to observe the morning or afternoon sheep-milking, watch the cheese-making operation, or see the newborn lambs in early spring. Just up the road, gardeners

© PAUL ITOI

Old Chatham

trade secrets at **A Country Garden at Antinore** (Shaker Museum Rd.; open daily; admission $4), where owners Pete and Carol Cox plant heirloom theme gardens for guests to enjoy. They also conduct gardening lectures and wreath-making classes in their home.

Shaker Museum and Library
In 1772, an Englishwoman named Ann Lee rose to the forefront of a radical movement within the Quaker society and led a small group of Shaking Quakers—so named for their tendency to break out in violent shakes during their worship services—to the New World to escape religious persecution. The United Society of Believers eventually established a leadership center in New Lebanon, New York, and grew to include some 6,000 members in 19 communities by the mid-19th century. Shaker beliefs evolved considerably over the years, but two ideals underpinned the religion: simplicity and celibacy. Above all, members strove to live a selfless and communal existence. Industrialization during the 19th century gradually eroded

the once-thriving Shaker community (along with other utopian social experiments like it), and the few remaining followers withdrew from society, leaving only traces of the culture.

You can spend several hours exploring the Shaker Museum and Library (88 Shaker Museum Rd., Malden Bridge, 518/794-9100, www.shakermuseumandlibrary.org; late May–late October Wed.–Mon. 10 A.M.–5 P.M.; $8 adults, $6 seniors, $4 children, $18 family), on the outskirts of Old Chatham. Founded in 1950, this remarkable museum contains one of the largest collections of Shaker artifacts and offers an informative introduction to the Shaker way of life. Among other values, the culture emphasizes high quality, precision, hospitality, invention, and systematic thinking. As a result, the industrious Shakers made fine furniture, tools, farm produce, and clothes. On display inside the museum are Shaker stoves, a washing machine, chairs, and textiles.

ALONG ROUTE 22
Taconic State Park
Just east of Route 22, at the intersection of the New York, Massachusetts, and Connecticut state lines, lies a hidden outdoor gem: the 5,000-acre **Taconic State Park** (Rte. 344 off Rte. 22, Copake Falls, 518/329-3993; open year-round). The park encompasses an 11-mile stretch of the Taconic Range—the vestiges of a mountain range that geologists believe stood taller than the Himalayas during the Ordovician time period, 450 million years ago.

The state has developed two areas for year-round use—Copake Falls and Rudd Pond—with extensive hiking, biking, and nature trails, as well as fishing, swimming, and camping. In winter, the trails belong to cross-country skiers and snowmobiles. The **Copake Falls Area** (518/329-3993) is located on State Route 344 or Valley View Road. To find the **Rudd Pond Area** (518/789-3059), turn off Route 22 at Route 62 in Millerton, and head two miles north.

The highlight of this wilderness area is **Bash Bish Falls,** at 80 feet, the tallest single-drop waterfall in Massachusetts. (The falls are located just over the state line.) Beginning about a mile

The Upper Hudson

upstream from the town of Copake Falls, a moderate one-mile hike through a hemlock and hardwood forest takes you to the base of the falls. The water cascades over a sheer granite cliff, landing in a pristine mountain pool. Cold temperature and strong currents discourage most hikers from taking a dip. The ecosystem supports a diverse population, including coyote, red fox, and brook trout. After the falls, the Bash Bish Brook winds its way through the Mid-Hudson Valley and empties into the Hudson River. Plan to get there before 10 A.M. to enjoy the view before the crowds.

South of the state park, Columbia and Dutchess Counties have teamed up to convert a 43-mile stretch of the old New York and Harlem Railroad into a pathway for walking, running, and cycling. A four-mile piece of the **Harlem Valley Rail Trail** (www.hvrt.org) now connects Ancram to the Taconic State Park entrance in Copake Falls. Lined in spots with weathered split rail fencing, the paved trail traverses the base of the Taconic Mountains. In several clearings, you can see the Catskill Mountains to the west.

According to local residents, Mohican Indian arrowheads, spears, and axes can still occasionally be found in the vicinity of Copake. Runners who depart from the town center can cross three state lines and still finish in under an hour. A tall clock and a Vietnam Veterans War Memorial at the intersection of Routes 22 and 7A marks the center of town, but there's not much reason to stop, unless it's for breakfast at the Hearthstone Inn.

Hillsdale and Catamount

When Hillsdale residents speak of "the mountains," they mean the Berkshires, not the Catskills. Located at the Massachusetts state line, the town is part sleepy Hudson Valley, part upscale New England. The first building you see rolling into Hillsdale from Route 22 North is a 1780s brick Dutch colonial named **Aubergine** (Rtes. 22 & 23, Hillsdale, 518/325-3412, www .aubergine.com), now the restaurant of chef and owner David Lawson and his wife Stacy. Lawson—a political scientist turned restaurateur—prepares French-inspired country fare in a cozy setting that takes his guests back 150 years in

time. His blend of traditional and inventive dishes attracts both weekenders from New York City and local residents for special occasions.

Catamount Ski & Snowboarding Area (Rte. 23, Hillsdale, 518/325-3200, www.catamountski .com), at the Massachusetts state line, is a great mountain to hit on a midweek snow day. With seven lifts and a new terrain park, the area draws families from across the Hudson Valley. The minimal lodge has stacks of blue lockers and cafeteria-style lunch fare. A heated tent next to the lodge houses a small gift shop with winter wear.

Austerlitz

The sale of abundant fresh blueberries helped early settlers pay their taxes in rural Austerlitz. Today, an annual Blueberry Festival commemorates the town's heritage. The Austerlitz Historical Society (518/392-0062, oldausterlitz@taconic.net, www.oldausterlitz.org) is in the process of creating Old Austerlitz, a museum site at the intersection of Route 22 and Harvey Mountain Road that collects and restores buildings, artifacts, and related town memorabilia. To date, the site includes a one-room schoolhouse from 1818 and an 1850s church. Next on the restoration list is a 1794 house called Morey-Devereaux (after its former owners), which will serve as a research library and lecture hall. The society sponsors events and workshops year-round.

Mount Lebanon Shaker Village

The Shakers established their second community in the northeast corner of Columbia County in 1785, and the site is now a National Historic Landmark. Eight families once farmed and lived here on 6,000 acres of rolling hills, forests, and fields. More than two dozen of the original buildings have been preserved as Mount Lebanon Shaker Village (at the intersection of Rtes. 20 and 22 in New Lebanon, 518/794-9500, www .shakerworkshops.com/mt_leb.htm; mid-June–mid-October Fri.–Sun. 10 A.M.–5 P.M.; adult $5, children $2, seniors $4.50, discounts for families, members, and groups). Visitors can view the original beams and chutes of the granary and the drying racks in the washhouse, as well as cemeteries, aqueducts, and the remains of several old mills. The site is a short drive from the Shaker Museum and Library, in Chatham, and the Hancock Shaker Village across the Massachusetts state line, in the Berkshires.

SPORTS AND RECREATION

Winter Sports

Catamount (Rte. 23, Hillsdale, 518/325-3200, www.catamountski.com) is open 8:30 A.M.–4 P.M. weekends and holidays, 9 A.M.–4 P.M. midweek, 5–9 P.M. Wednesday–Thursday nights, and 3–10 P.M. Friday–Saturday nights. All-day lift tickets cost $45 during the 2003-2004 season, with $15 days on Wednesdays and Thursdays.

Catamount Statistics
Base: 1,000 feet
Summit: 2,000 feet
Vertical drop: 1,000 feet
Trails: 29
Lifts: 7
Skiable acres: 110
Snowmaking: 100 percent of terrain
Snow report: 800/342-1840

Nordic skiers will find more than 15 wilderness areas with groomed and ungroomed trails across Columbia County. **Clermont** (Rte. 6 just off Rte. 9G, Germantown, 518/537-4240, www .friendsofclermont.org) opens its trails and grounds free to cross-country skiers. Or explore the carriage roads and six miles of trails on the grounds of **Olana State Historic Site** (5720 Rte. 9G, Hudson, 518/828-0135). **Lake Taghkanic State Park** (1528 Rte. 82, Taghkanic, 518/851-3631) has trails around the lake. **Taconic State Park** (Rte. 344, off Rte. 22, Copake Falls, 518/329-3993) has extensive trails in both developed areas, Copake Falls and Rudd Pond. Two cottages for rent year-round each have a refrigerator, stove, microwave, dishes and utensils, a bathroom with shower, and oil heat.

Hiking

Hikers can explore state forests, historic sites, and wildlife preserves in Columbia County. Olana, Clermont, and Martin Van Buren Park have well-maintained trails for nature walks and scenic views. To get further away from civilization, head to Beebe Hill State Forest (County Rte. 5, Austerlitz), Harvey Mountain State Forest (E. Hill Rd. off Rte. 22, Austerlitz), or the 5,000-acre Taconic State Park.

Swimming and Boating

Lake Taghkanic State Park (access from the Taconic State Parkway or Rte. 82, 518/851-3631) offers swimming and boating in a natural lake, while Taconic State Park allows swimming in the Rudd Pond area (Rte. 62 in Millerton, off Rte. 22, 518/789-3059). Queechy Lake in Canaan is another popular venue for swimming and canoeing. For Hudson River access, head to the boat launches on Front Street in Hudson or on County Route 35A (Northern Blvd.) in Germantown.

Fishing and Hunting

The New York State Department of Conservation stocks Kinderhook Creek, Claverack Creek, Roeliff Jansen Creek and the unfortunately named Ore Pit Pond in Taconic State Park with trout. Fly fishers head to the Taghkanic Creek or Bash Bish Falls. Queechy Lake and Kinderhook Lake allow fishing from car top boats only. A New York State fishing license is required at all locations.

Several state forests allow hunting in season: New Forge on New Forge Road off Route 82 in Taghkanic, Beebe Hill on County Route 5 in Austerlitz, and Harvey Mountain on East Hill Road off Route 22. Call the local state ranger for information: 518/828-0236. Taconic State Park permits bow and rifle hunting for deer only. Lido's Game Preserve is a private club in the town of Taghkanic (Berkshire Rd. off County Rte. 11, 518/329-1551).

Golf

A dozen golf courses are scattered among Columbia County's rolling hills. **Undermountain Golf Course** (274 Undermountain Rd., Copake, 518/329-4444, www.undermountain-golf.com; Mon.–Fri. 7 A.M.–7:30 P.M., Sat.–Sun. 7 A.M.–6:30 P.M.; $17.75 midweek, $19.50 weekend and holiday, $14.75 senior/junior) operates

The Upper Hudson

a public, 18-hole course with views of the Taconic Range, Berkshire Mountains, and Catskills.

Copake Country Club's (44 Golf Course Rd., off County Rte. 11, Copake, 518/325-4338, www.copakecountryclub.com, daily Mar.–Nov. 7 A.M. –7 P.M.; $19 weekday, $32 weekend) 18-hole par 72 course overlooks Copake Lake with distant views of the Catskills across the Hudson. The club offers car rentals, a pro-shop, lessons, and a restaurant.

Mountain Biking and Road Riding

Cyclists have many options for touring country roads and trails in this part of the Hudson Valley. An aggressive 83-mile road ride with a 60-mile option traverses nearly every major town in the county on back roads that meander by old homes, farms, rolling hills, and waterfalls (www.roberts-1.com/bikehudson/r/east/gt_columbia/map/index.htm). For an easier ride, the paved **Harlem Valley Rail Trail** (518/789-9591, www.hvrt.org) follows a set of old railroad tracks along the base of the Taconic Range. Access the path at Undermountain Road, off Route 22 in Ancram or at the Taconic State Park entrance in Copake Falls. Mountain bikers will find challenging terrain in both Taconic State Park and Lake Taghkanic State Park.

Steiner Sports (301 Warren St., Hudson, 518/828-5063, www.steinersports.com; Mon.–Fri. 9:30 A.M.–5:30 P.M., Sat. 9:30 A.M.–5 P.M.) carries high-end ski, bike, and kayak equipment in three locations: Hudson, Valatie, and Glenmont. Stop in for maps, supplies, and route advice.

Aviation

Private pilots and aviation enthusiasts should head to **Richmor Aviation** (Rte. 9H, Hudson, 518/828-9461, www.richmor.com), at the Columbia County Airport, for training and scenic flights.

ACCOMMODATIONS

Aside from a couple of modern hotels that cater to business travelers, places to stay in Columbia County tend toward the upscale. A number of unique bed and breakfast inns are scattered about the countryside.

Under $100

Wireless Internet in every room is a plus at the **St. Charles Hotel** (16–18 Park Place, Hudson, 518/822-9900, www.stcharleshotel.com; $80–98). Rooms are basic but adequate, and the location is within walking distance to the antique shops on Warren Street. You can get your morning coffee at the Starbucks on the premises.

$100–150

The **Hudson City B&B** (326 Allen St., Hudson, 518/822-8044, info@hudsoncitybnb.com, www.hudsoncitybnb.com; $109–189) occupies the former residence of Joshua T. Waterman, four-term mayor of Hudson beginning in 1853. The house is painted green with cream trim and sits within walking distance of the Warren Street antique shops. Its comfortable rooms are decorated in 19th-century furnishings.

The **Inn at the Shaker Mill Farm** (40 Cherry Lane, New Lebanon, 518/794-9345, www.shakermillfarminn.com; $55–85 per person, dinner $25) puts you within a short drive to Berkshire attractions, including summer performances at Tanglewood, 10 miles away. As the name implies, guestrooms occupy a converted 1834 mill, and owner Ingram Paperny has embraced the Shaker philosophy with zeal. Be prepared for bare-bones decor and a communal experience, including family-style meals.

$150–200

In a region dominated by Dutch colonial and Federal structures, the clay tile roof and stucco exterior of the **The Inn at Blue Stores** (2323 Rte. 9, Hudson, 518/537-4277, www.innatbluestores.com; $125–225) offer a welcome change of scenery. The Spanish colonial building, set on a farm, dates to 1908. Guests can enjoy afternoon tea in the garden or by the fire, depending on the season. Downtown Hudson lies 10 miles to the north. Each elegant room is accented differently with period furnishings to accommodate honeymooners and business travelers alike. A gourmet breakfast is included.

Farther north at the edge of the Berkshires, pine floors, antique trunks, and down comforters lend a cozy feel to guestrooms at **M The Inn at

Silver Maple Farm (Rte. 295, Canaan, 518/781-3600, www.silvermaplefarm.com; $105–290). Breakfast includes homemade breads and muffins.

Over $200

Next door to the restaurant of the same name, **M Swiss Hütte** (Rte. 23, Hillsdale, 518/325-3333, www.swisshutte.com; $110–180 per person per night, including breakfast and dinner) offers immaculate, recently renovated rooms with tiled baths and mountain views.

Campgounds

Woodland Hills Campground (386 Fog Hill Rd., Austerlitz, 518/392-3557, www.whcg.net; May–Oct.; $21 for tents, $27 for full hook-ups), near the intersection of the Taconic State Parkway and the Massachusetts Turnpike (I-90), has 200 sites for tents and RVs. Amenities include hot showers, laundry, and family activities.

Taconic State Park's (Rte. 344, off Rte. 22, Copake Falls, 518/329-3993; year-round) two recreational areas—Copake Falls and Rudd Pond—have campsites, trailer sites, and cabins available from mid-May until November. (Deer hunting is allowed in season, and camping is extended for hunters.) Reserve online through www.reserveamerica.com. Tent sites cost $13, and cabins cost $78–140. The Rudd Pond area is located off Route 22 on Route 62, two miles north of Millerton.

Camp Waubeeka Family Campground (133 Farm Rd., Copake, 518/329-4681, www.camp-waubeeka.com) has four rustic cabins, as well as campsites and trailer hook-ups. Cabins cost $60–65 per night; a basic tent site is $18.

FOOD

Along the Hudson—Route 9G

The owners of the trendy **M Red Dot** (321 Warren St., Hudson, 518/828-3657; Wed.–Sat. 5–10 P.M. and bar till 1 A.M., Sun. 11 A.M.–3 P.M., 5–9 P.M., and bar till 1 A.M.; mains $10–20) doubled the restaurant's space in 2003, so the place now seats 50 comfortably. Locals fill the place on weekend evenings, even in the dead of winter. Entrées range from a basic steak frites to the more exotic Thai beef salad. **Mexican Radio** (537 Warren St., Hudson, 518/828-7770; daily 11 A.M.–11 P.M.) opened in June 2003, just up the street from Red Dot. It serves upscale Mexican cuisine and has a sister restaurant in New York City. **Hudson Bakery and Grill**, at Warren and North 5th Street, is the place to go for breakfast.

Game in season is the theme at **Charlston** (517 Warren St., Hudson, 518/828-4990; mains $14–25), another long-standing Warren Street bistro. A new chef took over from owner Carol Clark in 2002, and the place continues to attract regulars with an eclectic menu. If a meal here inspires you to cook your own, pick up a copy of the *Wild Fish & Game Cookbook,* by John Manikowski (Artisan, 1997), a cofounder of the restaurant. Not only is Manikowski an accomplished outdoorsman, he wrote and illustrated his own book.

Wunderbar & Bistro (744 Warren St., Hudson, 518/828-0555; mains $6–14) up the street serves dependable Austrian and Hungarian cuisine at reasonable prices. The restaurant is open for lunch Monday–Friday 11:30 A.M.–2 P.M. and for dinner Monday–Saturday 5–10 P.M. with live music on Saturdays.

The atmosphere at **Paramount Grill** (225 Warren St., Hudson, 518/828-4548; Mon., Thurs., Sun. 5–9 P.M., Fri.–Sat. 5–10 P.M.; mains $16–23) is plain, but the restaurant's American menu has pleased local residents for years.

For ribs and southern fare, head to **Carolina House** (59 Broad St./Rte. 9, Kinderhook, 518/758-1669; opens Mon.–Sat. 5 P.M. & Sun. 4 P.M.; mains $14–21).

Along the Taconic State Parkway

An Indian head sign in neon pink and blue lights marks the site of the **West Taghkanic Diner** (Route 82, Ancram, 518/851-7117, www.taghkanicdiner.com; Mon.–Thurs. 7 A.M.–9 P.M., Fri. 7 A.M.–11 P.M., Sat.–Sun. 7 A.M.–10 P.M.; mains $4–13). Conveniently located at the intersection of the Taconic State Parkway and Route 82, this retro establishment has been serving breakfast and dinner all day long since 1953. Eggs, omelets, and pancakes average $4, and dinner mains including steak, seafood, pasta, and burgers are also on the menu.

The **Happy Clown Ice Cream Shop** is a favorite summer stop at the intersection of Routes 9 and 82 (Claverack, 518/851-2177; Apr.–Sept. daily 11 A.M.–9 P.M.). There is only outdoor seating.

Jackson's Old Chatham House (Village Square, Old Chatham, 518/794-7373; daily 11:30 A.M.–10 P.M.; mains $10–20) serves tavern-style food, including burgers, steaks, and pork chops. Nearby, the **Old Chatham Country Store** has homemade soups and sandwiches in a casual setting (Village Square, Old Chatham, 518/794-7151).

Along Route 22

Show up at **Ⅶ Aubergine** (Rtes. 22 & 23, Hillsdale, 518/325-3412, www.aubergine.com; Wed.–Sun. 5:30 P.M.; mains $24–32) in early May, and you may be treated to fresh tomatoes or herbs from Chef David Lawson's own garden before local farms have even planted their seeds. Lawson starts the seedlings in cold frames in late February or early March and heats the soil in his garden to lengthen the season for serving fresh-picked ingredients. When the leaves begin to turn in autumn, it's worth a visit just to see the view of Mount Alander from the dining rooms. Entrées range from a straightforward sirloin steak to the more adventurous crispy veal sweetbreads. The inn has several guestrooms upstairs.

A chalet straight out of the Swiss Alps, **Swiss Hütte** (Rte. 23, Hillsdale, 518/325-3333, www.swisshutte.com; lunch Tues.–Sat. noon–2 P.M. & 5:30–9 P.M., Sun. noon–3 P.M. & 5–9 P.M.; mains $23–28) is a restaurant and inn directly across the parking lot from the lifts at Catamount. A friendly golden retriever named Beano will likely greet you at the door. Owned since 1986 by Swiss-born Gert Alper (who is also the chef) and his wife, Cindy, the restaurant serves cheese fondue, homemade European-style hard rolls, and a full menu of hearty entrées in a cozy, mountainside setting.

The popular **Four Brothers Pizza** chain (Rtes. 9 & 9H, Valatie, 518/758-7151; daily 11 A.M.–10:30 P.M.; mains under $10) is open late, serving Italian, Greek, and American dishes. The restaurant is one of nine pizzerias in the Hudson Valley, and as the name implies, they were established by four Greek brothers, who immigrated to the United States.

To the south, the American cuisine at the **Hearth Stone Inn** (Rte. 22, Copake Falls, 518/325-5600; Mon.–Sat. 11:30 A.M.–9 P.M., Sun. 8 A.M.–9 P.M.; mains $8–12), in Copake Falls, is popular with skiers and hunters.

ENTERTAINMENT AND EVENTS
Performing Arts

Vladimir Pleshakov and Elena Winther converted a bank building into an acoustically tailored concert hall, the **Pleshakov Music Center** (544 Warren St., Hudson, 518/671-7171, www.pleshakov.com; tickets $20). On a typical Saturday evening, the center may host the Berkshire Symphony Players or the piano-duet owners.

After three decades of neglect, Hudson's 150-year-old city hall building reopened in 1998 as a local performing arts center, **Hudson Opera House** (327 Warren St., Hudson, 518/822-1438, www.hudsonoperahouse.org; Mon.–Sat. noon–5 P.M.; tickets $3–12). Artist exhibitions and concerts are hosted throughout the year.

Set in an 1847 schoolhouse, **The Spencertown Academy** (Rte. 203, Spencertown, 518/392-3693, www.spencertown.org; Feb.–Dec. Wed.–Sun. 1–5 P.M.) has a 140-seat auditorium and four exhibiting spaces. Events range from jazz and classical concerts to yoga classes.

North Pointe Cultural Arts Center (62 Chatham St./Rte.9, Kinderhook, 518/758-9234, www.northepointe.com; tickets $10–28) produces music, dance, and theater performances, as well as art exhibitions in the Village of Kinderhook.

The quaint **Mac-Haydn Theatre** (Rte. 203, Chatham, 518/392-9292, www.machaydntheatre.org; tickets about $20), on a hilltop overlooking the town of Chatham, specializes in musicals and runs a summer children's theater. The theater runs seven or eight shows per season.

Bars and Nightlife

Hudson residents congregate at the **Red Dot** (321 Warren St., Hudson, 518/828-3657; Wed.–Sat. 5–10 P.M., Sun. 11 A.M.–3 P.M. & 5–9 P.M.) after work to drink Morland Old Speckled Hen by the pint. In Hillsdale, **Mt. Washington Tavern** (Main St., Hillsdale, 518/325-4631) is a good place for après-ski refreshments.

For maritime entertainment, **Hudson Cruises** (518/822-1014, www.hudsoncruises.com) offers afternoon or evening cruises with dinner, dancing, and scenic river views. Boats depart from Waterfont Park on Front Street in Hudson at 7:30 P.M. Wednesday, 6 P.M. Friday, 2 P.M. Saturday, and 11 A.M. Sunday.

Festivals
Folk dancers and bluegrass music lovers attend the popular **Falcon Ridge Folk Festival** (Long Hill Farm, Rte. 23, Hillsdale, 860/364-0366, www.falconridgefolk.com) each July to watch up to 40 bands perform on three stages, with plenty of flat areas for camping.

Lebanon Valley Speedway (1746 Rte. 20, West Lebanon, 518/794-9606, www.lebanonvalley.com; Sat. mid-Apr.–Sept.; admission $22) holds stockcar races, monster truck rallies, and hot rod events.

The **Columbia County Fair** (Columbia County Fairgrounds, Rtes. 66 & 203, Chatham Village, 518/392-2121, www.columbiafair.com) is an old-fashioned fair with live music, a rodeo, tractor pulls, and amusement rides. It takes place on Labor Day weekend. And the Clermont hosts various festivals and educational events throughout the year, including a sheep festival in April.

SHOPPING
Antiques
As if the 70 independent antique shops on Warren Street in downtown Hudson weren't enough to choose from, the **Hudson Antiques Center** (522 Warren St., Hudson, 518/822-6522, www.hudsonantiques.net) has another 20 vendors, conveniently located under one roof. They sell a truly incredible range of rare goods, from Dutch antique furniture and art deco accessories to clocks, garden decorations, and custom upholstery. Most of the stores are closed on Wednesdays.

Away from the Warren Street bustle, **Copake Auction** (266 Rte. 7A, Copake, 518/329-1142, www.copakeauction.com) has specialized in the sale of Americana items for the past 50 years. Its

annual antique bicycle auction draws cycling enthusiasts from across the nation and overseas.

Books
Bookworms will want to spend an hour or two browsing the shelves at **Librarium Second Hand Books** (126 Black Bridge Rd., East Chatham, 518/392-5209) or **Rodgers Book Barn** (Rodman Rd., Hillsdale, 518/325-3610; Fri. & Mon. noon–5 P.M., Sat. 10 A.M.–5 P.M., Sun. 11 A.M.–5 P.M.) Better yet, save time for both. Each shop houses tens of thousands of titles in a converted barn that sets the mood for reading.

Farm Stands
There is at least one farm stand, or pick-your-own orchard in every town in Columbia County. Two farmers markets take place in Hudson during the growing season: **Hudson's Farmers Market** (8432 Rte. 22, 518/828-7217; Sun.–Thurs. 10 A.M.–6 P.M., Fri.–Sat. 9 A.M.–7 P.M.), at North 6th Street and Columbia Street, and **Hudson River Farm Market** (518/828-0935; Sun.–Thurs. 10 A.M.–6 P.M., Fri.–Sat. 9 A.M.–7 P.M.), at 17 North 4th Street. To the east, near Claverack, you can pick cherries, apples, and strawberries at **Hotalings** (518/851-9864), or apples and pears at **Philip Orchards** (518/851-6351).

Just north of Hudson on Route 9, **Van Wie Natural Foods** (6798 Rte. 9, Hudson, 518/828-0533, richardvanwie@aol.com, www.vanwienaturalmeats.com; Tues.–Sat. 10 A.M.–5 P.M.) offers organic-standard meat, including pork, beef, free range chicken and turkey, lamb, seafood, pheasant, duck, rabbit, goat and buffalo. All animals are raised without the use of chemicals, hormones, or antibiotics.

Several organic farms set up shop near Germantown in summer. **V.R. Saulpaugh and Sons** (1960 Rte. 9, Germantown, 518/537-6494) grows unusual varieties of eggplant, peppers, and squash. **Two Kids Organic** (409 Viewmont Rd., Germantown, 518/537-5108) specializes in heirloom tomatoes and beans.

Deer, buffalo, elk, antelope, and llama are just some of the animals that share the pastures at **Highland Farm** (283 County Rte. 6, Germantown, 518/537-6397). The farm sells venison and smoked venison products, breeds animals for zoos, and shelters endangered species, all under one roof. Farther north, **Sunset Meadows** (3521 Rte. 9, 518/851-3000, www.sunsetmeadows.com) is a large gourmet foods store and café located on Route 9, outside of Hudson. It carries more than 100 types of European beers and holds cooking demonstrations throughout the year.

INFORMATION AND SERVICES

The **Columbia County Office of Tourism** (401 State St., Hudson, 800/724-1846, www.columbiacountyny.org) has maps and brochures covering the county, as well as the greater Hudson River Valley region. The Columbia County Chamber of Commerce (507 Warren St., Hudson, 518/828-4417, www.columbiachamber-ny.com) can also provide visitor information.

GETTING THERE AND AROUND

By Bus

Adirondack Trailways (800/858-8555, www.escapemaker.com/adirondacktrailways) stops across the river in the village of Catskill, eight miles from downtown Hudson. Taxis are available, and some hotels offer free shuttle service.

By Train

Hudson is a two-hour train ride away from New York City's Penn Station. The **Amtrak Rail Station** (69 S. Front St., Hudson, 518/355-2287 or 800/872-7245, www.amtrak.com) is located at the water's edge. A one-way ticket from Penn Station to Hudson costs $37. You can hop a cab from the train station or rent a car from Enterprise Rent-a-Car.

By Car

From New England, turn off I-90 at Exit B2 to reach the northern end of the Taconic State Parkway, the speediest north-south route through Columbia County. Route 23 crosses northern Columbia County, connecting Hillsdale to Hudson. Route 9 and its many spin-offs form a major commercial corridor along the river, while the more rural Route 22 runs along the base of the Taconic Range at the eastern edge of the county.

The Capital Region

The Capital Region of Albany and Saratoga Springs marks the end of the tidal Hudson River and offers a symbolic bookend to a journey through the Hudson River Valley. After Albany and industrial Troy, the river becomes part of the Champlain Canal before veering west to its origin, high in the Adirondack Mountains.

Henry Hudson reached Albany in September of 1609 and had to turn the 122-ton *Half Moon* around when the river became too shallow. Word spread after that maiden voyage, and Fort Orange became one of the earliest and largest Dutch settlements along the river. Today's Albany is a destination in its own right, but with an international airport and brand new train station, the city also serves as a gateway to the more picturesque Catskills and North Country.

Must-Sees

Look for **M** to find the sights and activities you can't miss and **M** for the best dining and lodging.

M Empire State Plaza: The centerpiece of downtown Albany is a 98-acre plaza with an impressive collection of art displayed indoors and out (page 170).

crowded Empire State Plaza

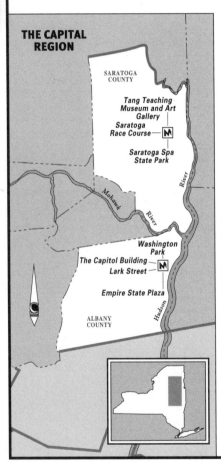

M The Capitol Building: Elaborate stone carvings line the imposing outdoor stairway that leads from the Empire State Plaza to the entrance of New York's state capitol building. Built by hand over a period of 30 years, the building defines the Albany skyline and serves as headquarters for the New York State Assembly (page 172).

M Lark Street and Washington Park: Downtown Albany has a bohemian enclave at the east end of Washington Park, with several blocks of eclectic boutiques and trendy restaurants (page 173).

M Saratoga Spa State Park: Natural hot springs, towering pine trees, and an outdoor concert venue are highlights in Saratoga's 2,300-acre park (page 181).

M Saratoga Race Course: The Saratoga racetrack is the oldest continuously operating thoroughbred track in the U.S., and the town's population triples during the summer racing season (page 182).

M Tang Teaching Museum and Art Gallery: Skidmore College has opened a state-of-the-art museum dedicated to presenting and teaching contemporary works (page 183).

COURTESY OF ALBANY COUNTY CONVENTION & VISITORS BUREAU

The Capital Region

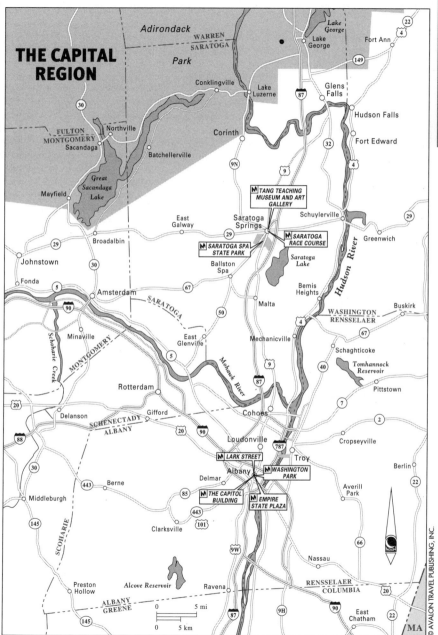

THE CAPITAL REGION

Adirondack

WARREN
SARATOGA

Park

Lake
George

Lake
George

Fort Ann

149

Conklingville

Lake
Luzerne

87

Glens
Falls

Hudson Falls

30

FULTON
MONTGOMERY
Sacandaga

Northville

Corinth

32

Fort Edward

Batchellerville

9N

9

Mayfield

Great
Sacandaga
Lake

East
Galway

M TANG TEACHING
MUSEUM AND ART
GALLERY

Schuylerville

Saratoga
Springs

29

Greenwich

Broadalbin

29

M SARATOGA SPA
STATE PARK

M SARATOGA
RACE COURSE

Johnstown

30

Ballston
Spa

Saratoga
Lake

Fonda

5

90

Amsterdam

67

Malta

Bemis
Heights

Buskirk

WASHINGTON
RENSSELAER

67

Minaville

50

Schaghticoke

MONTGOMERY

East
Glenville

Mechanicville

40

Tomhannock
Reservoir

5

9

Pittstown

Rotterdam

Mohawk River

87

7

20

Delanson

Gifford

SCHENECTADY
ALBANY

20

90

Cohoes

2

Cropseyville

88

Loudonville

787

Troy

Berlin

30

M LARK STREET

443

Berne

Delmar

M WASHINGTON
PARK

Averill
Park

22

Middleburgh

85

M THE CAPITOL
BUILDING

Albany

M EMPIRE
STATE PLAZA

145

443

101

Clarksville

66

Nassau

SCHOHARIE

Preston
Hollow

Alcove Reservoir

Ravena

RENSSELAER
COLUMBIA

20

ALBANY
GREENE

0   5 mi

0   5 km

145

87

9W

9H

90

East
Chatham

22

MA

PLANNING YOUR TIME

One day allows plenty of time to explore most of downtown Albany, but you'll need extra time to schedule a tour of the state capitol or Executive Mansion. Popular Albany itineraries include dinner downtown followed by an evening event at the Pepsi Arena, a weekend of historic colonial sights, or a day of holiday shopping at the malls.

The drive from Albany to Saratoga Springs should take about half an hour with light traffic; however, a large number of government workers commute into Albany each day, so be sure to time your drive to avoid the rush. Ideal as a weekend getaway, Saratoga Springs can also work well as a side trip from Lake George, or as a day of civilization before or after a multiday hike through the Adirondack backcountry.

Albany

From names like Ten Broeck to its annual tulip festival, New York's capital city retains much of its early Dutch roots. As the New York State capital since 1797, the city has also preserved much of its 19th- and 20th-century architecture. Walk a few of the city's historic blocks and you'll find many examples of the Italianate, Federal, and Greek Revival styles, in conditions ranging from perfectly restored to borderline rundown.

Governor George E. Pataki delivered his 10th State of the State speech to New York citizens in January 2004. And Albany today contains an appealing mix of architectural masterpieces, art collections, and historic sights. Meanwhile, students from several area colleges support a vibrant sports and nightlife scene. With a population of 100,000, the city is large enough to offer a rich urban experience, but compact enough that you can tour the downtown in a day. Unfortunately however, many parts of Albany have yet to recover from the economic turmoil of the mid-20th century. As a result, showy state government buildings alternate with equally powerful signs of urban decay.

DOWNTOWN ALBANY

The modern Empire State Plaza and giant Pepsi Arena have done much to revitalize downtown Albany since most of its factories shut down in the 1950s; however, the new and restored buildings contrast sharply with the low income neighborhoods that surround them. City leaders are targeting the dynamic technology industry—from nanotechnology to fuel cells—as a key source of future economic growth.

The majority of visitors find themselves in Albany for one of three reasons: a business convention, a children's school fieldtrip, or a concert or sporting event. Whatever the draw, it's well worth the time to absorb a slice of New York State history while you're in town.

Empire State Plaza

The centerpiece of downtown Albany is the 98-acre Empire State Plaza (State St., Albany), where most of the government's 11,000 employees show up for work each day. Ten dazzling skyscrapers surround an open plaza and fountain, including the Corning Tower, which at 42 stories is the state's highest building outside New York City.

In the 1960s, then-governor Nelson A. Rockefeller envisioned an architectural wonder and cultural center that would bring jobs and visitors to downtown Albany again. He commissioned Wallace Harrison, the same architect who built Rockefeller Center, and construction began in 1965. Thirteen years later, the city had a gorgeous new public space. The best view in town is found atop the **Corning Tower Observation Deck** (Mon.–Fri. 9 A.M.–3:45 P.M., Sat.–Sun. 10 A.M.–3:45 P.M.).

One of the most unusual sights on the plaza is a sculpturelike building called **The Egg** (Empire State Plaza, Albany, 518/473-1061, www.theegg .org), a custom-built performing arts center with two theaters and state-of-the-art acoustics.

Key to Rockefeller's vision was the incorporation of art into public spaces. (His mother, Abby Aldrich Rockefeller, had been instrumental in the founding of the Museum of Modern Art in New

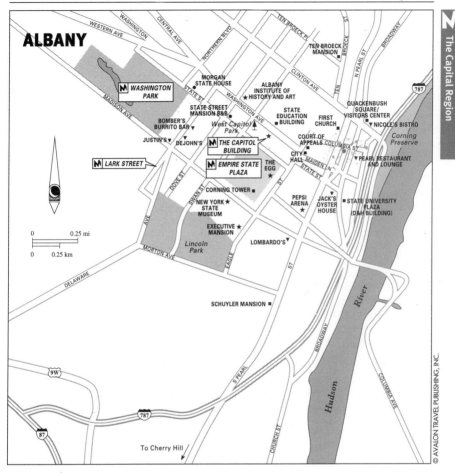

York City.) Accordingly, scattered throughout the plaza, inside and out, are pieces of the impressive **New York State Art Collection,** featuring the work of New York State artists from the 1960s and 1970s. It is considered one of the most important collections of modern art in the country.

Currently, there are 92 paintings, sculptures, and tapestries displayed on the concourse, in building lobbies, and in outdoor spaces. The collection is especially strong in abstract art. Alexander Caldwell and Mark Rothko are among the best-known artists in the collection. Visitors may view the works anytime government offices are open.

The **Plaza Information Office,** located off the main concourse, near The Egg, has information on maps and tours. Additional information booths are located at the north and south ends of the concourse. Take the Empire Plaza exit from I-787. There are several visitor parking lots around the plaza on Madison and Grand Streets.

New York State Museum

At the south end of the plaza, the **New York State Museum** (Madison Ave., Albany, 518/474-5877, www.nysm.nysed.gov; daily 9:30 A.M.–5 P.M.; suggested donation $2) began in 1836 as a center for geological and natural history exhibits. Over the years, it has maintained a core focus on geology, biology, anthropology, and history as they relate to the state. A photography exhibit in 2004 commemorated the 35th anniversary of the 1969 Woodstock Music Festival (see *The Western Catskills*).

The Executive Mansion

Governor Pataki lives in the New York Executive Mansion (138 Eagle St., 518/473-7521), one block south of the Empire State Plaza. The home was built in the 1850s and has housed governors and their families since 1875, including Theodore and Franklin Delano Roosevelt. Public rooms contain exquisite artwork and furnishings from the 18th, 19th, and 20th centuries. Guided tours are offered on Thursdays at noon, 1 P.M., and 2 P.M., except during the month of July (reservations required).

◪ The Capitol Building

The capitol building (Washington Ave., Albany, 518/474-2418) that towers over State Street hill, adjacent to the north end of the Empire State Plaza, looks more like a European castle than a U.S. state capitol. A stunning set of stairs climbs up to three grand archways, featuring elaborate stone carvings. Construction began by hand in 1867 and took 30 years to complete, by which time Theodore Roosevelt had become governor. The final price tag was an astronomical $25 million.

The New York State Assembly conducts its business inside. You can take a guided tour of the building Monday–Friday at 10 A.M., noon, 2 P.M. and 3 P.M., and on weekends at 11 A.M., 1 P.M., and 3 P.M. It's closed holidays. A number of lively inns and restaurants are clustered along State Street, within a short walk for business travelers and midweek lunch-goers.

From the Empire State Plaza, it is a short walk down State Street to Broadway and one of Albany's newest outdoor spaces: the **Hudson River Way** is a pedestrian bridge that crosses over I-787 to **Corning Riverfront Park,** where residents come to walk their dogs or read a book on warm afternoons. Along the path are a series of murals depicting Albany's long and colorful history.

Follow Broadway a few blocks further north to reach the **Albany Heritage Area Visitors Center** (Clinton Ave. and Broadway, Albany, 800/258-

State Capitol Building

3582; Mon.–Fri. 9 A.M.–4 P.M., Sat.–Sun. 10 A.M.–4 P.M.), a good place to get an overview of the history and culture of the Capital Region.

From there, it's a short drive to the handsome **Ten Broeck Mansion** (9 Ten Broeck Pl., Albany, 518/436-9826, www.tenbroeck.org), where the Albany County Historical Association has set up shop. The Federal-style home was originally built by Abraham Ten Broeck, a distinguished general and statesman who fought at the Battle of Saratoga and later served as mayor of Albany. More than two decades after the wealthy Olcott family had donated the renovated building to the city, museum staff discovered a fully stocked wine cellar in the basement. Many of the surrounding buildings in the once-exclusive Arbor Hill district have been converted into urban apartments.

◪ Lark Street and Washington Park

Many of Albany's events, including the popular spring tulip festival, take place in Washington Park (www.washingtonparkconservancy.com), a 90-acre green space in the center of the city that has been public property since the 17th century. Jogging trails circle a small lake and a handful of statues and monuments across the park. A bronze statue of Scottish poet Robert Burns was created by a local sculptor in 1888. The King Fountain was made of rocks from Storm King Mountain in Orange County. Though the park is well-loved, it's rarely crowded, and students can always find a quiet place to read. Playgrounds are a draw for kids.

At the east end of the park, bohemian Lark Street is Albany's answer to Manhattan's East Village and San Francisco's Haight-Ashbury. This is the neighborhood of choice for Friday drinks or Sunday brunch. Several blocks of shops and restaurants between State and Madison Streets got a fresh new look in 2003. You'll find everything from cozy cafés to chic new establishments serving Kobe beef.

The historic Center Square neighborhood, bound by Lark, State, Swan, and Jay Streets, connects the Lark Street district to the Empire State Plaza. Stroll through its quiet streets to see rows of brick, brownstone, and clapboard houses that are more than 100 years old.

Albany Institute of History and Art

For a lasting impression of Hudson Valley history and culture, head to one of the oldest museums in the U.S. Older than the Smithsonian, the Metropolitan Museum of Art, and the Louvre, the **Albany Institute of History and Art** (125 Washington Ave., Albany, 518/463-4478, www.albanyinstitute.org; Wed.–Sat. 10 A.M.–5 P.M., Sun. noon–5 P.M.; adults $7, seniors and students $5) dates back to 1791. The museum has increasingly broadened its focus over the years to include Hudson River School paintings, artifacts from colonial times, and 19th-century American sculpture. Beginning in 2004, the museum began a series of exhibits to bring to life the history of eight Albany neighborhoods.

ALBANY COUNTY

Historic Cherry Hill

South of downtown Albany, **Historic Cherry Hill** (523-1/2 South Pearl St., Albany, 518/434-4791, www.historiccherryhill.org; Apr.–Dec. Tues.–Sun. by guided tour; adults $4, seniors $3, students $2, children $1) was once the center of a working farm that belonged to the Van Rensselaer family. A hodgepodge of collections inside the 1787 Colonial-style home document the lives of four generations of the family, ending with Catherine Bogart Putnam Rankin, the great-granddaughter of Philip and Maria Van Rensselaer. On display are ceramics, silver, textiles, books, and photographs.

The home is also known as the site of a famous murder in 1827. Author Louis C. Jones chronicled the story in a book called *Murder at Cherry Hill* and also referred to the murder in a better-known book of ghost stories, *Things That Go Bump in the Night*. From I-787, take Exit 2.

Watervliet Shaker Historic District

In the shadow of the Albany airport stands an intriguing slice of history, the Watervliet Shaker Historic District and the site of the first American Shaker settlement (875 Watervliet Shaker Rd., Albany, 518/456-7890; Feb.–Oct. Tues.–Sat. 9:30 A.M.–4 P.M., Nov.–Dec. Mon.–Sat. 10 A.M.–4 P.M.). The first group of Shakers arrived here in 1776 with the founder of the movement, Ann Lee, and built a log cabin as the first communal dwelling. Over the years, the community grew to 350 people, and the last members left the site in 1938.

Visitors can explore several buildings, beginning with a museum in the 1848 Shaker Meeting House. Outside are an herb garden, barnyard, and network of trails around a nature preserve. Lee and other early members are buried in the Shaker Cemetery on the property. Guided tours are offered Saturdays June–October at 11:30 A.M. and 1:30 P.M.

John Boyd Thacher State Park

A short drive farther west, **John Boyd Thacher State Park** (1 Hailes Cave Rd., Voorheesville, 518/872-1237; admission $6) encompasses the Helderberg Escarpment, a six-mile-long limestone cliff that contains billion-year-old fossils and rock formations. Even amateur geologists will be able to spot the distinct change in rock formations as they climb and descend the staircases of the Indian Ladder, an 80-foot cliff on top of the escarpment. This geological wonder leads one back to the time when the area surrounding Albany was covered by a warm tropical sea. For an informative geology lesson, call to sign up for a guided tour with the park interpreter (518/872-0800).

Besides the geological wonders, the park offers panoramic views of the Adirondack and Berkshire Mountains and of Vermont's Green Mountains. Twelve miles of trails accommodate hiking, mountain biking, cross-country skiing, snowshoeing, and snowmobiling. Also on the premises are an Olympic-sized swimming pool, basketball and volleyball courts, playgrounds, ball fields, and picnic areas.

Rensselaerville

In the southwest corner of Albany County lies the 200-year-old hamlet of Rensselaerville, named for the Dutch patron who ran the local manor. Due to its remote location, the site was settled relatively late by colonial standards—in the 1780s—by Revolutionary War veterans from Long Island and New England. A number of handsome 19th-century buildings have been preserved along Main Street. Today, they house a mix of antique shops and restaurants. To get to Rensselaerville, take I-90 to Exit/Route 85 West and follow Route 85 for 12 miles.

SPORTS AND RECREATION
Winter Sports

Hockey and figure skating are popular winter activities in the Albany area. Empire State Plaza and Albany County Hockey Training Facility have rinks with public skate sessions. Nordic skiers will find trails at John Boyd Thacher State Park and at the 400-acre Five Rivers Environmental Education Center (56 Game Farm Rd., Delmar, 518/475-0291, www.dec.state.ny .us/website/education/5river.html). And for downhill skiers, Windham and Hunter Mountains are a half-hour away (see the *Upper Hudson* chapter).

Hiking

Four short hiking trails loop through John Boyd Thacher State Park, ranging .9–2.5 miles in length. The park also marks the northern terminus for the 326-mile Long Path, named for a line in a famous Walt Whitman poem, *Song of the Open Road:*

> *Afoot and light-hearted I take to the open road,*
> *Healthy, free, the world before me,*
> *The long brown path before me leading wherever I choose.*

The Long Path begins at the George Washington Bridge and meanders across the Hudson River Valley, eventually entering the park from the west.

Mountain Biking and Road Riding

The 41-mile-long Hudson-Mohawk Bikeway connects Albany, Schenectady, and Troy along the Hudson and Mohawk Rivers. Call 518/372-5656 or 800/962-8007 for a free map. The **Mohawk Hudson Cycling Club** (518/439-6678, www.mohawkhudsoncycling.org) organizes road and mountain biking trips within an 80-mile radius of the Albany-Schenectady-Troy area, including a September Century Weekend that begins in Saratoga Spa State Park and Mountain Bike Festival at **Grafton Lakes State Park** (Grafton, 518/279-1155) outside of Troy (Rensselaer County). Its 20 miles of multiuse trails, which now connect to neighboring trail systems, are popular with Albany-based riders.

In addition, several hundred cyclists participate each summer in the **Cycling the Erie Canal Tour** (518/434-1583, www.ptny.org; $495), an eight-day ride from Buffalo to Albany covering roughly 50 miles a day. The fee includes camping, meals, entertainment, and riding support. In its seventh year in 2005, the event is sponsored by Parks & Trails New York, a local nonprofit.

Stop by the **Down Tube Cycle Shop** (466 Madison Ave., Albany, 518/434-1711) in a convenient downtown location, for gear and information.

Golf

Capital Hills at Albany (65 O'Neil Rd., Al-

bany, 518/438-2208; $24), designed in 1929, maintains a challenging public course (18 holes) with tough closing holes and considerable elevation change. Rent a cart unless you're looking for a cardio workout. Ten miles north of Albany, **Mill Road Acres Golf Course** (30 Mill Rd., Latham, 518/785-4653; $12.50) has a well-maintained nine-hole course.

You can mix and match the four nine-hole courses at the **Town of Colonie Golf Course** (418 Consaul Rd., Schenectady, 518/374-4181; $22). The Red/White course combination has water hazards on six holes. You must pay for 18 holes, even if you only intend to play nine.

Swimming and Boating

Dutch Apple Cruises (1666 Julianne Dr., Castleton, 518/463-0220) operates several cruises per week from Albany through the Erie Canal. **Riverboat Cruises** (1 Terminal Rd., Clifton Park, 518/273-8878) offers day and evening tours on the *Nightingale III,* a 90-passenger boat. Both services depart from the eastern terminus of the canal in Clifton Park.

crew team on the Hudson in front of the Capitol

ACCOMMODATIONS

Albany's many business hotels are clustered downtown and near the airport. Unique properties are more difficult but not impossible to come by. Look near Washington Park and the Empire State Plaza.

Under $100

In 1997, Rensselaerville residents Steve and Marlene Omlor restored an 1806 home to create the **Catalpa House B&B** (Main St., Rensselaerville, 518/797-3483, www.catalpahouse.com; $65–90), named for a giant Catalpa tree that stands on the front lawn. The inn has six country-style rooms, two of which have private baths. The reasonable rates include breakfast and afternoon tea.

$100–150

In the shadow of the state capitol buildings, the **State Street Mansion Bed & Breakfast** (281 State St., Albany, 800/462-6780, www.statestreetmansion.com) is a three-story brownstone B&B with 12 amply furnished rooms and off-street parking.

Two heated pools and a day spa are among the modern amenities at ⓜ **The Desmond** (660 Albany Shaker Rd., Albany, 518/869-8100 or 800/448-3500, www.desmondhotelsalbany.com; $120–185), primarily a business hotel and conference center with well-appointed rooms in a complex of brick colonial buildings. There are two restaurants onsite: Scrimshaw serves *steak au poivre*, veal Oscar, and cedar-plank salmon in an 80-seat dining room. And Simpson's is a casual venue for all-American fare. Weekend packages include rooms and meals at discounted rates. Take Exit I-87 to Exit 4.

For a more personal touch in downtown accommodations, stay with the Stofelano family at **Mansion Hill Inn** (115 Philip St. at Park Ave., Albany, 518/465-2038 or 888/299-0455, www.mansionhill.com), in business since 1984. Several rooms feature the historical paintings of local artist Len Tantillo. An onsite restaurant, also family-run, prepares hearty American fare including rib eye and grilled whole quail with sausage and mushroom risotto.

$150–200

One block from the state capitol and the Pepsi Arena, the **Crowne Plaza Albany City Center** (corner of State St. & Lodge St., Albany, 518/462-6611 or 800/227-6963, www.cpalbany.com; $190–260) is one of the largest business hotels in downtown Albany. The facility includes 384 modern rooms on 15 floors, plus a health club and business center. High-speed Internet is a plus at the eight-story **Albany Marriott** (189 Wolf Rd., Albany, 518/458-8444 or 800/443-8952), a 350-room establishment located four miles from downtown.

Among the most posh in Albany accommodations is the four-room ⓜ **Morgan State House** (393 State St., Albany, www.statehouse.com; $160–200), where feather beds, robes, and down comforters make for a cozy night's stay. A 12-foot ceiling with skylights makes room No. 4B one of the best in the house.

FOOD

Downtown Albany

There are hundreds of restaurants to choose from in the Albany metropolitan area. A steady stream of politicians and financial executives support a diverse and upscale restaurant scene downtown. One of the oldest establishments is ⓜ **Jack's Oyster House** (42 State St., Albany, 518/465-8854; Sun.–Thurs. 11:30 A.M.–10 P.M., Fri.–Sat. till 11 P.M.; mains $16–28), a turn-of-the-20th-century tavern with a dark wood interior that creates a formal but not stuffy air. At the busy lunch hour, waiters dressed in snappy uniforms whisk about the dining room carrying trays of fresh oysters from the raw bar. Steaks pair well with the restaurant's private-label red wine from Silverado Vineyards in California.

Order in advance to try one of the famed soufflés at **Pearl Restaurant & Lounge** (1 Steuben Pl. on South Pearl St., Albany, 518/433-0011; Mon.–Fri. 11 A.M.–4 P.M., Mon.–Wed. 5–9 P.M., Thurs.–Sat. till 10 P.M.; mains $16–23). Additional specialties include salmon Genevieve, escargot, duckling, veal saltimbucca, and lobster bisque. Prices are moderate for the high quality of the food, and the restaurant offers free valet parking.

In 2004, the friendly owner of **DeJohn's Restaurant and Pub** (288 Lark St., Albany, 518/465-5275, www.dejohns.com; Mon.–Thurs. 4–11 P.M., Fri.–Sat. 4 P.M.–midnight; mains $13–20) renovated the space that was formerly known as Lulu's. The new three-floor restaurant has a basement sports bar and rear patio. The middle level is a casual restaurant serving pan-encrusted trout and several vegetarian options. The top floor has a banquet room.

Vegetarian dishes reign at **Shades of Green** (187 Lark St. at Washington St., Albany, 518/434-1830), where the menu includes burritos, chili, sandwiches, and yogurt smoothies.

For French cuisine in a romantic setting, make reservations at **Nicole's Bistro** (25 Quackenbush Sq. at Broadway, Albany, 518/465-1111; Mon.–Fri. lunch, Mon.–Sat. dinner; $25 prix fixe), at the Quackenbush House. In summer, courtyard dining next to a colonial herb garden is a plus. The restaurant also hosts occasional cigar nights.

There's a little bit of everything on the reasonably priced menu at **Quintessence** (11 New Scotland Ave. at Madison Ave., Albany, 518/434-8186; Mon.–Fri. breakfast, daily lunch and dinner)—Asian, German, Italian, Mexican, and more. Located near the Albany Medical Center, this diner is especially popular for weekday breakfast and late-night eats. On weekend mornings, enjoy live acoustic guitar over a mimosa made with fresh-squeezed orange juice.

More than 100 Italian restaurants are scattered across the Albany area, and a few of them manage to rise above the crowd: Locals choose **Lombardo's** (121 Madison Ave., Albany, 518/462-9180; Mon.–Fri. 11 A.M.–2 P.M. and 4–11 P.M., Sat. 4–11P.M.) for delicious and reasonably priced Italian fare. For northern Italian convenient to downtown, grab a table at **Café Capriccio** (49 Grand St., Albany, 518/465-0439; Mon.–Thurs. 5:30–10 P.M., Fri.–Sat. 5:30–11 P.M., Sun. 5:30–9 P.M.).

An eclectic basement restaurant with a small street-side patio, **Justin's** (301 Lark St., Albany, 518/436-7008; Sun.–Thurs. 5–10 P.M., Fri.–Sat. 5–10:30 P.M., café menu served daily 11:30 A.M.– 4 P.M. and 5 P.M.–1 A.M.; mains $17–23) is packed at almost any time of day on the weekend. The bar stays open till 4 A.M. daily. The corned-beef hash is deserving of its reputation. Wicker furniture, dim lighting, and dark paint won't detract from the experience of eating the *ropa vieja* sandwich made of braised Cuban brisket.

In business since 1976, **The Daily Grind** (204 Lark St., Albany, 518/427-0464, www.dailygrind .com; Mon.–Sat. 7 A.M.–10 P.M., Sun. till 8 P.M.) is a European-style coffee bar and café that roasts its own beans.

Albany also has its share of more exotic cuisines, including **Shalimar Restaurant** (31 Central Ave., Albany) for Indian and **Yono's** (Armory Center, 64 Colvin Ave., Albany) for Indonesian.

El Mariachi (289 Hamilton St., 518/432-7580, & 52 Central Ave., 518/465-2568; Mon.–Fri. 11 A.M.–10 P.M., Sat.–Sun. 1–10 P.M.) serves authentic Mexican fare in two downtown Albany locations. The full tequila bar and homemade sangria are a plus. Locals prefer the cheap eats and 25-cent Ms. Pacman at **Bombers Burrito Bar** (258 Lark St., Albany, 518/463-9636; Mon.–Sat. 9 A.M.–11 P.M., Sun. 9 A.M.–10 P.M.; mains $5).

With 50 years of experience, **Bob and Ron's Fish Fry** (1007 Central Ave., Albany) does seafood right. Impatient locals will stand in line forever for a basket of fish and chips. Meanwhile, **Paesan's** (289 Ontario St., Albany) has mastered the art of the thin-crust pizza. Most weekdays, a host of vendors congregate on the lawn behind the Capitol Building serving lunch to go. A slice of pizza or a couple of tacos are among the best deals around.

Albany County

Supersized plates of pasta and giant bottles of chianti define the southern Italian experience at **Buca di Beppo** (44 Wolff Rd., Colonie, 518/459-2822), outside of Albany.

ENTERTAINMENT AND EVENTS
Performing Arts

The twin theaters inside **The Egg** (Empire State Plaza, Albany, 518/473-1061, www.theegg.org) show theater, dance, music, and comedy.

Spectrum Seven Theaters (290 Delaware Ave., Albany, 518/449-8995) is the place to catch an indie film along with some of the best movie snacks around.

Founded in 1931, the **Albany Symphony Orchestra** (19 Clinton Ave., Albany, 518/465-4755, www.albanysymphony.com) plays at the Palace Theatre near Quackenbush Square. Its programs often emphasize contemporary or over-looked American works.

Bars and Nightlife

Albany boasts a colorful nightlife scene, with many bars and clubs along Pearl Street and Lark Street. The free alternative weekly *Metroland* (www.metroland.net) covers Capital Region happenings in exhaustive detail. Copies are available at many bars, restaurants, and convenience stores, and on many street corners.

Steps away from the Pepsi Arena, the martini bar at **Pearl Restaurant & Lounge** (1 Steuben Pl. on South Pearl St., Albany, 518/433-0011, www.pearlalbany.com) is open till midnight on school nights, 1 A.M. on Thursdays, and 4 A.M. on most weekend nights.

Jillian's (59 N. Pearl St., Albany, 518/432-1997; Sun. 11 A.M.–midnight, Mon.–Wed. 11–1 A.M., Thurs.–Sat. 11–3 A.M.; mains $5–10) is a three-story complex with a bar on each floor, plus a video café, dance floor, and numerous large-screen TVs. You'll find a wider-than-average selection of standard pub fare on the menu. A block away is the **Big House Brewery,** also three floors, with pool tables and a 3rd-floor dance club that often has an additional cover charge.

It's standing room only most nights at **Mahar's Public Bar** (1110 Madison Ave., Albany, 518/459-9416), near Washington Park. Beer afi-cionados are crazy about this tiny pub with a bar, limited seating, and old taps on the wall. There are 25 beers on tap and 300 bottles to choose from at any given time. Regulars keep their own mug on a shelf by the bar, and a free T-shirt goes to anyone who tries 50 different brews. Computerized menus keep track of which ones you've already sampled. Five hundred tastings get you a plaque on the wall. The food menu is intentionally limited.

Choose from among 30 wines by the glass and 160 bottles at **The Ginger Man** (234 Western Ave., Albany), a wine bar near Washington Park. Justin's Café (301 Lark St., Albany, 518/436-7008) draws a steady late-night crowd as well.

The college crowd descends on **Pauly's Hotel** after 10 P.M. most nights to listen to blues in a pub-style bar. Live bands often play at the **Lark Street Tavern.** A more refined alternative for live music is **The Larkin Lounge** (199 Lark St., Albany), which hosts local and national perfor-mances, including a Wednesday-night piano bar. **Quintessence** (11 New Scotland Ave. at Madison Ave., Albany, 518/434-8186) shakes martinis and serves a late-night weekend menu; a DJ spins tunes on Saturday nights.

Festivals

For almost 60 years, Albany residents have cele-brated their Dutch heritage with the annual **Albany Tulip Festival** (Washington Park, Albany, 518/434-2032), which coincides each year with Mother's Day in May. Sample an array of foods and live music while you admire the massive dis-play of flowers. For one Saturday each September, trendy Lark Street closes to traffic to host a wildly popular street fair, called **Larkfest,** with music, food, and entertainment.

Spectator Sports

Before visiting Albany, check the **Pepsi Arena** (51 South Pearl St., Albany, 518/487-2000, www.pepsiarena.com) website for upcoming events. You might be able to catch a monster truck show, the latest megaconcert, or an NBA game. The arena is the home to the AHL River Rats, Albany Conquest, and the Siena Saints col-lege basketball team.

SHOPPING

Albany's shopping malls draw consumers from hours away for a healthy dose of retail therapy. With anchor stores including Macy's, Lord & Taylor, Filenes, and JC Penney, the **Crossgates Mall** (1 Crossgates Mall Rd., Guilderland, 800/439-2011, www.shopcrossgates.com), in Guilder-land, a suburb of Albany, bills itself as the largest mall in New York State. For a more funky selection of clothing and locally made crafts, head to the shops on Lark Street. Among the many boutiques and antique shops is **Elissa Halloran Designs** (225 Lark St., Albany, 518/432-7090; Tues.–Sat. 11 A.M.–6 P.M., Thurs.–Fri. till 7 P.M., Sun. noon–5 P.M.), which carries women's apparel and handmade jewelry. Artists Cathy Frank and Ed Atkeson recently opened the tiny **Firlefanz Gallery** (292 Lark St., Albany, 518/465-5035, www.firlefanzgallery.com) on Albany's Center Square. Inside is a selection of jewelry, pottery, paintings, and sculpture.

Bookstores

Pop into the basement level **Lark Street Bookshop** (215 Lark St., Albany, 518/465-8126, www.larkstreetbookshop.com; Mon.–Fri. noon–9 P.M., Sat. till 8 P.M.) to browse used titles before a poetry reading or musical event. Sip a cup of a Fair Trade coffee while you listen or read. **The Book House of Stuyvesant Plaza** (518/489-4761) is another reliable independent bookstore featuring local authors in Albany's Stuyvesant Plaza strip mall. **Dove and Hudson** (296 Hudson Ave., Albany, 518/432-4518), on the historic Center Square, is much-loved for its collection of used titles.

Farm Stands

After checking out the Helderberg Escarpment, pay a visit to **Indian Ladder Farms** (342 Altamont Rd., Altamont, 518/765-2956) to pick your own apples, raspberries, and blueberries. You can also pick your own strawberries at **Altamont Orchards** (6654 Dunnsville Rd., Altamont, 518/861-6515, www.altamontorchards .com). **W.F. Ryan Produce** (114 Railroad Ave. Extension, between the Northway Mall and Filler Rd., Colonie, 518/459-5775; Mon.–Fri. 8 A.M.–

6 P.M., Sat. from 7 A.M.) is an indoor farmers market that stays open year-round.

INFORMATION AND SERVICES

The **Albany Visitor Center** (25 Quackenbush Square, Albany; 518/434-1217 or 800/258-3582, www.albany.org) has a wealth of information on local attractions.

GETTING THERE AND AROUND

As a major transportation hub for the Catskill and Capital Regions, Albany is easily reached by air, train, car, or bus. Many residents as far south as Dutchess County prefer to fly in and out of Albany International Airport than fight traffic around the New York City airports.

By Bus

Dozens of local bus lines serve the Albany metro area. Check the Capital District Transportation Authority website (www.cdta.org) for current routes and schedules.

By Train

One of the most pleasant ways to get from New York City to the Capital Region is to board an Amtrak train at Penn Station and follow the Hudson River for two hours north. Be sure to get a seat on the left side to catch the views the whole way north. Cabs are readily available from the Rensselaer Station (East St., Rensselaer).

By Car

Albany is a major metropolitan area with heavy traffic during commuting hours. I-87 and I-787 are the main north-south highways. The Albany Airport is Exit 13N on I-87. You can rent a car from all the major chains at the Albany Airport.

Saratoga County

For the 40-mile stretch from Troy to Fort Edward, the Hudson River becomes an industrial conduit for the Champlain Canal, a shipping channel built in the early 19th century that extends all the way to the Canadian border. A series of locks and dams enables ships to navigate the changing elevation. The most impressive feat of aquatic engineering takes place at Waterford, where the Hudson merges with its largest tributary, the Mohawk River. Managing an elevation difference of 165 feet, the **Waterford Flight of Locks** are the highest in the world.

Route 4 follows the Hudson shoreline northward, passing by a handful of historic sites: On October 17, 1777, British General Burgoyne surrendered to American General Gates in a decisive victory that convinced the French to join the American cause and marked the turning point of the Revolutionary War. **Saratoga National Historic Park** (Rte. 9, Albany, 518/664-9821; seven-day pass $3), in the town of Stillwater,

commemorates the battles of Saratoga. A nine-mile toll road ($5) open to motorists and cyclists reenacts the battles that took place on surrounding farmlands and woods. Park facilities include a visitors center, museum, and bookstore.

George Washington, Alexander Hamilton, and the Marquis de Lafayette all stayed at the summer residence of General Philip Schuyler, a few miles north in Schuylerville. Visitors can tour the **General Schuyler House** (Rte. 4, Schuylerville, 518/664-9821; adults $3, children $1) Memorial Day–Labor Day Tuesday–Sunday. Just off Route 4 is the 155-foot tall **Saratoga Monument** (Rtes. 4 & 32, Victory, 518/664-9821), built in 1877 to honor the historic victory.

Recently, local organizations have renamed Route 4 the **Lakes to Locks Passage** in an attempt to draw more visitors to the area. But other than these scattered historic sites, the prevailing mood along the Hudson here is one of ne-

General Schuyler House

glect. One abandoned factory after another serves as a poignant reminder that this region was once a busy port of commerce.

SARATOGA SPRINGS

History lessons aside, the main reason to visit Saratoga County is to explore the charming Victorian town of Saratoga Springs. Natural hot springs, world-class horse racing, autumn apple picking, and a vibrant artistic community that revolves around Skidmore College draw an enthusiastic crowd of students, weekenders, and permanent residents.

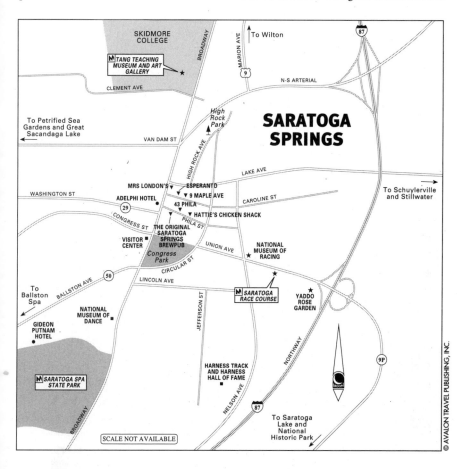 Saratoga Spa State Park

The Iroquois were first to discover the healing powers of Saratoga's natural hot springs, created by a layer of limestone in the ground that produces carbonated mineral water. Like the spa town of Baden-Baden in Germany's Black Forest, Saratoga's legacy as a spa resort dates back to the turn of the 19th century. Envisioning a well-developed destination for rest and relaxation, Gideon Putnam built the first tavern and boarding house and drew the first plans for a town around the hot springs.

In 1930, the state of New York got in on the action and built a Georgian Revival hotel in

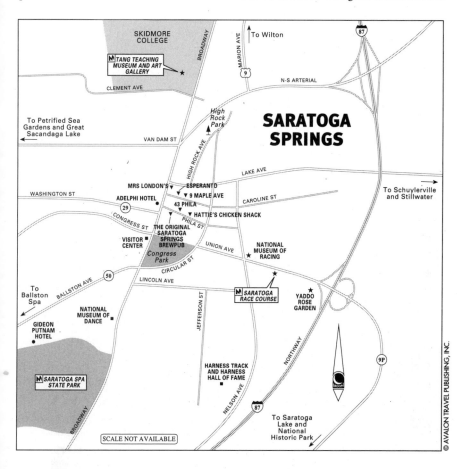

© AVALON TRAVEL PUBLISHING, INC.

Saratoga Spa State Park reflecting pool

Putnam's name. In its day, the Gideon Putnam Hotel hosted the likes of entertainers Bob Hope and Fred Astaire, as well as Chief Justice of the U.S. Supreme Court Charles Evans Hughes.

Today, Saratoga Spa State Park (19 Roosevelt Dr., Saratoga Springs, 518/584-2535) covers 2,300 acres of tall pines, steaming mineral baths, and tranquil walking paths. Visitors can access the mineral baths through the Gideon Putnam Hotel or the Lincoln Mineral Baths.

In addition to the great outdoors, the park holds several cultural attractions: There is no better way to spend a summer afternoon than listening to live music at the **Saratoga Performing Arts Center** (SPAC; Rte. 50, Saratoga Springs, 518/587-3330, www.spac.org). From opera and ballet to pop and rock 'n' roll, this custom-designed amphitheater offers something everyone. Initially conceived to give the New York Philharmonic a proper summer home, SPAC opened in 1966 and will celebrate its 40th season in 2005. Today, the New York City Ballet and Philadelphia Orchestra both move to Saratoga for summer performances May–September. The theater holds 5,000 people under an open shelter and has room for 7,000 more on the lawn.

SPAC also operates the **National Museum of Dance & Hall of Fame** (99 S. Broadway, Saratoga Springs, 518/584-2225, www.dance-museum.org; adults $6.50), in the old Washington Bath House (1918). The Greek Revival building contains five galleries full of photographs, videos, books, and costumes that document all forms of dance, from ballet to tap.

After a multiyear renovation that cost $5 mil-

lion, the original Roosevelt Bathhouse (1930) is back in business as part of the **Gideon Putnam Hotel** (Rte. 50, Saratoga Springs, 800/732-1560, www.gideonputnam.com; $165). Inside are a 13,000-square-foot spa with 42 private spa rooms. From Route 9, turn left onto Avenue of the Pines to reach the park entrance.

Saratoga Race Course

At the next exit on I-87 is Saratoga's other main attraction, the **Saratoga Race Course** (267 Union Ave., Saratoga Springs, 800/437-1611, www.nyra.com/saratoga). Featured in the contemporary book and movie *Seabiscuit,* the racetrack dates back to 1863, making it the oldest continuously operating thoroughbred track in the country. Horseracing became wildly popular in the 1940s and '50s, and the Saratoga Race Course has been a local institution ever since.

Saratoga's population of 27,000 literally triples during the month-long summer racing season, from the end of July through Labor Day weekend. Tickets are affordable, and the scene is at once traditional and exciting. Women still don their Sunday finest to watch from the grandstand. At the other end of the spectrum, diehard fans barbecue at their cars and watch from the parking lot without buying tickets at all. The hoopla concludes each year with the famous **Travers Stakes,** named for racetrack cofounder William Travers.

Grandstand tickets go on sale at 8 A.M. each morning for that day's races. Purchase them at the Union Avenue Gate, or at the Holiday Inn in downtown Saratoga Springs (cash only, limit four per person). You can also rent binoculars at the track for up-close viewing. Take Exit 14/Union Avenue from I-87.

National Museum of Racing

Across from the racetrack, an informative museum demonstrates what traits make the best thoroughbreds and recreates famous scenes on the track. Recent additions to the **National Museum of Racing** (191 Union Ave., Saratoga Springs, www.racingmuseum.org; Mon.–Sat. 10 A.M.–4 P.M., Sun. noon–4 P.M.; adults $7, students $5) archives include newspaper articles from the mid-19th century. Florida-bred

Skip Away and Kentucky-bred Flawlessly became the newest inductees into the museum's Hall of Fame in 2004.

Beyond the racetrack and museum on Union Avenue is the 400-acre Yaddo estate, an artist community established in 1900 and housed in an imposing Tudor mansion. Its terraced **Yaddo Rose Garden** (P.O. Box 395, Saratoga Springs, 518/584-0746, www.yaddo.org), modeled after classical Italian designs, has been gradually restored over the last 15 years.

Downtown Saratoga Springs

Broadway and Union Avenue both lead to the open lawns of **Congress Park** and the heart of Saratoga Springs. Kids will want to head straight to the park's working merry-go-round or to feed the ducks in the pond. The **Canfield Casino** (Congress Park, Saratoga Springs, 518/584-6920, www.saratogahistory.org; June–Sept. daily 10 A.M.–4 P.M., Oct–May Wed.–Sat. 10 A.M.–4 P.M., Sun. 1–4 P.M., closed Jan.; adults $4, seniors and students $3, under 12 free), a major attraction during the spa town's heyday, is now a local history museum.

Along Broadway, between Congress Street and Van Dam Street are a host of tempting options for shopping, entertainment, and dining out. To get oriented, stop by the information booth at the corner of Broadway and Congress. Then continue up Broadway to one of Saratoga's most famous landmarks, the **Adelphi Hotel** (365 Broadway, Saratoga Springs, 518/587-4688, www.adelphihotel.com; $155), a four-story Victorian that has stayed in business since the turn of the 20th century. Note the hand-painted stencils in the lobby before settling in for a drink in the garden out back. These days, the hotel is unfortunately surrounded by a sea of chain stores, including The Gap, Banana Republic, Eddie Bauer, and Starbucks.

⋈ Tang Teaching Museum and Art Gallery

North Broadway leads to the Skidmore College campus and an innovative museum that hosts programs with titles like "Why is Contemporary Art So Weird?" The Tang Teaching Museum and Art Gallery (815 N. Broadway; Saratoga Springs, 518/580-8080, tang.skidmore.edu, Tues.–Fri. 10 A.M.–5 P.M., Sat–Sun. noon–5 P.M.) combines an outstanding permanent collection with provocative lecture topics to engage an audience of students, as well as adults and children in the local community. Exhibits are designed to involve other college departments, from dance to history. Rooftop concerts are a favorite local pastime in summer.

Petrified Sea Gardens

West of downtown on Route 29 is a 30-acre outdoor museum called the Petrified Sea Gardens (off Rte. 29, Saratoga Springs, 518/691-0150; adults $3.25, students and seniors $2.25), where you can view stromatolite fossils that formed 500 million years ago, when the Hudson River Valley marked the edge of a tropical sea. Beyond the half-acre fossil area, walking trails lead to other glacial formations, a sundial park, and a Native American medicine wheel.

SPORTS AND RECREATION
Winter Sports

When a good nor'easter buries the North Country in snow, Saratoga Spa State Park becomes a winter playland, and the cross-country skiing is sublime. You can rent equipment at a ski shop at the golf course and ski 20 kilometers of trails. **Lapland Lake** (139 Lapland Lake Rd., Northville, 518/863-4974, www.laplandlake.com; Sun.–Fri. 9 A.M.–4:30 P.M., Sat. 9 A.M.–9 P.M.; adults $14, juniors $7) has another 38 kilometers of groomed trails for classic and skating-style cross-country. A four-kilometer portion of the trail is lighted for night skiing. Rentals and lessons are available. For off-piste skiing and snowshoeing, try one of the local apple orchards.

Hiking

As the gateway to the Adirondack Mountains (beyond the scope of this handbook), the Capital Region affords convenient access to some of the best hiking and backpacking in the northeast. Bugs and bears can be minor or major annoyances, depending on your tolerance. The steep and rocky terrain will challenge even the strongest of hikers.

Mountain Biking and Road Riding

The **Saratoga Mountain Biking Association** (518/587-0455, www.saratogamtb.org) maintains trails on 538 acres north of Skidmore College. Trails suit riders of all abilities, with single track, steep climbs, and fast descents. **The Bike Shop** (35 Maple Ave., Saratoga Springs, 518/587-7857, www.bicyclequest.com; Mon.–Fri. 10 A.M.–6 P.M., Sat. 9 A.M.–5 P.M.) has rentals, maps, and gear. **All Outdoors** (35 Van Dam St., Saratoga Springs, 518/587-0455) is another popular shop for cycling supplies. **Blue Sky Bicycles** (71 Church St., Saratoga Springs, 518/583-0600, www.blueskybicycles.com; Tues.–Fri. 10 A.M.–6 P.M., Sat. 9 A.M.–5 P.M.) sells cycling gear, maps, and high-end bikes. Visit the shop to stock up on supplies and ask for ride directions. Better yet, download a cue sheet online before you go. They don't offer rentals.

Golf

There are at least a dozen golf courses in the immediate Saratoga area. One of the best is **Saratoga Spa Golf Course** (60 Roosevelt Dr., Saratoga Springs, 518/584-3137, www.saratogaspagolf.com; Mar.–Dec.; weekends $30, weekdays $26), a 27-hole complex, with a 7,098-yard championship course. Before your round, you can hit a bucket of balls from the grass tees at the driving range. Private pilots should reserve a tee time at the **Airway Meadows Golf Course** (262 Brownville Rd., Gansevoort, 518/792-4144, www.airwaymeadowsgolf.com; weekends $27, weekdays $22), adjacent to an airstrip and skydiving school.

Slide into a GPS-equipped cart at the **Saratoga National Golf Club** (458 Union Ave., Saratoga Springs, 518/583-4653, www.golfsaratoga.com), and you'll forget about the $135 you paid to get away from the crowds. Elevation changes are a challenge at the relatively new **Saratoga Lake Golf Club** (35 Grace Moore Rd., Saratoga Springs, 518/581-6616; weekends $32, weekdays $26). Greens are in good condition.

Swimming and Boating

The busiest lake in the Capital Region is **Lake George,** 30 minutes from downtown Saratoga Springs along I-87. Known for its clear water and summer resort scene, the lake measures 32 miles long and 3 miles across, and several towns have public beaches. Scuba divers can explore underwater shipwrecks with remarkably good freshwater visibility. **Million Dollar Beach** has public parking. An **Antique Classic Boat Show** takes place in August.

In addition to Lake George, several smaller lakes offer ample space for aquatic adventures. You can rent a kayak, canoe, or rowboat from **The Kayak Shak** (Saratoga Outdoor Center, 251 Staffords Bridge Rd., 518/587-9788; $20 half day, $20 full day for kayaks) to paddle around **Saratoga Lake.** The larger **Great Sacandaga Lake** is a man-made lake that allows powerboats, personal watercraft, and fishing. Swimming and windsurfing are also popular summer activities. **Moreau Lake State Park** (605 Old Saratoga Rd., Gansevoort, 518/793-0511) has a sandy beach and wooded campsites, though it tends to be crowded in the summer time. Boating and fishing are allowed.

Fishing and Hunting

Anglers cast for largemouth bass, northern pike, and panfish in Saratoga Lake. You can rent a boat and stock up on tackle at **Lake Lonely Boat Livery** (378 Crescent Ave., Saratoga Springs, 518/587-1721). For more serious sport fishing and charter operations, head to Lake George, where the catch includes lake trout and land-locked salmon, as well as bass.

ACCOMMODATIONS

Overnight visitors to Saratoga Springs have more than 100 establishments to choose from, including business hotels, smaller inns, motels, and B&Bs: The newest option in town is the Marriott Courtyard, opened in spring 2004. The historic Gideon Putnam completed its overhaul in summer 2004. Expect higher rates during the month-long horseracing season.

$150–200

Enjoy high-speed wireless Internet access as you sit among the genuine antique furnishings in an elaborately decorated suite at the **M Adelphi**

Hotel (365 Broadway, Saratoga Springs, 518/587-4688, www.adelphihotel.com; $155). The property features 39 individually decorated guestrooms and a piazza that overlooks Broadway.

Six miles south of Saratoga Springs in the town of Ballston Spa, the newly opened Medberry Inn and Spa (48 Front St., Ballston Spa, 518/885-7727 or 800/608-1804; $125–175) has 11 rooms decorated in pastel colors and floral linens. Data ports and whirlpool tubs lend a modern touch to the 200-year-old property. There is a full day spa onsite.

Bob and Stephanie Melvin are your hosts at the Westchester House Bed and Breakfast Inn (102 Lincoln Ave., Saratoga Springs, 518/587-7613, www.westchesterhousebandb.com; $105–210, during the horseracing season $235–375), inside a colorful Victorian on a quiet residential street. Rooms are decorated in country-print wallpaper and lacy window coverings. Wireless Internet is an unexpected perk.

Over $200

Spacious and well-appointed guestrooms and suites cost up to $550 a night at the recently restored Gideon Putnam Hotel (Rte. 50, Saratoga Springs, 800/732-1560, www.gideonputnam.com; $195). You'll be walking distance to SPAC, but beware that rates go sky-high during the month-long horseracing season.

Campgrounds

You can pitch a tent or park an RV under the pine trees at the Whispering Pines Campsites & RV Park (550 Sand Hill Rd., Greenfield Center, 518/893-0416). Services include hot showers, swimming pool, a trout brook, and two ponds.

FOOD

Saratoga Springs

Don't leave Saratoga without sampling a pastry at ◼ Mrs. London's (464 Broadway, Saratoga Springs, 518/581-1652; Tues.–Sun. 7 A.M.–6 P.M., Fri.–Sat. till 10 P.M.; mains $6–12). Tempting first courses include grilled panini on ciabatta, pizzas, soups, and sandwiches.

Locals feared the worst when a financier from New York City purchased ◼ Hattie's Chicken Shack (45 Phila St., Albany, 518/584-4790) more than a decade ago, but the Saratoga landmark continued to serve the mouth-watering fried chicken that made it famous. Ownership changed hands again in 2001, and even with an updated menu, the restaurant draws crowds. Lighter salads and a few contemporary New Orleans–style dishes now complement the essential fried chicken.

The well-heeled leave the racetrack behind and retreat to 43 Phila (43 Phila, Saratoga Springs, 518/584-2720, www.43philabistro.com; Mon.–Sat. 11:30 A.M.–3 P.M. & 5–10 P.M.; mains $28–46) to savor a tender milk-fed veal rib chop for $46. *Steak frites* and swordfish round out the menu, and even the requisite chicken dish is prepared with a twist: hoisin sauce and kimchi. A block away on Phila is The Original Saratoga Springs Brewpub (14 Phila St., Saratoga Springs, 518/583-3209, www.saratogabrewpub.com; mains $7–25), where you can wash your burger down with a microbrew. Outdoor seating is a plus in summer. Vegetarians won't go hungry at Esperanto (6 1/2 Caroline St., Saratoga Springs, 518/587-4236). It has a tempting selection of quick eats, including burritos, pizza, and soups, as well as a number of international cuisines, such as Thai, Mexican, and Middle Eastern.

ENTERTAINMENT AND EVENTS

Performing Arts

The story goes that the Saratoga Performing Arts Center (Rte. 50, Saratoga Springs, 518/587-3330, www.spac.org) was originally built to keep the New York Philharmonic from moving to Vermont as its summer home. While the Philharmonic never came to Saratoga Springs, the new venue did become one of the largest producers of first-rate music, dance, and opera performances in the state. Recent concerts have included everything from Bon Jovi to the Grateful Dead. A night of ballet or opera will be unforgettable. For opera aficionados, Lake George Opera (480 Broadway, Ste. 336, Saratoga Springs, 518/584-6018, www.lakegeorgeopera.org) stages performances at the Spa Little Theater in Saratoga Spa State Park.

Bars and Nightlife

Between its racetrack spectators and student population, Saratoga Springs has earned a reputation as a party town: Jazz bars, dance clubs, and Irish pubs, as well as coffeehouses and wine bars, offer venues for spirited entertainment. Several of the late-night establishments are on Caroline Street.

At cocktail hour, head to the bar and outdoor garden at the **Adelphi** (365 Broadway, Saratoga Springs, 518/587-4688, www.adelphihotel.com). One block off Broadway, jazz aficionados settle in at the beautiful wooden bar of **9 Maple Avenue** (9 Maple Ave., Saratoga Springs, 518/583-2582, www.9mapleavenue.com; opens daily 4 P.M.) for a night of live music, well-made cocktails, and a large selection of single malts. The **Parting Glass** (40–42 Lake Ave., Saratoga Springs, 518/583-1916, www.partingglass.com) plays live Irish music. **Saratoga Gaming & Harness Raceway** (Crescent Ave., Saratoga Springs, 518/584-2110) has 1,300 video gaming machines.

Festivals

Each September since 2001, SPAC has hosted the popular **Saratoga Wine & Food Festival** (518/584-9330 ext. 3021, www.spac.org/calender/wine.html) drawing food and wine enthusiasts from across New England and the mid-Atlantic states. A selection of tapas and a premium sherry tasting were among the highlights of the 2004 event.

SHOPPING

Storefronts crowd both sides of Broadway in Saratoga Springs, offering a mix of boutique jewelry and apparel, high-end retail chains, and straight up kitsch. **Silverado Jewelry Gallery** (444 Broadway, Saratoga Springs, 518/584-1044) sells unique silver and semi-precious jewelry from a number of New York City artists. At the corner of Broadway and Phila, you can browse the selection of sun-dresses, hats, and handbags at **Lifestyles** (436 Broadway, Saratoga Springs, 518/583-1854). A block away, **Summerfield Lane** (386 Broadway, Saratoga Springs, 518/584-1266, www

Collamer building, downtown Saratoga Springs

.summerfieldlane.com) is a much-loved baby boutique and gift store. **Symmetry Gallery** (348 Broadway, Saratoga Springs, 518/584-5090, www.symmetrygallery.com; Mon.–Sat. 10 A.M.–6 P.M., Thurs. till 8 P.M., Sun. noon–4 P.M.), also on Broadway, features art glass works by local artists.

Farm Stands

Certified organic growers set up produce stands at the popular **Saratoga Farmers Market** (Saratoga High School, Saratoga Springs, 800/806-3276, Sat. 9 A.M.–1 P.M.) on Saturday mornings. If you're planning a whole meal, pick up some fresh-baked bread, organic beef, and smoked salmon while you're there.

Putnam Market (435 Broadway, Saratoga Springs, 518/587-3663, www.putnammarket.com) supplies the gourmands in town with an impressive display of cheeses and pâtés. Order sandwiches, desserts, and chocolates or pick up fresh fish to cook yourself. The adjoining wine store (Putnam Wines) offers free tastings every day and stays open on Sundays.

Visit **Bowman Orchards** (107 Van Aervunem Rd., Ballston Spa, 518/885-8888, www.bowmanorchards.com), **Charlton Road Apple Orchard** (140 Charlton Rd., Ballston Lake, 518/381-3601), or **Stetkar Orchards** (Fitch Rd., Saratoga Springs, 518/584-6839) for an afternoon of apple-picking and cider-sipping.

Bookstores

Browse through a wide selection of used books from every genre at **Twice Told Used Books**

(19 Phila St., Saratoga Springs, 518/587-2427, summer daily 10 A.M.–9 P.M.), and then hang out with a cup of coffee while you watch others pass through. Also on Phila, **Lyrical Ballad Bookstore** (7–9 Phila St., Saratoga Springs, 518/584-8779) displays some of its fine old books and prints in a former bank vault.

INFORMATION AND SERVICES

In Saratoga Springs, the **Saratoga County Chamber of Commerce** (297 Broadway, Saratoga Springs, 518/587-3241; daily 9 A.M.–5 P.M.) operates an information center near Congress Park late June–Labor Day.

GETTING THERE AND AROUND
By Bus
The Saratoga Summer Visitors Shuttle stops at Congress Park, Skidmore College, and SPAC. It does not operate on Mondays ($1 round trip).

By Train
Saratoga Springs is sporting a brand new rail station as of 2004 (West Ave., Saratoga Springs) with Enterprise and Thrifty car rentals onsite.

By Car
The Capital Region is a major metropolitan area with heavy traffic during commuting hours. I-87 and I-787 are the main north-south highways. The Albany Airport is Exit 13N on I-87; Saratoga Springs is Exit 14. You can rent a car from the Albany Airport or from several independent companies in the Saratoga area.

Know
the Hudson
River Valley

Abundant natural resources in the Hudson River Valley played a critical role in the development of trade and commerce in colonial America. The lush display of trees, bushes, and wildflowers as-

tounded Henry Hudson when he first sailed up the river. Native American and European settlers found ample water, arable land, and lumber, fish, and game to support their growing communities.

The Land

Nearly half the land in the Hudson Valley has been developed for urban, residential, and agricultural use, and the rest remains second- and third-growth forest. Elevation in the region ranges from 150 feet in the lowlands to 4,000 feet in the mountains. Lowlands consist of fertile farmland, rolling hills, marshes, and swamps. Mountainous areas feature sheer cliffs, escarpments, and rocky lookout points. In addition, the Catskill region is known for its red clay soil.

GEOLOGY

Dramatic rock formations in the Hudson River Valley tell a story of mountain-building, erosion, and glacial movement that began a billion years ago. According to Jill Schneiderman, associate professor of geology at Vassar College, the oldest exposed bedrock in the region is found in the Hudson Highlands of Orange and Putnam Counties. Limestone and shale marine sediments remind us that the valley was once the edge of a shallow, tropical sea, much like the Red Sea, complete with pink sand and delicate coral formations.

The Taconic Mountains were formed next in an event known as an orogeny, followed by the Acadian Mountains, which stretched as high as the Himalayas. Runoffs from the mountain range deposited sandstone and shale to create the Devonian Catskill Delta, which forms the Catskill and Shawangunk Mountains of today. Farther south, molten rock carved the sheer cliffs of the Palisades.

In recent geologic history, 40,000 years ago, glaciers carved the fjord we now call the Hudson River. When the ice melted, it formed glacial Lake Albany and a submarine canyon that extends 500 miles offshore from Manhattan.

GEOGRAPHY

The Hudson River Valley is bound by New York City and New Jersey to the south, New England to the east, the Adirondack Mountains to the north, and the Appalachian Plateau and Mohawk Valley to the west. At the center of the valley is the river itself, 315 miles long, 3.5 miles across at its widest point, and 216 feet at its deepest. The river originates from Lake Tear of the Clouds in the Adirondack Mountains and becomes navigable at Troy, above Albany. Dozens of tributaries feed the Hudson, draining the Catskill Mountains to the west and the Taconic Range to the east. The largest rivers and creeks include the Croton, Wallkill, Rondout, Esopus, and Catskill.

A second major river, the Delaware, traverses the western part of the region and empties into the Atlantic to the south.

AVERAGE TEMPERATURE BY MONTH		
Month	High	Low
January	34	15
February	38	16
March	47	26
April	59	36
May	70	46
June	78	55
July	84	60
August	82	59
September	74	50
October	62	38
November	51	30
December	39	21

CLIMATE

The Hudson River Valley enjoys a temperate, continental climate. Four distinct seasons range from the muggy days of summer to the crisp, clear-blue days of fall and below-freezing temperatures in winter. The first frost comes in late September, ending a growing season that lasts 160–180 days. According to U.S. Department of Agriculture Forest Service data, average rainfall is about 40 inches, while snowfall measures 165 inches at the mountaintops and 40–60 inches on the valley floor. Extreme weather events include ice storms and blizzards in winter and thunderstorms and the occasional hurricane in summer and fall. The fall-foliage season lasts mid-September through late October, with the peak typically around Columbus Day weekend.

ENVIRONMENTAL ISSUES

The Hudson River absorbed a barrage of industrial waste, raw sewage, and agricultural runoff during the late 19th and early 20th centuries. The river was on the verge of recovery by the 1970s, when scientists tested striped bass for polychlorinated biphenyls (PCBs) and found alarming levels of contamination. The discovery shut down all commercial fisheries along the river, and in 1977, General Electric (GE) was ordered to stop dumping PCBs into the river. But the Hudson was unable to heal itself. The Environmental Protection Agency finally agreed in 2002 to conduct a massive dredging effort to cleanup the river. The start date has been pushed back to late spring 2006 due to prolonged negotiations with GE.

By many accounts, the Hudson River is cleaner than its has been in a generation. American shad are considered safe to eat again, and the river continues to support an astonishing diversity of life. However, PCBs and the efforts to rid the river of them continue to pose a challenge the community.

Flora and Fauna

The constant mixing of saltwater and freshwater as far north as Albany creates a rich supply of nutrients that in turn support a remarkably diverse set of interdependent plants and animals.

TREES

Sixty percent of the entire Hudson River Valley is covered in second- or third-growth forest. Towering red and white oaks and a variety of northern hardwoods—white and yellow birch, sugar maple, hickory, basswood, and ash—comprise the majority of the deciduous forest. Acorns and beechnuts provide a key source of food for wildlife populations. Common conifers include blue spruce, hemlock, white pine, and yellow pine. The sand plains around Albany support the growth of pitch pine-scrub oak forests.

FLOWERS

Across the Hudson Valley, bright yellow forsythia mark the arrival of spring, adding the first splash of color to the barren winter landscape each May. Cultivated daffodils and tulips are close behind, and more than 100 different kinds of wildflowers bloom by midsummer, including goldenrod, buttercups, and daisies, as well as jack-in-the-pulpit, sarsaparilla, and winterberry.

MAMMALS

A variety of critters big and small make their home in wooded valleys, fields, and mountainous areas. Among them are the black bear, gray squirrel, coyote, raccoon, river otter, and bobcat. In addition, many of the Hudson Valley's suburbs are overrun with whitetail deer that munch on everything in sight, from geraniums to apple blossoms.

SEALIFE

The Hudson River once held a large number of saltwater creatures, including oysters, mussels, crabs, and turtles. Most of the shellfish are gone today—blue crabs are an exception—but the river still supports more than 150 types of fish, such as bass, shad, and sturgeon, many of which are prized catches for determined anglers. At the water's edge, muskrats, snapping turtles, and ospreys feed on cattails and other marsh plants.

BIRDS

Ornithologists flock to the Hudson Valley's wilderness areas to view more than 100 types of nesting birds, migrating raptors, and waterfowl. Among the more unusual species are the Red-Eyed Vireo, found in woodland areas; American Redstart, which arrives to nest in late spring to early summer; gray and yellow Canada Warbler, found at lower levels of the forest; and Western Wood-Pewee, which prefers the dense upper canopy. Wild turkeys, grouse, and pheasant are abundant in wooded areas as well. The noisy Pileated Woodpecker likes a moist habitat where it can feed on carpenter ants. Observing one in action is a treat. Mallard ducks paddle calm, sheltered waters across the valley, while Canadian geese enjoy spending the winter near local golf courses. And the American bald eagle has made a comeback along the Delaware River, with sightings as far east as Greenwood Lake.

REPTILES AND AMPHIBIANS

The Hudson Valley has its share of snakes, frogs, salamanders, and turtles. The friendly garter snake, water snake, and white striped milk snake are common. The only two poisonous snakes are the copperhead, found south of Kingston, and the timber rattlesnake, which lives in parts of the Catskills and along the river valley.

Come March, spring peepers fill the evening air with a familiar song. One of the most common amphibians in the region, peepers live anywhere that standing water is found. Other types of frogs and toads live at the water's edge, including wood frogs, bullfrogs, green frogs, and two dark-spotted frogs, the northern leopard and pickerel.

Motorists often encounter feisty snapping turtles crossing back roads to lay their eggs. Painted turtles are another common species. Less common are the box turtle, wood turtle, the yellow-spotted Blanding's turtle in the lower Hudson Valley, and the map turtle in the Hudson River. A dozen kinds of salamander also inhabit area rivers and ponds. The mudpuppy is found in the Hudson, while the hellbender lives in the southern part of the region.

INSECTS

Mosquitoes and mayflies are a nuisance in wet and wooded areas May through July, while fireflies light up the forest on hot summer nights. Deer ticks, found in fields and woods, can spread Lyme disease.

History

EARLY INHABITANTS

Anthropologists believe the earliest inhabitants settled the Hudson River Valley as many as 10,000 years ago. By the 17th century, three main Native American nations lived along the river: the Mahicans (Algonquin) claimed the east bank of the river, from Long Island Sound to Albany, as well as the west bank from Albany to Catskill; the Mohawks (Iroquois) lived in the Catskill area; and the Lenni Lenapes (Delaware) occupied the west, from the Catskills south to the Potomac. Modern town names like Wappingers, Tappan, Hackinsack, and Minnisink all refer to Native American tribes.

EUROPEAN EXPLORATION AND SETTLEMENT

Technically speaking, Giovanni Verrazano was the first European explorer to enter the Hudson River at New York Harbor in 1524. But it was Henry Hudson, commissioned by the Dutch, who made it famous. Hudson sailed the *Half Moon* as far north as Troy in 1609, in search of a northwest passage to the Indies. Hudson did not succeed and turned around when the river became too shallow near Troy, but Dutch settlers returned soon after to settle Fort Orange at present day Albany.

Despite ongoing conflicts, the Native American and European populations began to trade fur, tobacco, wheat, oysters, beans, corn, pumpkins, and other goods. Dutch settlements grew at Albany, Manhattan, and Kingston.

The Dutch introduced the patroon system of land management, in which an individual was granted proprietary rights to a tract of land in return for bringing 50 new settlers to the colony. When the English took over in the mid-17th century, they introduced a similar approach, the manor system. Robert Livingston, Frederick Philipse, and other historic figures were all benefactors of these preferential land-management practices.

a woman in traditional clothes, Constitution Island

REVOLUTIONARY WAR

Nearly two centuries after the first Europeans arrived, the Hudson Valley's communities found themselves in the crossfire of the war for independence. Major battles took place at Stony Point, Kingston, White Plains, and Saratoga. Soldiers wheeled canons along Route 23 between the Hudson and the Berkshires. George Washington established headquarters in Newburgh and other towns along the river, and West Point was fortified to keep the British out.

EARLY INDUSTRY

After the revolution, abundant natural resources created the foundation for industry in the newly independent country: tanneries, bluestone quarries, sawmills, and gristmills opened to support a growing population. Dairy farms and orchards flourished, and the first icehouses appeared along the Hudson.

STEAMBOAT TRAVEL

Inventor Robert Fulton shattered previous Hudson River records on August 14, 1807, when he made the first successful steamboat journey from New York to Albany in 32 hours. Backing the venture was Chancellor Robert R. Livingston, who had met Fulton in France a decade earlier.

Engines powered by steam would eventually revolutionize the transport of goods and passengers on the Hudson, spurring a new wave of economic development. Change might have proceeded at a faster clip, had New York State not granted Livingston a 20-year monopoly on steamboat travel between New York City and Albany. Livingston and Fulton were free to seize and impose fines on any competitors. But the sovereign state of New Jersey understandably objected to the arrangement, and the Supreme Court intervened to settle the dispute. In the landmark decision of 1824, *Ogden vs. Gibbons,* the court ruled to end the monopoly, setting a precedent for federal control over interstate commerce. In the wake of the decision, between 1819 and 1840, the number of steamboats on the river rose from 8 to more than 100.

RAIL TRAVEL AND RIVERSIDE ESTATES

The advent of the railroad brought a new wave of prosperity to the Hudson River Valley and Catskill Mountain towns. Summer resorts flourished in Greene, Sullivan, and Delaware Counties. Westchester County became a commuter base as early as the 1800s, when rail travel made it possible to reach New York City in just a few hours. In this era of prosperity, families including the Rockefellers, Vanderbilts, Philipses, and Van Cortlands built or expanded their sprawling country estates along the banks of the Hudson.

INDUSTRIAL REVOLUTION

Factories grew like weeds along the banks of the Hudson during the early 20th century, manufacturing everything from cars to paper to poultry. General Electric began to make appliances in Troy, and IBM settled near Poughkeepsie. As the industrial economy transformed into the information economy and jobs moved overseas, most of these factories shut down. Today's many abandoned plants in Beacon, Newburgh, Poughkeepsie, and other river cities testify to the volume of industry that once thrived across the valley. By the 1960s, the Hudson had earned designation as an industrial river—a body of water polluted beyond repair.

RECESSION AND REVIVAL

Modern auto, rail, and jet travel changed the region forever, sending would-be visitors to ever more exotic destinations in the same amount of time it once took to reach the Catskills from New York City. Farmers, manufacturers, and vacation resorts alike struggled to compete on the international stage, and most towns along the Hudson River fell into a deep and prolonged recession.

The economic boom of the late 1990s triggered a long overdue recovery for many area towns. Weekenders bought second homes, supporting riverfront restaurants and festivals from Newburgh to Kingston. To meet the needs of increasingly sophisticated palettes, local farmers began to experiment with boutique crops, such as heirloom vegetables, shiitake mushrooms, organic meat, and microgreens. Winemakers planted French hybrid grapes to produce award-winning labels. Together, these factors set the stage for the intriguing region visitors can experience today.

GOVERNMENT

New York State consists of 64 counties, 12 of which are covered in this handbook. Four of the group were established when the first New York General Assembly convened in 1683, with the rest to follow by the early 19th century. Several

COURTESY OF ALBANY COUNTY CONVENTION & VISITORS BUREAU

State Capitol Building

Hudson Valley cities, including Fishkill, Poughkeepsie, and Kingston, hosted the early state government, before it eventually settled in Albany.

THE PEOPLE

Historically, Hudson Valley immigrants were German, Dutch, or Irish. Today, area residents are a mix of commuters to New York City, farmers, small business owners, artists, students, second-home owners, and blue-collar workers. All major socioeconomic groups are represented, and the ethnic makeup has become increasingly diverse as new immigrants arrive in New York City and gradually make their way north in search of jobs and homes.

Getting There and Around

AIR

The Hudson River Valley is easily accessible from several international airports, including John F. Kennedy (JFK; Van Wyck Expressway, 718/244-4444), LaGuardia (LGA; Grand Central Pkwy, 718/533-3400), and Newark (EWR; I-95 and I-78, 973/961-6000) in the New York City area, as well as Albany (ALB; 737 Albany-Shaker Rd., Albany, 518/242-2200, www.albanyairport.com), Stewart (SWF; 1180 First St., New Windsor, 845/564 2100, www.stewartintlairport.com), and Westchester airports upstate. Numerous county and private airstrips provide local shuttle service.

Stewart and Albany offer convenient access to many Hudson River Valley attractions; however busier JFK and Newark airports often have better rates and more choice in flight times for travelers coming from afar.

Newark is closest to destinations in Orange and Rockland Counties, while JFK and LaGuardia serve Westchester and Putnam counties best. Newark also has the best public transportation to and from New York City. Its AirTrain service connects to NJ Transit and Amtrak, which offer frequent express trains out of Penn Station. Rail service to JFK is a trickier proposition that requires a long subway ride to Queens and then an AirTrain connection to the terminals. Information about all three New York City airports, as well as AirTrain services at Newark and JFK, is available at the Port Authority of NY & NJ website: www.panynj.gov.

Car services are often the best option for getting to and from Stewart and Albany airports, and listings are available on the airport websites; cabs, rental cars, and shuttle services are also readily available to most destinations.

TRAIN

Metro-North (800/638-7646, www.mta.nyc.ny .us/mnr/index.html) and New Jersey Transit (800/772-2222, www.njtransit.com) run commuter lines out of New York City's Grand Central and Penn Stations, reaching Poughkeepsie and Wassaic in the north, Port Jervis in the west, and Connecticut in the east. Metro-North offers discount rail fare and admission to popular destinations, including Boscobel, Clearwater, Dia:Beacon, Nyack, and Kykuit.

Amtrak (800/872-7245, www.amtrak.com) offers service beyond the commuter zone, following the eastern bank of the Hudson all the way to Albany and Saratoga Springs. Taxis are readily available at most major stations.

BUS

Greyhound (800/229-9424, www.greyhound .com) buses stop in major cities and towns throughout the valley, including Albany, New Paltz, Newburgh, Poughkeepsie, Saratoga Springs, and White Plains. **Shortline Bus** (800/631-8405, www.shortlinebus.com) and **Adirondack Trailways** (800/858-8555, www.escapemaker .com/adirondacktrailways.com) offer regional connections and package trips.

Public transportation gets less reliable the farther you travel into the countryside, but most counties run some sort of local bus system to connect major town centers and some rural areas.

BOAT

Several companies run daytime and evening cruises along the river. Major ports include Newburgh, Kingston, and Hudson. The Hudson River Sloop *Clearwater,* based out of Poughkeepsie, produces environmental education programs and riverfront festivals. **NY Waterway** (800/53-FERRY or 800/533-3779, www.nywaterway.com) runs commuter ferries as well as sightseeing tours to and from Manhattan. Some packages include admission to popular destinations.

CAR

Two major interstates traverse the Hudson River Valley: I-84 connects Pennsylvania to Connecticut through southern Dutchess County. And I-87, the New York State Thruway, runs from New York City to Albany and then on to Buffalo.

Toll Roads

The New York State Thruway (I-87) holds the record as the longest toll highway in the United States. It costs $7 to drive the length of the Hudson Valley stretch, from the New York City line to the downtown Albany exit. Exits are often 15 miles or more apart, so watch carefully for signs to avoid missing your turn. Occasional rest areas have gas, restrooms, and an array of fast food, including Starbucks.

The following five Hudson River crossings have a $1 toll in the eastbound direction:
• Bear Mountain Bridge (Westchester and Orange)
• Newburgh-Beacon Bridge (I-84)
• Mid-Hudson Bridge (southern Dutchess and Ulster)
• Kingston-Rhinecliff Bridge (northern Dutchess and Ulster)
• Rip Van Winkle Bridge (Columbia and Greene)

There is a $3 toll to cross the Tappan Zee Bridge between Westchester and Rockland counties, and $3 toll for the George Washington Bridge. All bridges and toll roads in New York State are equipped with the EZ-Pass (www.ez-pass.com) automatic transponder system, which is compatible with most systems in the northeast. If you want to use an EZ-Pass in a rental car, you must first call EZ-Pass to have the license plate registered on your account. Cash-only lanes are clearly marked at most toll plazas.

Highway Information

The best sources of real-time traffic updates for the Lower Hudson Valley and New York metropolitan area are AM radio 880 "on the eights" (1:08, 1:18, 1:28 etc.) and AM 1010 "on the ones" (1:01, 1:11, 1:21, etc.). **Radio Catskill** is a hydropowered community radio station serving the Catskills, the Upper Delaware, and Mid-Hudson regions (FM 90.5 and FM 94.5, www.wjffradio.org). In Albany, tune to **WAMC Northeast Public Radio** (FM 90.3 in Albany and FM 90.9 in Kingston, www.wamc.org).

Consult www.nycroads.com/crossings/hudson-river for bridge conditions. Also online is the New York State Travel Information Gateway at www.travelinfony.com/tig, with information by region.

The Taconic State Parkway

The scenic Taconic State Parkway runs north-south from the Sprainbrook Parkway, which comes out of New York City, to I-90 near the Massachusetts state line and offers convenient access to many of the Hudson Valley's inland towns. Unlike the six-lane interstates that run parallel to it, the Taconic has just two lanes in each direction with a wide, green medium in between. It crosses some of the prettiest woodlands, marshes, and fields of Westchester, Dutchess, and Columbia Counties, making it a popular route for motorists.

Several risks make the route also one of the more dangerous in the state. When driving the Taconic for the first time, take these factors into consideration:

Narrow lanes: The Taconic's narrow lanes are unforgiving, particularly on icy or wet roads. There are drains every few hundred feet on both sides and no emergency breakdown lanes. If you must stop for any reason, pull all the way onto the grass, as far as possible away from traffic.

Cross traffic: Except for a few of the busiest intersections, the Taconic does not have on- and off-ramps. After one too many accidents, the state closed most of the hazardous crossroads in Dutchess County, but many in Columbia County remain open. Watch for cars braking suddenly in the left lane to turn, or for cars accelerating slowly in the right lane.

Deer: The Hudson Valley supports a healthy population of whitetail deer, and many of them feed on the shrubs and bushes that line both

The Taconic near Chatham

sides of the Taconic. Watch for eyes at night, and remember that a deer caught in the glare of oncoming headlights will often freeze in its tracks. When you see one, others are likely feeding nearby.

Speed traps: The speed limit on the Taconic is 55 miles per hour, and New York State troopers are serious about enforcing it. Although traffic moves much faster during rush hour, troopers frequently lurk in the median to catch drivers who exceed the limit by as little as five miles per hour. Bulls Head Road near Rhinebeck and the town of Fishkill are known hotspots.

U.S. Route 9 and Route 9W on the east and west sides of the Hudson River are slower north-south routes through the valley.

Driving Guidelines

The maximum speed limit on New York State highways is 65 miles per hour, and limits are often lower through congested areas or on older highways. Seatbelts are required at all times, and it is illegal to talk on a cell phone while driving, unless you have a hands-free connection. Right turns on red are permissible outside of New York City, unless otherwise marked.

Rental Cars

Rental agencies are easy to come by in the Lower Hudson Valley, but more difficult as you venture north, until you reach Albany. Major brands cluster around the airports, and most sizable towns have at least one independent rental service.

Car rentals are generally much less expensive in the Hudson River Valley than they are at the New York City airports. If you are traveling from these airports to the Mid-Hudson region or farther and plan to stay more than a couple of days, try this cost-saving strategy: arrange a one-way rental at the higher airport rate, then return the

COURTESY OF WESTCHESTER COUNTY OFFICE OF TOURISM

Bicycle Sunday in Westchester County

car the next day and reserve a new vehicle at the lower upstate rate for the remainder of your trip.

BICYCLE

Mountain bikes are easier to find as rentals than road bikes, but a number of shops in the area cater to the cycling community. For example, The Bicycle Depot on Main Street in New Paltz rents aluminum road bikes in good condition. Cycling enthusiasts Ken Roberts and Sharon Marsh Roberts have posted a wealth of useful information, including maps online at www .robert-1.com/bikehudson. You can travel with bikes on Shortline Bus and Metro-North.

Washington D.C.-based **Escapades Bike Tours** (202/232-1531, www.bikeescapades.com/hud-son/index.html) organizes a seven-day fall-foliage tour in October for cyclists of all levels ($1,850). Average daily mileage is 25–45, depending on individual preferences and abilities.

Brooks Country Cycling Tours (P.O. Box 20792, New York, 917/834-5340, www.brooks-countrycycling.com) offers one-day trips to the Mid-Hudson region for $45 per person, ex-cluding transportation. Rentals are available—road and hybrid frames with or without toe clips—for $34.

R'Ode to Joy (5 Locust Crest Court, Pough-keepsie, 845/473-7520, www.rodetojoy.com) leads seven-day luxury cycling trips through the Shawan-gunk ($1,650) and Harlem Valley ($1,850) re-gions during the summer and fall. Top-notch accommodations and meals are included.

Tips for Travelers

STUDENTS

Students will find a range of programs at the Hudson Valley's many colleges and universities. The State University of New York has campuses in Albany, New Paltz, and Purchase. Private institutions include Vassar College, Marist College, Bard College, Skidmore College, and the Culinary Institute of America. Jobseekers should consult local newspapers and county websites for current listings.

FEMALE, GAY AND LESBIAN TRAVELERS

Women traveling alone should feel safe throughout the Hudson Valley, but be aware of surroundings when exploring urban areas like Newburgh and Poughkeepsie. While many of the Hudson Valley's towns are diverse in their makeup and progressive in their way of thinking, gay and lesbian travelers are still likely to encounter a quietly conservative attitude in rural areas.

TRAVELERS WITH DISABILITIES

With a few exceptions, travelers with disabilities will find most major attractions in the region to be easily accessible. Travel plazas along the New York State Thruway are fully accessible, and people with disabilities can purchase full-service fuel at self-serve rates.

FAMILIES AND PETS

Families will find many kid-friendly establishments across the Hudson River Valley. Restaurants often have special menus for children, and many historic sites and attractions offer reduced admission fees for families. Seniors and students also often receive preferential rates. Check with hotels and inns before making reservations.

Pets are welcome at many, but not all, outdoor spaces throughout the Hudson Valley. Inquire at inns and hotels before bringing Fido along. Restaurants do not generally allow pets inside.

ANGLERS AND HUNTERS

Trout fishing on lakes and streams is open April 1–October 15. You can fish for crappie, whitefish, shad, and perch year-round. Certain rivers and counties have additional restrictions. Trout fishing on New York City reservoirs is open year-round with size limitations. A free New York City Public Access permit is required to fish on the reservoirs. The application can be downloaded and printed from the Department of Environmental Protection at http://nyc.gov/html/dep/watershed/html/wsrecreation.html.

A wide variety of game is available for hunting in designated seasons within the Hudson Valley region. Deer, turkey, bear, ducks, and upland game are popular species. You'll know you're in a hunting town when you see signs advertising "hunter" breakfasts.

New York State is divided into four hunting zones: Northern, Southern, Westchester, and Suffolk. Seasons are divided into regular (for rifles), archery, and special firearms. Hunting season dates and regulations vary from year to year.

Before hunting or fishing, make sure you have the correct license, tag, and federal stamps. Licenses are available in many sporting goods stores. Contact the New York State Department of Environmental Conservation (518/357-2450, www.dec.state.ny.us) for the latest information.

Health and Safety

The Hudson Valley has a severe problem with ticks and Lyme disease. Wear long sleeves and pants when hiking in grassy or wooded areas, and always check for ticks when you return. Poison ivy is another nuisance that can cause minor skin irritation and itching.

Hypothermia is a concern for hikers, paddlers, and cyclists who may be subject to rapid temperature changes. Bring layers and plenty of fluid for any outdoor adventure.

Dial 911 for emergencies, or 0 for the operator. Area hospitals are open around the clock to treat injuries and illnesses. Bring proof of medical coverage.

Crime in New York State has dropped steadily over the past few years, and Hudson River Valley communities are known to be among the safest in the United States. Crime rates in the largest towns and cities measure average or better across the valley. Albany and Newburgh are the exceptions, with the highest crime rates in the region.

Information and Services

Businesses in New York are generally open Monday–Friday 9 A.M.–5 P.M. Banks close earlier, around 3 P.M., although some are open on Saturday mornings as well, and ATMs are accessible 24/7. Shops in tourist destinations stay open on Saturday and part or all of Sunday, and some grocery stores are open 24 hours. (Price Chopper is often open 24 hours, and ShopRite stores are generally open 6–1 A.M.).

Most stores, hotels, and restaurants accept credit cards for payment, but there are exceptions, so be sure to ask before you attempt to pay with plastic. The state sales tax is 4.25 percent as of January 2004, but when you add local county taxes, the markup usually exceeds 8 percent.

COMMUNICATIONS AND MEDIA

Post offices, found in even the most rural towns, are generally open Monday–Friday 8:30 A.M.–5 P.M. and Saturday 8:30 A.M.–noon.

Public libraries across the region offer Internet access for free or a nominal charge. In addition, Internet cafés and wireless hotspots have been making their way up the valley to Barnes & Noble, Starbucks, and a growing number of independent locations.

Telephone Area Codes

There are four main area codes in the Hudson River Valley.

518: Albany, Saratoga, Greene, Columbia
607: Parts of Delaware
845: Rockland, Putnam, Orange, Sullivan, Dutchess, Ulster, and parts of Delaware
914: Westchester

Maps

Jimapco publishes one of the best atlases to the region. The spiralbound *Hudson Valley Street Atlas* covers Greene, Columbia, Ulster, Dutchess, Sullivan, Orange, and Putnam Counties, with detailed maps of the largest cities (Kingston, Poughkeepsie, Newburgh, Middletown, Monticello, Catskill) and the tiniest hamlets (Maplecrest, Freehold, Ancram). The third edition is available at www.jimapco.com for $21.95. Hagstrom (www.hagstrom.com) publishes a laminated foldout map to the Hudson Valley and Catskills. Individual county maps from both companies are available in convenience stores throughout the region. Cyclists can print detailed route maps for scenic road rides on the website of cycling enthusiasts Ken Roberts and Sharon Marsh Roberts (www.robert-1.com/bikehudson).

Local Media

The *New York Times* is a daily national newspaper with regular coverage of upstate towns and issues. The *Poughkeepsie Journal* is a respected regional paper owned by a national publisher. Many other towns have small circulation newspapers, and several regional magazines contain useful information for travelers: *Hudson Valley Magazine* (Suburban Publishing, www.hudsonvalleymagazine.com), *Dutchess Magazine* (Taconic Press, dutchessmag@midhusdoncentral.com), *Westchester Magazine* (Spotlight Publications, www.westchestermagazine.com), and *Kaatskill Life* (The Delaware County Times, www.kaatslife.com).

Most local television networks are based out of New York City or Albany. Albany radio station WAMC 90.3 is an NPR-member station, as is WNYC 93.9 out of New York City.

Suggested Reading

FICTION

Adams, Arthur G., ed. *The Hudson River in Literature: An Anthology.* Fordham University Press, 1980. This anthology, which includes the writings of James Fenimore Cooper and William Cullen Bryant, provides a good overview of writers who wrote about and were influenced by the Hudson River Valley.

Cooper, James Fenimore. *The Leatherstocking Tales I* and *The Last of the Mohicans.* James Fenimore Cooper set many of his tales in the Hudson River Valley. These are two of his classic novels.

Irving, Washington. "Rip Van Winkle" and "The Legend of Sleepy Hollow." Many editions. Washington Irving lived in Sleepy Hollow and found inspiration for his writing in local residents and villages. These two classics are always worthy of another read.

George, Jean Craighead. *My Side of the Mountain.* Puffin Books, 1988. Many young readers have fallen in love with this story about a boy who runs away from home to the Catskills.

Goodman, Allegra. *Kaaterskill Falls.* Delta, 1999. This book, about three Jewish families who spend summers in the Catskills, is contemporary novelist Allegra Goodman's first.

HISTORY

Chernov, Ron. *Titan: The Life of John D. Rockefeller, Sr.* Vintage Books, 1999. This biography has sections on Kykuit and the Pocantico Hills and gives a good overview of the economy and culture that defined the Hudson River Valley in the 19th century.

Diamant, Lincoln. *Chaining the Hudson: The Fight for the River in the American Revolution.* Kensington Publishing, 1994. This book tells the story of defending the river at West Point.

Evers, Alf. *The Catskills: From Wilderness to Woodstock.* Overlook Press, 1982. This book is the definitive history of the Catskills.

Hall, Bruce Edward. *Diamond Street: The Story of the Little Town with the Big Red Light District.* Black Dome Press, 1994. This book tells the story of Hudson's red light district.

Ruttenber, E. M. *Indian Tribes of Hudson's River to 1700* and *Indian Tribes of Hudson's River 1700–1850.* Hope Farm Press, 1992. These present a thorough history of the Native Americans who first inhabited the valley.

Van Zandt, Roland. *The Catskill Mountain House: America's Grandest Hotel.* Black Dome Press, 1991. Roland Van Zandt offers in in-depth look at one of the most famous hotels in U.S. history.

CULINARY

Greenberg, Jan. *Hudson Valley Harvest: A Food Lover's Guide to Farms, Restaurants and Open-Air Markets*. Countryman Press, 2003. This fascinating overview of the region's microterroirs covers everything from heirloom beans to shiitake mushrooms. Chapters are organized by type of food.

Manikowski, John. *Wild Fish & Game Cookbook*. Artisan, 1997. Not only is Manikowski an accomplished outdoorsman, he wrote and illustrated his own book.

New York State Farm Fresh Guide Metro Region. New York State Department of Agriculture and Markets. This free guide on what to expect when and where is available through the New York State Department of Agriculture and Markets (718/722-2830).

The Valley Table. The Valley Table, Inc. This quarterly print publication maintains an informative website (www.valleytable.com) of local culinary news and events.

Zagat. *2003/04 Westchester/Hudson River Valley Restaurants*. Zagat Survey, 2003. Comprehensive restaurant listings with extensive coverage of Westchester County and select coverage across the valley. This guide does not cover Albany or Saratoga Springs.

TRAIL GUIDES

Henry, Edward G. *Catskill Trails: A Ranger's Guide to the High Peaks*. Black Dome Press, 2000. This pair of trail guides are an essential resource for hikers. Book 1 covers the Northern Catskills, and Book 2 covers the Southern Catskills.

Green, Stella and H. Neil Zimmerman. *50 Hikes in the Lower Hudson Valley: Hikes and Walks from Westchester County to Albany*. Countryman Press, 2002. Hikes on both sides of the lower Hudson, from the past vice president and president of the New York–New Jersey Trail Conference.

Kick, Peter. *Catskill Mountain Guide (Hiking Guide Series)*. Appalachian Mountain Club Books, 2002. A guide with more than 90 trail descriptions and a pull-out map by a local outdoorsman.

Kick, Peter. *25 Mountain Bike Tours in the Hudson Valley: A Backcountry Guide (25 Bicycle Tours)*. Countryman Press, 1996. Somewhat dated information on rail trails, bikeways, and shops.

NATURE

Boyle, Robert H. *The Hudson River: A Natural and Unnatural History*. W. W. Norton & Company, 1979. This is required reading for anyone who takes an environmental interest in the Hudson River.

Burroughs, John. *In the Catskills*. Cherokee Publishing Company, reprint edition 1990. One of America's first conservationists and a contemporary of Walt Whitman and John Muir, Burroughs writes about Slide Mountain and his hometown of Roxbury in a collection of eight essays.

Cole, Thomas. *Thomas Cole's Poetry: The Collected Poems of America's Foremost Painter of the Hudson River School*. George Shumway Pub., 1972. Cole was a poet as well as a painter. More than 100 of his poems and a chronology of his life are included in this edition.

Klinkenborg, Verlyn. *The Rural Life*. Back Bay Books, 2002. This memoir of life on a farm takes place largely in Columbia County.

Titus, Robert. *The Catskills: A Geological Guide*. Purple Mountain Press, 1998. This must-read for armchair geologists contains basic explanations and recommended fieldtrips.

Know the Hudson River Valley

TRAVEL ESSAY

Carmer, Carl. *The Hudson.* Farrar and Rhinehart, 1939. In the early 20th century, Carl Carmer wrote a guide to the region, filled with personal anecdotes and observations.

James, Henry. *The American Scene.* 1907. This book, first published at the turn of the 20th century, captures Henry James's reflections on his return to upstate New York.

Lossing, Benson J. *The Hudson: From the Wilderness to the Sea.* Reprinted by Black Dome Press, 1995. Lossing presents a 19th-century perspective of the region in a travel narrative format.

Lourie, Peter. *River of Mountains: A Canoe Journey down the Hudson.* Syracuse University Press, 1998. This contemporary travel narrative follows a paddler from the Adirondacks to New York Harbor.

Van Zandt, Roland *Chronicles of the Hudson: Three Centuries of Travel and Adventure.* Black Dome Press, 1992. This book captures an interesting cross-section of travel writing related to the Hudson River.

Internet Resources

Most New York State counties maintain a tourism website with information on attractions, activities, lodging, and dining out. In addition, most establishments maintain at least a basic website with general information. Here are some of the unique sites that cover broader issues and trends in the region.

I Love NY
www.iloveny.com
The central New York State tourism site contains trip ideas, event information, and more.

HV/Net
www.hvnet.com
Similar to I Love NY, this is a regional tourism site with a detailed calendar of events.

Historic Hudson Valley
www.hudsonvalley.org
This organization publishes information about visiting several National Historic Landmarks in the area, including Kykuit, Lyndhurst, and Montgomery Place.

Hudson Valley Magazine
www.hudsonvalleymagazine.com
This regional print publication has timely information for residents and visitors and articles about local food, business, and culture.

Black Dome Press
www.blackdomepress.com
This publisher has a large online catalogue of regional fiction and nonfiction titles.

Clearwater
www.clearwater.org
This organization gathers information about the ongoing clean-up of the Hudson River.

Index

Art Centers, Galleries, and Museums

Mansions

Acknowledgments

My sincerest thanks to the army of friends and family who contributed local insight, travel assistance, editorial input, and moral support during the research and writing of this guide. Your patience and enthusiasm made the project not only possible but also infinitely enjoyable.

Consummate travelers Mavis Morris and Charlie Wright shared their collective wisdom on gourmet dining and outdoor adventure across the region, with particular emphasis on Piermont, Columbia County, and Saratoga Springs. Mavis also steered me to the best art collections in the region and spent a generous amount of time editing an early draft of the manuscript.

Jenn and John Nisi scouted restaurants and wine trails in Dutchess and Westchester Counties and shared highlights of the annual Irish festival at Hunter Mountain. They both endured many months of research questions while planning their wedding at the West Park Winery. Jen Hauschildt and Kathy Herlihy added further insights to the Mid-Hudson chapter. Kathryn Goth relived her college days in a virtual tour of Albany's hotspots. Avid skier Tom Goth offered insider tips on the area's best slopes as well as custom photography services.

Rachel and Erik Lujbli led me through the shops of Warwick and along the shores of Greenwood Lake, while Tanya Lujbli introduced me to the Mt. Fuji Steakhouse and other notable restaurants in Orange County. Across the river, Hally and Greg Bayer and Ira and Cecilia Wolfson took a break from climbing the Gunks to share a weekender's view of the New Paltz area. Hally's careful read strengthened the Ulster County chapter considerably. Ali Garbarini put me in touch with Emily Klein, who shared impressions of Livingston Manor and Nyack.

As a Dutchess County native, my mom, Sue Goth, provided on-demand navigation assistance, a constant feed of travel-related information, and general support that reached above and beyond the call of parental duty. Grandma Charlotte Borchers sent clips from local newspapers throughout the year, while Barbara and Fred Borchers directed me to the latest developments in Kingston, Hyde Park, and Delaware County.

In researching the history of the Upper Hudson River Valley, I borrowed from the archives of Mary Jo and Gary Goth, who have recorded the comings and goings of seven generations of ancestors in the area. My grandparents, Joe and Ruth Goth, recalled the Catskills in the heyday of the summer boarding houses. My dad, George Goth, spent boyhood summers on a dairy farm at the base of Blackhead Mountain and taught me to tell a hard maple from a white oak. He and the entire Goth clan have kept the maple sugaring tradition alive and well on the family property in Greene County.

Deborah Claymon added a welcomed polish to the introduction and helped me see the Hudson River Valley from a visitor's point of view. Editorial intern Kristin Francosz proofed the entire manuscript from a home base in Paris, adding a number of pop culture references in the process. Virginie Boone and Bob Bestor provided early guidance.

My husband, Paul Itoi, logged countless hours as travel companion, information gatherer, and chief technology officer. His curiosity, patience, and encouragement were essential to the completion of the book.

Media relations professionals in each of the county tourism offices provided a wealth of current information and assistance. Special thanks to Joel Allen, Nancy Arena, Jill Brass, Rachel Carr, Susan Cayea, Annamaria Dalton, Jeff Levine, McKelden Smith, Traci Suppa, Crystalyn Thienpont, and Ingrid Williamson for their quick and thorough responses to my inquiries.

Finally, the team at Avalon Travel Publishing, including Grace Fujimoto, Rebecca Browning, and Amber Pirker, gave me an early vote of confidence and helped turn a collection of observations into a usable text.

I am indebted to all of these contributors, as well as others I may have omitted above, for giving generously of their time and experience throughout the life of the project.

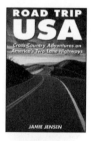

U.S. ~ Metric Conversion

1 inch	=	2.54 centimeters (cm)
1 foot	=	.304 meters (m)
1 yard	=	0.914 meters
1 mile	=	1.6093 kilometers (km)
1 km	=	.6214 miles
1 fathom	=	1.8288 m
1 chain	=	20.1168 m
1 furlong	=	201.168 m
1 acre	=	.4047 hectares
1 sq km	=	100 hectares
1 sq mile	=	2.59 square km
1 ounce	=	28.35 grams
1 pound	=	.4536 kilograms
1 short ton	=	.90718 metric ton
1 short ton	=	2000 pounds
1 long ton	=	1.016 metric tons
1 long ton	=	2240 pounds
1 metric ton	=	1000 kilograms
1 quart	=	.94635 liters
1 US gallon	=	3.7854 liters
1 Imperial gallon	=	4.5459 liters
1 nautical mile	=	1.852 km

To compute Celsius temperatures, subtract 32 from Fahrenheit and divide by 1.8. To go the other way, multiply Celsius by 1.8 and add 32.

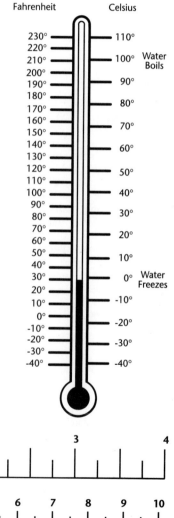

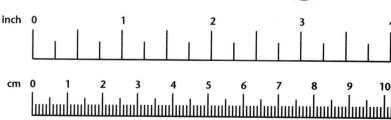

Keeping Current

Although we strive to produce the most up-to-date guidebook humanly possible, change is unavoidable. Between the time this book goes to print and the moment you read it, a handful of the businesses noted in these pages will undoubtedly change prices, move, or even close their doors forever. Other worthy attractions will open for the first time. If you have a favorite gem you'd like to see included in the next edition, or see anything that needs updating, clarification, or correction, please drop us a line. Send your comments via email at atpfeedback@avalonpub.com, or use the address below.

Moon Handbooks Hudson River Valley
Avalon Travel Publishing
1400 65th Street, Suite 250
Emeryville, CA 94608, USA
www.moon.com

Editors: Grace Fujimoto, Elizabeth McCue
Series Manager: Kevin McLain
Acquisitions Editor: Rebecca K. Browning
Copy Editor: Wendy Taylor
Graphics Coordinator: Amber Pirker
Production Coordinator: Amber Pirker
Cover Designer: Kari Gim
Interior Designer: Amber Pirker
Map Editor: Kevin Anglin
Cartographers: Mike Morgenfeld, Kat Kalamaras
Indexer: Deana Shields

ISBN: 1-56691-878-2
ISSN: 1554-2327

Printing History
1st Edition—May 2005
5 4 3 2 1

Text © 2005 by Nikki Goth Itoi.
Maps © 2005 by Avalon Travel Publishing, Inc.
All rights reserved.

AVALON
publishing group incorporated

Avalon Travel Publishing is an Imprint of Avalon Publishing Group, Inc.

Some photos and illustrations are used by permission and are the property of the original copyright owners.

Front cover photo: © William H. Johnson

Printed in United States by Malloy